D1189876

PRISONERS OF THE BASHAW

PRISONERS
OF THE
BASHAW

THE
Nineteen-Month Captivity
OF
American Sailors
IN
**Tripoli,
1803-1805**

FREDERICK C. LEINER

WESTHOLME
Yardley

Westholme Publishing, LLC
904 Edgewood Road
Yardley, Pennsylvania 19067
Visit our Web site at www.westholmepublishing.com

ISBN: 978-1-59416-386-9
Also available as an eBook.

Printed in the United States of America.

The race is not won by the swift,
Nor the battle by the valiant . . .
For the time of mischance comes to all.
And a man cannot even know his time.
As fishes are enmeshed in a fatal net,
and as birds are trapped in a snare,
So men are caught at the time of calamity,
when it comes upon them without warning.

Ecclesiastes 9:11-12

CONTENTS

Illustrations

ILLUSTRATIONS

A gallery of images follows page 118:

Barbary including Morocco Algier, Tunis and Tripoly, 1804

Merchant, Slave, & Arab

Preparations for war to defend commerce

Philadelphia, *off Tetuan, Morocco*

The Sailor's Description of Chase & Capture

Seaman's Protection Certificate

Captain William Bainbridge

First Lieutenant David Porter

Second Lieutenant Jacob Jones

Midshipman James Biddle

Perspective of the loss of the US Frigate Philadelphia

President Thomas Jefferson

Secretary of the Navy Robert Smith

Nicholas Nissen

Tobias Lear

Bombardment of Tripoli, August 3, 1804

Watching the bombardment from the Tripoli prison cell

James Leander Cathcart

Commodore Edward Preble

INTRODUCTION

THE GROUNDING OF THE US frigate *Philadelphia* on a reef off Tripoli (modern-day Libya) in October 1803 led to the capture of 307 American sailors and marines by a distant enemy in North Africa. This book is about what happened to the men in captivity: how they lived and labored, what they thought, and how they reacted to being slaves in an Islamic regime. No previous account of the Barbary Wars focuses on them and looks at the larger naval and diplomatic events from their perspective. These topics have been dealt with only in passing, or not at all, in the standard histories.

The *Philadelphia*'s officers and crew remained prisoners of the bashaw (a variation of the Turkish word "pasha")[1] for nineteen months, until the Tripolitan War ended in June 1805. The war came to be largely about them: the question for President Thomas Jefferson, for the diplomats and naval officers offshore, and even for the American people, was how to free their countrymen.

The Tripolitans treated the US naval officers far differently than the "people." For the officers, regarded as high-status gentlemen, the strain of captivity was, in large part, psychological. Even so, they considered themselves slaves, not prisoners of war. The crew worked as slave laborers, many serving as human pack animals. Often beaten, usually under-fed, they reacted to events and rumors around them. Some died in captivity. Some converted to Islam to escape their dreary lives. Others tried to undermine their captors.

This book raises larger, timeless questions about moral conduct in captivity, about the early American experience with the Islamic world, about slavery across cultures, and about the roles of diplomacy and force to redeem hostages from foreign lands.

Never before had the United States had so many of its people held captive in the Islamic world, and never before had the American public been riveted for so long on the news from Barbary. Some of the captives' letters, after a slow journey across the Atlantic, appeared in contemporary newspapers. They are rediscovered here and add context to a broadly Orientalist American view of the Arab world.

The irony of being slaves far away from America was not lost on the officers and crew. Some of the officers wrote thoughtfully about the nature of their slavery in the Islamic world. Unfortunately, only a few Americans questioned how their country could assert moral indignation about the captivity of a few hundred white Christian sailors when America held in slavery millions of black Africans, some of whom were Muslim.

This account also raises questions about the relation of force and diplomacy, as it captures the complexity of the negotiations, the role played by foreign diplomats, and the critical role of ransom money. The loss of the *Philadelphia* on the rocks off Tripoli is sometimes employed as proof of a core precept of principle and policy: the United States does not pay ransom for hostages. This bold statement is wrong historically and sometimes has caused tragic results. As the story of the American prisoners in Tripoli shows, history is not so tidy, and the lessons are not so clear.[2]

PROLOGUE

On the last day of October 1803, the frigate *Philadelphia* was sailing alone, close to the North African coast, seven or eight miles east of the city of Tripoli, hoping to intercept any ships trying to enter Tripoli harbor. Faced by Tripolitan threats to seize American merchant ships and enslave American sailors in the war that began in 1801, the US Navy had spent two years in intermittent and lackluster blockading that had achieved little. The *Philadelphia* was the lead ship of the third naval squadron sent to the Mediterranean to reassert the blockade.

At 9:00 AM, a *Philadelphia* lookout spotted a sail ahead and inshore of the frigate, standing in toward the harbor before an easterly breeze. Captain William Bainbridge immediately ordered his frigate to chase the strange sail, a small xebec cruiser, which hoisted Tripolitan colors and bore away for safety, toward the harbor. A xebec was a distinctive Mediterranean craft, often used by corsairs, with a forward-leaning foremast, billowing lateen sails, a wide beam, a narrow hull, and a pronounced overhanging bow and stern. In the age of sail, stern chases could be agonizingly slow. A slight difference in speed meant that catching up with a ship running before the wind might take hours. At about 11:00 AM, in about seven fathoms of water (forty-two feet), the *Philadel-*

phia came within range of the fleeing xebec. Bainbridge ordered the 18-pounder cannon in the bow to be run out and then to open fire. The *Philadelphia*'s bow chasers fired a 5-inch diameter, 18-pound cannonball that had a maximum range of just under three thousand yards. The gun crews began a slow, methodical fire, hoping a lucky shot would knock away a yardarm or dismast the fleeing corsair, but all the shots missed.[1]

As the frigate approached Tripoli, Bainbridge grew concerned about the depth of the sea because fully loaded, the *Philadelphia* drew about 18 feet of water forward and 19 1/2 feet aft. He ordered seamen to the bow and sides of the ship to take soundings. Each man used a deep sea line with knots for counting the depth and a lead weight at the end to make sure that the line reached bottom; the line was tossed ahead and pulled up when the ship was directly overhead. Oddly, for a ship blockading a foreign port, the *Philadelphia* did not have a reliable chart of the approaches to Tripoli. Bainbridge's first lieutenant, David Porter, at his station near the captain on the quarterdeck, reminded him that he had been in these same waters some months earlier, when he was the first lieutenant of the frigate *New York*. He assured Bainbridge there was ample water under the ship. Bainbridge deferred to his judgment. Even so, Bainbridge worried about sailing any farther inshore. Never lacking in self-confidence, Porter responded there was no danger yet, and there was time to try a few more shots to wing the xebec. At 11:30 AM, the leadsmen reported the ship was still in seven fathoms of water, speeding along at seven or eight knots. But all the *Philadelphia*'s shots missed, the xebec was clearly going to find sanctuary in Tripoli harbor, and Bainbridge decided to give up the pursuit.

The captain ordered the helm up, and the *Philadelphia* turned away, to head back to deeper water. Bainbridge sent Porter with a spyglass up to the mizzenmast top, a platform a third of the way up the rearmost mast, to look into the harbor to see how many enemy cruisers were in port. Porter started to climb up the rigging. The *Philadelphia* went another 1,200 feet, when the water suddenly shoaled. Then, with an appalling crash, the ship struck submerged rocks. A 1,240-ton ship cruising at seven or eight knots running onto an underground reef makes a grinding racket, and the big frigate shuddered as she came to a stop. She had run aground atop Kaliusa reef about three or four miles outside the harbor, with her bow all the way to the forechains—a third of the length of the ship—on the rocks. The forward part of the ship jutted out of water, and her stern sloped down on a steep angle on her port (left) side, the ship canted so far over that her "lee gun deck ports [were] on a level with the water's edge," as Porter later recounted.[2]

Marine Private William Ray, writing in the officers' wardroom, heard and felt the ship crash and lurch, and feet running on the deck overhead. Ray ran up the hatchway to the main deck and immediately saw the ship's bow up, and that she lay partly on top of the reef. Everyone looked shocked. Bainbridge was an experienced seaman, and whatever his emotions, he reacted professionally, with what Porter called "great coolness and deliberation." Bainbridge first tried to drive the *Philadelphia* over the reef by setting more sail, but she was stuck fast. He then ordered a ship's boat lowered into the water from the stern to take soundings to determine the depth of the water around the ship. The soundings revealed that the sea was deeper astern. Bainbridge ordered sailors aloft, to lay all sails aback, "loosed [the] top Gall[ant] Sails and set a heavy press of Canvass on the Ship, blowing fresh to get her off," to have his ship sail backward. Still, the frigate did not budge. Bainbridge then did what commanders classically do when ships run aground: he tried to lighten the ship. He ordered all the cannon run aft, meaning the crew began the herculean effort of rolling the cannon down the slanted deck. An 18-pounder cannon was an unwieldy monster, eight feet long and weighing more than two tons; the wooden carriage in which the gun was placed, with its iron ring bolts and linchpins, weighed hundreds of pounds more. Teams of men, spurred on by the bosun's mates' shouting or cursing encouragement, used brute force to push, pull, and drag the heavy guns aft, down the deck. But the frigate stayed stuck. Three heavy sea anchors were cast away over the bow, and Bainbridge ordered the water in the bilges pumped out, but the ship did not move. He then ordered most of the cannon to be tipped overboard, leaving only a few in the stern, to defend the ship against enemy gunboats that, having seen the *Philadelphia* in distress, were making their way out of the harbor toward the stranded frigate. One by one the cannon went over the side. Dumping the cannon did not free the *Philadelphia* from the reef, and the few cannon that remained on board could not be run out and trained around to bear on the approaching gunboats.[3]

With a growing sense of despair, Bainbridge called his officers to the quarterdeck to seek advice. As a last resort for lightening the ship forward, he ordered the *Philadelphia*'s foremast chopped down. When it fell, the main topgallant mast came down with it, still connected by some of the standing rigging. Still, the frigate did not budge. As Bainbridge put it, "our fate was direfully fixed," as was his ship. Three Tripolitan gunboats warily approached the frigate, even as more gunboats were seen being rigged in the port to come out. From a distance, the gunboats began firing their cannon. They aimed high, to spare the frigate's hull. No cannonball hit the hull of the *Philadelphia*, although several went through her rigging. Bainbridge ordered the taffrail, the handrail at the stern, cut away to make room for the few cannon left aboard to bear on the gunboats. The cannon thundered out, but the shots flew wide and over the enemy gunboats. Because the guns' muzzles did not protrude beyond the ship's sides, firing the cannon caused the frigate's own bulwarks to catch fire. While the blaze was quickly put out, the heel of the ship made her guns useless.[4]

With the Tripolitan cannonballs whizzing by overhead and more gunboats sailing out to join the fray, the bosun, George Hodge, approached Bainbridge and suggested a way to try to save the ship: a team of sailors would row a boat directly astern and drop an anchor in the water; when the anchor stuck fast to the bottom, sailors aboard the frigate, heaving together, would wind the anchor chain around the capstan again and again, pulling the *Philadelphia* off the reef by brute force, a maneuver called kedging. Bainbridge rejected the idea. He and Porter believed that none of the *Philadelphia*'s boats was large or sturdy enough to carry a heavy sea anchor, but even if a boat could handle the anchor, kedging would be in plain sight of the Tripolitan gunboats, which would close the range and direct their fire on the boat, and the sailors would all be sacrificed. Still, it is hard to understand why Bainbridge did not make any attempt, perhaps with another ship's boat sent out with a small carronade in the bow to provide covering fire, even if some of the Americans might have been killed.[5]

The *Philadelphia* was a big frigate with a large crew, including forty marines. Her situation was dire but not immediately hopeless. The Marine Corps had not yet received renown as a fighting force, but even in 1803, the marines provided a steady core of marksmen. At battle stations, the marines assembled on the quarterdeck and in the tops to shoot their muskets at enemy sailors and to repel boarders. Warships in the age of sail were equipped with boarding nets, which could be raised up the sides of the ships by blocks (pulleys) in the masts, to slow enemy attackers from coming aboard. Boarders attempting to come onto the *Philadelphia* would have to cut through the rope netting, even as the defenders fired on them with muskets and pistols. If Bainbridge had ordered the ship defended to the last extremity, Tripolitan sailors who made it through the netting would have to contend with more than three hundred American sailors and marines fighting them at close quarters, firing weapons, and slashing at them with pikes, boarding axes, and cutlasses. As Private Ray put it, even without her cannon, the crew had "every thing else to defend ourselves with," and with determined men, "we might . . . have kept off the enemy for that night." Not only would boarding have been perilous for would-be attackers, but also the gunboats would likely not have fired into the hull of the ship, given the Tripolitans' obvious goal of capturing the frigate in as undamaged condition as possible. And no one knew what a new day might bring. A gale of wind might blow the frigate off the reef; a storm might drive the gunboats back into port for days; perhaps a ship from a friendly nation might miraculously appear. Moreover, the American sailors and marines had not lost heart. The sailors at their battle stations called out to Bainbridge to defend the ship. It was Bainbridge's duty as captain to defend his ship to the utmost—but it was not to be.[6]

At 4:00 PM, Bainbridge again convened his officers on the quarterdeck, the Tripolitan gunboats arranged in a rough crescent on her windward (high) side firing cannonballs whistling over their heads. The officers agreed there was no hope in saving the ship from a coming attack, and immobilized as she was, no way of defending her if the Tripolitans aimed into the hull. Bainbridge later compared his situation to a man bound to a stake being attacked by a man with weapons. The twenty-nine-year-old Bainbridge had surrendered a ship before, the only captain in the then-six-year history of the US Navy to have done so. Now he was confronted with that nightmare again, lowering the Stars and Stripes from his once beautiful, but now mutilated, frigate. As Bainbridge wrote a few days later, the stress of "having withstood the fire of the Gun Boats for four hours & a reinforcement coming out from Tripoli, without the least chance of injureing them in resistance," was overwhelming. The only alternative to hauling down the flag, which he thought only "Fanatics" would support, was to blow up the ship, but Bainbridge thought that "such conduct would not stand acquitted before God or Man" and he had no right to consign 306 other men to their deaths just because he was the captain of the ship. Ray later thought the surrender was "unnecessary and premature," and it was true that the ship had not even been grazed by the cannon fire, and not a single man aboard had been killed or wounded. But Bainbridge thought that if they had tried to fight, "ten Gun boats carrying 18 & 24 pounders . . . which could take their Station on each Quarter . . . certainly would have cut us all to pieces."[7]

A few minutes before sunset, Bainbridge, in tears, ordered the colors down. According to Ray, the crew was shocked, and the quartermaster at the ensign halyards "positively refused to obey the captain's orders when he was ordered to lower the flag. He was threatened to be run through [with a sword], and a midshipman seized the halyards and executed the command, amidst the general murmuring of the crew."[8]

The commanders of the gunboats arranged warily around the frigate suspected the lowered flag was a ruse. Bainbridge had to send out Porter and Midshipman James Biddle in the *Philadelphia*'s barge to convince the Tripolitans that the surrender was real. One gunboat opened fire on the barge, but the American boat rowed onward, toward the gunboat thought to be carrying the Tripolitan flotilla commander. One of the nearer gunboats decided to seize the barge, sending out her own boat to row straight for the Americans. According to Biddle, twenty enemy sailors bristling with sabers and pistols jumped from the Tripolitan boat onto the barge, and "two seized Lieutenant Porter, and two others seized me. My coat was soon off, my vest unbuttoned, and my cravat torn from my neck. I thought, for my own part, I should not have time to count my beads; but we soon perceived, that their violence was only with the view of getting from us whatever money or valuables we might have concealed about our persons." Biddle lost his sword and money, except for twenty gold coins he had slipped into his boots, and the American sailors "were robbed of every thing except what they had on their backs, and even part of that was stripped off."[9]

Meanwhile, Bainbridge tried to make the *Philadelphia* a sorry prize. He ordered William Godby, the ship's carpenter, to take his mates below and drill holes in the frigate's bottom to scuttle her; he ordered the gunner, Richard Stephenson, to flood the magazine to ruin the gunpowder; he directed Midshipman Daniel Todd Patterson to destroy the signal book; and the crew tossed overboard everything that might be useful to the enemy. To record the exact spot where the *Philadelphia* grounded, Bainbridge had an officer take triangulated bearings with a compass of charted rocks on the coast, the spire of a mosque in Tripoli, and an old fort. But in all the last minute activity, Bainbridge made an unpardonable error: he forgot to destroy his orders and letter book, which would soon give Tripoli accurate intelligence about the US Navy and the squadron.[10]

In a pathetic scene, Bainbridge mustered the crew aft, told them their wages would continue to be accrued while they were in captivity, spoke hopefully of a rapid ransom once America learned of their capture, and asked them to bear up to what was coming. Before the Tripolitans arrived, the crew dashed below to grab whatever clothes and personal items they had stowed away, and the ship's slop chests were opened on the gun deck where the men helped themselves to extra clothing. They bundled up with several handkerchiefs around their necks and layers of shirts, trousers, and coats, and they crammed their pockets with food and their possessions. They provided a laughable image in a nightmarish scene to a literary-minded man like Ray, who thought they looked like buffoons, or like Falstaff in Shakespeare's plays.[11]

Then the Tripolitan corsairs swarmed aboard.

ONE

BARBARY

THE BARBARY POWERS was the name European countries gave to the Islamic regimes that stretched thousands of miles along the North African coast, the Maghreb, from the independent kingdom of Morocco in the west to Algiers, the largest and most powerful entity, to Tunis and to Tripoli. Morocco was ruled by a king (though often called an emperor), Algiers by a dey, Tunis by a bey, and Tripoli by a bashaw. While Morocco had the most strategic position, having ports on both the Atlantic and Mediterranean and holding the ground pinching the Mediterranean across from the British garrison at Gibraltar, the other powers were situated where they could easily interdict European trade with Mediterranean port cities. For centuries, the rulers in Barbary unleashed their corsairs on European merchant ships, capturing them as prizes, selling off their cargoes, and holding their crews and passengers as slaves for ransom. The corsairs were not pirates, although then and now they have been called that. Pirates are seafaring criminals, subject to no authority and operating outside any notion of law, but the Barbary rulers controlled their corsairs' actions and sometimes owned part of or the entire corsair vessel. The captures provided critical money for the Barbary treasuries. At the height of their power in the sixteenth century, the Barbary corsairs upended Mediterranean trade and etched fear deep into the imaginations of Europeans, a fear carried across the Atlantic to the New World, by their brazen assaults on the coasts of Spain, Tuscany, Sicily, the Greek islands, and as far off as Ireland, carrying off the populations of whole villages to bring back to Barbary. The seized Europeans were held as slaves and put to hard labor until they might be ransomed.

Western literature reflected the wide fascination with and deep fear of Barbary captivity. In 1575, corsairs captured the Spanish writer Miguel Cervantes, who was enslaved for five years in Algiers. Before Trinitarian friars supplied his ransom payment, Cervantes was a galley slave-rower, a subject he wrote about in two plays and in *Don Quixote*. Although the great English novel *Robinson Crusoe* (1719) is a shipwreck story, Daniel Defoe begins the tale with Crusoe's capture by Salé rovers (corsairs from Morocco) and his two years as a slave to the "Moors." The same fear and fascination gripped Americans. In 1794, Susanna Haswell Rowson, the first American best-selling novelist (and sister to two men soon to become naval officers), wrote the play *Slaves in Algiers*, which was staged at the Chestnut Street Theatre in Philadelphia. In 1797, Royall Tyler's novel, *The Algerine Captive*, appeared, in which the main character is captured and enslaved, though Tyler critiqued the slavery of blacks in America to be worse than Barbary slavery. Dozens of other Barbary captivity narratives, novels, and plays emerged from American authors around the turn of the nineteenth century.[1]

By the early eighteenth century, the Barbary powers were semiautonomous regimes, each with its own military and naval forces, finances, and diplomatic relations with the rest of the world. Although the Barbary powers had shed the historic control the Ottoman Turks had previously exercised, the sultan of the Ottoman Empire at Constantinople, as spiritual leader of Islam, retained a certain amount of influence. The Barbary rulers acknowledged their nominal dependence by paying annual tribute to the "Sublime Porte."[2] At the same time, all the European nations negotiated treaties establishing a system of annual tributary payments and "presents" to the Barbary powers, although over the centuries, they occasionally sent naval squadrons to the Mediterranean to bombard a Barbary city to lower the price. In exchange for money and gifts, the king, dey, bey, or bashaw would allow that country's ships to navigate freely to Mediterranean ports in southern Europe and the Levant. For example, between 1785 and 1790, Spain paid Algiers 4.5 million Spanish dollars; Britain and France each paid 15,000 guineas to Morocco in the 1780s. At the close of an inconclusive war in 1792, Venice paid Tunis 40,000 sequins. As late as 1798, Tunis sent a raiding force to the village of Carloforte on the island of San Pietro (off Sardinia) that seized nine hundred people and took them to Tunis to hold in slavery, for ransom. Tripoli was the weakest Barbary power, but even so, in 1795, Spain paid it 20,000 Spanish dollars and provided a ship and eighteen ship carpenters to build more corsairs as the price of a treaty, and Venice the same year paid 4,000 sequins to confirm its treaty and pay tribute in arrears.[3]

Slavery in the Barbary world for European and American seamen was not the same as slavery in the American South for black Africans. In the Maghreb, a Qur'anic distinction was made between captivity and slavery. European and American Christian seamen (mostly white, but some black) captured by Barbary corsairs could be ransomed by a monetary payment. While in captivity, they were treated as slaves, forced to contribute grinding physical labor, although some, for a fee, could bargain for easier treatment. Even as slaves, however, their work was supposed to cease before sunset, and they were not to be put to work on Fridays, the Muslim Sabbath. By contrast, in the American South, slavery was race based and perpetual (with rare instances in which slaves were manumitted). Further blurring the distinction was that the Islamic societies in the Maghreb also practiced race-based, perpetual slavery for black Africans. Still, the essential point for seamen ensnared in Barbary captivity was that they could hope for freedom, however distant a ransom payment might be.[4]

At the turn of the nineteenth century, the bashaw of Tripoli was Yusuf Karamanli. Born in 1766, Yusuf was an absolute ruler on a precarious throne. With a brief interruption in the 1790s, the Karamanli family had ruled Tripoli since 1714, and the family dealt with internecine and external threats. On his way to seizing power, in June 1790, Yusuf murdered his oldest brother, Ali, the heir to the throne, in front of their mother. Yusuf Karamanli's forces then laid siege to Tripoli (governed by his aging father) for two years, which created the chaos from the warring branches of the Karamanli family that allowed for a Turkish invasion to seize Tripoli to reassert Ottoman rule. Yusuf then came to symbolize a "national" leadership against Turkish hegemony, and after two more years of fighting, the Karamanlis regained power in Tripoli in January 1795. Yusuf deposed his other older brother, Achmet (known to the Americans as Hamet) that June. Hamet initially agreed to serve as Yusuf's regional governor in Derne, a city hundreds of miles east of Tripoli, but then realized he might not be safe from his brother and went into exile in Sicily, then in Tunis, then in Egypt.[5]

Yusuf was not a worldly man and may have been illiterate. Unlike several of his ministers, there is no evidence that he had seen any European city or traveled out of the Maghreb. At his court, Yusuf and his ministers spoke to foreigners in Italian, the lingua franca of the resident European consuls; he also could speak French. He was superstitious, deeply religious, strong, resourceful, a keen judge of people, and brutal in the treatment of his own subjects. William Ray described him as almost six feet tall, bearded, rather corpulent, with a "manly majestic deportment." Another American characterized Yusuf as "a white man of middling age, rather portly, and tolerably handsome," with two wives, one white and one black, and nine children. Mordecai Noah, the US consul to neighboring Tunis a decade later, referred to Yusuf's "shrewdness and sagacity," finding him "a frank, sociable man."[6]

Tripoli was the major city, port, and capital, of the Barbary power of the same name (although occasionally the whole entity was called Tripolitania). The country extended hundreds of miles, up to the border with Egypt, but except for the area adjacent to the seacoast, it was mostly desert. The city of Tripoli was built on low, sandy ground, in a crescent shape on a peninsula jutting into the sea. Like cities in medieval Europe, Tripoli was surrounded by a thick wall, twenty to thirty feet high, flanked by forts and entrenchments. Three gates controlled access to the city, all of which were opened at sunrise and closed at sunset. Immediately outside the walls of Tripoli were groves of olive trees, fruit orchards, and flower gardens. Along the shore, a mile outside the city, beautiful date trees grew in orderly rows, a stark contrast with the barren, pale sand of the desert and the white-walled, terraced houses in the city, the sky pierced by the minarets of several mosques.[7]

Tripoli's streets were crooked, narrow, and packed with coarse gravel. Private houses were built of a whitish local stone or cement and had no windows on the ground floor; their terraced roofs had pipes running down to cisterns below ground that held drinking water. Besides numerous mosques, the city contained a large synagogue and a Catholic church. There was a coffee bazaar where wealthy men exchanged information and rumors, "cook shops" where a dish of soup and meat could be had for a few coins, and fifty grog shops. The city had no newspaper, post office, college, bank, or courthouse. There were goldsmiths and silversmiths in small shops, all owned by Jews. No one knew how many people lived in the city, but if the estimate of more than thirty thousand is accurate, Tripoli was about as large as Philadelphia in 1800, and half again larger than Boston. The population was polyglot, with Arabs, Moors, Berbers (from the mountainous hinterland), Jews, Christian slaves (mostly Neapolitans), and a smattering of Greeks and Maltese.[8]

The bashaw was guarded by Turkish janissaries, salaried, heavily armed professional soldiers in lavish, colorful uniforms, formed from young boys (Christians by birth) from the borderlands of the Ottoman Empire. Enslaved and converted to Islam, the janissaries were raised to be soldiers, and in Tripoli they provided the nucleus of the bashaw's power. At the other extreme, many beggars lived on the streets, barely clothed. *Marabouts*, Islamic holy men, walked the streets handing out slips of paper with Qur'anic sayings that advised on policy, gave protection from bullets, prescribed cures for disease, and prophesied the defeat of enemies. They roamed the city and chanted from rooftops, threatening and praying, and to many Europeans they seemed "[d]irty, avaricious, [and] often completely mad." Yet they were held in great popular esteem, their very persons held sacred, and no matter what the crime, if an accused could escape to a *marabout*'s house, he was free from arrest.[9]

Although sea breezes meant that the temperature was often mild, the summer was blazing hot, and away from the coast, the heat and sand from the desert winds made it difficult to breathe. The harbor, protected offshore by rocks and shoals, was spacious but relatively shallow. The bashaw lived in an ancient castle in the northeastern corner of the city abutting the water. William Ray called the castle a "huge pile"; Mordecai Noah called it "an irregular shapeless mass," although internally, there were some elegant spaces filled with beautiful mosaics. The castle covered about an acre and rose to almost one hundred feet high. Ray described its front gate as a "narrow, dark, and sinuous passage [that] leads into a handsome square, or court-yard, with a piazza on each side, sustained by colonades of marble." The castle contained reception rooms, a council room for the *divan*—the bashaw's council of notables and ranking officials—a private mosque and apartments for the bashaw's extended family, a *seraglio*, an interior bombproof room if the city came under attack, quarters for five hundred servants and soldiers, an arsenal, a powder magazine, the mint, and storage areas for food. Beneath the castle was a labyrinth of passages and rooms where prisoners were housed or executed. The castle's seaward ramparts were lined with cannon, and artillery pointed in all directions.[10]

After the United States gained its independence in 1783, the British navy, which had protected American ships when America was part of the British Empire, no longer offered support. Indeed, as they were trading competitors, Britain had no interest in helping the Americans. The British regarded paying tribute to Barbary rulers as a "tax" that might suppress the trade of countries like the new United States, which might be less able to pay. With no naval protection, American merchant ships venturing into the Mediterranean were at the mercy of marauding Barbary corsairs. As secretary of state in 1790, Thomas Jefferson estimated that even before America achieved independence, between eighty and one hundred American merchant vessels, with 1,200 seamen, engaged in trading voyages into the Mediterranean each year. After independence, eleven American merchant ships were seized by Algerine corsairs, two as early as 1785. For more than a decade, the United States had tried to free its compatriots, officially and unofficially, through diplomatic negotiations; through the intercession of the Mathurin Brothers, a French religious order; and by raising funds at churches, by public subscriptions, by a national lottery, and by theatrical benefit performances. In March 1796, the administration of President George Washington finally agreed to ransom the eighty-five surviving American seamen held captive in Algiers, for the staggering sum of $642,000. Their ransoming had come none too soon. Six seamen had died of the plague only weeks earlier. Two others had gone blind, and several men were disabled by years of hard labor. In 1794, Congress had decided to create a navy to fight the Barbary corsairs and authorized funds for six frigates, but none of those ships were completed when the administration decided to pay ransom. Instead, the United States entered the same sort of treaties as European countries and made payments to Algiers, Tunis, and Tripoli.[11]

In 1796, at a time when Tripoli held no Americans captive, the bashaw, Yusuf Karamanli, along with his ministers, signed a treaty with the United States that provided that American merchant ships would not be molested by Tripolitan corsairs. In exchange, the US government paid Tripoli 40,000 Spanish dollars and some smaller "presents," pledged to provide an annual gift of shipbuilding materials (specifying a list of hawsers, cables, tar, pitch, rosin, wooden boards, masts, canvas, and anchors), and promised 12,000 Spanish dollars as a gift to the bashaw when any new US consul arrived in Tripoli. The bashaw pledged, in the words of the treaty, that when the money and materials were delivered, they would fulfill "all demands on his part," and "no further demand of tributes, presents or payments shall ever be made."[12]

The American consul in Tripoli was James Leander Cathcart, born in 1767 to a Scots-Irish family in Ireland. Cathcart had come to America as a boy, and during the Revolutionary War, at age twelve, he signed onto a privateer. While serving either as a privateersman or a midshipman in the Continental navy (as he later asserted), he was captured. Cathcart reasserted his British origins to avoid imprisonment, accepting a pardon and serving in the Royal Navy, although he later claimed he had been imprisoned and escaped. After the war, he reasserted his American status and returned to the sea. In July 1785, corsairs captured his ship, the *Maria*, off Cape St. Vincent in the Atlantic, and took Cathcart and twenty other seamen captive. He spent eleven years as a slave in Algiers. Cathcart again reasserted his British origins, petitioning King George III for assistance, and writing to William Wilberforce, the English abolitionist, for help. Neither effort succeeded, and Cathcart again reasserted his American citizenship. Through luck, thrift, using his wits, and networking, he improved his situation in Algiers, buying a tavern and a house with servants and philanthropically supporting the other American captives. By the end of his time in Algiers, he was the chief Christian clerk to the dey. When the United States finally negotiated the release of the slaves in Algiers—after 36 of the 130 men taken as slaves had died in captivity, most of the plague—Cathcart served as a mediator between the dey and the American negotiator, Joseph Donaldson Jr., which resulted in the treaty that gave him his own freedom. He returned to America and married fifteen-year-old Jane Bancker Woodside in June 1798.

In April 1799, he and his pregnant wife arrived back in the Mediterranean, President John Adams having appointed Cathcart the US consul to Tripoli. It must have seemed an inspired choice: Cathcart had spent a decade in the Maghreb, had read the Qur'an and could converse about Islam and the life of Mohammed, and had served under and negotiated with a reigning dey. Cathcart spoke and wrote Spanish, French, and Italian, but when asked by Yusuf Karamanli if he understood Arabic and Turkish, he responded that he had "a trifling knowledge of them but spoke them so miserably that [he] never made any use of them." A hefty man with a baby face, Cathcart was officious and overbearing. He was unpopular with his hosts and would bear the singular distinction of being declared persona non grata by three Barbary rulers. Many American naval officers and diplomats disliked him as well. But President Jefferson respected Cathcart, whom he called "the honestest & ablest consul we have with the Barbary powers: a man of very sound judgment & fearless."[13]

When Cathcart arrived in Tripoli, the bashaw's finances were in tatters. The Levantine Turks, who for more than a half-century had done much to build up the city's economy, had gradually departed, owing to the strife and political uncertainty in the 1790s. There had been famines in the late 1770s and the mid-1780s, followed by an onset of plague that reportedly killed one-quarter of the population, followed by the fighting within the Karamanli family and against the Ottoman-backed invaders. Tripoli's seaborne trade declined and never really recovered. Malta was Tripoli's primary trade destination. Tripoli sent cattle, sheep, and horses to the British island garrison, along with some grain, olive oil, and dates. Tripoli's imports were primarily luxury goods, naval stores, and ordnance, mainly from Malta, Marseilles, and Livorno. Twice-yearly caravans went into the interior of Africa seeking gold dust and black slaves. Camels carried goods to and from Tunis, to Tripoli's west, and east to Arabia. But with Tripoli's agricultural economy depleted, its finances relied on tributary payments from European powers and on punitively high taxes on Tripoli's Jewish minority, the merchants of the city.[14]

Yusuf often treated the Jews with disdain, but he granted Jewish merchants monopolies on trade in certain goods or with specific Mediterranean cities as quid pro quo for tax payments. As consul in Tripoli, Cathcart deplored his own dependence on the Jews. Because Jewish merchants brokered or financed nearly all of Tripoli's trade within the Maghreb and to the ports of southern Europe, and lent money to all the Barbary rulers, they had access to commercial and political information and were perceived to have insight into the Barbary rulers. The Jewish mercantile house of Bacri & Busnach in Algiers had already shown its importance to the United States by guaranteeing the entire treaty debt to Algiers in 1796, which allowed the Americans to be ransomed. Leon Farfara was the Bacri & Busnach agent in Tripoli. Cathcart relied on Farfara to loan the United States money, to translate Arabic and Turkish documents into Italian for him, and to provide information about, and pass messages to, the bashaw. When Cathcart first arrived in Tripoli, he borrowed money from Farfara to pay the American tribute promised to the bashaw upon the appointment of a new consul. Although Cathcart knew that Bacri & Busnach had instructed Farfara to advance any sum of money the United States might need, Cathcart did not like Jews, whom he regarded as cowardly, untrustworthy, and only interested in making money. His Jewish agents, he wrote, "never ask for any thing that is against the inclination of the Bashaw. When they are sent with a disagreeable message they go to the palace, drink a cup of coffee and bring a lie out [that the proposition had been declined,] without ever seeing [Yusuf]." Cathcart's letters are sprinkled with gross epithets against Jews. Still, Cathcart was not devoid of humanity, and he sympathized with "these poor Jews" when the bashaw instigated a pogrom when the rains failed in winter 1800: mobs desecrated the synagogue, robbed houses, and attacked Jews in the streets. In fact, most of the two thousand Jews in Tripoli lived in poverty and were confined behind gates locked at night in a squalid quarter of the city. Although Yusuf relaxed some humiliating regulations, Jews were subject to cruel and capricious treatment from the Muslim population, which by law they could not resist.[15]

By late 1799, Yusuf Karamanli, convinced that the 1796 treaty with the United States did not suffice, wanted more money. Cathcart reported these demands to President Adams's secretaries of state, first Timothy Pickering and then John Marshall, but in the age of sail, six months or more might elapse before he learned of his government's response. In fact, the foreign policy of the United States was focused on negotiating an end to the Quasi-War of 1798–1800 with France. The Quasi-War had deterred American merchant ships from sailing to the Mediterranean, which lessened the urgency of the diplomatic problems with Tripoli and the other Barbary regimes. As peace loomed with France—the Treaty of Mortefontaine was signed on September 30, 1800, but was not ratified by the US Senate until months later—and the resumption of American trade in the Mediterranean appeared imminent, Tripoli's demands became more important. The options before the United States, as with every other country trading in the Mediterranean Sea, were to pay tribute, to send warships to protect its commerce, or to order its merchant ships to withdraw from the area. The Adams administration allowed the situation to drift, despite Cathcart's pleas for a response.

After ratifying the 1796 treaty, the United States paid Tripoli $48,000 in tribute and presents in 1797; $12,000 in 1798; and $22,000 in 1799, when Cathcart arrived, although the promised naval stores often came late. The bashaw felt aggrieved by the payments in arrears and by the absence of a new consul at his court for two years after the treaty was signed, until Cathcart arrived in spring 1799. That year, Tripoli's corsairs began capturing ships of nations with which the bashaw had made treaties. Asking himself rhetorically how Yusuf would support his regime with trade to Europe at a low, Cathcart answered that he would send his corsairs to "sally forth and capture every vessel they fall in with," and that on the slightest pretext, Tripoli would soon attack American trade. In 1800, fearful of the corsairs, Ragusa (modern-day Dubrovnik) paid $100,000 to Tripoli, and the Dutch and the Danes each paid $40,000 and annual tributes of $5,000.[16]

Yusuf engaged in cunning diplomacy with Cathcart. First, he told Cathcart he had made peace with the United States for less than he had received from other nations but "he knew his friends by what he received from them." Then he showed "pique," Cathcart reported, that the United States paid more to Tunis than to Tripoli. Cathcart suggested that Yusuf might be assuaged for a year by a present of at least $10,000, but Cathcart knew that would be poor policy as it would only put off a reckoning, and he asked the administration to send a squadron of warships in case of an attack on American ships.[17] In May 1800, Yusuf wrote what is on its face an almost inscrutable letter to the president (then John Adams) in which he seemed to laud the Americans' cultivation of his good will and friendship. He stated that Cathcart had made it clear that the United States regarded Tripoli equally with the other Barbary regencies. If so, then Yusuf wanted this principle "followed by deeds and not by empty words," and he expected the United States would "endeavor to satisfy us by a good manner of proceeding," which everyone understood meant the bashaw wanted money, at least equal to what Tunis received. "We beg a speedy answer," the letter concluded, "as a delay on your part cannot but be prejudicial to your interests," which everyone understood meant the unleashing of his corsairs on American ships.[18]

The bashaw soon declared war on Sweden, and by November, Tripolitan corsairs had captured fourteen Swedish ships, condemned their cargoes, and put their crews into captivity. Yusuf made a huge demand for peace and ransom. In January 1801, the Swedes paid $240,000 to ransom their 131 captives, and an additional $10,000 to buy peace.[19] That Sweden, which sent a naval squadron to the Mediterranean, was willing to pay more than $1,800 per captive in ransom set a worrying precedent. The quick success with Sweden gave the bashaw what Cathcart called "enlarged" ideas about how to deal with the recalcitrant Americans, given that Barbary rulers no sooner negotiated peace and ransom with one country than they went to war against another. Through the bashaw's foreign minister, Mohammed Dghies, Yusuf told Cathcart in October 1800 that the United States would have to make a one-time payment of $225,000, thereafter maintained by annual tribute of $20,000. Cathcart responded that the poorest citizen in America would "lose their last drop of blood" before they would agree. The next day, Yusuf personally told Cathcart that there must be a fixed annual stipend, noting the 1796 treaty gave him nothing for maintaining peace. When Cathcart refused the demand, the bashaw gave the president six more months to respond to his May 1800 letter but added, "paid I will be, one way or the other." If the United States refused to provide tribute, Yusuf promised to declare war, capture American merchant ships, and hold their crews for ransom. Cathcart sent the bashaw's demand to the US consul in Tunis, William Eaton, who chartered a brig to sail immediately to America with the dispatches. In his covering note, Eaton expressed disbelief that the American diplomats in the Maghreb had heard nothing from the government in the nine months since Cathcart had first raised the alarm. Tripolitan corsairs were fitting out to capture American merchant ships, he wrote, and Cathcart was taking measures to evacuate his family from Tripoli. Eaton reminded Washington that to bow to Tripoli's demands inevitably would result in increased demands from Tunis and Algiers. He concluded: "If the United States will have a free commerce in this sea they must defend it. There is no alternative. The restless spirit of these marauders cannot be restrained."[20]

In November 1800, and again in January 1801, Cathcart sent circular letters to all American consuls around the Mediterranean announcing the bashaw's ultimatum, which he knew meant war. He asked the consuls to inform all American merchants and shipmasters that trading in the Mediterranean would be unsafe after March 22, 1801—or even before, "as these faithless people generally commit depredations before the time or period allowed is expired"—so that American merchant ships might "fly [from] the impending danger." Fly they did; nearly two dozen American ships sought shelter in Barcelona alone, and their masters wrote home asking for convoy protection, stating that their three hundred American seamen were in danger of enslavement.[21]

The bashaw's naval commander was born a Scotsman named Peter Lisle. Formerly the mate of a British packet boat, in 1794, his shipmates had accused him of theft, and he avoided punishment by coming ashore in Tripoli and converting to Islam, adopting the name Murad after a famous Muslim corsair. A year later, the bashaw named him the *rais* of the marine, or commander of the fleet. Murad, a consummate survivor, married one of Yusuf's daughters despite reputedly already having a wife and children at Wapping Stairs, on the banks of the Thames, in London. Murad was forty-two and had a blond beard, a foul temper, and a fine Scottish brogue. With war looming, he privately condemned the bashaw as a "fool" for giving the Americans time to get all their vessels out of the Mediterranean, and he "expected nothing more than to make a Scotch prize of [cruising for American ships] (i.e.) to be captured" himself.[22]

With the new Jefferson administration coming into office in March 1801, it was unclear to the American people what reaction the United States would have. Jefferson had long been opposed to paying tribute to the Barbary regimes, convinced, he wrote, that tribute was "money thrown away, that there is no end to the demands of these powers, nor any security in their promises. The real alternative before us is whether to abandon the Mediterranean, or to keep up a cruize in it, perhaps in rotation with other powers who would join us as soon as there is peace." A rural newspaper, the Burlington *Vermont Gazette*, wanted the country to turn its back on foreign entanglements, recognizing that with Tripoli having successfully extorted money from Sweden, now it would be America's turn. To use force "would be to lose a pound in hopes to gain a penny." Rather, the editors hoped that Jefferson would forego war, turn inward from the Old World, and "encourage domestic manufactures, open an asylum for distressed European artists, and facilitate inland navigation."[23]

Under the heading "The Bashaw & President," a Connecticut wit writing in the *Norwich Packet* took a satirical approach. Yusuf had demanded "a *douceur* [bribe], as a token of the sincerity of [American] friendship" and would estimate America's "friendship and sincerity according to the magnitude of the *douceur*." So, a huge gift he should get: "The President is therefore beseeched to send him the Mammoth Cheese."[24]

The newspapers in coastal towns that would suffer from the loss of trade expressed revulsion. The *Newburyport (MA) Herald* wrote that the demands of the bashaw "must excite a general emotion of indignation in this country." The United States had followed European practice in paying tribute to the "petty states of barbarians and pirates on the coast of Africa," which once may have been understandable, given their geography, "their connection with the Ottoman Porte, the desperate valor of their seamen, [and] the slavery to which they subjected their captives." But now new tribute was demanded, American trade was insecure, and "our citizens exposed to slavery upon every fresh wiff of avarice." This "extortion and humiliation" would "continue and increase until these villains feel our power." The US Navy was now strong enough to "wipe away the ignominy which lies upon us."[25]

Matters were taken out of American hands. Although Yusuf had promised to give the Americans until March 22, 1801, to respond to his letter, in February 1801, he declared the 1796 treaty void and sent out his corsairs to capture American merchant ships. Cathcart sent another letter to the diplomats around the Mediterranean, stating that war was unavoidable, and he advised all merchant ships to remain in port until they might be safely convoyed. Richard O'Brien, the US consul in Algiers, sent out his own warning letter, tersely observing that the bashaw "wants war and he should have it." The Tripolitan War began on May 14, 1801, when Yusuf ordered his janissaries to cut down the flagpole outside the US Consul house, a symbolic and effective method of communicating the severing of diplomatic ties and the onset of war.[26]

TWO

THE MEN

O N MAY 15, 1801, before the bashaw's declaration of war was known in Washington, President Jefferson asked his cabinet whether the United States should send a naval squadron to the Mediterranean and, if so, what its mission should be. The navy had ready a half-dozen ships left in commission after the end of the war with France. Congress was not in session, and it would take too long to call the dispersed senators and representatives back for their advice and consent. The executive branch would have to decide. The attorney general, Levi Lincoln, opined that without a declaration of war from Congress, the navy might defend American merchant vessels from attack, but it should not seek combat. Jefferson agreed. As a result, the objective of the squadron under Commodore Richard Dale was "to support the safety" of American commerce in the Mediterranean and "to exercise our seamen in nautical duty." The squadron was to convoy any American merchant ships that sought protection and defend them against attacks from any Barbary corsairs. If

Dale found that the bashaw had made good on his threats and declared war, then the squadron was authorized to attack Tripoli. But the president was under no illusions. He ended a letter on other subjects, stating, "Tripoli ha[s] demanded a large gratuity without the least foundation, but ha[s] declared there should be no rupture till an answer was received from us. [T]hat answer was of a nature to be sent only by the squadron. [B]ut I am afraid they have not waited."[1]

Dale, who had been John Paul Jones's lieutenant in the Revolutionary War, sailed off with three frigates and a schooner on June 1. On arriving in the Mediterranean, Dale learned of Tripoli's declaration of war, and he tried to establish a blockade of Tripoli. William Eaton, the US consul to Tunis, announced the blockade in a circular letter to European capitals on July 23. But Dale interpreted his orders—correctly—as not allowing his squadron to capture and make prizes of neutral merchant ships attempting to run the blockade, which meant that the most the navy could do was stop and try to persuade foreign merchantmen not to enter Tripoli.[2]

Dale carried a letter from Jefferson to Yusuf that Cathcart, if he were still present, was to deliver, in which the president said he hoped that the expressions the bashaw used in his May 1800 letter to Adams resulted from translation problems and that Tripoli had not broken the 1796 treaty. Dale's squadron of observation, the president wrote his "Great and respected friend," was to "superintend the safety of our commerce" in the Mediterranean and "exercise our seamen in nautical duties," and would, he hoped, not cause "umbrage."[3]

Dale established a base at the British bastion of Gibraltar and left a frigate to stand off the Rock to bottle up two Tripolitan warships fortuitously found there, thwarting their effort to get to sea. With hundreds of men to feed on the Tripolitan ships, no Gibraltar merchant would accept their bills of exchange in payment for provisions, and the British garrison commander refused to provide supplies. The Tripolitan sailors were reduced to serving as stevedores and carting materials around the harbor to obtain pocket money to feed themselves. Although Murad, the bashaw's naval commander, boasted about capturing American vessels, he did not try to sortie from Gibraltar to fight the American ship offshore. Murad demanded that a Ragusan brig in port carry his crews back to Tripoli, threatening to use force if the Ragusans declined, but that gambit did not work, as the American blockading ship refused to allow the Ragusan ship safe passage. Then the crew of one of Murad's ships mutinied, went ashore, broke into a British storage building, and literally ate the sweepings off the floor. But the wily Murad figured a way out of the trap. He sold his ships to Morocco, which raised its flag over them. Murad took passage on a British ship to Malta and then slipped back to Tripoli. His sailors crossed over to Africa in their "Moroccan" ships and made their way back to Tripoli as best they could.[4]

Having left one ship off Gibraltar, Dale proceeded with the rest of his squadron to Algiers, then to Tunis, to see if those regimes had begun hostilities against the United States. They had not. Dale arrived off Tripoli near the end of July. The bashaw refused to accept a gift of $10,000 from the United States to restore peace and insisted on annual tribute payments, a demand to which Dale did not deign to respond. But with distant logistical support, indecisive orders, and his crew falling sick, Dale's blockade, such as it was, soon disintegrated. When Dale's flagship, the frigate *President*, departed Tripolitan waters in early September, the blockade became nominal, "enforced" by American diplomats who refused to issue safe-conduct passports to shipping. Not surprisingly, such a blockade was porous. Dale's ships sailed home. What is remembered from the 1801–02 campaign is a single battle won by the schooner *Enterprise* in August 1801.[5] Although the 1801 campaign was inconclusive, with the force at hand, Dale's squadron was able to achieve some real results: Murad had been forced to abandon two of Tripoli's largest cruisers at Gibraltar, and no American merchant ship was captured while Dale's squadron was in the Mediterranean.[6]

On December 8, 1801, in his First Annual Message to Congress, President Jefferson reported that "Tripoli, the least considerable of the Barbary States, had come forward with demands unfounded either in right or in compact" and declared war on the United States. The president announced that "[t]he arrival of our squadron dispelled the danger" posed by the bashaw's corsairs. In the ambiguous style he often favored, Jefferson noted that without Congress's authorization, American naval forces were not permitted to undertake anything but defensive measures because under the Constitution, the decision to go to war was left to "the legislature exclusively," and Congress might "consider whether, by authorizing measures of offence, also, they will place our force on an equal footing with that of its adversaries." Even with that invitation, Congress did not formally declare war. On February 6, 1802, without additional appropriations, Congress authorized the president to arm and equip warships against Tripoli as he thought proper, making it lawful for the navy to "subdue, seize and make prize of all vessels, goods and effects" of Tripoli, and allowing Jefferson to order "all such other acts of precaution or hostility as the state of war will justify, and may, in his opinion, require."[7]

On different rationales, representatives of both parties thought there was no other choice. John Stratton, a Federalist from Virginia, wrote his constituents that "at its first appearance," the bill had met with some resistance from congressmen thought to be unfriendly to trade, but opposition quickly dissipated. Stratton stated that if he had voted against the law, he would have violated the duties he "owed humanity and the commerce of this country," because he was "fully persuaded that our fellow-citizens who are engaged in commerce have an equal right to protection with the planter who remains at home upon his farm." Indeed, agriculture and shipping were "so closely united," he concluded, that if Congress did nothing, farmers would be damaged because the market for their produce would be gone.[8]

William Dickson, a Republican from Tennessee, wrote his constituents that Tripoli had engaged in "a predatory war" against the United States and he thought it "not improbable" that Algiers and Tunis might join forces with Tripoli. Were that to happen, the short-term effects would be "disagreeable," meaning that more merchant vessels would be taken and more seamen thrown into slavery, but ultimately, it would justify the United States fighting a war that would end paying "a tribute as disgraceful as it is unjust."[9]

The president selected Commodore Richard V. Morris to command the second squadron, setting off in 1802. Morris was the son of Lewis Morris, a signer of the Declaration of Independence, but perhaps more important, he was the brother of the Vermont Federalist representative who, by withholding his vote on the thirty-sixth ballot, allowed Vermont's electoral vote, and therefore the 1800 presidential election, to go to Jefferson and not to Aaron Burr. Richard Morris had been a captain from the navy's founding but had never played a conspicuous role. His squadron consisted of most of the US Navy then in commission, five frigates and one smaller ship. His orders gave him broader discretion than Dale in prosecuting the war, and he was expected to "afford the most complete protection to our commerce." The administration thought that the 1801 campaign must have left an "impression" on Yusuf and that a stronger show of force by the second squadron might so over-awe the bashaw that he would be willing to restore peace without any tribute or payment. Secretary of State James Madison instructed Cath-cart, who had since fled with his family from Tripoli to Livorno, to be available to Morris to negotiate a new treaty with Tripoli.

But Morris was indecisive, and perhaps his lethargy owed to the fact that aboard his flagship he brought his wife, their young son, and their maid. As the consul to Tunis, William Eaton, acidly put it, the ships of the squadron spent more time in Gibraltar and other Mediterranean ports "drinking and wenching" than in blockading Tripoli. Morris finally arrived off Tripoli at the end of May 1803, nearly a year after his squadron arrived in the Mediterranean. After a skirmish with Tripolitan gunboats, and the capture of a large cruiser, the *Meshouda*, by one of the squadron's ships, the *John Adams*, Morris opened negotiations with Yusuf, although he unwisely declined to ask Cathcart, whom he disliked, to join him. The negotiation went nowhere. Although the bashaw was willing to discuss peace and tribute, and named his foreign minister, Dghies, as his negotiator, he wrote Morris, "I do not fear war—it is my trade—I understand it better than anybody." The bashaw demanded 200,000 Spanish gold dollars, and when Morris countered with an offer of $5,000, and $10,000 more in five years if Yusuf did not violate the treaty in the interim, Morris was sent packing with a verbal message that the business was at an end. A few days later, Morris sailed off, lifting the blockade, and the Tripolitan corsairs immediately put to sea. Rumor had it that six corsairs had "sailed in Quest of prey and that 4 other large cruisers would Immediately follow them & endeavour to get into the At-lantic." Jefferson recalled Morris, writing that he had "no expectation that any thing will be done against Tripoli by the frigates in the Mediter-ranean while under his command." Aghast at Morris's performance, Eaton wrote somewhat hyperbolically that "from his first arrival on the station, he never burnt an ounce of powder except at a royal salute fired at Gibraltar," and that for the seventeen months Morris commanded the squadron, he "was only nineteen days before the enemy's port!" Morris was recalled at the end of August 1803, and his performance was considered so inept that he was censured by a court of inquiry and dismissed from the navy.[10]

Richard O'Brien, the consul to Algiers, recognized that a favorable peace with Tripoli would come from "a close blockade and now & then other galling and distressing enterprizes." President Jefferson agreed that the best strategy would be a tight blockade. Still, imposing and maintaining a blockade of an enemy port thousands of miles away from America was not easy. Defending his lackluster conduct, Commodore Morris thought it was "impossible" to blockade Tripoli "without the aid of many small vessels, and a number of both large and small [warships], lying ready in the harbor of Malta for the purpose of relieving those on the station." One captain in Morris's squadron agreed, writing that because the Tripolitans had small galleys that drew little water and therefore could hug the coast, and could sail or row if there were no wind, no blockade would prevent supplies coming into Tripoli or ships from entering and leaving, and therefore a better idea to defend American merchant vessels in the Mediterranean from Barbary corsairs was to institute convoys. Nevertheless, the Jefferson administration believed that convoying was too passive and indecisive, and that the costs of war needed to be brought home to the bashaw. Furthermore, so many American merchant vessels were crisscrossing the Mediterranean that it was hard to imagine an effective system of convoys. On Independence Day 1802, Cathcart reported that at one time, twenty-four American merchant ships rode at anchor just in the harbor of Livorno.[11]

The president pointed out the problems of a blockade in his Second Annual Message to Congress, in December 1802. He scarcely commented on developments in the war but did inform Congress that "[t]o secure our commerce in that sea, with the smallest force competent, we have supposed it best to watch strictly the harbour of Tripoli. Still, however, the shallowness of their coast, and the want of smaller vessels on our part, has permitted some cruisers to escape unobserved," with the result that one American merchant ship, the brig *Franklin* of Philadelphia, had been captured and her crew brought to Tripoli, where they were being held for ransom.[12]

After two years of naval campaigns and Morris's lackluster performance, Jefferson's cabinet was frustrated and tired of the costs of foreign war and of funding the navy. As early as August 1802, Secretary of the Treasury Albert Gallatin, an inveterate foe of naval expenditures, wrote Jefferson that the United States needed to put "a speedy end to a contest which unavailingly wastes our resources." The United States was paying annual tribute to Algiers, and Gallatin thought it was "no greater disgrace" to pay tribute to Tripoli. For Gallatin, it was "a mere matter of calculation whether the purchase of peace is not cheaper than the expense of a war, which shall not even give us the free use of the Mediterranean trade." Not only was war costly, but Gallatin also argued that if Tripoli captured American-flagged merchant vessels, the United States would end up paying much more to ransom its seamen than it would pay in annual tribute.[13]

This argument made sense to Jefferson. From Monticello in March 1803, he wrote Secretary of the Navy Robert Smith that he had "never believed in any effect from a shew of force to those powers." The way the Barbary powers fought cost them little, Jefferson remarked, but any nation sending a force against them had huge costs, and it would be much cheaper to pay off Tripoli with money and presents. In April 1803, the cabinet voted unanimously that the United States might buy peace with Tripoli; surprisingly, when the cabinet secretaries were polled, Smith was willing to pay Tripoli the most, up to $50,000 for peace and $10,000 annual tribute. The president decided, as Madison wrote Cathcart the next day, that he was authorized to pay Yusuf $20,000 as a down payment for peace, and annual tribute of $8,000 to $10,000 thereafter, although the administration hoped it would not have to publicly admit to those terms in a treaty. In the context of negotiations with Yusuf, this authority seems hopelessly unrealistic. Months before, Cathcart reportedly had proposed through the Danish consul in Tripoli, Nicholas Nissen, to pay Tripoli $40,000 for a ten-month truce and $20,000 in annual tribute—terms that had been rejected. The bashaw's minister, Dghies, told Morris about Cathcart's offer, pointedly stating that Cathcart would not have made such an offer without authority. It is unclear why Jefferson and Madison thought Yusuf would be so cowed by the American naval presence or so desperate for peace to accept terms that were half of what he had rejected previously.[14]

Once Morris lifted the month-long blockade of Tripoli in June 1803, the effort to fight wavered. The US consuls in Algiers and Tangiers even provided passports to vessels carrying wheat bound for Tripoli, which damaged any credibility the United States might have had in the estimation of the Barbary rulers. Appalled, William Eaton wrote Madison:

[W]hat kind of a blockade is this, where the invested enemy is furnished with arms, am[m]unition and provisions under the guarantee of the passports of our ministerial agents! Is it pretended that these submissions are the preservative of peace? The calculation is erroneous. They tend rather to precipitate a war; because they show that we dread it; and, it is on weakness and submission that these brigands make war.[15]

Despite Gallatin's desire for a speedy end to the war, and the cabinet's interest in buying peace, the administration decided to embark on another naval campaign, and in spring 1803 formed a third squadron for the Mediterranean. Jefferson took the advice of the navy secretary to change the mix of ships for the new squadron. Instead of five frigates, which had been thought necessary for Morris's squadron in case Algiers or Tunis joined the war, the new squadron would contain two frigates (to provide firepower) and four brigs and schooners, smaller vessels that drew less water and therefore could more closely approach and blockade Tripoli. Revealing his true feelings about the navy, the president suggested to a Republican leader in the House of Representatives that as it was the administration's "purpose to keep only 2 frigates & the 4 small vessels in the Mediterranean this summer: That this therefore is the only force which need be absolutely provided" for the navy by Congress.[16]

For the command of the new squadron, Jefferson chose Edward Preble, a forty-two-year-old Maine native. In the Revolutionary War, Preble had served in the Massachusetts state navy, and with the coming of peace, he sailed for fifteen years as a merchant shipmaster. He was commissioned into the navy as a lieutenant in 1798 during the Quasi-War against France, and the navy agent at Boston had then called him "a smart active popular man, judicious & well qualified for his station." Preble was tall and thin, balding, his auburn hair cut short, with a stentorian voice and commanding presence. When he was promoted to captain in 1799, Benjamin Stoddert, then the secretary of the navy, wrote President Adams that Preble "ought to have been a Captain from the beginning." Preble was given command of the frigate *Essex*, which he sailed to the East Indies and back to protect American merchant ships in those distant waters from French privateers.

Preble was popular among his social equals and those who showed promise. To the common sailors—the jack tars—and to junior officers, he was a dour, choleric, dyspeptic man, an authoritarian with a hot temper and a ruthless sense of discipline who at first patronizingly referred to the young officers sent to run the ships in his squadron as "boys." He was virtually unknown to most of them because during the Quasi-War, he had been on the far side of the world on the *Essex* when they were on ships in the Caribbean, and since he had come home to Maine, he had not been recalled to active service because of a debilitating stomach ailment. Also, he was older, having been born in 1761 and having fought in the Revolution. No other captain in the squadron that was forming for the Mediterranean was even in his thirties. Preble would prove to be a dynamic leader. He was a consummate seaman, gave clear and decisive orders, and as a squadron commander would demonstrate that he was willing to shoulder responsibility and conduct war aggressively, thousands of miles from Washington.[17]

Preble's squadron consisted of six ships. Besides his own frigate, the 44-gun *Constitution*, not yet called "Old Ironsides," his squadron contained another frigate, the 36-gun *Philadelphia*, laid up "in ordinary" (in reserve and out of service) in Philadelphia; the brig *Argus*, just being completed at Edmund Hartt's shipyard in Boston; the brig *Syren*, building at Nathaniel Hutton's shipyard in Philadelphia; the schooner *Vixen*, finishing at William Price's shipyard in Baltimore; and the *Nautilus*, a sleek little schooner the navy purchased from a Baltimore merchant.[18]

On May 21, 1803, Secretary Smith ordered Captain William Bainbridge, then twenty-nine, to take command of the *Philadelphia*, moored in the Delaware River off the Southwark neighborhood of Philadelphia, just south of where the Gloria Dei (Old Swedes) Episcopal Church still stands, and to ready her for sea as quickly as he could.[19] Born in May 1774 in Princeton, New Jersey, Bainbridge had gone to sea at fifteen after briefly working as a clerk at a merchant's counting house in New York. As a teenager, he was the mate on the *Hope* on a voyage to Holland when a mutiny broke out that Bainbridge, armed with nothing more than a broken pistol, put down by beating the ringleader. As master of a merchant ship at nineteen, Bainbridge made trading voyages to Holland and the West Indies, using his fists to ensure he was obeyed. In 1796, on a voyage from Bordeaux to St. Thomas, his small ship, armed with four small cannon and just nine men, was attacked by a 9-gun British navy schooner; Bainbridge withstood the attack and, remarkably, compelled the British ship to surrender. On another merchant voyage to the West Indies, he met, wooed, and married Susan Heyliger, the granddaughter of the governor of St. Eustacia, in March 1797, on St. Barts, and brought her back to live in Philadelphia and Perth Amboy, New Jersey.

Bainbridge joined the navy as a lieutenant in August 1798, as the Quasi-War was beginning, to command the 14-gun schooner *Retaliation*. Bainbridge's autocratic attitudes ran up against the rising tide of Jeffersonian republicanism flowing into American society, even in the navy. The old idea, inherited from the British navy, was that captains were supposed to be aloof and unapproachable. The jack tars tested the system. In 1800, Bainbridge, by then a captain, commanded the frigate *George Washington*, and before the ship ever left her mooring in Philadelphia, a sailor named John Rea—something of a sea lawyer to be sure, who provocatively called himself a democrat—approached him, cap in hand, seeking the balance of his advance wages. Bainbridge exploded at him, "Don't speak to me in that manner, sir, begone—I don't allow a sailor to speak to me at all!" In an open letter to Bainbridge that he published after the *George Washington*'s cruise—and after being paid off—Rea provided numerous anecdotes to show Bainbridge's tyrannical nature. When the *George Washington* was sailing in the Atlantic, in punishment for Rea's sleeping on watch, Bainbridge ordered him tied to the spanker boom for three hours, then placed in irons, and then given a dozen lashes with the cat-o'-nine-tails, with Bainbridge urging the bosun to strike him harder.[20] With a complement of only one hundred sailors and marines on board, Rea asserted that over the course of the cruise, Bainbridge put fifty of the men in irons and flogged forty of them at the gangway, distributing a total of 365 lashes on their backs, with only one real crime (a theft) truly punishable. Bainbridge consigned an experienced bosun to thirty days in shackles and solitary confinement for telling "some brat of a Midshipman" to "Kiss his a——." Perhaps Rea's portrayal exaggerated Bainbridge's lack of human feeling, for Rea described him breaking a sword over a sailor's head, fracturing his skull, and having the man flogged after he was concussed and bleeding. With mock sincerity, Rea derided Bainbridge for not attending the funerals of seamen who died during the cruise and for not visiting ill seamen in the sick bay because it was too distressing. Rea ended his broadside with the biting insult that Bainbridge was not merely unfit to command a navy ship, but even unfit for "having a command in a Negro [slave] quarter." Despite Rea's screed, there is no record of the navy investigating Bainbridge or that Rea's open letter had any effect on his career.[21]

Bainbridge regarded sailors as misfits and lowlifes, and with the demoralizing and brutalizing floggings, it was not surprising that he was unpopular with the men of the lower deck. But to his young officers—by definition, "gentlemen"—he was avuncular and considerate. Midshipman William Henry Allen, who came aboard the *George Washington* in 1800, called his captain "a fine man much the Gentleman." Bainbridge called the midshipmen to his cabin, told them his home address in Philadelphia, and said they should call at his house to "refresh" themselves while they tended to their business ashore, as if he and Susan Bainbridge were their parents. A beefy, broad-faced man, tall and muscular with strong features, dark hair, and thick, long sideburns, Bainbridge had personal magnetism. Few questioned his seamanship or doubted his courage. Yet disgrace and defeat had wracked his career. In the Quasi-War, he surrendered the schooner *Retaliation* to French warships without firing a shot, the first American naval officer ever to strike his colors. In 1800, having anchored the *George Washington* within the range of the cannon at the dey of Algiers's palace, Bainbridge was ignominiously forced to convey the dey's tribute, including a menagerie of exotic animals—camels, tigers, lions, and antelopes—to the sultan at Constantinople. William Eaton, then consul to Tunis, remarked in a withering rebuke to Secretary of State Pickering, "Is it not somewhat humiliating that the first United States ship of war which ever entered the Mediterranean should be pressed into the service of a pirate?" Upon his return to the United States, Bainbridge was given command of the 32-gun frigate *Essex*, Preble's old command, which he sailed to the Mediterranean as part of Dale's squadron. The *Essex* was the frigate that spent months ensuring that the two Tripolitan cruisers in Gibraltar did not escape, and after those ships were sold to Morocco, she convoyed American merchant ships from Marseilles, Barcelona, and Alicante through the Strait of Gibraltar into the safety of the North Atlantic, returning to New York in July 1802.[22]

Bainbridge's new ship, the *Philadelphia*, was a 36-gun frigate, built by public subscription of the citizens of Philadelphia during the patriotic fervor in the initial days of the Quasi-War. In one week in July 1798, 177 Philadelphia merchants and entrepreneurs subscribed more than $100,000 to build the frigate in exchange for government "stock" bearing a 6 percent interest rate. It was an enormous sum of private money at a time when a skilled laborer might earn $1.50 per day. The *Philadelphia* was designed by Josiah Fox, a recent Quaker immigrant from England, trained as a draftsman in the Plymouth Naval Dockyard. Laid down on the banks of the Delaware River in the Southwark area of Philadelphia in July 1798, the *Philadelphia* was launched in November 1799. She was a beautiful, majestic ship, and at 1,240 tons, one-third larger than the typical 36-gun frigate of the time. Unlike the 44-gun American frigates such as the *Constitution*, which mounted 24-pounder cannon on her broadside, *Philadelphia* carried the conventional armament of British frigates, 18-pounder cannon, and thus she had fewer guns and less firepower than the *Constitution*. Like the largest American frigates, however, *Philadelphia* was designed with ultradurable, ultradense live oak wood for her internal structural timbers and with diagonal riders, a form of internal bracing that transferred the weight of the upper decks down to the rigidity of the keel, to prevent "hogging," the gradual sagging of the keel at the bow and stern. In the Quasi-War, the *Philadelphia* made a successful cruise in the West Indies, capturing several French privateers and rescuing American merchant ships that the French had already seized. In 1801, she made a cruise to the Mediterranean with Dale's squadron. Arriving back in Philadelphia in April 1802, she was laid up in ordinary, the sailing era's equivalent of mothballing, for a year, with her topmasts and rigging removed and put in storage ashore. The next year, she was called back into service and given to Bainbridge to command, for another deployment to the Mediterranean.

To ready a ship for active service that had been in ordinary for a year, Bainbridge faced enormous tasks. The *Philadelphia*'s 160-foot-long hull needed its worn or missing copper sheathing replaced, and fissures in the seams needed to be caulked. These were noxious and dangerous tasks for shipyard workers because there was no dry dock in America, and for repairs below the waterline like coppering and caulking, the ship was deliberately grounded ("careened") on soft sand or mud at high tide, to allow workers to make repairs below the waterline, one side at a time, during low tide. The yard workers or the skeletal navy crew also had to set up her rigging, both the standing rigging (the stays and shrouds to keep the masts standing) and the running rigging (the halyards, braces, and sheets, which turned the position of the sails and yardarms to allow the ship to catch the wind). The topmasts had to be mounted on the caps of each mast, and the yardarms had to be raised and crossed. At the same time, gunpowder, shot, spare spars and sails, cordage, tons of food (including biscuit, peas, salted pork and beef, and rum), and huge butts containing fresh water had to be swayed, carried, or rolled aboard, and accounted for and stowed in a way to keep the ship in trim.[23]

In the middle of June 1803, Secretary Smith directed Captain Bainbridge to recruit his crew, not to exceed 320 men. The *Philadelphia* was authorized to sign up 110 able seamen at ten dollars per month and 110 ordinary seamen and boys at five to eight dollars per month, their pay depending on Bainbridge's assessment of each man's experience and ability.[24] As was customary, the navy allowed Bainbridge to appoint his own petty officers: quartermasters, coxswains, gunners' mates, and the like. The commandant of the Marine Corps, Lieutenant Colonel William Burrows, supplied a detachment of marines, and the secretary of the navy assigned the *Philadelphia* commissioned and warrant officers.

In the age of sail, recruiting a navy crew was always difficult, not only because of the higher wages paid to seamen on merchant ships but also because of the hardships and dangers of serving on a warship afloat. A jack tar's life at sea at the turn of the nineteenth century was often wet, usually uncomfortable, and occasionally terrifying. Sailors could expect harsh discipline, low pay, unappetizing food, no privacy, repetitive tasks like the morning drudgery of "holystoning" the deck (seamen on all fours, using a soft sandstone to scrub, smooth, and whiten the wooden deck), and brief moments of terror in battle or surviving monstrous waves and storms. While the US Navy did not resort to the hated British wartime practice of impressment—the forcible seizure of seamen and anyone else caught up by a press gang in seaport towns—assembling a crew relied on unsavory practices. Many American seamen came aboard through "crimps," landlords or their agents who housed seamen in dingy waterfront boardinghouses. In exchange for a seaman signing or placing his *X* on a certificate, the crimp advanced money for food, liquor, lodging, and clothes. The crimp, who acted as a surety for his recruits, delivered the seaman onto the ship with the certificate (which bound the seaman to service), and in payment for his debt collected the seaman's advance wages.[25]

With war renewed between Britain and Napoleonic France in spring 1803, Commodore Preble's initial belief was that crews for the squadron would be recruited easily. He initially believed that the European war would depress wages in the merchant service, and foreign seamen in American ports would volunteer for the US Navy because they "dare not trust to the protection the Merchant Service affords them, and are sure of being safe from impressment with us." In fact, the war in Europe raised seamen's wages, and it was difficult to recruit a crew in Boston and Providence, Rhode Island, for his command, the *Constitution*.[26]

The other ships destined for Preble's squadron suffered from the same shortage. Following British practice, the American navy held recruiting "rendezvous" in seaport towns, near a market or outside of a tavern, where a fifer trilled out patriotic tunes to the rum-tum-tum of a marine beating a drum. The musicians and a lieutenant or midshipman in charge of the recruiting party looked smart in uniform and offered a tankard of ale or rum, and advance pay, to a recruit inside the tavern, even though the law forbade enlisting men who were intoxicated.[27] Joining the navy held out the prospect of worldly adventure and prize money and promised regular, if low, pay, food, and liquor (the grog ration), which represented a certain kind of freedom, an escape from toil and drudgery ashore, a chance for a life not behind a plow or at a workman's bench. Young men often joined the navy to get away from poverty, a creditor, a woman, or a difficult family relationship. No wonder that Herman Melville, who served in the navy forty years later and wrote a semifictional novel, *White-Jacket*, about his experiences afloat, claimed the navy was "the asylum for the perverse, the home of the unfortunate. Here the sons of adversity meet the children of calamity, and the children of calamity meet the offspring of sin." One source of recruits was young men apprenticed to a trade, who may have been ill used by their masters or just bored. Runaway apprentices escaping to sea were so common that advertisements in newspapers—such as that promising a five-dollar reward for seventeen-year-old runaway Thomas Foster, a cooper, with a "dark complexion, black eyes, small rings in his ears, short sailor jacket, and blue nankeen trousers, green spotted waistcoat and check[ed] shirt"—warned shipmasters "not to harbor or take off" such young men "at their peril." When seventeen-year-old able seaman James Durand signed up for the navy at a rendezvous in Baltimore in spring 1804, with his pay set at twelve dollars per month, he wrote that his "old master received my advance, forty eight $ and he furnished me with all the necessities" for the voyage to the Mediterranean.[28]

New York City produced many of the new seamen for Preble's squadron, 140 for the *Constitution*, 40 for the *Philadelphia*, and 100 for the *Argus*. Desertion was a problem from the moment the sailors or their crimps got hold of their advance pay, as the following advertisement in the *New York Evening Post* reveals:

100 *DOLLARS REWARD.*
DESERTED from the naval rendezvous at New-York the following seamen, recruited for the United States brig Argus, viz. James Graham 20 years old, light complexion and hair, about 5 feet 5 inches high, born in New-York; John Williams, 21 years old, light complexion and hair, born in New-York; Moses Cox, 32 years old, dark complexion, eyes and hair, 5 feet 9 inches, born in Portland; and John Thompson light complexion eyes and hair, 5 feet 2 inches high, 19 years old. A reward of 25 dollars for each of the above will be paid on delivering them to the subscriber; and a further award of 50 dollars for William Clark, Grocer, who became surety for the above men, he lived at 33, Division street, New-York. He is an Irishman, about 5 feet 9 inches high, long dark hair, marked with the small pox.
JOSHUA BLAKE, Rendezvous Office
Front street near Fly-market.[29]

Despite low pay, harsh conditions, and Bainbridge's reputation, the *Philadelphia* took on more than 250 landsmen, ordinary and able seamen, and marines. The identities and backgrounds of most of the men who joined the ship in 1803 are lost to time. Unlike the officers, some of whom were socially prominent or later became famous, the jack tars of the lower deck did not have their portraits painted by Gilbert Stuart or Rembrandt Peale, nor have their letters been preserved in archives. Even many of their names are uncertain. To be sure, there is a list of the crew of the *Philadelphia* returning from the Mediterranean in summer 1805 published in the official navy document collection about the Barbary Wars, even though the *Philadelphia*'s log book, journals, and muster rolls were all lost when the ship was captured. On the 1805 list are two Thomas Browns, two James McDonalds, three John McDonalds, no less than four John Smiths, even two John Stouts. Many of the names on the list are obvious aliases. Some men who enlisted in the navy used aliases to evade the law, avoid debt collectors, or escape domestic troubles; others assumed new names when they emigrated from Europe or deserted from the British navy; and many seamen routinely sailed under false names. A large percentage of the sailors and marines serving aboard US Navy warships in the early years of the nineteenth century were foreign-born or just foreign, mostly English and Irish, but others were from France, Scandinavia, and Germany, with a smattering from other places.[30]

For some of the *Philadelphia*'s sailors, however, some historical trace remains. In 1796, Congress enacted a law enabling seamen who could prove their native American birth or who were legally naturalized to receive a paper called a seaman's protection certificate. In those prephotograph, prefingerprint, prebiometric-data days, the paper, carried on the seaman's person, certified American citizenship and provided a government identification that might provide protection from impressment into a foreign navy. In applying for a protection, each seaman provided information about his background and a physical description, including his name, age, birthplace, racial designation if he was not white (such as a "free man of color"), height, hair color, eye color, complexion, scars, distinguishing skin marks, and tattoos. The applicant signed the paper under oath or left his mark. As a result, information survives for about a dozen sailors in the *Philadelphia*'s crew:[31]

William Adams was rated an able seaman, meaning he had experience at sea and was able to go aloft or respond to any need. He was a local man, born in Southwark, Philadelphia, who received his protection in October 1801. When Adams signed on to the *Philadelphia*, he was twenty-nine and described as five feet, seven and three-quarters inches tall, with a fair complexion but "pitted with the small pox [and] has lost his right eye."

Richard Brothers was rated an ordinary seaman on the *Philadelphia*, meaning he had previously served afloat and had basic skills. Brothers received his protection in 1797. By the time he mustered onto the *Philadelphia*, the Delaware native was twenty-five and five feet, two inches tall, his face described as "a little pitted with the Small Pox."

Thomas Cleghorn, another ordinary seaman, received certificate no. 7592 in July 1801. He was described as five feet eight, with dark hair and dark eyes, and "a Cast in his Right Eye" (likely a "sleepy" eye). Born in Philadelphia, he was thirty-nine in 1803.

Joseph Edwards, an ordinary seaman, received certificate no. 7835 in October 1801. He was a Philadelphia native, twenty-eight in 1803, stood five feet seven, and had gray eyes; the rest of the handwriting on his application is illegible.

James Francis, rated an ordinary seaman, received certificate no. 7925 in October 1801. Francis hailed from Perth Amboy, New Jersey. He was twenty-four in 1803 and was described as five feet seven, with a fair complexion, brown hair, and a "large mark of the smallpox on his left breast."

John Mitchell was rated as a quartermaster, a petty officer responsible for manning the helm of the frigate and sometimes for flag hoists and signaling, implying he was a steady, capable sailor. He was born in Philadelphia, received his protection in 1799, and was thirty-one in 1803. He was five feet eight, had black hair and dark eyes, was "marked with the small pox," and bore a large scar on his left hand.

John Morrison received certificate no. 6718 in 1801, and was twenty-two in 1803. An able seaman, he was born in Newburyport, Massachusetts, stood five feet seven, and had brown hair and brown eyes. He had scars on his cheek and nose and a crucifix tattoo on his left arm. Morrison served as captain of the foretop aboard the *Philadelphia*. Topmen were an elite group of able seamen who scrambled out on the yards, day or night, in any weather or sea, to loosen, bring in, or reef the sails. Topmen had to be "[d]aring, acrobatic, and with a *sang froid* that won the respect of their fellows." The captain of a top led the seamen stationed on the mast, and the fact that he was given that position meant he was a savvy, responsible sailor who could set an example or take charge in emergencies.[32]

Christian Myres, whose last name may have been "Myers" or "Meyers" (nineteenth century cursive handwriting occasionally being nearly unreadable) received certificate no. 7440 in June 1801. Rated an ordinary seaman, Myres hailed from the Germantown, just north of Philadelphia.

He was twenty-two in 1803 and described as five feet five, with light hair, blue eyes, a large scar on his right leg, and a small scar on his left wrist.

Thomas Williams, rated an ordinary seaman, received his protection certificate in September 1801, when he was twenty-seven. Williams, who signed his application before a Philadelphia alderman with an X, was born in Charleston, South Carolina. The alderman sized him up as five feet one-half inch and wrote that Williams was marked "with a cut on his right arm, one on the crown of his head, mark'd with the small pox, [and had] a burn on his right arm."

Samuel Woodruff, rated a quarter gunner, hailed from Cape May, New Jersey. A quarter gunner was a petty officer who assisted the gunner's mate in keeping the ship's cannon in proper order. A warship carried one quarter gunner for every four cannon. Quarter gunners were so lovingly attached to their guns, knowing each cannon's idiosyncrasies, that captains sometimes used them as aimers if single shots, not broadsides, were needed. Woodruff received his protection certificate in 1796, and when he signed onto the *Philadelphia* in 1803, he was thirty-five and described as having a fair complexion and being five feet six, with brown hair and a small scar on his nose.

There were free black sailors in the *Philadelphia*'s crew, although there is no record of the number of black men who signed onto the frigate. In August 1798, when the navy was first being organized, the then secretary of the navy, Benjamin Stoddert, ordered that "No Negroes or Mulatoes are to be admitted" into the service. Presumably following that order, in July 1803, Commodore Preble wrote to a recruiting officer for the *Constitution*, "You are not to Ship Black Men." Nevertheless, the orders that Secretary Smith sent to each captain in summer 1803 did not prohibit recruiting black seamen, and men were entered on the ship's muster roll without any reference to color. There was a "John Robinson" rated as an ordinary seaman on the *Philadelphia*, and a John Robinson received a protection, certificate no. 5553, in August 1800. If the references are to the same man, Robinson was a free black man, born in Annapolis, Maryland, twenty-eight in 1803, five feet four, with a scar on the calf of his left leg.[33]

Undoubtedly there were other free black men on the *Philadelphia* and on each of the ships of Preble's squadron; in the pre-Jim Crow navy, black seamen were not listed or categorized separately. And although it was against the law, there may have even been a few fugitive slaves serving on navy ships.[34]

When the *Vixen* sailed from Baltimore to the Mediterranean, a newspaper article mentioned that as she fired a cannon salute to the town, a gunner's mate put a match to a cannon, not realizing it was still being charged with powder. The match caused a small explosion that "carried off" the forearm of the gunner's mate and blew him over the side into the water, where he would have drowned but for "a negro [sailor] on board [who] jumped over and supported the sailor until the boat picked him up." Black seafarers made up approximately one-sixth of the seamen applying for protections in Philadelphia in the early nineteenth century, which suggests that black seamen made up a substantial part of the pool of possible recruits for ships such as the *Philadelphia*. The prejudice that black men faced on board ship came mostly from officers. There was no segregation, although black sailors and white sailors tended to mess separately. With their lives dependent on each other, and with the need to work together on ropes and sails and guns, the surviving evidence suggests that black sailors lived and worked alongside white sailors with less racial antagonism than in the land-based world—certainly less than in the slave-based American South. There may have been friendships or at least camaraderie across racial lines, as suggested by the black *Vixen* sailor diving overboard to save his wounded white comrade from drowning.[35]

From the 853 surviving individual records of seamen who received seamen's protection certificates in Philadelphia from 1796 to 1803, which is a reflection of the local American seamen available for enlisting on the *Philadelphia* in May 1803, some tentative conclusions can be drawn about the frigate's sailors. The median height of a Philadelphia-enrolled mariner was only five feet six. A significant number bore the marks of smallpox, whether from surviving the full onslaught of the disease, which in the 1770s John Adams had called the "King of Terrors," or from the inoculation, which usually gave the patient only a mild case. And a large percentage of their seamen protection certificates bear an *X*, not a signature, and even those who knew how to sign their names might not have been able to write anything more than that. Of the applicants for seamen's protection certificates, 37 percent were illiterate. No women served aboard the *Philadelphia*, nor (as far as it is known) did any woman enroll as a man.[36]

One of the last men to sign on to the *Philadelphia* was William Ray, an exception to the overall lack of literacy afloat. His life story is also reasonably well known. Born in Salisbury, Connecticut, in 1771, Ray was raised in upstate New York. Although he had just a "common school" education, Ray had memorized much of Milton's *Paradise Lost* and Pope's "Essay on Man" before he was twelve. He survived smallpox (which means he was pitted with its marks) and grew up to become a quarrelsome, contentious man, an egalitarian with fervent Jeffersonian Republican political views. Unique among the *Philadelphia*'s crew, Ray was an aspiring poet. He struggled to earn a living as a teacher and storekeeper, always teetering on insolvency, and he was once jailed for bankruptcy in upstate New York. Although he was married with a daughter (he eventually would have three daughters), he does not mention his wife or children in his autobiographical sketches. In 1803, Ray accepted a job as the editor of a Philadelphia newspaper at a salary of thirty dollars per month. As he traveled south, his horse died, he fell sick, and when he arrived in Philadelphia after his recovery, the job had been given to another man. With no friends or family in Philadelphia, and having run out of money, on July 3, 1803, in what he described as "a paroxysm of half despair and half insanity," he signed on to the *Philadelphia*. Although listed on the ship's books as a marine private, he was "taken into the wardroom to write for the officers." Almost immediately, Ray complained that a warship "was no place to find repose"—how could he have thought otherwise?—and he winced at the severity of naval discipline. From the moment he stepped aboard, "[t]here was almost one incessant outcry of men writhing under the rope's end or the cat[-o'-nine-tails]."[37]

On July 12, 1803, the *Philadelphia* warped out of the city of her birth and began to sail down the Delaware River to the open ocean. She had gone only about ten miles—just south of what is now Philadelphia International Airport—when she ran aground near the lower end of Little Tinicum Island, apparently misjudging the depth of the water at half-tide. She was undamaged and soon refloated, but it was an omen of what was to come.[38]

The *Philadelphia* sailed downstream to New Castle, Delaware, to take on fresh water and some final stores before entering the Atlantic. The last recruits came on board, the forty men who signed up at the rendezvous in New York, brought down to New Castle in a pilot boat by the frigate's second lieutenant, Jacob Jones. The frigate's purser, Keith Spence, a Scottish immigrant via Portsmouth, New Hampshire, where he had left his wife and daughters—his son Robert Traill Spence was a midshipman going out to the Mediterranean in another ship in the squadron—also joined the frigate. Spence was the oldest man on the ship (and perhaps in the entire navy), having been born in 1735, in the Orkney Islands, and he immigrated to New England before the Revolutionary War. He had not been successful as a merchant. He joined the navy during the Quasi-War, serving as purser, the warrant officer in charge of all the accounts and stores, on a succession of ships. A purser faced liability for losses and pilferage, but in addition to his pay, he received a commission on the issuance of the daily allowance of food, as well as a percentage of the receipts for goods sold to the crew, including clothing ("slops") and tobacco. The job of purser could be lucrative. In his letters, Spence refers to his position affording him a chance to advance to an "independent" financial position. As one might expect, many seamen regarded pursers as predatory. Without identifying Spence by name, William Ray questioned "the justice in [the purser] charging seamen fifty cents a pound for tobacco—fifty cents for a jack-knife, and more than one hundred per cent on all his slops—when, by law, he is allowed to charge no more than ten per cent? Where does the amount of this enormous profit go?" Spence immersed himself in the enormous paperwork relating to the inventory of supplies and the receipting of provisions for a major warship departing for extended service overseas, and he wrote his wife, Polly, on July 26 that he had "never been so busy, working explaining and managing matters." He noted, "We have now everything and every man aboard (our complement 325 men) and shall sail the first puff of fair wind."[39]

The officers of the *Philadelphia* used their time while the ship was in the Delaware River to organize the crew, with the petty officers pushing, cursing, or striking inexperienced sailors into place. At sea, a warship was a large, rigidly hierarchical community isolated from the rest of mankind, subject to the will of her captain. As Melville put it, "a ship is a bit of terra firma cut off from the main; it is a state in itself; and the captain is its king." Particularly for new sailors, this way of life took time to understand. Each sailor was assigned to a watch, station, and quarter bill, a mess for communal eating, and a berth. The watches divided the crew in half, to serve the ship in shifts, day and night. Shipboard tasks were further organized by "divisions": waist, afterguard, foretop, maintop, mizzen top, and forecastle. For every one of the thousand tasks and evolutions the ship might go through, from lifting or casting an anchor, to setting, trimming, or reefing the sails aloft, to bracing the yards around, to firing the guns, each man had his station. Many tasks required strength and stamina, and men had to work together to develop highly particularized skills with the sails or the guns. The navy did not tolerate laziness or shirking, and bosun's mates made sure that a seaman moved along briskly and obeyed orders promptly by "starting" him, using a three-foot-long, hardened, twisted rope end called a "colt" to strike a sailor's back or buttocks through his clothes.[40]

At the time, one sailor, Samuel Leech, described a warship as a vast machine—the Industrial Revolution was giving prominence to machines—"in which every man is a wheel, a band, or a crank, all moving with wonderful regularity and precision to the *will* of its machinist— the all-powerful captain." More recently, to those of a leftist cast, the regimentation of time and task, together with the brutal discipline aboard ship, acting on a mass of barely literate, "expropriated," "motley" "workers," suggests a "proletariat." Had they understood that freighted term, it is doubtful that jack tars would have embraced that characterization. Rather, sailors represented more of a counterculture whose hard-drinking, cursing, bawdy, carousing ways rejected social hierarchies. Sailors were conscious of a brotherhood among shipmates, which contained a strong sense of egalitarianism, but, perhaps paradoxically, many went to sea to find freedom from the tedium and regimen of work on land.[41]

While the *Philadelphia* lay moored off New Castle, Secretary Smith's orders arrived. In his early forties, Robert Smith had been a leading admiralty lawyer in Baltimore before Jefferson appointed him to the Navy post on the recommendation of his older brother, Samuel Smith, a Republican congressman (who also had served as acting secretary of the navy), after a half-dozen other men spurned Jefferson's offer of the position. Robert Smith ran the navy in an administration that was indifferent about, and sometimes hostile to, the very idea of a navy. In setting forth his principles before seeking the presidency, Jefferson had written in 1799 that he supported "a naval force only as may protect our coasts and harbors" and not "a navy, which, by its own expenses and the eternal wars in which it will implicate us, will grind us with public burthens, and sink us under them."[42] The Naval Peace Establishment Act of March 1801, passed by the lame duck Federalist Congress to preserve a semblance of a navy before the Republicans came to power, limited the navy to just six ships in commission, and seven laid up in ordinary. The other sixteen vessels were sold at auction. The law allowed the navy to retain 9 captains, 36 lieutenants, and 150 midshipmen, and at times during Jefferson's administration there were scarcely 1,000 officers and sailors in the entire establishment. In 1801, Jefferson reduced the number of privates in the Marine Corps to 400, along with 31 commissioned officers, and there were serious, repeated efforts in Congress to abolish the corps. Although Smith had a few clerks and a bookkeeper in the Navy Department, he had no officer or staff to advise him on operations, construction, repairs, or personnel. He personally managed nearly everything. Although the navy employed agents in the ports to handle local contracts for supplies, the secretary approved plans to build ships, oversaw repairs, chose midshipmen, appointed officers for each ship, and directed operations through voluminous correspondence with far-flung officers. At the same time, he served in the president's cabinet. On top of all that, Smith directed a war in the Mediterranean, five thousand miles away, without a telegraph or radio communications, a remarkable achievement for one man. Smith's ability to keep the navy funded despite budgetary battles with Treasury Secretary Gallatin, and at the same time win Jefferson's friendship, reflected his easygoing personality and courtly manners.[43]

"It is the command of the President," Smith wrote Bainbridge, that "as soon as your vessel is in a state of readiness, you proceed to the Mediterranean & place yourself under the command of the Commanding Officer of the American Squadron," soon to be Edward Preble. Once in the Mediterranean, the *Philadelphia* was to "subdue, seize and make prize of all vessels, goods, and effects belonging to the Bashaw of Tripoli or to his subjects." The administration doubted that Bainbridge would be able to take any prizes, and Smith observed, "Our main object is the protection of our commerce and this we are to effect by depriving the enemy of the means of annoyance." The United States was not looking to expand the war. Smith reminded Bainbridge to respect the rights of other nations and warned him that "[w]e shall scrupulously & without indulgence examine that conduct which shall bring us into collision with any other power." Smith made provision for funds to be available for contingencies from merchants in London and Livorno, and the navy had agents at Gibraltar and Marseilles who would support the squadron. Smith closed by wishing Bainbridge success and glory.[44]

THREE

THE CRUISE

THE *PHILADELPHIA* PUT TO SEA ON July 27, 1803. She enjoyed pleasant weather and a fine westerly breeze, making the Strait of Gibraltar in twenty-six days, a fast passage in the days of sail. Harsh naval discipline prevailed. Captain Bainbridge ordered sailors flogged for drunkenness, sleeping on duty, and cursing at and talking back to officers. One marine caught napping a second time was put in irons, where he remained until the frigate went aground off Tripoli four months later.[1]

The harsh discipline correlated to the heavy doses of alcohol served out daily to all hands. Each man aboard was entitled to a half-pint of rum, called "grog" after the nickname of a British admiral from a half-century before. Navy rum had an alcohol content about twice as high as rum bottled in modern times. The rum was diluted with water, usually at a ratio of three parts water to one part rum, and lemon or lime juice was added, when available, to prevent scurvy. Sailors could also purchase sugar from the purser to add to their grog and make it into a kind of rum punch. In a twice-daily ritual, before noon and in the late afternoon, the men were called up by their mess to the main deck, and each man downed his tot on the spot at the grog tub, although on some ships, warrant and petty officers could drink theirs at their mess table. Herman Melville described the ritual, and the importance of serving out grog:

At the roll of the drum, the sailors assemble around a large tub, or cask, filled with the liquid; and, as their names are called off by a midshipman, they step up and regale themselves from a little tin measure called a "tot." No high-liver helping himself to Tokay off a well-polished sideboard smacks his lips with more mighty satisfaction than the sailor does over his tot. To many of them, indeed, the thought of their daily tots forms a perpetual perspective of ravishing landscapes, indefinitely receding into the distance. It is their great "prospect in life." Take away their grog, and life possesses no further charms for them.

Given the amount and the potency of navy rum, many men were inebriated every day. No wonder that the word "groggy" entered the general vocabulary. While it took the edge off the harshness of life at sea, grog made some men stupid and others belligerent, leading to accidents and injuries, as well as to conduct—drunkenness, insubordination, mistakes—that was punished.[2]

Bainbridge was a severe disciplinarian. A dozen lashes from the cat-o'-nine-tails was a bloody ordeal for the offender and a dehumanizing spectacle for the massed crew. The punishment ceremony was ritualized. The officers, in full uniform, assembled on the quarterdeck, the marines were drawn up at attention, and the crew mustered to the main deck to witness punishment. The prisoner was brought up, guarded by a marine and the ship's master-at-arms. The captain read out the offense and recited the penalty. The prisoner's shirt and waistcoat were removed, and he faced a grating set up vertically on the main deck or he bent over the capstan. His hands were tied to the grating above his head or to the capstan. The bosun took the cat-o'-nine-tails from its special bag and awaited the order to "Lay it on." The "cat" consisted of nine cords of braided cotton, eighteen inches or two feet long and a quarter of an inch wide, affixed to a handle. When the captain ordered the punishment to begin, the bosun spread the cords of the cat with his fingers, and then, tossing the cords over his shoulder, he would swing his arm violently around, whipping the cords across the victim's bare back. The first blow often was enough to cut open the prisoner's flesh. After each blow, the master-at-arms called out the number of lashes. When the ordeal was over, the victim's bindings were cut down. If he was able, the victim could return to duty. Some men withstood twelve or more lashes without a murmur. Others wept or fouled themselves, and some needed the care of the ship's surgeon. The "standard" flogging of a dozen lashes was said to leave a man's back looking like raw meat. Witnessing such punishments caused some men to desert at their first opportunity.[3]

In stridently condemning naval discipline, William Ray was an outlier. Early nineteenth-century America allowed a slaveholder near-absolute rights over his slaves, fathers near-absolute power over their children, and artisans control over the lives and welfare of their apprentices: the navy's treatment of its men was an accepted practice. Beatings and floggings were the norm for a pupil who angered his tutor and for minor crimes in the civilian world. Most sailors understood the need for discipline afloat and did not object to flogging unless it was excessive or arbitrary.[4]

Under naval regulations, officers were not subject to flogging or other forms of corporal punishment for disciplinary infractions, although they might be court-martialed or summarily dismissed from the service. Still, the discrepancies in punishment for the men of the lower deck and for officers for similar offenses were not lost on anyone, even if the discrepancies were understood as inherent to the social hierarchy of that era. During Edward Preble's tenure in command of the Mediterranean squadron, a marine private named William Johnson was court-martialed for sleeping at his post on board the frigate *Constitution* while she lay moored in Syracuse harbor in Sicily, a friendly port. He pleaded guilty, but by way of mitigation he testified that his duty had been "uncommonly hard, being two hours on & two hours off post" for the previous twenty-four hours. Taking account of Johnson's "youth, former good character, and apparent penitence," he was sentenced to fifty lashes. Three months earlier, when a young lieutenant, Joseph Maxwell, was found asleep on watch while his ship, the brig *Syren*, cruised off the enemy (Tripolitan) coast, Preble referred to Maxwell's "almost unpardonable" neglect of duty, but because it was the first complaint against him, and because his commander interceded on his behalf, Preble decreed his punishment to be an admonishment read out on the quarter-deck of his ship. John Rea, the sailor who raised this disparity in treatment between officers and enlisted people in his 1802 open letter to Bainbridge, commented sarcastically, "It is a fine thing to be an *Officer*—it makes a man a *gentleman*; he ought therefore, to be excused, though the charge of *all* is upon him."[5]

For his part, William Ray chaffed at the idea of young midshipmen with unchecked power over seamen old enough to be their fathers. The "chief cause of so much tyranny," he wrote in his memoir, "is the practice of giving [midshipmen] warrants to boys." He also got in a political swipe, claiming that "every cruel officer that we had on board was a warm partisan for British precedents, and of course a serious federalist." While acknowledging that discipline and subordination were needed in the navy, he despised a "coxcomb of an officer" who punished men for slight errors or when they were trying to do their duty but were ignorant of what needed to be done. Foremost in Ray's loathing was Midshipman James Biddle, a bantam-sized twenty-year-old who seemed obsessed by the need to be shown deference. One morning during the *Philadelphia*'s cruise, Biddle checked to see that the marines' hammocks were properly stowed. Two marines responded to him by calling out, "Here," omitting "sir," which, Ray insisted, was the customary practice among the marines on board. Biddle "flew into the most outrageous passion," seized the end of the mizzen halyards, and started to flail away at the marines with "twenty to thirty blows," which did them little damage. "Lucky for them," Ray concluded, Biddle was "no Mendoza," the famous English Jewish boxer.[6]

Biddle represented everything Ray despised. Biddle was from a wealthy family of ardent Federalists, a political party premised on social distinction, deference from below, and *noblesse oblige* from above. Biddle had attended the University of Pennsylvania, but the victories of Commodore Thomas Truxtun in the Quasi-War excited many young patriotic men to enter the service, and the Biddle family succeeded in getting James a midshipman's warrant and placing him on board Truxtun's next command, the frigate *President*. Despite Biddle's lack of sea time and combat experience, and despite his family's politics, the Jefferson administration retained him as one of 150 midshipmen under the Naval Peace Establishment Act of 1801, and he was assigned to the *Philadelphia* in summer 1803. With his need to be shown respect and his quick resort to blows to make himself obeyed, Biddle made a poor impression on Ray. But it is not hard to imagine that the jack tars tried to bait and undermine a small, slight, insecure young man.[7]

Ray, who also was to become a vehement critic of Bainbridge, admired him on the voyage across the Atlantic. In a poem composed at sea, he compared Bainbridge to "stern Ulysses" or "Achilles bold," writing,

> *The martial look of Bainbridge shall inspire*
> *The dauntless ardor of heroic fire;*
> *His sword shall triumph in the vengeful blow,*
> *And deal destruction to the recreant foe.*

As the *Philadelphia* steered for Gibraltar, Bainbridge exercised the men at quarters, firing the massive 18-pounder cannon in broadsides over the open ocean. Looking back on the voyage, Ray made fun of how "truly ludicrous" it was for three hundred men to run around the ship with cutlasses and battle-axes pretending to cut and stab when there was no one there. At the time, however, he was not so cynical and captured in a poem how thrilling it was to go to quarters:

> *"Clear ship for action!" sounds the boatswain's call—*
> *"Clear ship for action!" his three mimicks bawl;*
> *Swift round the decks, see war's dread weapons hurl'd,*
> *And floating ruins strew the watery world!*
> *"All hands to quarters!" fore and aft resounds.*
> *Thrills from the fife, and from the drum head bounds;*
> *From crowded hatchways scores on scores arise,*
> *Spring up the shrouds and vault into the skies!*
> *Firm at his quarters each bold gunner stands,*
> *The death-fraught lightning flashing from his hands!*
> *Touch'd at the word, tremendous cannons roar,*
> *The waves rush, trembling, to the viewless shore!*[8]

The *Philadelphia* sailed into Gibraltar Bay on August 24, 1803. The American squadron, led by the *Philadelphia*, had arrived at Gibraltar at a critical moment. Earlier that month, Richard O'Brien, the US consul in Algiers, had written to the US consul at Cadiz that two Tripolitan "galoetas," each with three lateen sails, four cannon, fifty to sixty men, and

"13 benches of oars," had arrived at Algiers and would "sail in a few days for the coast of Spain, no doubt in search of American unarmed vessels." O'Brien asked the consul at Cadiz to warn masters of American merchant ships and to provide this intelligence to captains of any US Navy warships who might "be informed in time to prevent the threatened evil."[9]

Captain Bainbridge paid a call on John Gavino, the consul at Gibraltar, and learned that Tripolitan corsairs had been seen off Cape de Gata at the southeastern corner of Spain. The next morning, Bainbridge ordered his ship back out to sea to find them. On the evening of August 26, abreast of Almeria Bay, the *Philadelphia* came upon a large armed ship—not a "galoeta"—and a merchant brig, sailing in company. The *Philadelphia* forced the cruiser to "heave to" by firing several cannonballs in front of her, but the brig took advantage of a stiff breeze and fled into the murky darkness. The strange warship answered the *Philadelphia*'s hail that she was from Barbary, a generic explanation that did not satisfy the Americans. Bainbridge demanded she send a boat over to the *Philadelphia* with her papers, which revealed she was a Moroccan warship called *Mirboka*, carrying twenty-two guns, under a *rais* named Ibrahim Lubarez. By "not making ourselves known to the officer who came on board," who presumably thought he was on a British frigate, Bainbridge learned that the fleeing brig was the *Mirboka*'s American prize, the *Celia* from Boston. Bainbridge sent his first lieutenant, John Cox, with a boatload of armed sailors to the *Mirboka*. They searched the Moroccan ship and below deck found the *Celia*'s master and seven seamen in irons. Bainbridge "instantly ordered all the Moorish Officers on board the frigate" and seized the *Mirboka*. Conveying her one-hundred-man crew over to the *Philadelphia* and manning the Moroccan ship with an American prize crew took time, and the *Celia* escaped into the darkness. But the next afternoon, Bainbridge spotted the *Celia* rounding Cape de Gata, and by midnight, she was retaken. The *Philadelphia* escorted both into Gibraltar.[10]

Although the United States and Morocco supposedly were at peace, the American officers and crew might hope for compensation for saving the *Celia* and capturing the *Mirboka*. In fact, in 1795, two years after Mulay Suleiman became emperor of Morocco, he had called in James Simpson, then the US consul at Gibraltar, to discuss how much the

United States should pay him in annual tribute, only to realize he was dealing with the country whose independence his father had recognized in 1777. He decided that no tribute was necessary. But that was then; it was now unclear if the emperor had declared war. If the *Mirboka* was a "good prize" under the law of nations because the United States was at war with Morocco, each officer, sailor, and marine aboard the *Philadelphia* stood to gain a monetary share from the capture and sale of the *Mirboka*. And because the *Celia* had been in the hands of the Moroccans for more than twenty-four hours, her recapture by the *Philadelphia* might entitle every man aboard the frigate to a share of "salvage."[11]

Leaving the *Celia* and *Mirboka* in Gibraltar Bay, Bainbridge immediately set the *Philadelphia* out to sea again, this time in response to information from Gavino that another "Moorish frigate" of thirty guns was in the Atlantic off Cape St. Vincent. The American frigate searched for ten days but saw nothing but open ocean. "We should have been staid out longer, notwithstanding the encumbrance of our Prisoners," wrote Spence, the purser, "but the Captain thought it indispensibly necessary to see Commodore [Richard V.] Morris before he went to America, so that Government might have full information respecting this unexpected rupture with Morocco." Returning to Gibraltar Bay, the *Philadelphia* found the newly arrived frigate *Constitution*, under the new commodore, Preble.[12]

With Preble aboard the *Constitution* was the Jefferson administration's consul general to the Barbary powers—the chief American diplomat in the Maghreb—Tobias Lear. A native of Portsmouth, New Hampshire, and a Harvard graduate, Lear had served as George Washington's secretary during his presidency and in his retirement at Mount Vernon. In those years, Lear met every important person in the new republic, handled Washington's correspondence, and helped manage his sprawling farms and investments. Washington regarded Lear as indispensable, keeping him on even after discovering that he had once pocketed accounts payable to Washington to service his own debts. When Washington was called back to service to command the army during the Quasi-War, he made Lear part of his military family, and Lear used the title "Colonel" for the rest of his life. Despite twice marrying into the general's extended family (two of his wives died) and constantly being in the great man's orbit, in the mid-1790s, Lear developed Republican sympathies. Lear was at Washington's bedside when he died in December 1799, vetted his papers, and allegedly destroyed Washington's letters that excoriated Jefferson for having maligned Washington when he was president.[13] Given the veneration accorded to Washington, had any of his letters blasting Jefferson come to light, they might have damaged Jefferson's standing. After Jefferson became president, he kept Lear employed in lucrative federal jobs, first sending him to Saint-Domingue (now, Haiti) as US consul general. When Lear had to abandon that post in 1802 as a result of revolutionary upheaval and French military intervention, Jefferson appointed him in 1803 to the far distant post in Barbary. Accompanying him aboard the frigate *Constitution* was his new wife, Frances Dandridge Henley Lear, one of Martha Washington's nieces, to take up residence in Algiers.

Lear was a complex figure. He had strong friendships, such as with Commodore Preble, his childhood schoolmate at the Governor Dummer Academy in Massachusetts, but he also made implacable enemies. Mordecai Noah, the consul to Tunis a decade later, provided a damning portrayal, writing that "Col. Lear possessed no extraordinary acquirements," merely the excellent manners of a gentleman. From Washington, Lear "had acquired a portion of his prudence, without any of his energy; [he was] cold, calculating and timid." Lear was outwardly self-assured and dedicated to bolstering his country's position in the world; unique among American diplomats, he got along with the Muslim rulers in Barbary.[14]

After the *Mirboka*'s prize crew (made up of sailors from the *Philadelphia*) sailed her into Gibraltar Bay, three of the American sailors deserted to the frigate HMS *Medusa*, claiming to be British subjects. The *Medusa*'s captain, Sir John Gore, refused to give them back to Bainbridge, noting the three "were known to be [British] when they were enter'd as part of the *Philadelphia*'s Crew, and having again placed themselves under the Flag of their Liege Sovereign cannot possibly be given up either to the United States or any other Foreign power, whatever engagements they may have enter'd into." Indeed, Gore requested that two other men on the *Mirboka* be released to him as they "wish[ed] to return to their Duty and Allegiance." Preble demanded the return of the three sailors, asserting in lawyer-like fashion that he knew of no British subjects on the ships in his squadron; he knew them "only as Citizens of the United States, who have taken the Oath of Allegiance to our Government." Still, he did not regain the deserters.

Three more sailors from the prize crew of the *Mirboka* then deserted—Gore must not have been exaggerating—none of whom Preble could get back. A few days later, four more sailors deserted from the *Philadelphia*, three to the *Medusa*. Desertion was a constant plague in the early navy, but ten sailors belonging to the *Philadelphia* in the space of a few days was extraordinary. While it may seem odd that American sailors deserted to the British navy, and not the other way around, William Ray asserted some sailors had been so "ill used" by Bainbridge that they said they were treated better as pressed men in the British navy. Besides, jack tars switched between the two navies with surprising frequency, based on self-interest and the reputation of the ship they might decide to join. Gibraltar was a major base in the Mediterranean, and British-born sailors among the crew of the *Philadelphia* decided to find a British ship eager for their skills where they might avoid a disciplinarian like Bainbridge.[15]

The first news of the *Philadelphia*'s encounter with the *Mirboka* reached America by the merchant brig *Harriot*, under a Captain Adams, which arrived in Newburyport, Massachusetts, on October 26. Buried in its shipping news column, the local paper reported that in arriving in forty-five days, the *Harriot* "Left at Gibraltar, 10th Sept. brig Celia, Bowen, of Boston—a few days before Capt. A. arrived at Gibraltar, the frigate Philadelphia, Capt. Bainbridge, brought in a Moorish ship of war of 26 guns, who had previously taken the Celia of Boston, when on her passage to Alicant[e], and had her in co. 9 days."

The news, of course, spread like wildfire, to Boston and Salem, then down the coast to New York, Philadelphia, Baltimore, and Washington.[16]

When President Jefferson learned of Morocco's hostile action, he fully backed Bainbridge. Navy Secretary Smith conveyed the president's thanks to Bainbridge through Preble, praising the "vigilance and foresight exercised by him in the whole conduct of this business and the rapid movements he subsequently made to arrest the Mischief intended us." Jefferson informed Congress that the *Mirboka*'s hostile act was "without cause and without explanation," and it was "fortunate that Captain Bainbridge fell in with and took the capturing vessel and her prize." The administration hoped the episode did not augur war with

Morocco. Reportedly, Secretary of State Madison understood that the king of Morocco had ordered his cruisers to capture American merchant ships, and the *Celia* had been taken as a result. The arrival of Preble's squadron in the Mediterranean in early September allowed a substantial force to make a demonstration of power at Tangiers. Madison predicted that Preble "would probably propose to return the cruiser upon receiving assurances of future good conduct," and the United States could hope that "friendly arrangements will be entered into, [and] everything restored to its former footing."[17]

After learning of Bainbridge's capture of the *Mirboka* and recapture of the *Celia*, Preble wrote King Suleiman of Morocco, demanding to know if he had declared war against the United States.[18] Preble's initial reaction to Secretary Smith was to complain that like Algiers or Tripoli, Morocco sent out its cruisers, "and if they prove successful, it is war, and we must purchase peace, suffering them to keep all they have taken, but if they are unfortunate and we capture their Cruizers before they have taken any thing valuable it is not war altho the orders for Capturing our vessels are found on board." He mused, "I know not how long we shall be obliged to submit to this sort of treatment, the Moors are a deep designing artfull treacherous sett of Villains and nothing will keep them so quiet as a respectable naval force near them."[19]

The king responded to Preble that he had not authorized his cruisers to capture or molest American merchant ships. He indicated he would punish the governor of Tangiers, a man named Hashash, who, the king said, had unleashed the *Mirboka*. Hashash survived only by the intervention of European consuls. Suleiman proposed meeting the American commodore at Tangiers on October 10. Preble brought most of his squadron to Tangiers and anchored within three hundred yards of the city. An officer aboard the *Syren* wrote that the king arrived "in all the pomp of eastern magnificence, escorted by 15,000 cavalry and 5,000 foot [soldiers]," whereas Preble arrived with the guns of the massed ships of his squadron, which "were ranged immediately under their batteries, and with a determination, should negotiacion fail, to commence an immediate attack upon the town." After Suleiman indicated he wanted peace, Preble ordered the *Constitution* "dressed" in her flags, and a twenty-one-gun salute boomed out to honor the king. Suleiman returned the compliment by sending out to the squadron ten bullocks, twenty sheep, and abundant poultry. Preble and Colonel Lear went ashore, where Suleiman talked of peace, disavowed having given hostile orders, and promised both to confirm in perpetuity the treaty made between the United States and his father and to restore all American property. On October 12, Preble and Lear received a copy of the order from the king to his provincial governors, bearing the royal seal, restoring peace. To cement the deal, Preble returned the *Mirboka* and her crew to Morocco, but in his letter to Secretary Smith he noted sardonically that the ship was "such a miserable piece of naval architecture that I do not believe we have an officer in our service that would be willing to attempt to cross the Atlantic in her [for a prize court proceeding] for ten times her Value."[20]

The news that there would be no war with Morocco arrived in America with a merchant ship in Salem, Massachusetts:

PEACE WITH MOROCCO.
Capt. Mugford, who arrived here on Tuesday night [November 22, 1803] in 33 days from Gibraltar, brings the agreeable intelligence, that our differences with the Emperor of Morocco have been settled; and that the ship taken by Capt. Bainbridge had been restored, and sailed for the Emperor's dominions.[21]

President Jefferson praised his naval commanders. Informing Congress that the king had disavowed the actions taken by the *Mirboka* and all differences had been adjusted amicably, Jefferson referred to Preble's "promptitude and energy" and "the proper decision of Captain Bainbridge, that a vessel which had committed an open hostility, was of right to be detained for inquiry and consideration." Jefferson asked Congress to indemnify the captors of the *Mirboka* for their "interest."[22] Congress ultimately appropriated $5,000 compensation for the *Mirboka*. Under the prize law in place, Bainbridge received three-twentieths of this amount, or $750, his officers received smaller percentages, and the approximately 260 sailors and marines collectively received seven-twentieths of the whole, or about seven dollars per man.[23]

With Lieutenant Cox having sailed in the *Mirboka* as prize master, David Porter came aboard the *Philadelphia* at Gibraltar to fill his place as first lieutenant. Born in the North End of Boston in February 1780, Porter grew up in Baltimore, where his father, a sea captain, was in charge of the signal station on Federal Hill. Young Porter went to sea at age sixteen with his father, sailing to the West Indies and then to Saint-Domingue. While his ship took on cargo at Jeremie, a British press gang tried to board, which the Americans resisted with force. Several men were killed, one by Porter's side; the Britons retreated. On his second voyage, Porter was twice impressed onto British warships and escaped both times, showing pluck and resourcefulness, and making his way home by working his passage, once via Copenhagen. Porter entered the US Navy as a midshipman in April 1798 and was assigned to the frigate *Constellation*, under Thomas Truxtun. Truxtun ran a taut ship, demanding much from his midshipmen and trying to weed out lazy young men from the nascent officer corps. Young Porter had the gumption to approach Truxtun to say he was considering resigning from the service, when he received this epic reply:

Why you young dog! If I can help it you shall never leave the navy! Swear at you? Damn it, sir—every time I do that you go up a round on the ladder of promotion! As for the first lieutenant's blowing you up every day, why, sir, 'tis because he loves you and would not have you grow up a conceited young coxcomb. Go forward and let us have no more whining.

Under Truxtun, Porter fought in an epic battle of the Quasi-War, showing his courage when the *Constellation* captured the French frigate *Insurgente* in February 1799. In the din of battle, on his own initiative, Porter climbed up the rigging to secure the foretopmast, which had been damaged by a cannonball and was swinging loosely. When the *Insurgente* was captured, he went over to the prize with Lieutenant John Rodgers, and with eleven sailors managed to sail the leaking, battered French ship through rough seas and heavy weather into St. Kitts, going without sleep for three nights, with a loaded cannon pointed down the hatchway to keep 173 discontented French prisoners below deck. Porter was promoted to lieutenant that October. Already in the war with Tripoli, he had distinguished himself, serving as first lieutenant of the schooner *Enterprise* in summer 1801 when she pummeled a 14-gun Tripolitan vessel, and as a lieutenant on the frigate *New York* in Morris's squadron.

Yet Porter had a dark past. In March 1802, while searching in Baltimore for some seamen who had taken their advance wages and deserted,

Porter stopped in a Fells Point tavern for "refreshment." There he was confronted by the barkeep, a man named McGlossin or McGlassin, who may have been drunk. McGlossin spoke disdainfully of the navy and its recruiting practices and ordered him out. In the inevitable fracas outside the tavern, McGlossin knocked Porter down and started stomping on him. Porter drew his sword and stabbed the man, killing him. A crowd gathered and started to pelt Porter with stones, forcing him to escape into the harbor by boat. Secretary Smith initially ordered Porter to be turned over to the state for trial, but when it became clear that Porter had acted in self-defense, Smith asked the Maryland authorities not to prosecute him, and a *nolle prosequi* was granted. Nevertheless, Porter's killing a man was notorious, and rumor had it that the navy kept him in the Mediterranean to let memories of the incident fade before he next set foot in America.

A smallish man with nervous energy and a mercurial temper, Porter did not make a good initial impression on the crew of the *Philadelphia*. His son, David Dixon Porter, who wrote a highly sympathetic account of his father's life, acknowledged that as a lieutenant, Porter was sometimes "too severe" with his sailors. William Ray saw Porter ordering two sailors flogged who did not respond quickly or obsequiously enough to him, and then had them flogged again for not pulling their hats off when addressing him. Nothing better could be expected from a man, Ray wrote, who had "deliberately stabbed a man in Baltimore, and had to fly from the pursuit of justice, and dare not return to America for fear of the halter."[24]

While the *Philadelphia* was moored in Gibraltar Bay, four shipwrecked American seamen came aboard. Seamen stranded in a foreign country had to find their own way home. They typically had no money, much less enough to pay for a passage. If they found an American ship, they normally had to serve on board to pay their way by working. To Gavino, the consul at Gibraltar, a short-handed American frigate must have seemed an ideal place to direct the four shipwrecked seamen and dump his responsibility. Without informing Bainbridge in advance, he had James Ingerson, Daniel Shays, Nathaniel Brooks, and Charles Rhilander rowed out to the *Philadelphia*. Although Bainbridge asserted the "people willingly came on board," that was only because Gavino told them they were being given passage on a ship bound to America. When the *Philadelphia* upped anchors the next day and set sail to go farther into the Mediterranean, the four seamen approached Bainbridge (which may have been an ordeal in itself), explained Gavino's falsity, and asked to be put ashore. With the ship underway, Bainbridge did not, as he later reported, "gratify their whim." Over time, Bainbridge was able to persuade one of the four to join the navy voluntarily, but the others refused to enlist. Nevertheless, Bainbridge stated grimly, they "were made to do duty"—forced to serve. Ray asked in his memoir, "Was this any better than impressing?," and one is hard-pressed to defend Bainbridge's conduct. Although three of the four did not join the navy, they all were paid and were treated as part of the crew.[25]

In giving Preble command of the Mediterranean squadron, Secretary Smith had ordered him to begin "an effectual blockade" of Tripoli, to be maintained as long as the weather allowed. On September 16, 1803, two months before Preble announced the blockade in letters to diplomats scattered through Europe, he decided to send the *Philadelphia* and the brig *Vixen* to begin the blockade, which Morris's squadron had lifted three months earlier. Bainbridge was to convoy any American merchant vessels in Malaga, Spain, that wanted an escort and to voyage east as far as he thought would benefit the service. The *Vixen* would accompany the *Philadelphia*, subject to Bainbridge's orders. Both vessels were to sail along the southern coast of Spain to flush out any Tripolitan cruisers, and Preble directed that the *Vixen* stay "well in shore to look into the Bays, and snug places." En route to the coast of Africa, they could stop at Malta. Preble allowed Bainbridge some discretion with the *Vixen*: "you may make such use of her as may to you appear most proper." But their goal was Tripoli, where the *Philadelphia* and *Vixen* were to reestablish the blockade and "annoy the enemy by all the means in your power." Bainbridge was "not to allow the vessels of any nation to enter, or have commerce with Tripoli, but you have a right to treat as an enemy, whoever attempts to enter that place, or carry any thing to it, without your leave, while it is blockaded by you." When "the Season makes it dangerous to cruise on the Coast of Tripoli," Bainbridge could shelter the *Philadelphia* and *Vixen* in Malta.

The coast of North Africa was known to be a dangerous place. Commodore Morris noted that from Cape Bon in Tunisia to the Gulf of Sidra, "every where the soundings are irregular, the water generally shoal," and that even far out of sight of land, ships went aground on reefs and banks, "consequently the navigation is dangerous in the best seasons." With the two ships expected to arrive off Tripoli in mid-October, Preble informed the secretary of the navy that "[a]s the winter is fast approaching I conceive there will soon be very little danger from the Tripolines until the spring opens[;] in the mean time Capt. Bainbridge will be able to keep them in check with the *Philadelphia*, and *Vixen*."[26]

The Americans did not really worry about the Tripolitans as a naval force. The most up-to-date description of Tripoli's maritime strength came from the Danish consul in Tripoli, Nicholas Nissen, sent to Cathcart in September 1803. Nissen, who called his rendering "an exact statement," reported that Tripoli could put to sea a 14-gun brig, two xebecs mounting 12 and 10 guns, a schooner building on the strand that would carry 10 or 12 guns, four small galliots, each armed with a few cannon, and ten gunboats. The gunboats stayed close to Tripoli harbor, relying on the shoals and reefs off the coast to prevent larger vessels from approaching too close. Even so, the Tripolitan fleet was less than it seemed. Its officers were largely untrained, unskilled navigators, and the crews were mostly landsmen brought aboard by a local type of impressment. If met at sea, Cathcart noted, the Tripolitans would fire one "broadside, and then set up [a] great shout, in order to intimidate their enemy; they then board you if you let them with as many men as they can."[27]

Keith Spence, the purser, wrote his wife Polly that for perhaps twenty months, the *Philadelphia* would be in the Mediterranean, fighting the Tripolitans, and that he did not expect another opportunity to post a letter to America until the spring. The *Philadelphia* sailed from Gibraltar on September 23, 1803, and called at Malaga but found no American vessels going farther into the Mediterranean. After taking on fresh water, the *Philadelphia* proceeded along the Spanish coast as far as Cape St. Martins, speaking to all vessels she encountered but gaining no intelligence about any Tripolitan corsairs. She then turned south, came in sight of the island of Galitta, on the African coast, then passed the Bay of Tunis, but still did not see any ships. Off the southern coast of Sicily, the frigate spotted and chased a 22-gun Tunisian cruiser, but when the *Philadelphia* brought her to, she carried the passport of the US consul, and there was no basis to stop or seize her. The *Philadelphia* arrived at Valeta, Malta, on October 3, and landed spare masts and naval supplies for the future use of Preble's squadron at the British Naval Dockyard. While the *Philadelphia* lay moored in Valetta harbor, two more sailors deserted. One of them, named Walker, had been flogged a few days earlier on David Porter's orders for what Ray claimed was no discernible fault, and Walker had said that if he could not desert, he would jump overboard to drown himself. Although years later Porter's son claimed that in his few weeks aboard the frigate Porter had won Bainbridge's favor by "exacting strict obedience and attention to duty from all under him," Ray, who was there, claimed that there was "a general murmuring among the men of insufferably bad usage."[28]

On October 5, the *Philadelphia* and *Vixen* sailed from Malta; two days later they arrived off Tripoli to begin the blockade. They remained on what Bainbridge called "this solitary station" without seeing an enemy corsair except under the protection of the bashaw's forts in Tripoli. Bainbridge expected to remain offshore until late November, when the weather would force them back to Malta. On October 19, the *Philadelphia* hailed an Austrian Empire brig coming out of Tripoli, from which Bainbridge learned that two Tripolitan corsairs were out on a cruise. Presuming they likely would have sailed west, Bainbridge used the discretion in Preble's orders to direct Lieutenant John Smith, the commander of the *Vixen*, to sail to Cape Bon, where Bainbridge thought the *Vixen* might encounter the enemy. In any case, he realized the *Vixen* would be safer there than if she stayed off Tripoli, where gales blow with great violence offshore. The next day, the *Vixen* sailed off.

What seemed to Bainbridge to be a sensible decision would have terrible consequences. On October 31, sailing by herself, the *Philadelphia* ran aground on the Kaliusa reef a few miles off Tripoli, having given up the chase of a Tripolitan xebec. As the sun set, after four hours of desperately trying to free the frigate from the rocks, Bainbridge surrendered his ship and the 307 men aboard.[29]

As the Star and Stripes came down, and as the Tripolitan corsairs swarmed aboard, the United States was confronted with the worst foreign crisis the new republic had yet faced. If the *Philadelphia* could be refloated, repaired, and taken into Tripolitan service, she might undermine America's maritime advantage in the Mediterranean and even embolden Algiers or Tunis to join in the war. Worse, more than three hundred Americans were about to become prisoners in a far-off land,

and it was far from obvious how they could be freed, and at what price in lives and money. The Tripolitan War, which had been about the right of free navigation of the seas, would have a new focus: how to keep alive and free captive Americans. Yet the government in Washington would not even know of the surrender of the ship and the imprisoning of her men for months to come.

FOUR

CAPTIVITY

BOATLOADS OF ARMED TRIPOLITANS began to come aboard the stranded *Philadelphia* and immediately started to plunder the crew and strip the ship of everything of value. Theoretically, when a corsair captured and boarded a ship, the boarders were entitled to seize small items of personal property found among the surrendering crew, and other property was placed around the mast for distribution to all, with no man taking more than his just share. That may have been the theory, but on the *Philadelphia*, there was an orgy of stealing, with every Tripolitan sailor grabbing all he could.[1]

The Americans were ordered off the ship. Dr. Jonathan Cowdery was one of two surgeon's mates aboard the *Philadelphia*, and his diary, published in newspapers and as a pamphlet in 1806, is one of the eyewitness accounts of the Barbary captivity. Cowdery, believing he would be safer if he aligned himself with someone in charge, found a Tripolitan officer who, through his gestures, assured him of his friendship. Cowdery carried his trunk of clothes, but his new "friend" signaled him that he could not take it and it would be safe with him. The Tripolitan "hurried [him] over the side of the ship, while his other hand was employed in rifling my pockets, from which he took about ten dollars." Cowdery passed down into one of the Tripolitan boats, where he found the "Turks" stripping the other surgeon's mate, Nicholas Harwood, and the carpenter, William Godby, of their possessions and outer clothes. Three boarders confronted Cowdery with drawn sabers and cocked pistols and wrested his frock coat off his body, "picking its pockets, and quarrelling with each other for the booty." Cowdery saw his chance and jumped into the next boat, which was almost filled with *Philadelphia* officers, with whom he thought the Tripolitans might be more circumspect. The boat set off for the city, with *Philadelphia* sailors rowing themselves into captivity, Tripolitans "standing with drawn sabres over our heads."[2]

As the boat came close to the shore, two Tripolitan sailors hit Cowdery on the side of his head, searched him, and took away his surgical instruments, a pocket book (which they returned since it contained his papers but no money), a silver pencil, and the handkerchief he was wearing around his neck. Sailing Master William Knight recounted that "as we were going they began to Rob us of wa[t]ches cravats money some of their coats—the Capt. treated no better than other officers—every article taken but what they stood in." Bainbridge's gold epaulets and his cravat were ripped off him. He wrote later that he and his officers "lost everything except what was on our Backs, and part of that tore off Our Pockets picked, Watches and Money taken, even to Pocket handkerchiefs & Gloves." Only by struggling was he able to save a miniature portrait of his wife, Susan.[3]

The officers' boat landed at the foot of the bashaw's palace. An officer recounted, "It was just dark when we approached the beach, which was covered with people, armed and shouting most hideously, and landed, amidst the shouts of the populace, by whom we were pushed about rudely." As other boats neared the beach, the crew was pushed or thrown into the sea, left to swim ashore or drown. Ray was "thrown headlong into the waves, foaming from a high breeze, when the water was up to our armpits," and left to wade ashore. All survived the landing onto the African coast. The Americans were ordered into the palace, through a row of armed guards who cursed and spat on them.[4]

Captain Bainbridge and the other officers were brought into the palace first, taken through narrow corridors and up flights of stairs into an ornate, marble-floored hall covered with rich carpets. The bashaw, Yusuf Karamanli, received them with his *divan* about him, flanked by guards. Yusuf sat on a raised throne, inlaid with tile and covered with velvet cushions. He was dressed in a white turban and a blue silk robe embroidered with gold, and on his diamond-studded belt were pistols inlaid with gold and a gold sword. The officers were paraded before him. The bashaw counted them, a broad smile on his face. Through an interpreter, he asked: How many men were on the frigate? How many guns did she carry? Were her guns made of brass? How much gunpowder did she carry? Did she carry money? Where was the squadron commander? Where was the schooner *Enterprize*? After he got answers, the officers were given supper, and the bashaw's foreign minister, Mohammed Dghies, led them out of the castle to the house formerly occupied by Cathcart, the US consul. Dr. Cowdery described it as "a very good house, with a large court, and roomy enough for our convenience." Bainbridge received permission to contact the Danish consul, Nicholas Nissen, who visited the Americans that first night and promised he would help them as much as he could. That night, Nissen gathered all the bedding he could find, which he brought to the American consul's house, along with some food and drink. By 2:00 AM, the officers were left to sleep on mats and blankets spread on the tile floor. All the officers, with a few seamen who acted as their stewards, a total of forty-three men, were consigned to the American consul house.[5]

The sailors and marines were not so fortunate. After they waded out of the surf, they passed through a double file of armed soldiers up to the castle. A gate opened to reveal a dark, winding stairway, which led to a large hallway lined with more armed soldiers, some of whom jostled or spit on them. They were brought before the bashaw after he was done with the officers, but the sailors and marines were given nothing to eat. They laid down to sleep in a piazza near the bashaw's audience hall, open to the night air, some in their own wet clothes, some in ragged, old, dry clothes Neapolitan slaves brought them.[6]

For the crew, the next morning, November 1, the first day of captivity, began with a weird encounter that seems straight out of Shakespeare's witches in *Macbeth*. A bent old woman, described by Ray as "an old sorceress" and "a frightful hag," came to visit the Americans on the piazza. Ray later learned that she was regarded by the bashaw as an "enchantress" and a "prophetess," and supposedly, she had predicted the capture of the *Philadelphia*. Ray recounted that she "looked round upon us, and raised a shrill cry of *bu-bu-bu-bu*, struck her staff three times upon the pavement, and then went through and examined us." Ray was spooked by the old woman, but her only action was to choose a black sailor to be a cook in the castle.[7]

Yusuf then came to visit them with his retinue. Using Murad, the Scottish-born *rais* of the marine as a translator, the bashaw asked the crew if Bainbridge was a coward or a traitor. They responded that he was neither. Yusuf could not understand the surrender and said his gunboats would not have attacked the stranded frigate at night. He ridiculed Bainbridge for being a coward. Then he suggested that Bainbridge was more likely a traitor because he could not imagine a captain unacquainted with the waters and without an adequate chart sailing in shallow water so recklessly. The bashaw asked about America's naval strength, and the men responded with a "surprising" number of ships. Murad, bearded, dressed in a turban and loose fitting clothes, a curved dagger at his waist, asked if there were any skilled "mechanics" among the crew, and after he found out that the frigate had armorers (blacksmiths), sailmakers, coopers, and carpenters, they were selected to work on special projects in the port and around the city.

The rest of the men were counted and marched out of the palace, through narrow alleys to an old magazine used as a storeroom for sacks of grain, lumber, and old munitions, which months earlier had housed the Swedes captured and held for ransom. Once the American sailors hauled these materials away, the magazine was to be their quarters. Ray estimated the space to be fifty feet long, twenty feet wide, and twenty-five feet tall, with an overhead skylight and two grated windows in front. It was a dismal place, dark, smoky, and floorless. The enlisted men were ordered out, counted again, and each handed a twelve-ounce loaf of black bread, their only food for the day. Their guards, whom Ray called "overseers," "drivers," or "keepers," then ordered them back into the magazine, where they were counted a third time. This constant counting worried the Americans, who feared that every time "all hands" was called, they were about to be separated from each other, with some moved into other parts of the country. That did not happen. But on the first day, they learned that anyone who did not show immediate respect to their drivers by pulling off his hat was beaten. Ray, the man who winced at floggings in the navy, witnessed that day a *bastinado*, the ancient punishment in Barbary. The wrongdoer was thrown on his back, his feet placed through and twisted around by ropes attached to a wooden yoke until they were raised up, horizontally, and then the soles of his feet beaten with a three-foot wooden bat. As night drew in, there were no hammocks or even straw on which they might sleep, and the 260 sailors and marines of the *Philadelphia* lay down on an old sail spread over the damp, pebbly earth of the magazine.[8]

When Bainbridge woke up on November 1, the first day of his captivity, he felt the full weight of his loss of the ship. Although his officers were literally in his presence, he put his quill pen to paper, asking them to give their written opinion of his conduct the day before. He hoped it would be a balm to his feelings—Bainbridge said a testimonial "in some measure [might] alleviate my feelings which are beyond description." But he also told them that he would submit the paper to Washington, thinking the president himself would want to know what the officers thought. Bainbridge might also have wanted their opinions in writing against the day when they all might be freed, the navy would formally inquire into his conduct, and his officers would testify about him in court: a signed statement would corral all the officers in support, if later any had doubts. The officers responded immediately and sympathetically:

SIR: We, late officers of the United States frigate *Philadelphia*, under your command, wishing to express our full approbation of your conduct concerning the unfortunate event of yesterday, do conceive that the charts and soundings justified as near an approach to the shore as we made; and that, after the ship struck, every exertion was made, and every expedient tried, to get her off, and to defend her, which either courage or abilities could have dictated. We wish to add, that, in this instance, as well as every other since we have had the honor of being under your command, the officer and seaman have distinguished you. Believe us, sir, that our misfortunes and sorrows are entirely absorbed in our sympathy for you.

The four lieutenants, the sailing master, the lieutenant of the marines, the surgeon and his two mates, the eleven midshipmen, the purser, and the four warrant officers each signed the testimonial.[9] In a private letter to Vice President Aaron Burr, a family friend, Midshipman Biddle echoed the testimonial (which he had signed), writing that "the shoal we run upon was never laid down on any chart yet published, nor ever before discovered by any of our vessels cruising off this coast; consequently, the charts and soundings justifying as near an approach to the land as we made, not the smallest degree of censure can be attached to Captain Bainbridge for the loss of the ship." Years later, Dr. Thomas Harris, Bainbridge's friend, who spoke with Bainbridge before writing the earliest biography about him, wrote that the officers' letter left the captain "much gratified." Yet Bainbridge was sufficiently self-aware to understand that his ranking over his officers, and the fact that he had solicited their support, diminished the worth of the testimonial. At the time, he wrote his wife, Susan, that he attributed his officers' support "to a generous wish on their part to sustain me in my affliction." Regardless, Bainbridge sent the letter to Secretary of the Navy Smith.[10]

Bainbridge began his own letter to Smith, "Misfortune necessitates me to making a communication, the most distressing of my life." Bainbridge provided an account of the chase, the grounding—he referred to the *Philadelphia* as being "wrecked on Rocks," but of course she was not "wrecked"—his efforts to get the frigate off, the surrender, and the plundering. He plaintively stated that "[s]triking on the Rocks was an accident not possible for me to guard against" because the reef was not on his charts and he had the leadsmen sounding the depths. Bainbridge made clear that his officers and men were not at fault, and in fact had "done every thing in their power worthy of the character & stations they filled." While in captivity, the officers would support themselves on "as equinonomical a plan as possible" on credit from Preble and American diplomats, while "the Crew will be supported by this Regency."[11]

In addition to his letter to Secretary Smith, Bainbridge wrote Commodore Preble with the "distressing information" of losing his ship "by being wrecked on rocks about four and a half Miles from the town of Tripoli." Bainbridge defended sending the *Vixen* to Cape Bon but acknowledged that had he not "sent the Schooner from us, the Accident might have been prevented," and even if the *Philadelphia* had run aground, the presence of the *Vixen* could have deterred any Tripolitan gunboats or cruisers from approaching. He informed Preble that none of the Americans had even a single change of clothes, and that he would be gouged in negotiating bills of exchange for ready money, meaning the officers in captivity would have to "rely on [the squadron] aiding and assisting us." The American officers survived initially on a $300 loan from Richard Farquhar, a Scottish merchant from Malta who happened to be in Tripoli and witnessed the loss of the ship and the officers and men being stripped of everything, and who later provided Preble with intelligence about Tripoli.[12]

Bainbridge also wrote the US consul in Malta, Joseph Pulis, asking for $300, along with certain medicines that Drs. John Ridgely, Harwood, and Cowdery would need to treat the officers and men while in captivity. Pulis informed Preble of Bainbridge's request, and Preble responded that if Bainbridge had asked for ten times that amount, Preble would honor the request. Given the slowness of communications, Bainbridge had to borrow $500 from Dghies, the bashaw's minister, for which Bainbridge had to give him a bill of exchange on a merchant firm in Livorno, at 15 percent loss to the drawer (Bainbridge).[13]

As soon as he learned of the disaster, James Leander Cathcart sprang into action. His priority was to ensure that the news of the loss of the *Philadelphia* got to America. He asked a merchant ship captain in Livorno to carry his dispatch, and the letters from Tripoli, to Barcelona, so the papers might be consigned to the first ship sailing to the United States from there. If none were ready to sail immediately, the captain was to give the mail to the US consul at Malaga for forwarding home.[14] Cathcart also used funds at his disposal to buy two suits of clothes for every member of the crew and sent Danish consul Nicholas Nissen 3,000 Spanish dollars to distribute to the "sufferers." Finally, Cathcart opened a line of credit for Nissen with a firm in Naples if Nissen chose to draw on it, or Nissen could draw bills of exchange upon Cathcart himself. Bainbridge did not use Cathcart's proffered line of credit, choosing to rely on credits established by Preble, and later, on credits opened by George Davis, the US consul in Tunis, and Lear, perhaps because Cathcart had no official position after he departed from Tripoli. In just the first month, Preble put a line of credit worth $6,000 at the disposal of William Higgins, a British merchant in Malta, for Bainbridge's use, drawing from ten bills of exchange on a firm called Mackenzie & Glennie in London.[15]

For his part, Lear sought to initiate a $10,000 line of credit in Tunis for the benefit of the captives. He blamed the Bacri & Bushnach house in Algiers for the absence of ready money. One of the Bacris told Lear that their house would have to forward money to their agent in Tunis, but Lear interpreted that comment as an effort "to throw obstacles in the way" to favor a Jewish merchant. As late as January 1804, Bainbridge complained that the officers needed credit, although ultimately, the captive officers' money problems were solved.[16]

Nicholas Nissen visited the officers every day and soon became the savior of the beleaguered Americans. Only thirty-one years old in 1803, Nissen had been brought up as the son of an officer in the Prince Frederick's (Prins Frederiks) Regiment of the Danish army, although rumor had it that his real father was Count Johann Struensee, the German doctor who became royal physician to Denmark's manic-depressive King Christian VII, lover to Queen Caroline Matilda, and de facto regent before being toppled by a coup, and then executed, in 1772, the year of Nissen's birth. As a teenager, Nissen received a commercial education while a clerk for the Danish Asia Company for five years. He passed the *examinatus juris* in 1792 (the law examination for the "uninitiated"— those who could not read Latin—after taking the law course from the University of Copenhagen) and was employed in the College of Commerce from 1793 to 1797, rising to clerk. In 1799, Nissen was appointed the Danish consul in Tripoli, although he took up the post a year later.[17]

Bainbridge asked Nissen to serve as the Americans' commissary, supplying provisions and other goods, for which Bainbridge could pay with lines of credit. The Danish consul also acted as the Americans' postal service: through him, they might send and receive letters to and from the outside world. For a few days, the Tripolitans allowed the officers to walk on the rooftop terrace of the consul house, which commanded a view of the port, the sea beyond, the town, the bashaw's palace, and the adjoining countryside. Dr. Cowdery took advantage of the opportunity to climb up to the roof on the first day. From that vantage point, he sadly observed the *Philadelphia* still "on the rocks, full of Turks, and surrounded by their boats, and a constant stream of boats going to, and bringing off, the plunder of the ship. We could see these robbers running about town, with our uniform coats and other clothing on." Within days, however, the bashaw ordered the officers off the terrace, sent some masons into the consul house to wall up the passageway to the rooftop, and placed a guard at the front door to prevent the officers from going onto the street. Passersby in the street jeered and mocked the Americans and, as an unnamed midshipman witnessed, "point[ed] the finger of scorn at us." To be made "the sport of such villains" infuriated the midshipman, but he realized there was nothing he could do except try to remain stoic. Although every officer signed a parole of honor, written in French, by which they promised not to escape as *quid pro quo* for freedom of movement about the city, when the bashaw refused to allow them to leave the consul house, in the officers' minds he broke the agreement they had just signed.[18]

The newly imprisoned Americans thought of their loved ones, thousands of miles away, and wanted to send home the calamitous news of their capture before their families and friends imagined the worst. Sailing Master William Knight, referring to the "Malencholy Loss of the *Philadelphia* on the Rocks off tripoly," ended his letter to a Philadelphia friend that the officers were young, and "hope[d] to out live" their captivity. He expected "to be Redeem'd in the space of 3 or 4 years, [We have a] house to live in plenty to eat at present [and I am] ... in fine spirits. ... Father & Mother must excuse me for not [writing] two letters, tell Mother not to grieve at my [plight]. [I] live in hopes to see her again."[19]

Purser Spence wrote his wife Polly, "I am a prisoner ... to the Bashaw of Tripoli." Spence referred to the chase, the crashing onto the reef, and trying to free the ship, after which "we were at last reduc'd to the mortifying necessity of giving ourselves up." All he had were the clothes he wore. Dghies had offered to resell to the officers their own clothing—he had bought or expropriated eight trunks plundered from the officers when the ship was captured—but the officers declined to pay the $1,200 demanded. Nor did the officers buy other clothes at exorbitant prices in the *souk*, the market. Spence expected "our body sufferings will be nothing. For the mind, I cannot promise so much," but he vowed to "keep up my Spirits" because while he lived "I never will despair."[20]

Nicholas Harwood wrote to his brother-in-law in Maryland about "the most melancholy instance" that "ever happened." Harwood, a native of Annapolis, and an 1800 graduate of St. John's College, had been appointed a surgeon's mate prior to the *Philadelphia*'s sailing.[21] Harwood described the chase of the Tripolitan ship and firing "several Shot to bring her too, but she kept in and Capt. Bainbridge being not acquainted with the coasts, or at least no rocks being laid down in the Charts we unfortunately ran on a Rock." They had "gallantly Defended the Ship— but, alas, we were obliged at last to strike our Colours" and were now prisoners, having been "stripped . . . of Everything." But Harwood added that "as yet we are treated kindly and we are assured by the Danish Consul we shall be treated with humanity." Harwood hoped "that America will ransom us as soon as possible. But if our Country should not redeem us, I request it as a particular favor that no exertion on the part of my friends to release me will be maid. For never would I consent to leave my Brother Officers and Seamen in Bondage."[22]

In another letter written on the first day of captivity, an unidentified officer wrote to his family in Philadelphia that it was his turn to use one of the two quill pens the officers possessed. He narrated the events of the chase, grounding, and plundering, although by "scuffling," he had saved his great coat, money, and watch. The officers had promised each other not to leave Tripoli "until we are all ransomed together." Nissen had been a great help, but "none of the other consuls have been near us—they all hoisted their flags this morning [indicating they were in residence]. If the Danish consul had not behaved as well as he has, we should have been badly off."[23]

It was true that the other consuls were disappointing and offered little help. The Dutch chargé d'affaires, an Italian from Livorno named Antoine Zuchet, wrote that P. N. Burstrom, the Swedish consul, had "lowered himself" by congratulating the bashaw about the capture of the *Philadelphia.* Zuchet had, in his own eyes, remained "neutral" and had not written Bainbridge to offer sympathy because Yusuf would have been informed, and diplomats had to tread "very carefully" with the bashaw. Nissen, braver and more humane than the other diplomats in Tripoli, wrote the Danish consul in Marseilles about what he called "the deplorable event" and referred to the obvious advantage the bashaw now had with his hands on 307 Americans. They had thus far been treated "as soft as possible, but the Populace here strip[pe]d them of everything," and he was doing what he could "to render their position supportable."[24]

The officers' mutual promise not to leave any behind—not to accept ransom individually before they all could depart together—reflected the high sense of honor binding naval officers. At times in the centuries-long history of Barbary captivity, wealthy families or friends of captives privately funded ransom for their relative or friend. The family of at least one officer tried to do so. Midshipman James Biddle was the son of Charles Biddle, a former lieutenant governor of Pennsylvania, a wealthy man who mixed with the leaders of the republic, having hosted George Washington and having introduced Aaron Burr to his future wife, Theodosia. One month after word of the *Philadelphia* debacle reached America, Phineas Bond, the British consul in Philadelphia, wrote his counterpart in Tripoli at the request of his old friend, Charles Biddle, to try to "soften the rigor" for "every Individual of this Ship's Company" but requested "particular attention" be paid to James Biddle. Charles Biddle established personal lines of credit for his son with the governor of Malta, Sir Alexander Ball, and with George Davis, the US consul in Tunis, for 600 Spanish dollars. Davis passed word of the funds to Nissen, and both men assured James Biddle that they would supply him with anything he needed. Biddle might have used these credits to ransom himself. But he refused his family's efforts to free him, keeping his word not to abandon his brother officers and to remain in prison forever or be liberated together.[25]

In a letter to his wife in Perth Amboy, Bainbridge could be more revealing of his own worries than in an official letter to Preble or Secretary Smith. He began: "With feelings of distress which I cannot describe, I have to inform you, that I have lost the beautiful frigate which was placed under my command, by running her a-foul of rocks. . . . After defending her as long as a ray of hope remained, I was obliged to surrender, and am now with my officers and crew confined in a prison in this place."

He wrote of his anxiety at the realization he would be separated from Susan for a long time and his haunting fear that he would be censured by his countrymen. Distraught, Bainbridge admitted that he wished "Providence" had let a shot strike him down while the *Philadelphia* lay on the rocks. He feared his career as a naval officer was as lost as his ship, that his honor was tainted, and that the government and American people would treat him with disdain. But he counted on Susan to stand by him, so that even "[i]f the world desert me, I am sure to find a welcome in her arms."[26]

Bainbridge gave his letters (to Commodore Preble, Secretary Smith, and Susan), and his officers' letters as well, to Nicholas Nissen, who handed them off to a British merchant ship captain in the port of Tripoli, who set sail and found the *Vixen* at sea and delivered them to Lieutenant John Smith. Realizing the urgency of the news, Smith sailed west along the coast of Africa, hoping to find Preble, and left a copy of Bainbridge's letter to Preble at Malta with Pulis, the consul. If he missed Preble as he sailed west, Smith resolved to sail all the way to America, if necessary, to make sure the information reached Washington as soon as possible.[27]

The contrast between how the officers and the enlisted men were treated in Tripoli could not have been greater. Because of the higher status of officers as gentlemen, the Tripolitans did not put them to work, and they generally had ample food and a reasonable place to sleep but were kept closely confined in the consul house. The enlisted men—sailors, petty officers, and marines—were treated as slaves, forced to work all sorts of manual labor every day, but were out and about the city, in the open air. The so-called mechanics among the sailors—the coopers, smiths, sailmakers, and carpenters—worked in gangs, repairing and building ships in the harbor. Ten other men were selected to be cooks and waiters in the bashaw's castle. Most of the sailors and marines were used as human pack animals, to haul and carry supplies, one day offloading stores from boats at the wharf to the magazine in the bashaw's navy yard, another day hauling the barrels and bags of wet gunpowder salvaged from the *Philadelphia* from the quay to the castle, and many days yoked to carts carrying stones to build masonry fortifications. Ray observed that there were few wagons in the city, but the Tripolitans never used horses, camels, or asses to haul materials, but rather "made our people perform the part of draft animals." Other men labored in construction gangs, mixing cement from sand, water, and limestone, and hauling troughs of cement to sites around the city, where other sailors and marines built or repaired walls of houses and forts.[28]

Without their daily dose of grog, the jack tars were desperate for alcohol when they were done with their labor for the day. Some had been able to hide coins in their clothing when they left the *Philadelphia*; others, according to Bainbridge, were so "infamous" that they "rob[bed] the last Jacket from their ship mates, to sell for liquor to get drunk on." In one of his tirades, Bainbridge railed that "there never was so depraved a set of mortals as Sailors are; under discipline they are peaceable & serviceable; divest them of that, and they constitu[t]e a perfect ra[b]ble." Sailors were notorious for their thirst for alcohol, and their ability and desire to get drunk. Samuel Leech, who served in the British and American navies, wrote, "To be drunk is considered by almost every sailor as the *acme* of sensual bliss." Once the entire crew was "aground" in Tripoli, there were no officers to watch over a grog tub, but there were opportunities in the evening, after work and before they were locked into the magazine, to drink. Ray reported that the liquor in Tripoli was a powerful spirit he called "aquadent"—*aguardiente*, a liquor distilled from dates—sold from stalls in the *souk* or from booths along the castle's walls. There were also grog shops, kept by Jews and Greeks, selling *aguardiente* to what Ray called "profligate Mohammedans," as well as to sailors who had a few of the local coins, called *buckamseens*. Given their uncertain existence, their devil-may-care attitude, and the absence of the officers, some of the sailors got drunk even on the first evening, caused a ruckus, and were beaten by their overseers.[29]

For food, instead of the salted beef and salted pork served out aboard ship, the crew was fed two small loaves of cheaply made black barley bread, full of chaff and straw, with olive oil, and sometimes a dish then completely novel to Americans called *couscous*. There was little food, and what they were fed was almost completely carbohydrates. On the third day of captivity, some of the Americans were allowed to go to the *souk* to purchase vegetables, and the bashaw allowed the crew to retrieve from the frigate some barrels of salt pork and salt beef. When the meat was shared out, the men were so hungry they ate it raw. The magazine where they slept did not have enough space for the 260 American seamen and marines to all lie down at the same time, forcing some to sleep sitting up or even spend all night standing and talking. In what would become a Hollywood cinematic staple for American POWs throughout time, some of the sailors acted in an insolent, facetious manner to their guards—what Ray called displaying "the invincible spirit of our tars"—responding to their discomfort with "caper[s], sing[ing], [and] jest[ing] ... as if they had been at a feast or wedding."[30]

Some European observers could scarcely believe what had happened. Zuchet, the Dutch chargé d'affaires, wrote to Amsterdam that the Americans should have "carried on fighting" because not a single cannonball had struck the frigate, and none of the gunboats "dared to approach them." He thought the surrender suggested panic or misconduct. He reported that Yusuf celebrated his "great victory," attributing the success to Allah, and the forts and ships in the harbor fired their guns in celebration. Bryan McDonogh, the British consul, reported to London that the *Philadelphia* was "lost on a Reef of Rocks in the entrance of this Harbour" and "finding it impossible to get the Frigate off [was] obliged to surrender." He predicted Yusuf would make "the most exorbitant demand ever known in any of the States of Barbary" to ransom their freedom.[31]

On the first day of captivity, the bashaw demanded that William Godby, the *Philadelphia*'s carpenter, repair the damage to the bottom of the ship. Six feet of water were in the hold, but Godby and his mates had done a poor job of drilling holes in the hull to scuttle her, as Bainbridge had ordered. With his carpenter's crew and fifty sailors, Godby worked through the night of November 1 to repair the holes and pump out the water. That night, a gale of wind and a heavy sea lifted the frigate off the reef. Mortified, Bainbridge had to report that his ship, seemingly so fixed on the rocks, and which he had reported was a "wreck," was now floating free. He wrote Preble reporting "a strong Westerly wind that came on about 40 hours after we struck, which raised the Sea, so as to enable them to get her off." Bainbridge realized that the freeing of the *Philadelphia* "still adds to our calamity," but he insisted that on October 31, it had been "impossible" to float the ship. He asserted that he had "surrendered to the rocks," but "We were not Gods to foresee the Wind, and to know that the Sea would so rise" after the surrender. Adopting the tone of a sea lawyer, Bainbridge took consolation in recalling that "it is not the first instance where ships have been from necessity (of running aground) obliged to surrender, and afterwards got off by the enemy, which could not have been effected by the ships company; witness the *Han[n]ibal* at Alge[c]iras, the *Jason* off St. Malo, and several others."[32]

With the water pumped out of the frigate's hold, a flotilla of small boats towed the *Philadelphia* into the harbor, where they moored her under the guns of the castle. Within two weeks, the Tripolitans recovered the *Philadelphia*'s cannon from the sea bottom, which they remounted on the frigate. The ship was a shambles. Zuchet reported that the captors had robbed everything they could get hold of and smashed what they

could not steal. Yusuf renamed the captured frigate *Gift of Allah* and gave the command to Murad, his *rais* of marine, who raised his flag aboard. Nissen reported that the bashaw ordered a foremast from Malta to replace the original, which had been cut away to lighten the ship in the efforts to get her off the shoal.[33]

Although the enlisted men were treated as slave laborers, Spence, an officer, was not treated badly in any physical sense. Given to introspection, he mused that he found himself in "so distressing a condition," loaded metaphorically "with the Chains of Slavery," anticipating he would "suffer the deepest anxiety." He thought about his changing fortune over the years. After less than one week as a prisoner, there was "no price too high" for freedom. Shrewdly, he estimated that "[e]ighteen months, or two years, is as short a time as we can reasonably calculate upon" until the country redeemed them from slavery, "and even that short space will appear an eternity."[34]

The *Philadelphia*'s officers were subject to capricious treatment. In mid-November, a letter arrived from a Tripolitan sailor captured on the *Mirboka*, interred at Gibraltar, who complained of harsh treatment. This accusation was a canard. Ray wrote that the *Mirboka* prisoners were "not insulted or abused" and were given as much food to eat as they wanted. Ray described the Tripolitan sailors as "meagre" and "grisly," and notwithstanding their Islamic faith, they devoured salted pork and drank grog with gusto. Mohammed Dghies sent his *dragoman* (interpreter or guide) to Bainbridge, informing him that if he would order Preble to release the eighty Tripolitan prisoners, the American officers could remain in their quarters in the consul house, but if he refused, the officers would be punished. Bainbridge replied that the reports of mistreatment must be mistaken, but in any case, he served under Preble and could not order him to do anything. He agreed to write Preble for information. But this solution was unacceptable to the bashaw, which the Americans learned that night when a Tripolitan officer arrived at the consul house and told them in broken English, "Tonight nothing; tomorrow the castle." The next morning, the Americans rose early, ate breakfast, and were ready when, at 9:00 AM, guards arrived to escort them. Bainbridge ordered his officers to form a column in order of seniority, and off they marched through the alleys "amidst crowds of gaping people." The guards led them to what Bainbridge called the "loathsome prison of our Crew." An unidentified officer wrote home that the prison was "the most dreary place imaginable," the walls covered with damp and mold, "the vaulted ceiling hung with cobwebs," the ground "broken and uneven" and infested with vermin, the only light through a grated window in the roof, plunging them all into "Stygian darkness." Midshipman Biddle bemoaned the fact the three hundred officers and men were crammed into a space that he estimated was only eighty feet by twenty feet. There was no furniture, and when tired of standing, the officers had to find a place to squat or lay on the ground. They spent the day without food, and Cowdery reported they "were scoffed at by our foes until night." Murad, the bashaw's *rais*, visited Bainbridge, urging him to agree to the bashaw's demand. Bainbridge replied that he was a prisoner, and the bashaw could "lop off his head, but he could not force him to commit an act which is incompatible with the character of an American officer." Perhaps realizing Bainbridge was an immovable object, Yusuf allowed the officers to return to the consul house that night, Dghies telling Bainbridge that they could stay there until he heard more about the treatment of his people in the hands of the Americans.[35]

In fact, Bainbridge did write Preble about the episode, and Preble responded that the prisoners "were well treated while I had the command of them; and I have every reason to believe, they were, before I arrived at Gibraltar." He suggested that Bainbridge tell Dghies that the *Mirboka* and her people had been restored to Morocco, even though the Americans thought they were really Tripolitans. Danish consul Nissen reported to Copenhagen that the bashaw was satisfied by Bainbridge writing to Preble; besides, he reported, the initial report may have been a fabrication, written to obtain compensation for the sailors from the bashaw upon their return or so the bashaw would send gifts to their families.[36]

In an era of fluid national allegiances, many foreigners served on American ships, even as they carried papers attesting to their American citizenship. As Danish Consul Nissen reported from his own inspection, "Among the crew are found naturally people of all sorts and nations." Because seamen seeking to avoid their pasts used aliases, and because American naturalization laws varied by state, it is hard to track the number of foreigners aboard American ships. Five years later, in 1808, when the Navy sought an accounting of the nationalities of its sailors, the returns from the New York Navy Yard showed that of the 306 enlisted men

on that station, 150 were foreign nationals. "Foreign" was almost a eu-
phemism for Irish or English; 134 of the 150 were from the British Isles;
only 126 of the 306 enlisted men were native-born Americans.[37] The na-
tive-Briton sailors on the *Philadelphia* had sworn an oath of allegiance
to the United States when they enlisted in the American navy but were
regarded by Britain as having an inalienable loyalty to the king. In a classic restatement of the position, a British diplomat in Lisbon wrote his
American counterpart, "The Spirit of the British Constitution requires
the Services of all our seafaring Men, for the general defence of the
Country, whenever our fleets may stand in need of them[;] . . .
cons[e]quently ever[y] British Sailor who enters into the Service of another Country when called upon to serve His Majesty is guilty of a
breach of Duty, and is in effect a deserter from his profession and the
cause he is bound by allegiance to espouse."[38]

In a secret passage in a letter to Preble, written with lime juice as his
ink, Bainbridge asserted that the "greater part" of the sailors from the
Philadelphia, three-quarters of them, were "English subjects, not naturalized in America." He mused that if Horatio Nelson, the admiral commanding the British Mediterranean fleet, "was to claim them, and to
enforce his demand, would it not be policy in the United States, to accede
to such a measure?" Bainbridge thought that "Interest"—meaning there
would be fewer seamen to ransom, so the United States might save
money—"and Humanity, would . . . sanction an acquiescence."[39] To be
fair, there was ample precedent for American merchant seamen to avoid
Barbary captivity by claiming protection under other flags—countries
that had treaties with the Barbary regimes and paid tribute as *quid pro
quo* for their seamen not to be held as slaves for ransom. As recently as
June 1802, the Philadelphia-based merchant brig *Franklin* had sailed
from Marseilles bound to the West Indies. Off Cape Pallas, she was
boarded by one of the 4-gun Tripolitan galliots Consul O'Brien had
warned about and was brought into Tripoli. Two officers and a seaman
from the *Franklin* asserted they were British subjects because they had
been born in Ireland, and they were duly released to the British consul.
Two others asserted French citizenship, and they were delivered to the
French consul, leaving "but four [Americans] in captivity, Namely Capn.
Morris[,] his carpenter and two Negroes." By the end of the year, through
the dey of Algiers, O'Brien negotiated the release of the four Americans

for $6,500, which came to $1,625 for each captive, an exorbitant amount per capita, certainly setting another bad precedent for any negotiation with the bashaw over the *Philadelphia*'s crew.[40]

Nevertheless, Bainbridge's idea was unwise. If Nelson were to make a successful appeal to the bashaw, then Bainbridge might be consigning some of his sailors to their deaths. Consistent with Bainbridge's estimate that three-quarters of the *Philadelphia*'s sailors were British, Ray believed that one hundred of them were deserters. Desertion from the Royal Navy was a capital offense. Although many captains might forego punishing a deserted seaman who returned voluntarily, for those whom the British Navy found after deserting, the punishments could be draconian. During the War of 1812, when British captains on the North Atlantic station wanted to handle deserters "informally," the mean punishment was twenty-six lashes. But if a captain wanted to make an example, he could have a deserter court-martialed. Twenty-seven sailors were court-martialed for desertion, receiving sentences up to five hundred lashes. Punishments of hundreds of lashes, known as "flogging around the fleet," meant that the poor man was whipped with dozens of strokes from a cat-o'-nine tails on a ship, and rowed successively to every ship on that station for the same proportion of the sentence.[41] Many men flogged around the fleet did not survive the ordeal. With Bainbridge knowing that perhaps one hundred of his sailors were deserters from the Royal Navy, it is far from clear just how humane his idea was. On the other hand, as a flogging captain himself, Bainbridge may not have cared much that a severe flogging was the price his "British" American sailors had to pay for their freedom from Barbary captivity.

Regardless of their individual fates, an appeal to Nelson on the basis that the American sailors were in fact British would have meant that a high-ranking US naval officer would have formally conceded that issue. Bainbridge's concession would be tantamount to agreeing with the British that those sailors' papers and oaths of allegiance were fraudulent, and perhaps would throw into doubt the right of Britons to become naturalized American citizens. Those would have been ruinous positions for the most contentious issue in Anglo-American relations, the impressment of sailors. As Bainbridge knew, Preble had already refused to yield on this issue in his letters to Sir John Gore, attempting to get the return of sailors who had decamped to the *Medusa* while in Gibraltar bay. Not surprisingly then, Preble rejected Bainbridge's idea, even though he knew that British sailors dominated the lower decks of American ships. As far as Preble was concerned, having signed up on a US warship, having taken an oath of allegiance to the United States, and having been paid Treasury dollars, the sailors and marines of the *Philadelphia* were going to stay American, whether they were Americans or not.[42]

Nevertheless, Gavino, the consul at Gibraltar, passed on a rumor, perhaps true, perhaps apocryphal, to the officers of the *Argus* that "140 of the crew of the *Philadelphia*, have claimed protection of Lord Nelson, as being British subjects, but that he refused to interfere." Within days of the *Philadelphia* running aground, several American sailors who claimed to be British subjects approached the British consul in Tripoli and asked for protection. McDonogh took their names and said he would write to London to seek their release, although no such letter has been found in the British archives. It is possible that McDonogh wrote Nelson, or that he wrote another British naval officer who told Nelson, that there were 140 Britons held captive. But Nelson was far from sympathetic, reputedly commenting that if he were to do "anything in the Business, it would be to have the Rasc[a]ls all hung" for deserting.[43] And even if Nelson had intervened, the bashaw may not have been willing to give up the massive payday that so many captive sailors represented. In the immediate aftermath of the *Philadelphia*'s grounding, Bonaventure Beaussier, the French consul, gained access to the frigate's papers (which Bainbridge had failed to destroy), determined that four Frenchmen served on the frigate, and went directly to the bashaw to seek their redemption under the terms of the Franco-Tripolitan treaty. Yusuf pointed out, not unreasonably, that where the treaty called for the repatriation of French subjects, it did not contemplate Frenchmen serving on ships fighting Tripoli, and he refused to produce the four men. But the bashaw candidly told Beaussier that there were also 170 Britons in the *Philadelphia*'s crew (Yusuf referred to them as "deserters"), and if he granted Beaussier's request, he would have to grant a similar request if the British consul demanded those men, since Britain had most-favored-nation status. Turning over 170 Britons would deprive him of most of the ransom he would seek to extract for the same men as "Americans" from the United States.[44]

In addition to the Britons and Frenchmen, at least two sailors from the *Philadelphia* "announced themselves" as Danes to Nissen. But Denmark did not have a treaty with Tripoli that called for the repatriation of Danes held captive. Although Nissen was a generous man and gave a few coins to one of them, Jens Andersen, who was ill, he did not attempt to take custody of them. With the crew being supported by the Americans, he did not further subsidize the Danes in the crew, or, as he put it, he did not feel "entrusted with the right to give someone support at Our Majesty's expense, which they had no right to."[45]

If they could not be saved from Barbary slavery by foreign consuls, individual sailors and marines could decide to "free" themselves by collaborating. Because their work as slave laborers was unrelenting, and it was unclear if they ever would be rescued, a sailor could turn against his fellow tars to provide information or to work as a foreman, or he could become a Muslim, taking advantage of the Qur'an's teachings that a fellow Muslim must not be enslaved. The officers and crew called the collaborators "renegades," a term passed down from the Middle Ages to describe a Christian who embraced Islam to escape slavery. John Wilson was an example of a renegade who "turned Turk." "John Wilson" was not his name, as he was a Swede who had entered the US Navy under an alias. Wilson was a quartermaster, and Bainbridge said Wilson was once one of his favorites among the crew. But in the very first days of captivity, he became a renegade, telling Yusuf numerous lies to ingratiate himself. Somewhere in his travels, Wilson had learned Arabic, and he took advantage of his language skills. First he told the overseers that the officers were planning an escape, which was the reason the bashaw ordered the terrace on the consul house closed off and soldiers posted on the roof. Then he told the bashaw that the *Philadelphia* carried a large amount of gold, which had been tossed overboard before the surrender, leading Yusuf to order divers to search around the reef, where, of course, they found nothing. Giving his word of honor, Bainbridge assured the bashaw that Wilson was lying, but Yusuf sent for the captain's steward and told him he would be beaten if he did not tell the truth about the gold. Under intense questioning, the man denied there was any gold, and he was released.

Wilson became a full-throated traitor. Ray recalled that Wilson "mingled amongst us, and acted as a spy, carrying to the Bashaw every frivolous and a thousand false tales." When Yusuf passed by, Wilson called on the men to doff their hats and give three cheers, and although "some of our silly asses swung their hats and brayed," most of the sailors stood silently. In reward for his cooperation, the overseers made Wilson a foreman, which did not sit well with the sailors who had been his shipmates. Wilson spewed insults against Bainbridge and his officers, not fearing a repercussion because he could seek protection from Burstrom, the Swedish consul. Preble wrote Burstrom that Wilson had sworn allegiance to the United States and had heaped abuse on the officers, and that Preble hoped Burstrom was "not so far lost to every sense of honor & humanity, as to support a scoundrel." Ultimately, Preble's letter went undelivered because it was unnecessary. In late November, Bainbridge, who temporarily was allowed out of the consul house, confronted Wilson in front of the rest of the crew, called him a traitor, said he would be hanged if he ever returned to America, and then threw a metal chain at him. After that, as Ray put it, Wilson "put on the turban." Bainbridge referred to Wilson as "the greatest Villain I ever knew;" he had "turned *Renegado*," embracing Islam and going over to the enemy.[46]

Wilson did not always get favorable treatment from his new protectors, and his was not an easy existence. He quarreled with Murad and received five hundred *bastinadoes* for his contumacious conduct. In late January 1804, Wilson told the bashaw that the crew was armed and about to rise against the regime. Yusuf ordered an immediate search, which, not surprisingly, found no weapons. According to Dr. Cowdery, Yusuf was intimidated by the idea of a rising and placed more guards over the officers. To prove his worth to his new compatriots, Wilson presented himself as a great engineer and demonstrated how to fire "hot shot" at a target. In that era, shore batteries equipped with a furnace could heat cannonballs until they were glowing fireballs. Wooden ships with their canvas sails were especially vulnerable to red-hot shot. The British defense of Gibraltar during the Spanish siege of 1782, in which land batteries fired hot shot at the Spanish fleet, causing three huge ships to catch fire and explode, was clearly an example the Tripolitans wished to emulate. But the technique of heating cannonballs in specially designed furnaces to the right temperature was difficult and dangerous.[47] To Cowdery's pleasure, Wilson only "succeeded indifferently," although Yusuf awarded him eight dollars. Wilson wanted to earn his keep by "teach[ing] the Turks how to throw bombs, [fire] hot shot, and [toss] hand grenades; and to alter and improve the fortifications." Wilson's efforts did not help Tripoli much, but he set a pernicious example. Within three months of the crew becoming captives, three more sailors "turned Turk"—a German-born seaman, Lewis Hacksener, who had been a steward for the officers; Thomas Prince, a seventeen-year old ordinary seaman from Rhode Island; and Peter West, a member of the carpenter's crew, who later supervised the building of gunboats for the bashaw. A midshipman wrote home that the four had "turned Traitors" and "made their appearance with their heads shaved and a Turkish habit on."[48]

On the other hand, there were American sailors who tried to take advantage of Yusuf's naivete, and with jack tar impudence they tried to play him. One was gunner's mate George Griffith. Pretending to copy Wilson's example, Griffith passed the word through the overseers to the bashaw that he could build a furnace to cast cannonballs for hot shot. Yusuf gave Griffith a work crew and promised him $100 for the first cannonball he produced. After Griffith expended vast amounts of money building a furnace and experimenting with molds, the demonstration day arrived. Griffith's furnace could not melt iron to cast the cannonballs, and then the furnace cracked apart. Cowdery realized that Griffith never intended to cast a shot.[49]

But the situation confronting the American sailors was not amusing. Only a month into their captivity, Cowdery recorded in his diary that "[o]ur men complained of their hard usage, in being compelled to lie on the cold damp ground, to eat bad bread, to work hard, and to be bastinadoed by their drivers." Ray wrote of a day in late November 1803 when he and fifteen other sailors were set to work boring cannon. The work took all their strength, and they had no food that day until late in the afternoon and nearly collapsed. Still, some of the gang were able to drift off in the late afternoon to find *aguardiente* to drink, and they predictably got drunk and were beaten. There was never enough food, and although the sailors devised a system of saving some loaves of bread overnight to have something to eat in the morning, the dawn light often revealed that the bread ration had been stolen by other ravenous sailors.[50]

With no hope in sight, Charles Rhilander—one of the merchant seamen who had come aboard at Gibraltar—tried to kill himself, but as he was cutting his throat, an overseer intervened. Rhilander survived, although Ray depreciated his wound as a "scratch" and chalked up the attempted suicide to too much alcohol. Yet before two months of captivity elapsed, Ray himself thought slavery was so harsh that "life became insupportable," and every night when he went to sleep, he "sincerely prayed that [he] might never experience the horrors of another morning." But seamen are hardy and resourceful people who make the best of their circumstances. By the end of November, the sailors and marines began to build themselves cots, using as bedposts whatever pieces of lumber that they could find around the bashaw's shipyard, weaving a net of ropes in lieu of a mattress, the whole contraption suspended from spikes already in the walls. The sailors lucky enough to make cots were able to sleep high off the ground, into something resembling the hammocks they slept in aboard ship: they thought it was pure luxury.[51]

Little information has survived about how the enlisted people governed themselves while imprisoned in Tripoli. During the War of 1812, at Dartmoor, the infamous English prison that housed thousands of Americans, committees were selected to draw up rules to preserve order and discipline. It is likely the *Philadelphia*'s crew did the same. Used to hierarchy aboard ship, the senior seamen likely took the lead in setting rules about food, cooperation with the regime, and general conduct. Indeed, the petty officers or senior seamen formed the natural cadre of leadership to adjudicate any quarrels or mete out petty discipline. The men were used to their eight-man messes aboard ship, and Ray described a system of messes implemented in captivity. Eating in messes also allowed the men to more easily share food purchased at the *souk*. Although their physical labor was exhausting, and the crew was chronically underfed, the sailors summoned enough energy in the evening hours inside the prison to do what sailors always did in passing the time, spinning tall tales, smoking their pipes if they could buy Turkish tobacco at the *souk*, and singing sentimental or bawdy songs. Samuel Leech may as well have had the *Philadelphia* sailors in mind when he wrote that someone watching the "song, the dance, the revelry of the crew, might judge them to be happy. But I know that these things are often resorted to because they feel miserable, to drive away dull care."[52] Sailors were notoriously addicted to all sorts of games of chance, and undoubtedly several sailors had brought playing cards and dice with them into captivity, or they could be fashioned out of bones or scraps of wood. The favorite card games among sailors of that era were twenty-one, brag, and keno, and the imprisoned tars likely enjoyed playing them. A group of *Philadelphia* sailors carved two scale models of a ship, made from scraps of materials from the bashaw's navy yard, and rigged and painted the models. They presented one to the British consul and were mortified when he paid them only one dollar; the other, presented to Yusuf, at least yielded a gold doubloon.[53]

One might think that cast into captivity in Barbary, working as slaves, men might have turned to religion. It was demoralizing to be a captive in a faraway land, with no contact with friends and loved ones, and they might be captives for years or forever. It was painful and demeaning to be beaten by overseers, and it was debilitating to never have enough food. Moreover, the Arabs, Turks, and Moors were regarded as alien people, with their different Islamic faith, look, and customs, and it might seem natural that the sailors and marines would turn to their Christian faith for comfort. But that was not their reaction. Except for scattered references invoking God's help, none of the surviving letters or documents refer to prayer or God. The *Philadelphia* did not carry a chaplain. There is no suggestion that the sailors and marines organized their own services with a lay leader. As a matter of Qur'anic teaching, Christian religious services likely would have been tolerated in Tripoli; in the grand *bagnio* (prison for slaves) of Algiers, the largest slave-holding Barbary power, there was a small chapel where Catholic prisoners took Mass. Yet in Tripoli, on Christmas Day 1803, while Yusuf allowed Neapolitan slaves to attend Mass, "no relaxation was allowed" for the Americans. Of course, most seamen in that era were irreligious, in fact were nonbelievers.[54]

Their spiritual health aside, the situation confronting the enlisted people was unsupportable only weeks into their captivity. At sea, a sailor's diet, in the words of one historian, was "unhealthy, monotonous and revolting" and may have lacked essential vitamins and nutrients, but at least a diet of salted meat, ships' biscuit, and a half-pint of rum per day provided ample calories. After one month of captivity, with only two small loaves of coarse bread and a little oil, occasional vegetables, and a little meat to eat, the jack tars were famished and falling sick. In November 1803, the crew took collective action, writing a group petition for a redress of grievances. Their tone was respectful, even obsequious, but their points were clear:

To His Excellency the Grand Bashaw of Tripoli:

The Petition of the American prisoners humbly sheweth—That when your petitioners were captured, in the United States frigate *Philadelphia*, they were plundered of all their clothing, and are daily sickening and suffering most intolerably by the inclemency of the season, and by not having any thing more to sleep on to keep them from the cold, damp ground, but a thin and tattered sail-cloth: and also, that your petitioners, not receiving sufficient food and nourishment to enable them to endure the hardships and perform the hard tasks assigned to them, are frequently most inhumanly bastinadoed for the lack of strength which adequate nutriment would restore and supply. Your petitioners, therefore, pray that his Excellency, consulting his interest as well as his honour, by contributing to our relief, would graciously be pleased to grant us more comfortable clothing, and more nutritious food; and your petitioners, while they continue your prisoners, will remain your most faithful, industrious, obedient and humble servants.

The next day, Yusuf ordered two barrels of salt pork from the frigate be brought to the enlisted men, who, Ray recounted, devoured "their crude dividend." Although the petition brought only fleeting relief to half-starved men, it showed that the bashaw understood that his self-interest lay in keeping his captives alive. One week later, an officer wrote home that "[o]ur crew are kept at hard labor, nearly naked, and on the worst of fare, and scarcely sufficient of that to satisfy the cravings of nature."[55]

In mid-November, Dr. Cowdery began to visit the sick sailors of the *Philadelphia* when the Tripolitans allowed it. Cowdery was thirty-six, born in April 1767 in Sandisfield, Massachusetts, in the Berkshire Mountains. He likely studied medicine under his father, Dr. Jabez Cowdery, growing up in rural Vermont and Massachusetts. He married in 1789 and had two children, but when his wife died in 1796, he left his children to be raised by their grandparents. After practicing medicine in Massachusetts, Connecticut, and New York, Cowdery joined the navy as a surgeon's mate in January 1800, and in July 1803 shipped out on the *Philadelphia*.[56]

In Tripoli, a small house with a sand floor, about half a mile from the consul house, was given over for the sick Americans. When it became clear that the bashaw refused to provide anything better to them than what Cowdery called "sour filthy bread," Captain Bainbridge asked Nicholas Nissen to supply them with fresh food from the *souk* and contracted with the Danish consul to supply beef and vegetables for soup every day. After a few days, Cowdery's trips to the sick expanded. The authorities allowed him to go to the *souk* to try to buy medicines, a mostly fruitless endeavor, and he was granted permission to call on a Spanish physician resident in Tripoli for medicine for an ailing Dr. Ridgely. By early December, the bashaw sent for Cowdery to treat him for some undisclosed ailment and directed him to get whatever medicines he needed for treating his family. When Yusuf recovered, Cowdery was treated like a distinguished guest. Increasingly, he filled the role of court physician, treating the sultan's representative at Tripoli and the officers, ministers, and leading families of Yusuf's regime. His new stature gave him freedom of movement around Tripoli not allowed to any other American. His hosts frequently questioned him about America and the navy, and while he embellished the naval strength of the United States, he was feted with coffee and sweets.[57]

After a month in captivity, Midshipman James Biddle took quill to hand to write Aaron Burr. Biddle provided the vice president with an account of the loss of the ship, the plundering of their clothes and possessions, and the first weeks of captivity. He first referred to himself and his shipmates as "prisoners of war" but immediately corrected himself, stating he "should have said slaves, for we certainly are in the most abject slavery, our very lives being within the power and at the very nod of a most capricious tyrant." Only God knew how long they would be slaves, he wrote, although Biddle recognized that the duration of their captivity would depend on how quickly the government would take "effectual measures." But he ended, "While we are here, our lives must be in constant jeopardy and uncertainty."[58]

At about the same time, Spence, the purser of the *Philadelphia*, wrote his wife, Polly. After a month of captivity, he was "well, comfortably clothed, fed, and lodged." As to his daily existence, his "wants were small and [his] enjoyments still smaller." He had landed at Tripoli with just the shirt on his back, but he had got another, and with two shirts, he expected to have enough clothes for a year. The officers' lodgings at the consul house were comfortable enough, but the forty-three of them were completely confined there, with guards at the door. Captain Bainbridge had his own room, the officers shared a second room, the eleven midshipmen had a third room, and two large rooms were given over for a dining room and a sitting room. As high-status gentlemen, the officers had their own stewards and cooks, and they dined together, able to access the lines of credit to purchase provisions. Consul Nissen was a daily visitor, and they enjoyed his company and conversation. Spence called him "a sensible, intelligent man" and "our only friend." Each day, Nissen sent a servant over with enough food for them all. Indeed, Cowdery reported that they had plenty of pomegranates, dates, and oranges—fresh fruit that would never have been available aboard ship on a lengthy cruise. Nissen also furnished each officer with a mattress and a blanket. The officers, isolated in the consul house, had little enough to occupy their time: conversation among themselves, letter writing, eating, walking the piazzas, and reading. Soon, widespread depression settled in, one officer writing home, "Our chief support is sleep; we mostly retire to rest at 7 o'clock, and in the morning when we awake, the iron bars around the windows pronounce too plainly that we are prisoners."[59]

Spence asked Polly not to worry about him, but he feared she was sorrowful; if she could look on his "misfortune" with "a philosophick eye," he himself would regard it "with almost perfect indifference." Although he longed to hear from her, he realized that Tripoli was "so remote and unconnected with every part of Christendom that there is hardly a chance" that her letters would arrive. He also reported wistfully that "[n]one of our vessels have yet appeared in these seas." He hoped he would be free in eighteen or twenty months, speculating that the timing of their release depended on how much Congress was willing to spend to ransom them, but the longer they debated, the higher the price would be for their freedom, and it was "[d]istressing to us all to think how great it will be."[60]

During one of Nissen's first visits with the American officers, Bainbridge told him he missed his books, which, like everything else, had been stolen when the ship surrendered. Without seeming to take notice, Nissen returned to his consul house and packed two large baskets with books from his own library written in English and French. Then Nissen learned that many of the books plundered from the Americans could be purchased in the *souk* for a modest price. He bought all of them and sent them over to the officers the next day, to their surprise and joy. Bainbridge insisted on repaying him for the books, and the officers now had a library from which they all could find solace in their isolated world.[61]

The infusion of books reminded Bainbridge that the hours of enforced captivity could be used to train his young officers. At the beginning of the nineteenth century, the US Navy had no formal educational institution for officers and would not open the Naval Academy until 1845, though its leaders sought to improve the minds and skills of its midshipmen. In summer 1803, Secretary Smith had hired a mathematician to assist "Gentlemen of the Navy in the study of navigation," and he invited all midshipmen not assigned to active duty to come to Washington to be tutored, albeit on half-pay. Just before the *Philadelphia* sailed, Smith wrote Bainbridge of "the great importance of instructing our Midshipmen in the line of their profession & for this purpose, every opportunity, not incompatible with the good of the service, must be allowed them."[62]

Paternalistic to his young charges, and with the good of the service in mind, Bainbridge created a "school for officers," deciding that each morning, time would be set aside to instruct the midshipmen in mathematics, navigation, and tactics. Less than a week into their captivity, Bainbridge wrote Lieutenant Porter (although Porter shared quarters with him and he could have just spoken to him, Bainbridge wanted his orders memorialized) that he would not allow "the distressing time spent here" to be "entirely lost." He directed Porter to announce that after breakfast each day, the eleven midshipmen "will repair to their room to study navigation, and read such books, as in our possession, which will improve their minds." Bainbridge personally set the course of instruction, which was not only to provide substantive knowledge but also to ensure his junior officers understood that they were entering upon a profession and that hard work was required to master the necessary skills. Thereafter, Bainbridge took little part in the teaching. Depressed over the loss of his ship, he passed many days shut up in his room, writing letters and dealing with the demons that assailed him. In his stead, Porter and Lieutenant Jacob Jones were the principal instructors.[63]

Jones was one of the best-educated officers from the *Philadelphia*. At thirty-five, he was older than his captain and almost old enough to be the father of some of the midshipmen. Educated in Greek and Latin at a private academy in Lewes, Delaware, and trained as a physician, he had spent several years as a doctor in Dover, but frustrated at his lack of business, he began to study law. Through family connections, Jones was appointed the clerk of a county court in his native Delaware, but that life did not suit him either, and he opened a store, and then operated a farm. Jones's first wife died in 1799, he remarried, and he had an infant son who died before his first birthday. His personal problems and his desire for a more active life may have driven Jones to get away from Delaware. He sought and received a midshipman's appointment in May 1799, during the Quasi-War. It was a striking indication of the character of the man: midshipmen typically were teenagers; Jones became a midshipman at thirty-one. Promoted to lieutenant in 1801, Jones was retained when the Jefferson administration reduced the officer corps, and in spring 1803, he received orders to the *Philadelphia* as second lieutenant. In a navy notable for overbearing officers, Jones was quiet and reserved. With dark hair, a beaked nose, and chiseled features, he was later described as "a man of exceedingly plain tastes and thoroughly democratic in his tendencies," and in a navy sometimes besotted with drink, Jones promoted temperance. William Ray, who had nasty comments about many officers, wrote that Jones was a "calm, mild and judicious officer, beloved by all the seamen."[64]

The other main teacher at the "school for officers" was David Porter. Unlike the calm and reserved Jones, Porter was full of energy and activity, and according to an early biographer "never suffered himself to sink into despondency [from his captivity] but applied himself closely to his study." Porter immersed himself in learning history, drawing, French, mathematics, and grammar. He had been at sea almost constantly since he was sixteen, and he used the time of his captivity to become a fine writer and artist. Porter and the other officers mastered French well enough to speak, write, and read the language.[65]

Porter and Jones proved capable teachers. Several of the midshipmen, including Biddle, James Renshaw, and Daniel Patterson, later rose to high commands in the navy. Bainbridge boasted to Preble, "Our prison represents a College of Students," and then he added cryptically—perhaps touting his midshipmen's ability with trigonometry—"Your triangles [used to plot a ship's position on a chart] would fly a long time before we would see them." Through Nissen, the officers apparently obtained from the *souk* one of their books on trigonometry and one of their pilfered sextants, which they used to determine the sun's highest azimuth, essential for plotting latitude. Sextants were of no use to Barbary mariners, given that they were littoral sailors, sailing from landmark to landmark, a strange weakness for the civilization that developed celestial navigation.[66]

But the principal subject for the midshipmen and junior lieutenants at the "college" was naval tactics. The junior officers used wooden blocks to represent ships and moved them around the floor of their consul house prison to solve tactical problems, with various enemy ships to engage or evade and the wind coming from various directions and at various speeds. This systemic playing with wooden blocks on the floor represents the first known instance of wargaming in the US Navy.[67]

In autumn and winter 1803–04, the officers also whiled away some of the time by staging plays. There is a long tradition of American soldiers and sailors immersing themselves in theatrics while in winter quarters or during "down time" overseas. During the winter at Valley Forge during the Revolutionary War, Washington's military family performed Joseph Addison's *Cato*, a play with themes of liberty, republicanism, honor, and duty, before a large audience, including the general. During World War II, Frank Loesser (who later wrote *Guys and Dolls*) collaborated on a series of camp musicals called *About Face* and *Hi, Yank!* with scripts and scores performed by and for the troops. Likewise, Bainbridge's officers performed four plays: *The Castle Spectre*, a Gothic drama set in medieval Wales; *The Heir at Law*, a comedy; *The Stranger*, a German play in translation that Richard Brinsley Sheridan altered; and *Secrets Worth Knowing*, another comedy. All these works appeared in an anthology of plays that appeared on the London stage in 1797–98, which Nissen must have bought at the *souk*. According to an early history, the officers "were busily occupied some time in preparing the scenery, then the [costumes], then in rehearsing, and finally, after great exertions for three or four weeks, the theatre was opened." The scenery was made with whatever materials they could find or have delivered. The "dresses of the ladies were formed of sheets, while black silk handkerchiefs [which naval officers wore around their necks as part of their uniforms] sewed together furnished suits of wo[e]; and leaves and paper completed the materials of the female toilet." The performance created conversation and criticism, which "kept [the officers] alive, and sometimes cheerful for a fortnight," until they began to prepare the next play.[68] To modern eyes, these plays are wooden and ponderous. For instance, *The Heir at Law* features stock humor: the character of Dr. Pangloss (derived from the character of that name in Voltaire's 1759 novel *Candide*) is a greedy and pompous teacher, fond of pontificating with literary quotes. Still, one can imagine the officers enjoying putting on a play, unbending a little bit from naval hierarchy, and the midshipmen playing—and being made fun of for playing—the female roles with falsetto voices. Regardless of whether putting on plays was fun, learning lines and performing theater absorbed time from the heavy hours in captivity.

FIVE

REACTION

IN THE DAYS OF SAIL AND BEFORE THE TELEGRAPH, radio, or the internet, the news of the loss of the *Philadelphia* came slowly and indirectly to Edward Preble. On November 24, 1803, more than three weeks after the disaster, off the southwest corner of Sardinia, the British frigate *Amazon* hailed Preble's flagship, the *Constitution*. The British captain passed along what Preble called "the melancholy and distressing Intelligence" that the *Philadelphia* had run aground, her officers and crew had been taken prisoner, and, after she had come off the rocks, the Tripolitans had brought the frigate into their harbor. Preble understood immediately that the loss of the *Philadelphia*, her possible addition to the Tripolitan navy, and the effect of more than three hundred Americans being held as slaves to the bashaw, changed the entire dynamic of power in the Mediterranean. In his diary, he called the blow "alarming," and even if the resulting weakness of his squadron did not bring Tunis and Algiers directly into the war against the United States, he knew the war against Tripoli would not end soon.[1]

Preble needed more information and immediately altered the *Constitution*'s course for Malta, where he arrived on November 27. Awaiting him was the copy of Bainbridge's letter to him that Lieutenant Smith had left with the US consul. Initially, Preble could not believe that Bainbridge had surrendered a 36-gun frigate without anyone even being wounded. He wrote Secretary Smith that the surrender of the *Philadelphia* "distresses me beyond description." The loss of one of his two frigates would not only affect the campaign against Tripoli, but worse, it damaged America's standing in the Barbary world. He mused, "Would to God, that the Officers and crew of the *Philadelphia*, had one and all, determined to prefer death to slavery; it is possible such a determination might save them from either." The loss of the *Philadelphia* blasted Preble's hope for a peace treaty with Tripoli by the spring. He asked for more ships, to "compleatly Blockade Tripol[i] and annoy the Coast, as to lessen the Bashaw's demands . . . and perhaps oblige him to sue for peace." While Preble doubted "the *Philadelphia* will ever be of service to Tripol[i]" because of the city's shallow harbor and the lack of officers and seamen with the expertise to operate a ship of her size, he would have to "hazard much to destroy her—it will undoubtedly cost us many lives, but it must be done."[2]

The news of the disaster spread slowly and shows the uncertainties in a world with a wind-dependent communications network. In Algiers, Colonel Lear learned the news only on December 12. His initial reaction was to treat the information as a false rumor. He wrote George Davis, the consul in Tunis, that his *dragoman* had just told him that an American frigate had run aground off Tripoli, surrendered, and had then been freed from the rocks. Lear refused to credit it because no ship had come into Algiers for the past twelve days, and he assumed that if the news had come overland through Tunis, Davis would have let him know. Lear consulted Bacri & Busnach, and despite the merchants' usually superior information, they knew nothing about such a disaster. Lear concluded that the news might be true, but it would so upset American relations with Barbary that he would "pretend to give no kind of credit to the tale."[3]

Adverse winds and storms prevented the news from getting to Gibraltar, and thus to the Atlantic world, for weeks. The schooner *Vixen*, carrying the news, sailed from Malta for Gibraltar on November 19. After twenty-two days and not having traveled one-third of the way, she reversed course for Malta, and then sailed into Syracuse, in Sicily. Her captain, Lieutenant John Smith, reported that he made every effort to get to Gibraltar but had been buffeted by "constant Gales of Wind" and been compelled to return. The *Vixen* simply could not sail west. Instead, on December 15, Preble sent the schooner *Nautilus* to Gibraltar carrying Midshipman Christopher Gadsden, who was to hand deliver Preble's and Bainbridge's letters to Secretary Smith in Washington by the fastest merchant ship he could find sailing to the United States. Gavino, the consul at Gibraltar, booked passage for Gadsden on the only America-bound vessel, departing for Georgetown, South Carolina, the same day (January 4, 1804) Gadsden arrived in Gibraltar. The news was so critical, but communications so uncertain, that Preble sent quadruple sets of the letters home on different ships.[4]

Word of the *Philadelphia* disaster reached America only in March 1804, as reports drifted in on merchant ships from the Mediterranean carrying foreign newspapers. The first account appeared in the *Boston Commercial Gazette* on March 8, which contained a few sentences below a dire headline:

Loss of the U.S. frigate *Philadelphia*, Captain BAINBRIDGE.

We are sorry to say that the above mentioned frigate has been lost on the coast of Tripoli, and the officers and crew, we fear, condemned to slavery. The following are the particulars which have reached us, respecting this unpleasant affair.

From the London Courier, Jan. 23.

ITALY, DEC. 25. The American ship Philadelphia, Capt. Bainbridge, of 44 guns, which blockaded the harbor of Tripoli, pursuing a Tripolitan zebeck too far, ran aground, and the crew, consisting of 350 men, were made prisoners by the Tripolitans.[5]

As more foreign letters and accounts flowed into the ports, north and south, and then after Midshipman Gadsden landed and made his way to Washington, newspapers across the land carried the news in greater detail, including that the crew "have met with very severe treatment" and were "ill-used." The news spread unevenly, and some of the reports contained false information. Charleston, South Carolina, received word from a passing ship, from the late-arriving Midshipman Gadsden:

Loss of the Frigate Philadelphia.

Capt. GEDDES, of the schooner Thetis, in 20 days from St. Jago [Santiago] de Cuba, informs, that a few days since he spoke a vessel from Gibraltar, bound to Georgetown, on board of which was a Mr. GADSDEN, who informed that they had dispatches for the American government, giving an account of the loss of the Frigate *Philadelphia*, which vessel went on shore in the Bay of Tripoli, in a severe gale of wind. All the crew were made prisoners by the Tripolitans.[6]

Despite his initial reaction to the news of the debacle, Preble wrote Bainbridge showing some humanity. Recognizing Bainbridge's psychologically devastated state, Preble wrote that he felt "most sensibly for the misfortunes of yourself, your officers, and your crew," and Bainbridge's situation affected his "friends too powerfully to be described." Preble had "not the smallest doubt, but that you have *all* done everything which you conceived could be done, to get the ship off." He assured Bainbridge that "in *me* you have a *friend*," and he promised his utmost to bring relief to the prisoners through the line of credit he established at Malta. Preble hoped Bainbridge would not let his "misfortunes bear too heavily on your mind." With "God bless and preserve you!" he advised Bainbridge to take consolation in knowing that he had done his duty and that all his officers thought so. But Preble was not so positive in a letter to his wife, Mary. Ruminating on the cruelty of war, Preble wrote that he pitied "poor Bainbridge. I know not what will become of them. I suspect very few will ever see home again."[7]

On December 10, Preble decided he needed to scout the coast of Tripoli for himself. He planned to send a boat into the port under a flag of truce to see how the bashaw was treating the captured Americans and, incidentally, to learn the number and disposition of enemy ships. He expected Yusuf's demand for ransom would be enormous. But Preble would not make the same mistake Bainbridge made, of sailing alone off the poorly charted coast of the enemy. Instead, he ordered the *Enterprize*, commanded by a young lieutenant named Stephen Decatur, to sail with him. But adverse winds, day after day, prevented them from leaving Syracuse. The *Constitution* and *Enterprize* finally weighed anchor and sailed a week later.[8]

The *Constitution* stopped briefly at Malta. Preble sent an officer ashore to wait upon the governor, Sir Alexander Ball, to tell him why

Preble had come to Valetta, which would soon become a base for the American squadron. Preble then gathered British merchant William Higgins, US Consul Joseph Pulis, and Scottish merchant Richard Far- quhar aboard the flagship. Farquhar had been in Tripoli when the *Philadelphia* went aground, had loaned Bainbridge money, and had brought back intelligence—erroneous as it turned out—that the bashaw demanded $3 million in ransom for the captives. Such a demand was "ridiculously extravagant," Preble reported to Secretary Smith, and added that he hoped that when the campaign season arrived, he would make the bashaw "feel the force and Weight of our shot so effectually, as to check the extravagance." Preble floated to Smith the idea of American support for Yusuf's brother, Hamet Karamanli, then rumored to be in Alexandria, to topple the regime of his brother. Hamet had been exiled from Tripoli for years, and after what Yusuf had done to their oldest brother (murdering him in front of their mother), he feared for his life. Preble asked Higgins to purchase "some necessaries" for his brother of- ficers in captivity. Preble directed Pulis, who unfortunately did not speak English, to hire a vessel to carry the "necessaries" and Preble's letters to Tripoli. Pulis had brought on board the *Constitution* an Italian doctor, Pietro Crocillo, who had just returned from Tripoli, and he told Preble that he witnessed the *Philadelphia*'s capture and had seen the officers and crew manhandled and spat on as they came ashore.[9]

The *Constitution* and *Enterprize* then went back to sea, bound for the Barbary coast. On the morning of December 23, the *Enterprize* saw a distant smudge of land, Tripoli, and at nearly the same moment spotted a ketch under sail. A ketch was a small, two-masted vessel with a tall mainmast and a mizzenmast placed far aft, widely used throughout the world for local trade or fishing. The *Enterprize* gave chase and caught up with her. Preble signaled to Decatur to bring the ketch to the *Consti- tution*. As she neared, Preble had English colors run up the *Constitution*'s halyard and hoisted out one of the *Constitution*'s boats to bring back the ketch's commander. According to the *Constitution*'s log, "[s]he showed about 20 men who seemed to confer together waiting the Issue. When we haul[e]d down the English & hoisted American Colors the People on board the vessel appeared to be in the greatest confusion." The three ships lay about nine miles off Tripoli. The ketch, the *Mastico*, looked to Preble to be about sixty or seventy tons in size. She carried two cannon, flew Turkish colors, and, according to her master, was bound to Benghazi and then Constantinople. The Ottoman Empire was at peace with the United States, and there was no basis for seizing a Turkish ship if she was legitimate. Her master was Turkish, and she had a crew of seven Greeks and four Turks, which was typical of an Ottoman ship. But everything else raised Preble's suspicions. The *Mastico* had on board two Tripolitan officers, ten Tripolitan soldiers, and forty-two slaves (thirty young black women and twelve black boys) belonging to Yusuf, intended as gifts for the sultan, Selim III. Moreover, the *Mastico*'s papers were in Arabic, not Turkish. Crocillo, the Italian doctor who had come aboard the *Constitution* at Malta and was now serving as a surgeon's mate, told Preble he recognized the Tripolitan officers; they had served on the gunboats that had fired on the *Philadelphia*, and he said the master of the *Mastico* had boarded the *Philadelphia* and plundered her officers and sailors. Preble saw for himself that the *Mastico*'s officers carried American sidearms. According to Midshipman William Henry Allen, "the rascal" who had stripped Bainbridge's epaulets off his uniform and taken Porter's sword was brazenly wearing their kit. Preble wrote Bainbridge, "Has any of your Officers lost a Gold Watch with three or four hands one of which is broken? Tell Lt. Porter I found his Sword & Belt in bad hands, and shall take care of it for him." Clearly, Preble could not let the *Mastico* go about her business. He ordered the *Mastico*'s crew transferred to the *Constitution*, but he left the forty-two slaves on the ketch, with two Tripolitans to care for them. Preble sent over several sailors with a midshipman to take charge as prize master, with orders to sail the *Mastico* into Syracuse, where he would arrange for her papers to be translated. Late that afternoon, Preble sent her off, with the *Enterprize* to convoy her.[10]

Preble spent another two days off Tripoli. His plan to send a boat into Tripoli under a flag of truce had to be abandoned, as a gale blew in that threatened to fling the *Constitution* ashore. She veered off, set a course for Sicily, and by year's end sailed into Syracuse harbor with the *Mastico* and *Enterprize*.[11]

But the American officers in the consul house had seen the warships far offshore, a tiny beacon of hope for the captives. Spence wrote Polly that the "Commodore's ship, and two smaller vessels, appear'd off this harbor for a few hours; but a threatening sky and an approaching gale onshore, made them haul off; and we have not since seen or heard any thing of them." Had there been time, Bainbridge told Spence he would have asked the bashaw for permission to send Spence out to the *Constitution* to arrange for money and supplies, and to get news. As of the end of 1803, two months into their captivity, the prisoners had received no letters from Preble or anyone else in the squadron.[12]

Nonetheless, Bainbridge kept writing Preble, hoping his letters got through. In a December letter, he repeated that the crew had been kept at work by the Tripolitans, "the mechanics at their respective Trades, the others at various work." With one gang, Ray was sent to work repairing the walls of the castle, but as he had no masonry skills, his job was to carry dirt, stones, mortar, lime, and sand. Other men were sent into the countryside to cut wood for boat building, while another gang bore cannon, a third worked at the mint coining *buckamseens*, and a fourth carried mortar mixed in cisterns in various parts of the city. Godby, the *Philadelphia*'s carpenter, and his mates were building a schooner, and then a gunboat. Godby seemed a bit too eager to work for his new masters, and when he came back to his quarters one night, intoxicated, and began to boast to his messmates about his privileges, a fistfight erupted, which, according to Ray, left him "shattered." Bainbridge recognized the benefit the bashaw received from the labor of the *Philadelphia*'s people, but if they refused to work, he considered that "they cannot receive much worse treatment than they do, for they are only allowed bread scarcely sufficient for them to subsist on, and the Interest the Bashaw has in their lives" prevented him "from starving them entirely." Bainbridge wanted to order his crew not to help strengthen the bashaw's defenses but suggested it would have more weight coming from Preble than from him, an astonishing admission from a captain about his own relations with his crew.[13]

Preble got the letter and responded in an open letter to the entire crew that "the fortune of War has made you prisoners to the Bashaw," but not his slaves. "Whether you will be Slaves or Not," Preble wrote, "depends on yourselves." He called on them not to work for the bashaw and not to be intimidated by threats. Rather, Preble posited, they should insist on being treated as prisoners of war. If the bashaw forced them to work by physical punishments, he would retaliate on the Tripolitans captured on the *Mastico*. He warned, quite falsely, that if any of the sailors voluntarily served the bashaw's regime and later were redeemed, the United States would "undoubtedly" put them to death as traitors. He asked them to stand firm and hoped that the time of their liberation was not far distant.[14]

Preble also wrote Mohammed Dghies, admonishing him that the captive American sailors had to be treated as prisoners of war, and "*humanity & justice*, as well as the general usage of Nations, forbid your treating them as *Slaves*." Preble stated, again quite falsely, that the United States would only ransom prisoners, not "slaves." By contrast, Preble informed Dghies that the "Tripoline Officers, Soldiers & Black people" captured on the *Mastico* were not treated as slaves, and had retained all their clothing, possessions, and money. He asked Dghies to consider a prisoner exchange. Preble sent the two letters (the first addressed to the crew, the second addressed to Dghies) under cover to Bainbridge, leaving their delivery to Bainbridge's discretion. Bainbridge gave Preble's letter to Dghies, who responded weeks later that he would not undertake another negotiation, but Bainbridge withheld the letter for the crew, informing Preble "it would only be attended with unpleasant consequences." He was certainly correct. Just as the crew could not resist doing their duty on board ship under navy regulations enforced by the cat-o'-nine-tails, so too could they not avoid laboring for the bashaw, enforced by the *bastinado*.[15]

While the officers studied, played war games on the floor, and staged plays, and while the crew acted as human pack animals and construction crews, diplomats and Commodore Preble wondered how much it would cost to ransom the three hundred Americans in captivity. Everyone realized they would have to await a decision from President Jefferson, who was thousands of miles, and therefore many months, away. Lear wrote Preble that he could do "nothing more in this business untill advices are received from our Government" except "to alleviate, as much as possible the bonds of captivity and slavery, with which our unfortunate countrymen are oppressed; and obtain every information in our power respecting the views & expectations of the Bashaw of Tripoli." He consulted with Bacri & Busnach. "The Jews estimate," Lear wrote, that Yusuf's price would be $500,000 "for Ransom & a peace; but this is out of the question." O'Brien, the former consul in Algiers, came up with a precise, if wholly imaginary, price of $282,800 to ransom them, along with an additional $100,000 to buy peace, but wrote Preble that paying such an amount would give Algiers and Tunis an incentive to make excessive demands for themselves. Worse, he reasoned, after a round in which Tripoli would wrangle more money from the Swedes, Danes, Dutch, and Spaniards, "it would be our turn again." To bring Tripoli to reasonable terms, O'Brien wrote, force was needed "to enter the port of Tripol[i] to attack, fire on the Town," and land three or four thousand men in an amphibious attack.[16]

The officers in captivity themselves had no idea how much the bashaw would demand to ransom them, and they had heard "not a syllable" on that critical subject. One officer wrote home that it was "impossible" to guess what the bashaw would demand and no basis to come up with even an approximation. However high, he hoped the United States would "not too eagerly come into their terms." He realized that "although the government ought to conceive [itself] bound to rescue us from captivity," the United States would be humiliated and show "an excess of sensibility" by accepting outrageous terms for their ransom; he hoped the Jefferson administration would reject paying $1 million, or even $500,000. Rather, a show of naval strength would force the bashaw to deal more reasonably, even perhaps obviating the need for paying money.[17]

In Malta, however, Preble met an Englishman, Patrick Wilkie, the agent victualler for the British navy, who had spoken with the bashaw's agent in Malta, a shady merchant named Gaetano Schembri, to provide Yusuf's "indirect proposals." Wilkie listed Tripoli's terms: Yusuf would not insist on money for peace *per se*; he wanted only a small present when a new consul was appointed; he would return the *Philadelphia* "as is" in exchange for a new schooner; and he wanted $500 for every man he held captive. Preble hoped he could swap the sixty people on the *Mastico* in a man-for-man exchange before paying ransom, which would net to about 240 Americans to ransom at a cumulative cost of $120,000. Preble assumed that these terms were real, but Yusuf also demanded annual tribute for maintaining peace, a condition that made a deal impossible. Preble concluded, "This we never ought to accede to, as it would stimulate the avarice of the other Barbary Powers and probably induce them to make War upon us."[18]

Preble wrote Bainbridge that he hoped to be able to exchange the "cargo" of Tripolitan officers for some of the American officers. Indeed,

even after the Neapolitan government agreed to house the *Mastico* prisoners, whom Preble wanted off his ship because "their want of attention
to cleanliness" might endanger the health of his crew, he retained eight
of her officers on board, thinking he could trade for Bainbridge. The
Tripolitans would not trade for anyone; Bainbridge wrote Preble that
Yusuf would not give "an orange [a] piece for his subjects." But Preble
expected the bashaw to lessen his demands if the Americans could destroy the *Philadelphia* and if he could borrow mortar boats to bombard
Tripoli. Preble recognized that the bashaw "seems already to be convinced that he has something to dread" or he would not be willing to
take about $120,000 when his initial demand was $3 million. Preble concluded wistfully that "[i]f it was not for the situation of our unfortunate
Country Men, I should be sorry to have peace with the Bashaw, until we
could oblige him to beg for it as a favour, and sign any treaty that might
be dictated to him. I am anxiously wishing for the favourable season to
arrive, when we can keep constantly near Tripol[i]; closely blockade their
ports, and annoy their Coast, to prevent the possibility of their Vessels
cruising, destroy their commerce, and distress their City."[19]

In a mid-January letter to Bainbridge, Preble referred to the capture
of the *Mastico* and wanted to know more about the nationality of the
vessel and the reaction in Tripoli to the capture. He asked for an update
about his officers and crew, "what distinction" the Tripolitans made between the officers as gentlemen and the crew, and what they provided
by way of provisions. But the letter was also meant to buoy Bainbridge's
spirits. Preble wrote, "Keep up a good heart and for God's sake do not
despair. Your situation is bad indeed but I hope ere long, it will be better.
Rest assured my dear friend that every exertion of mine shall be made
to lighten your captivity and to release you."[20]

On January 2, 1804, the US minister to France, Robert R. Livingston,
wrote the French foreign minister, Charles Maurice de Talleyrand-
Périgord, that he had just learned that the *Philadelphia* had been lost
off Tripoli, and the officers and crew were all being held captive. Livingston asked Talleyrand to approach the first consul, Napoleon Bonaparte, to intervene with the bashaw. Livingston appealed to Bonaparte's

"humanity" and suggested that if he could release these "unhappy Men" from slavery, Bonaparte would add to his glory. And, Livingston wrote, Bonaparte had a real interest in the matter, since he needed American trade to support France's war effort against Britain. Yet Livingston's approach was loaded with irony. The United States, which now sought French help, had been at war with France less than four years before, and one of the immediate causes for that war was Talleyrand's incessant demands through intermediaries called X, Y, and Z, for tribute from the Americans.[21]

Bonaparte responded positively. As Livingston observed, France had reason to help the Americans. As the British naval blockade of France started to bite, the French needed American grain to help feed its people and armies. Although in 1798, Napoleon had led the French army on an invasion of Egypt, which was under the Ottomans' suzerainty, by 1804 he was trying to use the Ottomans against the British in the Mediterranean and elsewhere. If Bonaparte could broker a successful peace between the Americans and the Tripolitans, he would get credit with both the Americans and the sultan. Talleyrand wrote the French consul in Tripoli, Bonaventure Beaussier, that the first consul was "touched with the most lively commiseration for [the Americans'] misfortune." Bonaparte wanted Beaussier to "to alleviate their situation, and to obtain their deliverance," and he was to do everything he could to "ensure the success of this negotiation." The goal, Talleyrand wrote, was "a solid and advantageous peace to both parties." Bainbridge did not trust Beaussier—"France would be found to be a good mediator," he wrote Preble, "but not to be negotiated thro' their Consul"—but there was no question that Bonaparte had influence with the bashaw.[22]

Just as Livingston had approached Talleyrand for French help, the US consul at St. Petersburg, Levett Harris, approached Count Aleksandr Vorontsov, the chancellor of Russia, asking for Tsar Alexander I to intercede with the sultan. Although the Russians were traditional enemies of the Turks, having fought for decades over access to the Black Sea and influence in the eastern Mediterranean, Harris believed the Tsar's help could be decisive. Alexander commanded his diplomats to aid the Americans, instructing the Russian ambassador at Constantinople, Andrei Yakovlevich d'Italinsky, to seek a *firman*, or decree, from the Sublime Porte to the bashaw, ordering the release of the American prisoners. Ultimately, the Russian overture fizzled out.[23]

Even the Swedes joined the cavalcade of European powers pledging to help the United States. James Monroe, the US minister to the Court of St. James's, wrote his Swedish counterpart in London, who wrote the Swedish chargé at Constantinople, asking him to intervene with the sultan to try to free the captives, and he also asked the chargé to write Burstom, the Swedish consul in Tripoli, to help "the unfortunate prisoners."[24]

The initiative of American diplomats seeking European intervention to help free the *Philadelphia* captives, which seems so obviously appropriate, was embarrassing to the president of the United States. In April 1804, having learned of the actions of Livingston, Harris, and Monroe, Jefferson wrote Robert Smith:

I have never been so mortified as at the conduct of our foreign functionaries on the loss of the *Philadelphia*. They appear to have supposed that we were all lost now, & without resource: and they have hawked us in forma pauperis begging alms at every court in Europe. This self-degradation is the more unpardonable as, uninstructed & unauthorized, they have taken measures which commit us by moral obligations which cannot be disavowed. The most serious of these is with the first consul of France, the Emperor of Russia & Grand Seigneur. The interposition of the two first has been so prompt, so cordial, so energetic, that it is impossible for us to decline the good offices they have done us. From the virtuous & warm-hearted character of the Emperor, and the energy he is using with the Ottoman Porte, I am really apprehensive that our squadron will, on [its] arrival, find our prisoners all restored. If this should be the case, it would be ungrateful and insulting to these three great powers, to chastise the friend (Tripoli) whom they had induced to do us voluntary justice. Our expedition will in that case be disarmed and our just desires of vengeance disappointed, and our honor prostrated.[25]

SIX

PRISONERS OR SLAVES

Sunset on December 15, 1803, marked the start of the thirty-day Muslim holiday of Ramadan. The day began with a bang, the batteries firing volleys to announce the holiday. Ramadan is a time when Muslims may not eat or drink during the day, but feast at night. In walking the alleys of Tripoli to visit his patients in the evening, Dr. Cowdery was impressed by the illuminated houses and mosques, and the general sense of rejoicing he found among the people. Passing a coffeehouse, Cowdery was spotted by Murad, the Scottish-Tripolitan *rais* of marine, who called him over for a coffee and conversation.[1]

At the end of the holiday in mid-January 1804, at the start of the Bayram festival, Bainbridge and Porter were invited to a levee with the bashaw, his family, the *divan*, and all the foreign consuls. After they were formally presented, Yusuf asked them to sit on embroidered couches. Neapolitan slaves served sherbet and coffee, and then sprinkled the Americans with attar of roses and frankincense before they were ushered out of the bashaw's presence. After stops at the prime minister, drinking more coffee while sitting under an arcade, and then at the bashaw's uncle, who tried to talk to them in Italian, they went to the house of Dghies. He greeted Bainbridge and Porter as old friends, offered them tea, coffee, fruits, and cake served on fine French porcelain, and on their departure wished them a speedy liberation.[2]

Bainbridge valued Dghies as a humane and amiable man who mediated between the bashaw and the captives, always trying to alleviate the harshness of their conditions. He probably did not know that in 1801, Dghies told Cathcart privately that the bashaw had no reason to declare war on America, which Dghies had tried to prevent, but Yusuf disregarded his advice, "being surrounded by a set of mercenaries." Dghies added that the bashaw's strategy was to capture American ships and enslave American citizens to oblige the United States "to come, cap in hand, and sue for peace," reasoning that America was "at too great a distance to send a considerable force into the sea." Cathcart respected Dghies's candor. Dghies reputedly had been educated in Italy and had lived in France, speculating in grain to amass a fortune that he left invested in Europe. Dghies was, in Bainbridge's estimation, a man "of much penetration and a great politeness and has the entire confidence of the Bashaw." Shrewd and well informed, Dghies had served as an ambassador at various European courts and had studied the law of nations. He was sometimes incapacitated, however, with eye problems that were leading to blindness.[3]

While Bainbridge and Porter had coffee and cake, the enlisted men were being exhausted by work that wore them down past their endurance. Their overseers selected 150 men in late December to raise from the strand, east of the city, a wrecked boat. The taskmasters drove the seamen and marines into the water, up to their armpits, to shovel sand into baskets and carry them to the beach. "The chilling waves," Ray reported, "almost congealed our blood," but their overseers enjoyed their misery and kept them in the water from sunrise to two o'clock, when they were allowed out of the water for their first meal of the day, bread and *aguardiente*, and to rest. Then the Americans were forced back into the water until sunset. When they returned to the magazine, they had no dry clothes to change into and slept wet on the ground. Not surprisingly, many became sick.[4]

That winter, Cowdery made his mark as a doctor indispensable to his hosts. He was called to treat the bashaw's eleven months old infant, who was dangerously ill. Whatever he did must have worked; the next day, the child was pronounced "better," and after that the bashaw thought Cowdery could do no wrong. The bashaw invited him to visit his gardens, about two miles outside the city. Cowdery and Achmet, the *dragoman*, walked there, and as they passed out of the gates of Tripoli they came upon a man's head sticking on a pole, a murderer who had been caught and punished. Of course, in that era, it was not unique to Barbary to find heads on poles: during the Terror of the French Revolution just a decade before, the American minister to France, Gouverneur Morris, had been nauseated to see the highly civilized Parisians cut the heads off and disembowel aristocrats, and parade the parts around the streets. In any event, Cowdery turned tourist. He visited the Roman arch dedicated to Augustus Caesar (which still stands) and walked or rode into the interior of the country, visiting gardens and orchards, with Dghies and the bashaw's son serving as guides. After writing extensively about these wanderings, without any transition, he noted in his diary on January 3, 1804, "John Hilliard died in the evening."[5]

After Cowdery's laconic phrase about Hilliard's death appeared in print, William Ray excoriated Cowdery, complaining that he enjoyed the gardens rather than taking care of a "languishing sailor, in a dreary cell." He contrasted Cowdery ministering to the bashaw and his family with his barely mentioning the suffering of his own countrymen. Hilliard died of the flux, what today is called dysentery, and Ray thought that with proper medical attention, Hilliard might have lived.[6]

Ray's criticism raises some sharp questions but may have been misplaced. It is possible that the *Philadelphia*'s doctors divided responsibilities for the sick and injured, and that Ridgely or Harwood cared for Hilliard. But even if Cowdery supervised Hilliard's care, he thought he knew about a treatment for dysentery, noting in one letter that "[d]iarrhea and [d]ysentery have often appeared among our crew, but on a free use of carbonate of soda (Natron) which is found in abundance in this country ... it soon disappears." Cowdery may have tried this treatment on Hilliard, but even with medical attention, many in that era died of dysentery. In fact, three months after Hilliard died, Cowdery himself was "violently afflicted with the dysentery" for more than two weeks, and there is no indication of his treatment or what was done to care for him that was not done for Hilliard.[7]

In a way, Hilliard lived on. Ray, moved by his friend's death, wrote "Elegy on the Death of John Hilliard." He passed the poem on to the officers to read, and "G"—perhaps Midshipman James Gibbon—wrote home, mentioning "a marine, whose extraordinary merit has attracted the notice and attention of all the officers; his name is Ray." "G" enclosed several of Ray's poems, including his elegy. Within weeks, the poem was published in a Philadelphia literary magazine, *The Port Folio*, and by the end of the year, it was republished in a half-dozen newspapers around the country. The first and last stanzas of the elegy recount:

> *HILLIARD, of painful life bereft*
> *Is now a slave no more*
> *But here no relative is left*
> *His exit to deplore!*
>
> . . .
>
> *But foes, and a barb'rous kind,*
> *Surround him as he dies;*
> *A horror to his fainting mind,*
> *And to his closing eyes.*[8]

When the *Constitution* was moored at Malta in early 1804, Commodore Preble initiated contact with the British consul in Tripoli, Bryan Mc-Donogh, a man he did not know but who came recommended by Richard O'Brien. In the face of the newly announced US Navy blockade of Tripoli, which the British promised to respect, Preble had agreed to the request of the British governor of Malta, Sir Alexander Ball, to allow one thousand bullocks, already ordered from Tripoli for the British army garrison in Malta, to be shipped. When that ship sailed to Tripoli, she would carry letters, newspapers, and clothing for Bainbridge and his officers—not for the crew—and Preble asked McDonogh to ensure they were delivered. More generally, Preble asked him to help the American prisoners, and he asked him to approach the bashaw to learn what the ransom demand would be. Having seized the *Mastico* and sixty Tripolitans, Preble hoped the bashaw would be willing to negotiate an exchange.[9]

Preble was to be disappointed in every respect. McDonogh did not even acknowledge receiving Preble's letter for two months. When he did, he assured Preble that "nothing has been, or shall be wanting on my part, to render every assistance in my power" to the American captives. Yet he had not approached the bashaw respecting the ransom demand because McDonogh "thought it prudent, to remain at present silent." In fact, he did nothing for the Americans. In a letter written after the bashaw ordered McDonogh out of Tripoli in April 1804, one American officer noted that his "conduct towards us on our arrival, at this place was far from being friendly." When they were made captive, "we knew not for several days that there was such a man [as a British consul] in Tripoli." He met with the officers once, a week into their captivity, and although he offered to provide help, he did nothing. He was no friend to America; McDonogh truckled to the bashaw, "congratulating him upon his good fortune in obtaining so valuable a prize as our ship, and with so many slaves thus suddenly becoming his!"[10] Preble would have to find another interlocutor.

On January 8, 1804, Keith Spence, the *Philadelphia*'s purser, wrote his wife, Polly, that "our situation here . . . is much better and more comfortable than we could have expected; and the treatment of captives in general [is] infinitely less rigorous than the tales of travelers, and the cries of Captives, would lead you to believe." If one had to be a slave, then Tripoli was "the place to be." The crew received more food than black slaves in the West Indies or in the American South, "their duty is not as hard" as slaves in America, nor had he "seen or heard of a Slave in chains since I have been here." The problem, Spence stated with considerable arrogance, was only that the crew was given food "they have not been used to." Spence wrote condescendingly that "the labour they perform is not hard, nor has any of them been punished but for such faults as justly deserved it, such as getting drunk [and] fighting." While Spence thought the crew was treated with a light touch and could legitimately grouse only about the food, he thought he and his fellow officers faced the real hardship, albeit psychological. The thought that they were slaves threatened to demoralize the officers. To Spence, prisoners might be exchanged during the war or freed by peace, but slaves' freedom had to be purchased. Spence refused to recognize his slave status, for he would be a slave only if he allowed his mind to be "displaced, debauch'd and brutalized." He was determined to "let the misfortune sit as lightly on my mind as possible, knowing that my life is yet of some consequence to those I have left behind."[11]

In another letter to Polly a month later, Spence again reflected on his status, noting that "Slavery, next to death, is certainly the greatest evil that can befall man." Although his slavery might be temporary, it weighed heavily on his mind. He recalled that "the moment the ship struck the rock, our fate appeared to me inevitable. Every circumstance that led to it, or tended to increase its severity, pass'd thro' my mind, with rapidity and regret." As an older man, he contrasted how keenly he felt "the loss of liberty," but he could face the physical privations of captivity better than some of the younger officers, for whom "close confinement, low diet, want of Clothes, etc. appeared great hardships." Since they had been captured, they had never been allowed out of the consul house and could see the outside world only "thro' the gratings of our prison windows." But a week earlier, in February 1804, the bashaw had given permission for the American officers to walk around the city, escorted by their *dragomen*. Some of his brother officers had already been out, enjoying a walkabout, but Spence had not yet left the consul house because the freedom to walk around the city seemed "so small." But there was some welcome news too. Letters from Commodore Preble had finally arrived, and the officers learned that he had established an unlimited line of credit for them in Malta. This meant Bainbridge might pay for food, clothes, and other goods in the *souk* for the officers and men of the *Philadelphia*. Spence wrote, "You see my dear, we are now comfortably situated, and all provided for."[12]

In fact, the officers lived remarkably well. If they were confined under a form of house arrest, at least the consul house was large and airy, with piazzas lengthy enough to take exercise by walking up and down—more room than they would have had pacing a quarterdeck at sea. Their food was plain, but at least it was wholesome, whatever fruits and vegetables Nissen's man would bring, plus eggs and muffins for breakfast and supper, and beef or mutton, with a soup, for dinner, occasionally finishing with tea. They even had their own stewards to serve them. Well might one officer write home that "this mode of living" agreed with him, and he "never enjoyed better health."[13]

When the bashaw finally allowed the officers to leave the consul house, most, though not Spence, took advantage of the exercise and the change of scenery. They went out into the town and countryside in groups of six, under escort. Midshipman James Renshaw thought "the dissagreeable situation in which we are placed" was "alleviated by our being permitted occasionally to visit the Gardens of the Bashaw which is the only satisfaction we have ever experienced since our captivity." The countryside was laid out in wheat and barley fields, and there were orchards of olives, figs, and fruit trees interspersed with flower gardens.[14]

Spence's letters home were not always upbeat. He ruminated in one letter to Polly on "how heavily the days pass." Their three-month captivity seemed like three years. Although he assured her that he was physically comfortable, he suffered psychologically. "Time," he wrote, "limps and lags behind like a weary traveler; and if I murmur or complain of his tardiness, he lifts his ugly [scythe] and threatens to cut me down." The sun seemed to stand still at noon, the stars seemed stationary at night, as he looked up to them "watch after watch." Spence found it hard to sleep and felt forsaken. When he could sleep, his dreams were troubled, filled with "fantastic figures and dreary prospects" that, through the "magic lantern of dreams and visions, plays before my imagination."[15]

Spence did not record anything further about his dreams. While psychological conclusions across cultures and generations are highly speculative, the dreams of young British officers captured early in World War II and held prisoner in Laufen Castle, a German prisoner-of-war camp in Bavaria, may illustrate the subconscious thoughts and strivings of the American officers in Tripoli. According to a modern psychological study, those seventy-nine British officer POWs in World War II dreamt more of their imprisonment, possible escape, and food, and less about friends, sexuality, and aggression, compared to the male norms of the era. Most frequently they had bland dreams about the tedium of life in their castle-prison, with only occasional dreams of release, reunion with loved ones, and gorging on favorite foods. Their sexual dreams featured distant, unattainable women. While it is impossible to know what Bainbridge and the other officers dreamt about, it may be that, like the British officers 140 years later, their subconsciouses dealt mostly with imprisonment, escape, food, and the tedium of life in confinement, where time, as Spence put it, limped behind.[16]

The Americans had scarcely any contact with Arab women; even if there had been no cultural barriers, women were strictly off limits to Christian slaves. The sailors and marines might see women in passing as they went out on their daily work gangs or late in the day, when the sailors went to the market to buy vegetables or to find *aguardiente*. Even then, the women they might encounter were garbed head-to-toe, what Ray described as "wrapped and muffled up in blankets, which conceal their shapes and faces." Few Americans had ever seen women dressed like that, but Ray described the encounters briefly and without judgment. Yet the only man who claimed to glimpse women in a less-restricted context was Ray. On one of the early days of captivity, he was one of four men chosen to bring some goods through a warren of alleys and passageways to a private home. Their overseer led them into the courtyard of the house. There, much to their surprise, the sailors found themselves "surrounded by a dozen beautiful females, who came from the piazzas above." They had been brought into a *seraglio*. Ray's description is highly charged and eroticized:

[T]o us, this was a novel sight; for the ladies were exposed to view, as much as the half-naked belles of our own towns. They were fantastically wrapped in loose robes of striped silk; their arms, necks and bosoms bare. Their eye-lids stained round the edges with black. Their hair braided, turned up, and fastened with a broad tinsel fillet. They had three or four rings in each ear as large in circumference as a [silver] dollar. Several of them were very delicate and handsome. They brought us dates, olives, oranges and milk. They expressed or manifested great surprize at our appearance, and, like other ladies, were full of giggling and loquacity.[17]

This episode was a unique sailor encounter with women, and with beautiful, scantily clad women at that—if the story is not a figment of Ray's imagination. In America at that very time, it was sensational to see a "half-naked belle" in public. In winter 1803–04, a mob of boys swarmed around nineteen-year-old Baltimore socialite Elizabeth Patterson Bonaparte on the streets of Washington, DC, on her way to a ball.

She wore a sheer dress "so transparent," one onlooker wrote, that she was "an almost naked woman," the dress leaving her back and bosom "uncover'd." Strangers looked through windows to see her, and the guests inside were thrown "into confusion, and no one dared to look at her but by stealth." Given that reaction in America, it must have been positively hallucinatory for Ray and his fellow sailors to be immersed in such a scene in Tripoli, met by "fantastically wrapped" women. True or fabulist, Ray's story of exposed women, their bare skin revealed, gives a snapshot of the thoughts and longings of an American sailor in captivity.[18]

The lack of access to women in Barbary, and the reality of more than 250 enlisted men and boys packed together (not to mention the officers), raises the question of homosexual relations among the Americans. The image of a jack tar was that of an idealized heterosexual man who found a woman in every port and who lived a spartan life at sea, dreaming of the opposite sex. Homosexuality is not a subject that any captive in Tripoli wrote about, and more generally, little is known about homosexuality in the American navy in the age of sail. The US Navy's first court-martial in which the charge was sodomy was only in 1805. Usually, the navy dealt with homosexual conduct informally. When rumors of same-sex contact circulated aboard ship, the officers typically sent a petty officer to investigate. If his report indicated that a homosexual act occurred, the sailors involved might be flogged with a cryptic reference in the ship's log about "uncleanliness," or they might be discharged and put ashore at the first opportunity. As first lord of the Admiralty in the early twentieth century, Winston Churchill supposedly referred to the Royal Navy in the age of sail as held together by "nothing but rum, sodomy and the lash." In the British navy at the time, the ships' boys, young teenagers, were apparently sometimes the object of homoerotic affections; according to the list compiled by Spence on the return from Tripoli, the *Philadelphia* shipped ten boys in her crew. But diary references, ships' logs, and court-martial records suggest that homosexual conduct in both navies was rare, the subject of intense hostility, and difficult to conceal afloat. Among the enlisted people themselves, the discovery of same-sex contact produced what one British historian called "a kind of ribald horror." Homosexual conduct was widely reviled in contemporary society, and even forty-five years later, when Melville wrote *White Jacket*, the subject was so taboo that he referred to same-sex contact as an evil "so direful" as to "hardly bear even so much as an allusion." Nevertheless, when seamen were cut off from "shore indulgences," Melville alluded to some succumbing to "[t]he sins for which the cities of the plain were overthrown ... [in] these wooden-walled gomorrahs of the deep." A decade after the captivity of the *Philadelphia*'s sailors, an American POW named Josiah Cobb in England's Dartmoor Prison during the War of 1812 recounted that the "unpardonable sin" was "but seldom done;—howsoever depraved were the Rough Alleys [a criminal gang among the prisoners] in other respects, there had been but two or three instances of this heinous sin being committed," although one wonders how Cobb knew this. During the nineteen months of captivity in Tripoli, when three hundred Americans were cut off from "shore indulgences," some sexual activity among officers or sailors and boys may have occurred. For the officers, kept in close confinement, there was almost a complete absence of privacy. In addition, there was an intense concern with honor and a manly image. Although the sailors and marines went about their daily tasks in and around the city, they were under guard, and their wardens hardly would have permitted men to drift off together; at night, they were massed within the four walls of their prison, their bedding slung along the walls or on the ground in one common space. The lack of privacy, social opprobrium, ostracism, and punishment if caught *in flagrante delicto* were all constraints against sex between men, and there is simply no evidence of homosexual conduct among the captive officers and men of the *Philadelphia*.[19]

Barbary including Morocco Algier, Tunis and Tripoly by William Faden, published 1804, London. (*New York Public Library*)

Merchant, Slave, & Arab, woodcut of Maghreb inhabitants, drawing by A. Earle. From Mordecai Noah, *Travels in England, France, Spain, and the Barbary States in the Years 1813-14 and 15* (1819).

"Preparation for war to defend commerce. The Swedish Church Southwark with the building of the frigate *Philadelphia*," William Birch, 1800. (*New York Public Library*)

Frigate *Philadelphia*, off Tetuan, Morocco, engraving by Wells for *The Naval Chronicle* (1803). (*Naval History & Heritage Command*)

"The Sailor's Description of Chase & Capture," by George Cruikshank, 1822. Although portrayed by a British cartoonist, given the international and racial make-up of the U.S. Navy, this print captures lower deck life. The sailors do not share a common uniform but enjoy their grog and story-telling. (*Library of Congress*)

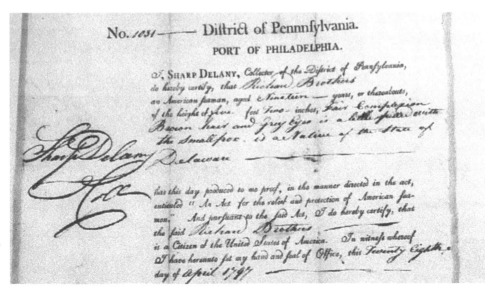

Seaman's Protection Certificate for Richard Brothers, ordinary seaman on the *Philadelphia*. (*National Archives*)

Captain William Bainbridge. (*U.S. Naval Academy Museum*)

First Lieutenant David Porter. (*U.S. Naval Academy Museum*)

Second Lieutenant Jacob Jones. (*New York Public Library*)

Midshipman James Biddle. (*Naval History & Heritage Command*)

The officers of the *Philadelphia*, all portrayed in 1814–15.

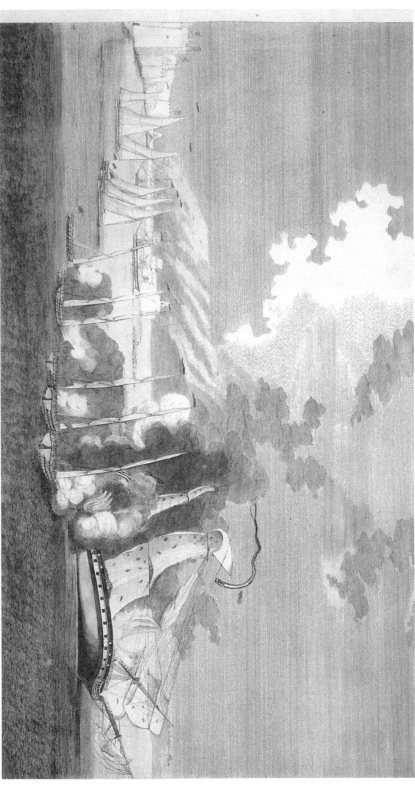

"A perspective of the loss of the US Frigate *Philadelphia* in which is represented her relative position to the Tripolitan Gun-boats when during their furious attack upon her she was unable to get a single gun to bear upon them." Engraving by Charles Denoon, a sailor who was aboard the *Philadelphia*. (*Library of Congress*)

President Thomas Jefferson. (*The White House*)

Secretary of the Navy Robert Smith. (*Naval History & Heritage Command*)

Nicholas Nissen, Danish Consul to Tripoli and friend to the American captives. (*Den Kongelige Kobberstiksamling, Statens Museum for Kunst, Denmark*)

Tobias Lear, Consul General to the Barbary Powers.

Bombardment of Tripoli, August 3, 1804, by Michael Felice Corné. Of this painting, Commodore Edward Preble wrote, "When last at Boston I delivered [to] the Navy agent a painting of the first Attack on the Tripolitan shipping & Batteries by the Squadron which I had the honor to Command. The view of the Town & situation of the squadron & enemies naval force is tolerably correct." (*U.S. Naval Academy Museum*)

George Gibbs's painting, "Watching the bombardment from the Tripoli prison cell," from James Barnes, *Commodore Bainbridge* (1897). (*Author's photograph*)

James Leander Cathcart, Consul to Tripoli, who Jefferson called "the honestest & ablest consul we have with the Barbary powers."(*Naval History & Heritage Command*)

Commodore Edward Preble. (*U.S. Naval Academy Museum*)

Stephen Decatur, portrayed as a captain, circa 1815. (*National Portrait Gallery*)

Burning of the Frigate *Philadelphia* in the Harbor of Tripoli, by Edward Moran, 1897. (*U.S. Naval Academy Museum*)

"Blowing Up of the Fire Ship *Intrepid* . . ." Sept. 1804. (*Library of Congress*)

The Jamahiriya or National Museum (Red Castle Museum) in Tripoli is housed in a wing of the Al-Saraya al-Hamra Fortress. This building is the ruins of the bashaw's castle. (*David Stanley/Creative Commons*)

SEVEN

THE RAID

A S 1803 TURNED INTO 1804, the strategic outlook for the captured Americans was bleak. Zuchet, the Dutch chargé d'affaires, thought the United States might try to ransom them but imagined it would cost at least one million Spanish dollars. The navy could launch an attack, but he predicted that would be "costly without achieving much; the town [Tripoli] can be destroyed, but then the 307 prisoners will be abandoned and they will be massacred."[1]

Bainbridge also thought a bombardment or a blockade would be ineffective. "Nature," he wrote, "has strongly guarded the Harbour of Tripoli by Rocks & Shoals," and "the Town is too well fortified for our shipping, by an attack, to make an impression on it." He depreciated the effect of a blockade because it would not prevent Tripolitan corsairs from slipping into and out of port. Even if a blockade would cut Tripoli's trade with southern Europe, the immediate area around the city supplied ample food to feed the population, and, if necessary, the city could circumvent a blockade by bringing in food and supplies from Tunis "in small boats along the shore, or brought on Camels, for a small expense; as these animals are numerous here, land carriage is exceedingly cheap." Bainbridge concluded, "The Bashaw will never be forced to terms, [unless] he considers his own safety endangered; and he is only Vulnerable to the United States one way; that is by eight or ten thousand men landing near his Town." To Bainbridge, a land attack or ransoming were the alternatives for their freedom.[2]

The loss of the *Philadelphia* cost Preble's squadron more than one-third of its firepower. Worse, there was a chance the squadron's loss would become the enemy's gain. Tripoli might repair the *Philadelphia* and find enough seamen to man her. If Yusuf opted to sell the frigate, he might find a ready buyer in Algiers or Tunis, and there were rumors that the bashaw's agents in Malta were seeking a buyer. If the *Philadelphia* fell into the hands of another Barbary power, the chance of a wider war increased. Preble was thousands of miles away from the United States, and his depleted squadron was months from any reinforcements the Jefferson administration could dispatch. Preble had no staff or senior captain to consult. Yet the goal was obvious. He had to destroy the *Philadelphia*, and he would "hazard much to destroy her."

Destroying the frigate would not be easy. The Tripolitans had brought the *Philadelphia*, renamed the *Gift of Allah*, into the harbor. She had her own cannon to defend herself and was moored within range of the castle's cannon and shore gun batteries, said to be 115 heavy guns. In the harbor were gunboats and a few armed ships, with a thousand Tripolitan sailors. The bashaw had called in his soldiers and could mass twenty-five thousand men around the city.[3] The US squadron now consisted of one large frigate, Preble's own *Constitution*, and five smaller vessels: the *Argus, Syren, Vixen, Nautilus*, and *Enterprize*. The harbor of Tripoli was shallow, and Preble could not risk running the *Constitution* aground. One option Preble had, in theory, was to send his smaller ships, which drew less water, into the harbor, sail near the anchored *Philadelphia*, and hit her with their lighter cannon. But that idea was rash. No captain in the days of sail would lightly choose to sail frail wooden ships before the concentrated fire from protected, shore-based cannon. The approach of an American squadron, dependent on the wind, would take hours. There would be no surprise. The smaller ships might be battered or even sunk, and the nearest base for repairs was several days' sail away, at Malta.

But the rashness of a direct attack suggested the wisdom of the opposite. There was in the arsenals of European navies a standoff weapon, the mortar boat, known then as a bomb vessel. The ugly, squat mortar placed on the forecastle of an anchored bomb vessel was a formidable weapon, capable of blasting a 196-pound explosive shell against a target up to four thousand yards away in a thirty-second, high-arcing flight. The French navy was the first to deploy bomb vessels and in 1682 and 1683 had used them to bombard Algiers, destroying much of the city, forcing the dey of Algiers to free 1,600 Christian slaves and sign a peace treaty with France that lasted a century. Whether Preble knew this history is unclear. But on his return from the cruise to Tripoli—perhaps he thought of bombs as he gazed at the distant shore at the end of December—he set out to acquire such vessels. In January 1804, he wrote Cathcart to ask if he could procure two bomb vessels "compleat" from the French navy at Toulon, or from anywhere he could find them. Preble asked Cathcart to let him know "Where—When and on what terms." Along with the ships Preble also wanted "one or two good Bombardiers" who "understand their business." A few days later, Preble wrote two American merchants in Livorno that he wished to purchase or charter two or three bomb vessels to act against Tripoli that spring and asked if they could be acquired there or at Naples. He later sent a ship to Messina, in Sicily, to see if bomb vessels were to be had there. As Preble knew, with all the good will in the world, he would not have his bomb vessels until at least the spring, and maybe much later. He needed another way to change the status quo.[4]

While Preble weighed his alternatives, he had a devil of a time getting the Arabic papers of the *Mastico* translated. Preble noted that the ketch "was under Turk's Colours and the Captain says belongs to the [sultan] and was bound to Beng[h]az[i]. The papers will be translated in a day or two, and if the Captain tells [the] truth, I shall release her together with a Turkish Officer and all the Crew which the Captain claims, amounting in all to twelve." He expected to release the *Mastico* as soon as it cleared quarantine—the Neapolitans had such fear of disease from the Barbary coast that the *Mastico* only cleared quarantine twenty-nine days after her arrival. When Preble received a batch of the translated papers, he learned that one of the *Mastico*'s officers was a "chouix" (a high-ranking messenger) of the bashaw, who, after loading goods at Benghazi, was ordered to sail to Constantinople where he was to present twenty black slaves as a gift to the sultan. The day the *Mastico* cleared quarantine, Preble learned from an English merchant captain who had been in Tripoli that the *Mastico* had flown Turkish colors, but when the *Philadelphia* ran aground, she took more than one hundred Tripolitan soldiers on board, hoisted the Tripolitan flag, and sailed out to join the attack. When Bainbridge surrendered, these men boarded the *Philadelphia*, plundered the American sailors, brought them into Tripoli, and paraded them before the bashaw. Hearing this information, Preble decided that the *Mastico* was a legitimate prize.[5] "Having acted hostile towards our Flag," Preble summed up the matter, "If a Tripoline, [s]he is a prize; if a Turk, a pirate.[6]

All of a sudden, Preble realized that the *Mastico* was a new weapon. She was a ketch, rigged in the Barbary manner, and her appearance was familiar to lookouts and seamen in Tripoli because, after all, she was a local vessel. Moreover, she had just sailed from Tripoli, and her reappearance would not cause alarm. Precisely because the *Mastico* sailing into the harbor would be routine, Preble had a means of launching a raid into the heart of the enemy's port so as to be able to attack and destroy the *Philadelphia*. On January 29, 1804, he ordered the ketch, which he renamed *Intrepid*, readied for a cruise.[7]

To command the *Intrepid*, Preble chose Stephen Decatur. Decatur, who had served in the navy since 1799, was an energetic, well-built man a little less than six feet tall, with a large, aquiline nose, high forehead, and curly brown hair. Decatur had spent several years at the Episcopal Academy of Philadelphia and the grammar school of the University of Pennsylvania, but he was no scholar. In fact, he found writing a difficult chore and may have been mildly dyslexic. Despite the dashing figure he cut in his navy blue and gold-laced uniform, Decatur had not had an opportunity to distinguish himself in combat. But there was an aura about him. During the Quasi-War, Robert Traill Spence, then a midshipman on the *United States*, thought Decatur had the "form and look of a hero" and seemed to embody the ideal of Homer. Two years later, in 1802, when Decatur was a lieutenant on the *New York*, an officer observed that he held "a boundless sway over the very hearts of the seamen at first sight."[8]

Decatur's charismatic leadership qualities were critical to Preble, but Preble did not know Decatur well. Though Decatur had never served as an officer on one of his ships, he had been under Preble's eye when they captured the *Mastico*, and he impressed Preble. When the *Constitution* and *Enterprize* returned to Syracuse, Decatur reportedly went to Preble with a plan to take the *Enterprize* into Tripoli harbor to burn the *Philadelphia*. Preble rejected Decatur's plan because if it failed, he could not afford to lose the *Enterprize* from his already depleted squadron, but he promised Decatur the command of the expedition if he could figure out a better way. The newly renamed *Intrepid* was the better way.[9]

Preble's January 31, 1804, orders to Decatur were concise. He was to take command of the *Intrepid*, proceed to Tripoli with the *Syren* under the command of his friend Lieutenant Charles Stewart, "Enter that Harbor in the night, Board the Frigate *Philadelphia*, burn her and make good your retreat." Preble would lend him five midshipmen from the *Constitution*, and Decatur was to seek seventy officers and sailors to volunteer for the hazardous mission. "On boarding the Frigate it is probable you will meet with Resistance," Preble noted, so "it will be well in order to prevent alarm to carry all by the Sword." Decatur was to carry, or make, the necessary "combustibles," and Preble advised him where to light the fires belowdecks on the *Philadelphia*. Inadvertently punning on the names of Decatur's ships, Preble wrote that the mission relied on Decatur's "Intrepidity & Enterprize." The immensity of the task for Decatur and his volunteers struck Preble deeply; the final sentence in his orders read, "May God prosper and Succeed you in this enterprize."[10]

Soon, five midshipmen from the *Constitution* arrived aboard the *Intrepid*, including a promising nineteen-year-old from Connecticut named Charles Morris. Preble also sent Decatur a Maltese pilot, Salvadore Catalano, who knew Arabic and was familiar with the harbor of Tripoli.[11]

After Preble dispatched his orders, but just at the time *Intrepid* and *Syren* sailed, Preble received intelligence about the target. He noted in his diary, "From information which I have received from Tripol[i], [*Philadelphia*] is now in the Harbor with all her Guns mounted: but that she has no ammunition on board and only a Guard of about 30 Men."[12]

Rumors swirled about the *Intrepid*'s mission. Watching the *Syren* and *Intrepid* sail near sunset on February 3, Nathanial Haraden, the sailing master of the *Constitution*, noted in the log that they were "bound on some Secret Expedition." Midshipman Ralph Izard Jr., the son of a signer of the Declaration of Independence, wrote his mother in South Carolina in the tone of a boy going to a party. "This evening, my Dear Mother, I sail for Tripoli on board of a prize . . . for the purpose of burning the Frigate *Philadelphia* which is now in the possession of the Tripolitans." He hoped to have "the happiness of seeing the *Philadelphia* in flames. We shall astonish the Bashaws weak mind with the noise of shot falling about his ears. Perhaps some shot 'more lucky than the rest may reach his heart' & free our countrymen from Slavery."[13]

With a fair wind, it takes only a few days to sail the 240 miles from Sicily to the African coast. But after a brief calm, in early February 1804, the weather turned quickly. The Mediterranean is notorious for violent storms, and a forbidding blast of wind and huge waves began to fall on the small American ships. The *Syren* and the *Intrepid* arrived off Africa late in the day on February 8. The weather had not improved. The *Intrepid* anchored close to shore and sent a boat out to determine if the raiders could cross the breakwater and enter the harbor. In the boat were the pilot, Catalano, and Midshipman Morris. Close to the entrance to the harbor, Morris found the surf breaking over the bar. Catalano and Morris returned to the *Intrepid*, and before a council of the officers, Catalano "declar[e]d that if we attempted to go in we would never come out again for the breakers were tremendously high." There was a murmuring among the officers, questioning Catalano's courage. Morris agreed with Catalano and told the officers so, but he worried that they might think him "shy." Despite expressions of disapproval, Decatur listened to Morris and Catalano and decided to postpone the attack.[14]

Almost immediately, the weather showed that Catalano and Morris were right. Both the *Syren* and the *Intrepid* were blown about, driven by a heavy sea and a strong northerly wind, making the African coast the lee shore that all sailors dread. Waves started to roll in, higher and higher, seawater surging over the gunnels of the *Syren* as the brig rolled to port and starboard with each crest and trough.[15]

There was nothing to do but ride out the storm. Day after day, the wind whipped about, and the spray and water surged on board the two little ships. Conditions on the *Intrepid* were cramped, dirty, and disgusting. Decatur and four officers occupied the small cabin. Morris, five other midshipmen, Catalano, and eight marines slept on a loft laid over the water casks in the hold. Their space was so low that no one could sit up. The forty-five sailors slept in the hold, among the water casks. Things were not much better on deck, which was pitching and rolling in the gale, with little room to move about. Below deck, the Americans were attacked by lice left behind by the Tripolitan slaves. The surging and rolling of the little *Intrepid* in the rough weather jostled the sailors about, and many were sickened, not helped by the smell from the bilges. When they left Syracuse, each officer was allowed only one change of linen, so after days of tossing about in storms, everything was damp. Their food, hastily stowed in Syracuse and probably left over from the Tripolitans— Morris stated that "no time was allowed to prepare stores" because the *Intrepid* sailed within an hour of receiving orders—proved to be putrid, crawling with maggots, so rank that sailors, not a mollycoddled bunch, could not stomach their rations. Most ate only navy biscuit, bad water, and their ration of grog.[16]

Decatur brought his officers and men together and disclosed his plan of attack. He would lead the assault after the ketch lashed onto the *Philadelphia*. Sixty men would scramble up the side of the frigate. With fifteen men, Decatur would secure the spar deck. The rest of the boarders, following, would be divided in three divisions, under his three lieutenants. They would use only blade weapons—cutlasses, tomahawks, and pikes—to gain control of the rest of the ship. Once they had possession, they would retrieve the combustibles from the *Intrepid*, and sailors in each division would run them down to assigned parts of the ship and set her ablaze. Sailors not boarding would be sent out in the *Intrepid*'s boats to prevent enemy reinforcements from intervening. Finally, Dr. Lewis Heermann, a German émigré who was a surgeon's mate, would be left behind in command of the *Intrepid*, because Decatur had run out of officers. Decatur gave Heermann seven men. He anticipated that the Tripolitans on the *Philadelphia*, "when pressed hard, will be apt to retreat from the spar deck and board the ketch." If they did, Decatur warned, "your safety will consist of giving no quarter." Without the *Intrepid*, the Americans could not escape, and Decatur told the doctor "at all events, to defend her to the last man."[17]

The attackers tried to launch their assault on the evening of February 15. The *Syren* and *Intrepid* stood in toward the harbor, but it was a dark night, and Stewart, the commander of the *Syren*, reported he "could not determine our position not having seen the town[.] We were therefore obliged to stand off again." The two American ships went back out to sea.[18]

The next day, February 16, 1804, they tried again. At 11:00 AM, the *Intrepid* set a course for the harbor. The Americans did not want to sail in too early, and light winds allowed the ketch to appear to be trying to reach the harbor before night. When still far enough off to be unseen from land, Decatur ordered small sails to be put overboard in the water, attached to the sides with lines, to act as drags. Decatur also ordered the entire crew below, except for the six or eight seamen needed to navigate the *Intrepid*. Only warships carried large crews, and he did not want to cause suspicions for anyone casually training his telescope on the approaching ketch. As an added precaution, he ordered those on deck to wear Maltese-style clothes.[19]

As the *Intrepid* slowly wafted in toward the harbor, Decatur ordered British colors hoisted. Given her appearance, it would have been understandable for Decatur to fly no flag at all, or Turkish or Tripolitan colors as a *ruse de guerre*. But flying the British flag would not be alarming, since the British Mediterranean squadron frequently sent small ships into Barbary ports for supplies. The British consul ashore, McDonogh, responded to the *Intrepid* flying British colors by hoisting the Union Jack, an acknowledgment of having seen the flag in the offing. McDonogh could not have known the mission of the *Intrepid* (or that the ketch was the *Intrepid*). Yet to anyone ashore who might have had doubts about a small ketch approaching the harbor in the late afternoon, it was reassuring nonetheless. The ruse worked perfectly. Cowdery wrote in his diary that at 5:00 PM, he was told that two English merchantmen were standing in for the harbor. The sighting cheered the crew, according to William Ray, because the sailors assumed the two vessels were American and had come with proposals to negotiate their release.[20]

After the days of storms, the attack was at risk because the wind was dying. Sailing down to the bottom of the harbor took hours. The drags were taken up as it grew dark; the *Intrepid* was still two miles off the eastern entrance to the harbor. In the early evening, Decatur called his officers together. The *Syren*, as planned, was about a mile astern. The officers agreed that it was too risky with a dying and fickle breeze to wait for the *Syren* to provide more men. Decatur decided to proceed with the attack without waiting, murmuring to Morris, paraphrasing Shakespeare's *Henry V*, "The fewer the number the greater the honor."[21]

Slowly, the *Intrepid* entered the harbor. The water was smooth. There was enough moonlight for the few men on deck to make out the bashaw's castle and prominent buildings and minarets. The Americans slipped by a battery that did not open fire. The *Philadelphia* lay directly ahead. The *Intrepid* sailed right at her. Near the frigate were several small gunboats. Behind the *Philadelphia*, Morris could see the whitewashed walls of the city.[22]

As the *Intrepid* drew close to the *Philadelphia*, Decatur passed the word, quietly, for his men to gather on deck in their assault groups. They lay down, armed with their swords and pikes and tomahawks, resting in anxious silence. The silence was broken as the *Intrepid* was only a hundred feet away from the looming frigate when a lookout on the *Philadelphia* hailed, in Arabic, to demand what ship was that, and what was she doing. Standing next to Decatur was Salvadore Catalano. Hailing back and forth with the Tripolitan lookout across the shrinking gap of water, Catalano bought time. He called out that the ketch was from Malta and had lost her anchors in the gale, and asked if she could tie up to the anchored frigate for the night. The lookout relayed the message to an officer and then called back with permission. As the *Intrepid* neared the much-larger *Philadelphia*, the wind shifted. Now blowing directly from the frigate toward the ketch, the wind pushed the *Intrepid* about twenty yards away from the *Philadelphia*.[23]

The *Intrepid* lay wallowing in the water, motionless, directly under the cannon of the frigate, what Morris called "a moment of great anxiety." Decatur motioned to his ranking lieutenant, James Lawrence, to lower the *Intrepid*'s boat and run a line from the bow of the ketch to the bow of the *Philadelphia*, which was quickly made fast. At the same time, Decatur whispered to Midshipman Thomas Anderson to gather several sailors—without any quick movements or noise—man a boat being towed astern, row over to the frigate's stern, and toss up the line to tie down. With lines between the ketch and the frigate fore and aft, the sailors on the *Intrepid* would literally pull themselves to the *Philadelphia*. The boat was manned and began to row across. But a Tripolitan boat, perhaps from the frigate, perhaps from a nearby vessel, having seen the ketch being blown away from the frigate, began to row toward the ketch. The two boats met between the ketch and the frigate. Without a word, the Americans handed their line over, the two lines were knotted together, and each boat rowed back to its own ship. There now were the precious links between ketch and frigate. Anderson passed the line up to the *Intrepid*'s deck. The *Intrepid*'s crew began to haul the rope in, dragging their ketch closer and closer to the frigate by brute force.[24]

In seconds, only a few yards separated the *Intrepid* from the *Philadelphia*. From the deck of the frigate, a Tripolitan sailor looked down into the ketch, realized who the men massed on her deck with cutlasses and pikes must be, and screamed, "Americanos! Americanos!" The ketch nudged up against the frigate. Decatur and Morris were the first two to jump onto the tumblehome of the *Philadelphia*, but in seconds, in Heermann's memorable phrase, the "boarders hung on the ship's side like [a] cluster [of] bees." Up the side they went, over the rail onto the frigate's spar deck. In front of this torrent, a few Tripolitan sailors jumped overboard, and others who tried to fight were overwhelmed by American tars and marines stabbing and slashing with their weapons. In a few seconds of frantic fighting, the Americans seized control of the spar deck. Only one American was slightly wounded. The Americans had not fired a single shot. Heermann recalled:

After the first exclamation of "Ali Mohamed!" the sound of voices and the clashing of arms, left, during the contest nothing of distinct perception to the ear; and the fire of small arms now commencing from the two cruizers close by (xebecs) and followed soon after by the cannon of the bashaw's castle and other batteries, together with the whooping and howling on shore, filled the air. . . . Some of the Enemy in retreating, had gone up the rigging, some in the channels, some jumped overboard, and others [hid] in the hold of the ship.

According to Midshipman Izard, about twenty Tripolitan sailors were "cut to pieces" and others jumped overboard, although Heermann reported that only a few were killed, one wounded man was made a prisoner, and the rest escaped by jumping into the water, to swim ashore.[25] The assault parties went below, but there were no more defenders. Decatur ordered the assault groups to lay their combustibles. Men dashed back to the *Intrepid* to get the charges. What happened in the next few minutes is murky. Heermann heard one of the American lookouts on the *Philadelphia* call out "in quick succession the approach of [the] enemy's boats, and their retreat, with an interval of time just sufficient

Chart drawn by Midshipman F. C. De Krafft on board the *Syren* off Tripoli, 1804. The location of the *Philadelphia* is marked with an "M" to the right, near the castle and forts of Tripoli. (*Library of Congress*) to execute the order which grew out of it—of killing all prisoners." Heermann was the only participant to report that the Americans killed their prisoners. Although he did not identify who gave the order, Decatur was the only officer who could have given such a command.[26]

The combustibles were laid and then lit, setting fire to the berth deck and the forward storerooms, which contained turpentine, paints, canvas, and other flammable materials. The fires erupted violently and began to spread throughout the ship. Morris had been the first onto the *Philadelphia*, but Decatur made sure he himself was the last man off. He stood on the frigate's rail, making sure every American sailor and marine was accounted for and back aboard the ketch. Morris recounted that "the bow of the ketch had already swung off from the ship when he joined us by leaping into the rigging of the ketch."[27]

Less than fifteen minutes after the Americans set foot on the *Philadelphia*, fires were bursting out of her ports. At about 10:40 PM, the *Philadelphia* erupted into flame and "the castle & Batteries then commenced the fire on the *Intrepid*, all around the frigate & in every direction." Morris called the spectacle "magnificent," as "[t]he flames in the interior illuminated her [gun]ports and, ascending her rigging and masts, formed columns of fire, which, meeting the tops, were reflected in beautiful capitals." The fire of the immolating frigate was so enormous that "[t]he walls of the city and its batteries, and the masts and rigging of cruisers at anchor, [were] brilliantly illuminated, and animated by the discharge of artillery."[28]

One of the captive midshipmen in the consul house wrote home:

We had all turned in early in the evening, and were fast asleep in our prison, when we were awakened by a most dreadful noise, accompanied by repeated discharges of artillery. We jumped up, ran to the window, and with great surprise, beheld our ship engulfed in flames. It was a grand, and awful sight, and viewed by us with infinite delight. . . . She burned a long time with great fury, and the guns which had been loaded, being heated, were discharged at intervals with a tremendous roar, adding greatly to the sublimity of the scene.[29]

Cowdery wrote in his diary that at "[a]bout 11, at night, we were alarmed by a most hideous yelling and screaming from one end of the town to the other, and the firing of a cannon from the castle. On getting up and opening the window which faced the harbour, we saw the frigate *Philadelphia* in flames." Another captive officer wrote that they "were awakened by the report of a cannon, and on opening our windows, beheld the frigate *Philadelphia* in flames, which raged with great fury." No scene could be "more grand or awful," the frigate "blazing from stem to stern, and to the very tops of her masts, all her ports so distinctly seen, that they might be counted—the cannon roaring from the castle and the adjacent batteries." They watched, mesmerized, for an hour, until the *Philadelphia*'s cables had burned off, allowing her to drift onto some rocks, out of their sight.[30]

The captive sailors and marines in the magazine could not see what was happening but heard women screaming, guards running in the prison yard, the cannon from the bashaw's castle thundering out—a scene of complete tumult. But they did not know what was going on.[31]

The *Philadelphia* was a bonfire and burned for hours, down to her waterline, destroyed. Despite the hundreds of cannonballs fired at the *Intrepid* none hit her, and she slowly sailed out of the harbor into the safety of the open sea.[32]

The frigate burned so speedily that there was nothing the bashaw could do, although he saw *Gift of Allah* destroyed with his own eyes. When the light of dawn showed the once majestic ship was destroyed, the Tripolitan overseers began exacting revenge on the crew. "Much earlier than usual," William Ray wrote, "our prison doors were unbolted, and the keepers, like so many fiends from the infernal regions, rushed in amongst us, and began to beat every one they could see, spitting in our faces, and hissing like the serpents of hell. Word was soon brought, that the wreck of the frigate *Philadelphia* lay on the rocks." The crew could not restrain themselves from cheering and joking about the destruction of their ship, which only "exasperated [the Tripolitans] more and more, so that every boy we met in the streets, would spit on us and pelt us with stones; our tasks doubled, [and] our bread [was] withheld."[33]

Two days later, on the morning of February 19, the *Intrepid* and *Syren* arrived back in Syracuse. As they made their way into the harbor, Preble asked by signal flag if they had succeeded in their mission. Stewart, commander of the *Syren*, hoisted in reply, "We did." As the two American ships made their way to the anchorage, the sailors of the squadron crowded aloft on their ships (the *Constitution*, *Nautilus*, and *Vixen*) and gave three raucous cheers and waved their hats as the victors passed by in triumph. In his letter that day to the secretary of the navy, Preble reported the success of the expedition and stated that the conduct of Decatur and his men "cannot be sufficiently estimated—It is beyond all praise."[34]

The burning of the *Gift of Allah* threw Yusuf into a rage. The gunners of his batteries had missed the *Intrepid* as she departed, and he unleashed his fury on them. Zuchet recorded that he "beat them upside down and sideways," except for those lucky enough to find refuge in the mosques. After Yusuf's preening over the capture of the frigate, there now was humiliation, but Zuchet surmised that "his political side required him to try to hide his chagrin and he forced himself, as much as he could, to try to show indifference over the loss, saying that it was only a punishment from Heaven and had nothing to do with the valor of his enemies." But Yusuf could and did react against the officers and crew of the *Philadelphia*. The crew was given additional grinding work. Two days after the raid, the entire crew was turned out to get the remains of the frigate off the rocks, but they could not clear the wreck, despite Godby, who was in charge, beating some of the men "to court favour from the Turks." The bashaw placed a strong guard over the crew at night and refused to provide meat in their rations. The officers, who only eight days earlier had been allowed to walk in the countryside, were once again confined to the consul house, with their guard doubled and soldiers again posted on the roof. Yusuf forbade the officers from sending or receiving any letters—a prohibition that lasted only three weeks—and ordered a prison built for the officers inside his castle, below the interior courtyard, with an iron grill placed over the space. A French visitor in Tripoli noted, "Were it not for his hopes of a heavy ransom, they would most assuredly experience some more distressing marks of his displeasure."[35]

After discovering the bodies of Tripolitan sailors after the attack on a nearby beach, Yusuf assumed they had been murdered after surrendering. He told Beaussier, the French consul, about the discovery of the bodies of three Tripolitan sailors who had been repeatedly stabbed. Beaussier reported to the Foreign Ministry in Paris, "The bashaw has no doubt that they were massacred after their seizure, and then thrown into the sea. If the fact is true, he does not blame the American [prisoners] for it, but rather the leaders of the expedition" that burned the ship. Dghies wrote Bainbridge that the dead sailors from the *Gift of Allah* had been found covered with wounds. Dghies, a minister in a land that Americans routinely termed inhabited by "barbarians," asked, "How long has it been since Nations massacred their Prisoners?" Bainbridge passed the letter on to Preble, who expressed regret for the lives lost in burning the *Philadelphia*, but noted, "the Men who were killed in taking possession of her, had a right to expect their fate from the opposition they made, and the alarm they endeavoured to create. Our People were few in number, and had everything to apprehend from an attack by their Cruisers and armed boats[.] The Officer who conducted the expedition has not reported to me any Massacre or inhumanity."[36]

The day Decatur and Stewart returned to Syracuse with the news of the destruction of the *Philadelphia*, Preble reported to Secretary Smith that the loss of the ship damaged Yusuf because he could not raise money from selling her. Preble hoped that before the end of the summer, the bashaw would seek a treaty "without a cent for Peace or Tribute" and asserted he would rather spend his life fighting the Tripolitans than paying a penny for either. A month later, Preble wrote Robert R. Livingston in Paris that the United States wanted a real peace but "we never would purchase Peace, or pay [the bashaw] Tribute." He had asked Naples, he reported to Livingston, for a loan of gunboats and bomb vessels, and if he got them, he would attack Tripoli and "oblige the Bashaw to sue for Peace as a favour in three days after I reach his Coast."[37]

~ EIGHT ~

REINFORCEMENTS

WORD OF THE *PHILADELPHIA*'S LOSS on Kaliusa reef arrived in the United States in March 1804. The capture of three hundred Americans came like an electric shock to the whole country. Even before President Jefferson officially informed Congress, the families and friends of the officers and crew of the frigate submitted a petition to the House of Representatives, and another petition was submitted by "sundry other inhabitants of the City of Philadelphia," asking the government to "take such measures as may be deemed effectual and proper to rescue, from the deplorable state of slavery" the men of the *Philadelphia*.[1]

Thomas Fitzsimmons, a former Federalist congressman and a Philadelphia civic leader who had led the citizens committee that had raised money for and supervised the construction of the *Philadelphia* in 1798, wrote Secretary of State James Madison to determine whether private Americans, "friends of the prisoners" as he put it, could pool their funds to alleviate their plight or to ransom them. The urge to try to rescue family and countrymen held captive is timeless, and Fitzsimmons represented those wishing to rally the public to secure the captives' release. In the early 1790s, efforts to privately redeem Americans held captive in Barbary were derailed by President Washington, who sought to resolve the issue through diplomatic channels, and by then-Secretary of State Jefferson, who tried to deter Algiers from seizing more American sailors and holding them for ransom by convincing the dey that the United States was too poor to pay and feigning indifference to the captives' fate. The argument against private relief was that it would show the Barbary rulers that Americans would pay any price for the captives' freedom, undermining the government's efforts.[2]

With that precedent, it is not surprising that Madison replied privately to Fitzsimmons that sympathy for the captives needed to be balanced against the "superior consideration" of the public good. A "too unbounded" generosity to fund their support or release might spur further aggressions by the Barbary regimes to seize Americans. In the meanwhile, Madison assured Fitzsimmons, the captives were "amply supplied," the French consul in Tripoli might have already intervened to "soften the rigor of their situation," and the navy's attacks might lower the demands for ransom. Madison acknowledged there was no law prohibiting private citizens from providing relief, but he asked Fitzsimmons to consider whether private efforts might thwart diplomatic negotiations and "protract the sufferings of those unhappy men." In the face of the administration's request for restraint, the effort of private citizens to ransom the captives fell silent.[3]

A year later, the *Charleston (SC) Courier* recounted that initially, feeling for their enslaved countrymen ran "like electric fluid, from city to town, from town to village, from village to hamlet" and that from "every part of the Union the hand of Bounty was opened, and [an] immense subscription promised" to free the captives and "speedily restore them to liberty[,] . . . to air, to comfort, to joy—to America." But the government "chilled" that impulse, concerned that the more Americans strove to free the captives, the higher the ransom demand would soar, stifling in its birth the "noble design" of the people to donate their money to rescue the captives.[4]

On March 20, 1804, President Jefferson formally notified Congress of the "wreck" of the *Philadelphia* and that the officers and crew "had fallen into the hands of the Tripolitans," attaching Bainbridge's letter to Secretary Smith. Jefferson advised Congress that the disaster required an increase of the naval force sent to the Mediterranean, which would necessitate additional funding. Within four days, both houses of Congress passed a bill laying on an additional 2.5 percent *ad valorem* duty on all imports into the United States and an additional 10 percent duty on all goods imported on foreign merchant ships to defray the costs of putting back into commission, manning, and employing whatever warships the president thought expedient to fight Tripoli and, if necessary, other Barbary powers. The collected money for Barbary operations would be called the Mediterranean Fund so as not to indicate a regular appropriation for the navy. In addition, the president was authorized to borrow up to $1 million for naval expenditures, and the bill authorized the administration to "hire or accept on loan in the Mediterranean sea, as many gun boats as he may think proper." Jefferson signed the bill into law on March 26, 1804. The new law did not provide money to ransom the captives, an omission not lost on Federalist-leaning newspapers, like the *New-York Herald*, which hoped that the administration did "not mean to suffer our gallant Tars to languish in hopeless captivity." The *Herald* was "sure that the people of our country, will not behold without emotion 300 of our fellow-citizens, galled by the chains, and smarting beneath the lash of the most cruel and ferocious of barbarians."[5]

Remarkably, the bill was signed into law just one week after the news of the *Philadelphia* disaster had arrived in Washington. Even arch Republicans who on theoretical grounds rejected maintaining a navy felt the expenditure was necessary. John Fowler, a Republican congressman from Kentucky, informed his constituents that money for the navy for the coming year would not be cut, as it had been each year under the Jefferson administration, but, including the Mediterranean Fund, would rise to $1,650,000. That sum, he wrote, "may perhaps surprize you." But the country had been "forced into the maintenance of a naval force." With the *Philadelphia* having run aground and three hundred Americans in slavery overseas, it would be an inappropriate moment to forego a navy, but Fowler admitted that for him, American trade to the Mediterranean was "not worth the expense [of a navy] or the injury [the seamen held for ransom] to which it subjects the nation."[6]

With Jefferson's direct involvement, the navy reacted immediately to the news of the disaster overseas. Orders went out to prepare four frigates for service in the Mediterranean and to recruit hundreds of sailors in New York, Philadelphia, and Baltimore to man the reinforcing squadron. There was a sense of national purpose as marines and sailors were enrolled and dispatched to the ports where the navy scrambled to ready its ships, and orders coursed through the country for gunpowder and salted beef and pork and the hundreds of other things that a naval squadron sailing overseas needed.[7]

Representing the leading veins of public opinion, newspapers expressed sympathy for Bainbridge for running his ship on the rocks and concern for the captive Americans. While calling the loss of the *Philadelphia* "truly distressing" and a "national misfortune," the Worcester, Massachusetts, *National Aegis* presumed the "disaster" was "one of those inevitable misfortunes, which no human foresight could have seen." The *Aurora*, a leading Republican newspaper in Philadelphia, referred to the events as "a national calamity" and knew that there was no American "who does not sensibly feel for the situation of his fellow citizens made captives." A column published in several northern newspapers called the surrender of the frigate and imprisoning of her men the most "severe calamity" to befall the country since the Constitution had been adopted fifteen years before. Even if the bashaw were to demand a million dollars or more for the officers and crew, the *New Hampshire Sentinel* editors opined from Kenne, New Hampshire, that "there is not an American patriot in existence who would not cheerfully pay his proportion of the ransom."[8]

But inevitably, there were recriminations and political finger pointing. The Federalist Party, still reeling from the 1800 elections in which Jefferson narrowly edged John Adams to become president and Congress passed into Republican hands, was months away from the 1804 presidential contest. Federalist-leaning newspapers reacted to the surrender of the ship and crew by condemning the frugality of the administration for sending an inadequate squadron off to the Mediterranean and by attacking the "philosophical" president who skimped on the high-seas navy, a proud Federalist legacy. The Philadelphia *True American* commented that the loss of the *Philadelphia* meant the war would be prolonged, and "great expense will be necessary to repair the loss and strengthen the force; and a number of our brave men are gone into a cruel captivity, who must be redeemed at an enormous sum. This is economy with a vengeance."[9]

Some Federalist newspapers thought they hit a nerve by exposing the fact that when she went aground, the *Philadelphia* was alone in blockading Tripoli. The *New York Evening Post*, founded by Jefferson's nemesis, Alexander Hamilton, in 1801, and edited by William Coleman, was a leading voice of Federalism. The *Evening Post* attacked the very notion that the *Philadelphia*'s grounding was an accident or unpredictable. No, the paper hastened to state, it did not reproach Bainbridge; Coleman's target was Jefferson. Noting that Jefferson boasted in his Second Annual Message that he sent "the smallest force competent" to the Mediterranean to protect American trade, the *Evening Post* exploded in wrath that he "sends a single Frigate to invest the harbor of Tripoli. This may have been a pretty scheme for a knick knackery philosopher, but it was a very curious mode of warfare" for a responsible commander in chief. Coleman reckoned the loss of the frigate, the ransom of the captives, and buying a peace with the bashaw would cost millions of dollars. Economy in government expenditures was all well and good, the *Evening Post* concluded, but "not that miserable, starveling, niggardly species of economy which, by saving a dollar, ruins a nation."[10] In a similar vein, the leading Federalist paper in Boston, the *Columbian Centinel*, editorialized, "The present administration boast[s] loudly of its wisdom, as well as economy. But the loss of the frigate *Philadelphia* is but a poor comment on either. Had there been a single tender in company with that frigate, we should not now have to deplore the fate of above Three Hundred of our countrymen in slavery."[11]

Republican-leaning newspapers answered that Preble had dispatched the *Vixen* to accompany the *Philadelphia* but that Bainbridge had ordered her away. The *Aurora* quoted Bainbridge's letter in which he acknowledged that if he had not sent the *Vixen* away, the accident might have been prevented, to show that the absence of an escort could not be attributed to the administration. Another Republican-leaning paper ridiculed the *Evening Post*, stating that Coleman and his newspaper did not "absolutely accuse Mr. Jefferson, or his Secretary of the Navy, of planting the rocks in the Mediterranean, on which the *Philadelphia* foundered, nor does he intimate that Captain Bainbridge . . . was in league with the Tripolitans, and that he [deliberately] ran the ship aground." But Coleman's invective against the president was misguided. Preble himself thought his squadron was fully adequate, and he had discretion to employ it as circumstances required; and no one could have predicted the grounding, since the shoals were not on any chart. Other newspapers observed that no one criticized the adequacy of the squadron when Bainbridge captured the *Mirboka* and Preble had demonstrated American power to the king of Morocco.[12] After a few weeks of invective, the newspaper war died down.

Everyone knew it would take months for the ships to be readied, manned, and sailed to the Barbary coast. But the sailing orders to Commodore Samuel Barron, in command of the reinforcements, only went to him on June 6, and the squadron was not able to put to sea until July 1, eight months after the *Philadelphia* had gone aground and only a few weeks before Preble's squadron, more than five thousand miles away, was about to start its long-awaited attacks on Tripoli.[13]

The situation in the Mediterranean quickly entered American popular culture. At the Southwark Theatre in Philadelphia, after a performance of a comedy called *John Bull, or, an Englishman's Fire-side*, promoters advertised a new one-act play, *A New Wreath for American Tars*, which concluded with a "reproduction of the burning of THE FRIGATE PHILADELPHIA." In Providence, at Mr. Aldrich's Assembly Room, a concert included composer James Hewitt's overture in ten parts "descriptive of the Capture and Burning of the Frigate Philadelphia." New Hampshire newspapers published a song, set to the tune of "Yankee Doodle," of which the last stanza rang out:

> *A million granted for defence,*
> *To gain our friends' dismission,*
> *Is ready for departure hence,*
> *And call'd the new emission.*
> *Three frigates bear it o'er the sea,*
> *To urge its circulation,*
> *To set the Philadelphia free,*
> *Or awe the barbarous nation.*[14]

Later, at the New Theatre in Philadelphia, a farce was staged called *American Tars in Tripoli*, which was to conclude with "a grand

panorama" of the "exact situation of the engagement with the Tripolitans." In Manhattan, promoter Joseph Delacroix prepared a summer
benefit (for himself) at his New Vauxhall Garden Theatre (Lafayette
Street, from Fourth to Eighth Streets) of a theatrical spectacular of the
events in the Mediterranean, with thirty-foot-long paintings of the port,
fortifications, and city of Tripoli, and the burning of the *Philadelphia*,
to be concluded by fireworks and a "GRAND FUE DE JOIE." Even the
turf was affected by the war: in Rhode Island, the owner of a fifteen-
hand-high racehorse called Young Bashaw advertised that he was "to be
let to mares on very reasonable Terms."[15]

NINE

BLOCKADE AND DIPLOMACY

B ACK IN THE MEDITERRANEAN, even as the *Intrepid* raiders were making their way to Tripoli, Preble ordered the ships of his squadron to begin the blockade interrupted when the *Philadelphia* ran aground. To enforce the blockade, Preble ordered one captain to "capture all Tripoli[tan] or other Vessels on which Tripoli[tan] property is laden which you may happen to fall in with. You are not to suffer the vessels of any nation to enter or to have commerce with Tripol[i], but have a right to treat as an Enemy whoever may endeavor to enter that place or carry any thing to it whilst blockaded by us." In directing the movements of his small squadron, Preble tried to ensure that sufficient force would be available to blockade Tripoli. Although in early 1804, only the schooner *Nautilus* and the brig *Syren* were on blockading duty, by spring Preble was able to station most of his squadron off Tripoli. When he arrived there in the frigate *Constitution* in June, five US warships were in sight, and with the port kept closely blockaded, he hoped that the bashaw would "soon be sick of the War."[1]

The goal of the blockade was to persuade the bashaw to negotiate peace by preventing military supplies from entering Tripoli, cutting off contact with the outside world, and even depriving the local population of food. Bainbridge thought a blockade would be useless, writing Preble that it was the "wrong system to pursue" as it created a "great risque" to blockading ships "without the least effect, except the Interest of a few Jewish Merchants. The Country abounds with plenty, and every super-fluous supply can readily be got from Tunis by Land. The situation of their Harbour, and coast is such, that their small cruisers which are the most dangerous, can always go to Sea, and return into port in spite of the most vigilant cruisers stationed off here." Preble brushed off the crit-icism, concluding that a blockade would have "a good effect." The truth was, with the ships that he had, it was all he could do.[2]

The offshore blockading squadron stopped a half-dozen ships and made prizes of several trying to run the embargo. On February 16, 1804, the same night that Decatur's men burned the *Philadelphia*, the schooner *Nautilus* captured a Maltese brig, *Santissimo Crocifisso*, twelve or fifteen miles off Tripoli. Ostensibly cleared for Djerba (in Tunis, west of Tripoli), the *Santissimo Crocifisso* was brought to the east of Tripoli, standing in for the harbor. Preble recorded that her capture was "in sight of the fire made by the burning of the Frigate in that Harbor." The *Santissimo Cro-cifisso* carried a cargo of hemp, wine, scantling, and bales of linen and merchandise. The commander of the *Nautilus*, Richard Somers, sent a prize crew aboard the brig with orders to sail her into Syracuse to let Preble sort out what to do.[3]

A month later, on March 17, the *Syren* captured the brig *Transfer*, which had managed to evade the blockade and enter Tripoli two days after Decatur's expedition burned the *Philadelphia*, delivering a cargo of gunpowder and other stores and taking on a cargo of six thousand gallons of olive oil and horses for the return voyage to Malta. The *Syren*'s commander, Charles Stewart, reported to Preble that the *Transfer* had departed from Tripoli that morning despite the *Syren* sailing close in-shore. Stewart sent the *Transfer* with a prize crew into Syracuse. After Preble had her surveyed to determine a fair price, he brought her into the navy to use in his squadron, renamed *Scourge*.[4]

A few days later, the *Syren* stopped a polacre, the *Madonna di Cata-paliani*, a Greek-built ship flying Russian colors from Tripoli bound to Malta with a cargo of sheep and bullocks. She had arrived in Tripoli from Smyrna in December 1803, carrying gunpowder, shot, ship timber, cannon, and seventy-five Turkish soldiers recruited for the bashaw. The pilot admitted under oath that everyone aboard "knew of the blockade of Tripol[i] by our Squadron previous to our sailing from Smyrna" so that her papers read she was bound for Djerba in Tunis, but the master had directed the pilot to guide her into Tripoli. Stewart sent her into Syracuse as well.[5]

In May, the brig *Argus* stopped a Spanish ketch, the *Virgine Del Rosario*, leaving Tripoli, and in June, the *Argus* and *Vixen* seized a ketch, the *St. Jean Baptiste*, flying Ligurian colors. Both were sent into Malta, but on diplomatic protests by Spanish and French diplomats, Preble decided to let them go.[6]

Two centuries later, it is impossible to know how successful Preble's blockade was. Although the small ships of the squadron intercepted a few vessels seeking to enter Tripoli, no one has been able to determine the number of ships that slipped through the blockade. If any records were once created and still exist of ship entries and departures kept by the bashaw's regime, no one has found them. While the blockade must have deterred some ships, others slipped by, and goods and money were brought in over land by camels from Tunis, as Bainbridge asserted. Beaussier, the French consul, reported to Paris that an Austrian ship, sailing from Livorno to Djerba, landed a shipment of 80,000 dollars promised by the Batavians as tribute for Tripoli, showing a hole in the blockade. On the other hand, Zuchet observed that there was suffering and discontent among Tripoli's population because of a lack of food. The blockade contributed to the scarcity, exacerbated by Yusuf ordering a mass conscription in response to the American navy offshore; with farmers under arms, they were not tending to their crops. But there was enough food to feed the population. Nor was the fighting ability of Tripoli diminished. Nissen suggested that the squadron blockade the eastern ports of Tripoli, such as Benghazi, because "many vessels enter there from the Levant with powder etc." William Henry Allen, a midshipman who came out to the Mediterranean in the reinforcing squadron in summer 1805, wrote home that "we well know that Tunis has *last winter* covered small boats (with their papers) bound to Tripoli; *loaded* in Malta with *musquetry & powder* and have arrived there." The fact that Spanish carpenters and American slave-prisoners were able to build and arm gunboats on the strand suggests there was sufficient timber, naval stores, and cannon.[7]

Blockading an enemy's coast was trying, mostly sailing back and forth off the coast, a few miles offshore, in all weathers, keeping a sharp lookout for small vessels creeping along the shore. Occasionally, the vessels from the squadron closed with the shore to fire on ships carrying grain, on gun batteries, or on concentrations of Arab horsemen. Bold captains like Stewart and Somers sometimes sent in their launches and barges to land marines and sailors on the African sands to burn coastal craft or just to test the enemy. In his journal for April 29, 1804, Midshipman Cornelius de Krafft scribbled that in the mid-afternoon, his ship, the *Syren*, tacked in toward shore west of Tripoli, trailed by the *Argus* and *Vixen*. The carronades on the three ships "commenc'd a brisk fire on the fort & a small Battery close on the beach, & continued the sport 'till ½ past 6. The enemy's shot flying over & in every direction of us but to no effect."[8] Henry Wadsworth, another midshipman, captured the essence of those brisk fights. He wrote a friend in America that the *Vixen* had come upon and chased a galley, forcing her to run ashore. "The *Vixen* anchored close in and made a riddling sieve of her in a short time: she was laden with wheat which they got on shore, the Musketry from shore fired thro[ugh] the *Vixen*'s sails & 4 men were killed in the *S[y]ren*'s boat." He added, "The Boats of the squadron frequently go on shore at a distance from the Town for Sand to scrub our decks & for amusement, to chase & be chased by the Natives, but they always retire before the people begin to collect. The [Tripolitan] Gun Boats . . . often get under way & work about the Harbor & the Bank to the Eastward . . . & once or twice we have been at it with long shot, but this the commodore [Preble] has now forbid as it practices them in firing."[9]

As his small ships blockaded Tripoli, Commodore Preble began a flurry of diplomatic activity to free the captives. The United States had no diplomatic representative with the Ottoman Empire, but Preble knew that Bonaparte had pledged French assistance. He decided to send the *chouix* captured on the *Mastico* to the French ambassador in Constantinople, General Guillaume Brune, with a letter about the capture of the

Mastico and announcing the proclamation of the Tripoli blockade. He also wrote to the British emissary in Constantinople, as well as to the chief of the Ottoman navy, the "Capitan Pasha" (a corruption of the Turkish "Kapudan Pasha") asking for the intervention of Sultan Selim III. Preble's overture was extraordinary because less than four years before, when Bainbridge's *George Washington* arrived in the Bosporus, the Sublime Porte was unfamiliar with the Stars and Stripes flag, and no one had heard of the "United States." In writing the Capitan Pasha, Preble pointed out that the *Mastico* was flying Turkish colors, but after the *Philadelphia* went aground, the *Mastico* hauled that flag down, hoisted Tripolitan colors, and "went out to the attack." Preble's point was that "by the Piratical interference of the Vessel of a friendly Nation, was the crew of one of our Frigates made prisoners." Based on the friendship between the United States and the Ottoman Empire (a convenient diplomatic fiction), he asked for Selim III to issue a *firman* to the bashaw, ordering him to free the officers and crew of the frigate and punish those who committed "this flagrant violation of the law of Nations." Preble feigned astonishment that the bashaw allowed such a piratical transaction. Although he professed confidence that the sultan would come to Bainbridge's relief, there is no evidence that the Sublime Porte did anything.[10]

Tobias Lear, the consul general to the Barbary powers, was the obvious man to lead a diplomatic overture to Tripoli, but in spring 1804, he opted to remain in Algiers, given the tensions with other Barbary powers. Instead, Preble would conduct negotiations himself, and he asked Lear to send him Richard O'Brien, the former consul in Algiers. O'Brien, the child of Irish immigrants who settled in Maine, was originally a mariner, making transatlantic voyages before the Revolutionary War. He was an officer aboard the brig *Jefferson* in the Virginia State Navy during the Revolution and was captured by the British, languishing as a prisoner for two years. After the war, he resumed his life at sea. In July 1785, Algerine corsairs captured the ship on which he was master, the *Dauphin*, 240 miles off the rock of Lisbon. He survived eleven years as a slave. O'Brien was freed in 1796 along with Cathcart (who was then his friend but became his malevolent enemy), and then, like Cathcart, O'Brien returned to the Maghreb as US consul in Algiers. Cathcart tried to warn Preble away from O'Brien, claiming he was weak and would be "the mere echo of the Algerine Jews," fulminating that he was "arm'd with all the mean intrigue & low artifice of that sink of perfidy and corruption the Sanhedrim of Algiers." Preble and Lear disregarded Cathcart's diatribe. Lear sent O'Brien, knowing that his "knowledge of the language, Manners, and Politicks" of the Maghreb would be useful. Lear gave Preble the full extent of his authority, writing that if Preble could ransom the captives at $500 per man without an annual tribute payment, he should not hesitate to conclude a treaty. Although Lear had not received any revised instructions from Madison since the loss of the *Philadelphia*, if the bashaw would agree to make peace without any annual tribute, he thought paying even $600 per man was acceptable.[11]

In February 1804, Gaetano Schembri, the bashaw's consul in Malta, arrived in Tripoli on private business and told Yusuf he was authorized by Preble to negotiate for the Americans. French Consul Beaussier, who was likely debriefed by the bashaw himself, reported to Paris that Schembri exaggerated the strength of American naval forces in the Mediterranean and what was amassing to attack Tripoli; told the bashaw the Americans were in contact with Hamet Karamanli, Yusuf's brother; and, preposterously, said the Americans had little interest in ransoming the officers and crew of the *Philadelphia* because they would be shot as traitors as soon as they were freed. Schembri also advised Yusuf to sign a treaty and then begin the war anew when the US squadron departed. Then, Schembri reportedly said, the bashaw could have his revenge for the burning of the *Gift of Allah* and the murdering of his people. On behalf of the Americans, Schembri offered $150,000 to ransom the captives but then said Preble would pay $200,000 or more. Beaussier wrote the French foreign minister that Preble could not have chosen a negotiator "more inept, less skillful, and more capable of advancing absurdities, contradictions and falsehoods." Yusuf reportedly gave Schembri a diamond pin for his efforts but told him that since he was his consul, the Americans would not accept such a proposal emanating from Tripoli.[12]

The first report to the Americans of Schembri's activities was in the postscript of a letter Dghies wrote to Bainbridge. The bashaw's minister mentioned that "Mr. Sch[e]mbri Ambassador sent by the Commodore is closely engaged with His Excellency the Bashaw in the Negotiation with which he is charged." Bainbridge, completely in the dark, informed Preble of a rumor that Schembri had "offered any sum which they would demand; and if he was charged by you with a commission to negotiate he did not steer in the proper channel." Bainbridge passed Dghies's letter along to Preble, who responded that Schembri had "no more authority from me than I have knowledge of him, and I assure you I never spoke to, or saw him since I was created. When the Bashaw chooses to propose a Negotiation I will attend to it." Bainbridge relayed to Dghies that Preble disavowed Schembri and that his involvement was both improper and unauthorized.[13]

It must have been a considerable surprise to Preble to then receive a long letter from Schembri himself that not only discussed his diplomatic intervention but also blithely requested the American squadron relinquish three ships that he either owned or on which he had freighted cargo, the *Transfer*, the *Santissimo Crocifisso*, and the *Madonna di Catapaliani*. Schembri claimed that in February, he decided to act as an intermediary for the Americans and sailed on the *Transfer* with a passport Preble had given to Sir Alexander Ball to carry cattle for the British army garrison in Malta. Schembri met with Yusuf, with the goal of "discovering the sentiments of the Bashaw, and endeavouring by a faithfull representation of the power & preparations of the United States to induce him to wa[i]ve those pretentions to tribute upon which he had formerly insisted." He had succeeded in persuading Yusuf "to treat with [Preble] upon the sole conditions of Ransoming such Americans [who] were at that time prisoners in his possession." While in Tripoli, however, Schembri also looked out for his own business interests, recognizing "a favorable opportunity of obtaining payment of a large sum then due to him from the Bashaw [and shipping] several Butts of Oil, & Iron on board the *Transfer*." Schembri was so certain that his actions would benefit the Americans that the *Transfer* sailed from Tripoli in daylight, while Preble's "Cruizers were actually in sight," and consequently was surprised, he wrote, that not only was the *Transfer* seized but so were the other two ships, for what Schembri characterized as inconsequential violations of the blockade.[14]

Preble was outraged. Schembri's three ships had flagrantly violated the blockade and had "prostituted" Preble's passport for "infamous purposes," violating the faith Sir Alexander Ball reposed in him by giving him a passport. But the violations of the blockade were not the real issue. Calling Schembri an "Insolent Medlar" in diplomacy, Preble blasted his "ill timed officiousness," which had done real "mischief," and hoped the British government would punish Schembri for his "iniquitous proceedings."[15]

At nearly the same time, an authorized French negotiation with the bashaw began. Livingston, the US minister in Paris, sent Preble a copy of French Foreign Minister Talleyrand's instructions to Beaussier, implementing Napoleon's desire for a peace advantageous to both America and Tripoli. When the *Constitution* arrived off Tripoli on March 27, 1804, Preble ordered a gun fired and a white flag of truce raised, which the Tripolitans answered with the same, meaning a truce was in effect and they were willing to allow the Americans to approach. Preble sent Midshipman Ralph Izard ashore with letters for the captured officers and one for Dghies, and he also carried Talleyrand's instructions for Beaussier and a letter from Preble to Beaussier requesting a meeting. Preble asked Dghies for permission to send a boat ashore with clothing and medical supplies for the captive seamen and marines, including 280 sets of straw hats, shoes, shirts, trousers, and duck jackets, and he suggested that the officer Dghies sent with his response could talk with the Tripolitan prisoners lodged on the *Constitution*. Dghies responded that he had not previously answered Preble's letter imploring him not to treat the American enlisted men as slaves because of "how you treated our Prisoners against all laws." But if the *Constitution* was holding a Tripolitan prisoner seized when the *Philadelphia* was burned, he asked Preble to "send him on shore, and then we will treat with you in some Negotiation." Confusing Dghies's accusation about Decatur killing prisoners on the *Philadelphia* for an assertion about his own treatment of prisoners from the *Mastico*, Preble replied that he was "at a loss to know how I have merited the imputation of having treated Prisoners contrary to the dictates of humanity." He reiterated that he had "a prisoner that was taken out of the *Philadelphia* at the time she was set on fire; he was wounded, but from the kindness and attention he has received is now well in health. I cannot however consent to send him on shore, until a Cartel for the exchange of Prisoners is settled. But you may . . . send an Officer to converse with him."[16]

When Midshipman Izard went ashore with the dispatches, he visited Bainbridge and the other officers. Izard was the first contact they had with a free American since the *Philadelphia* went aground five months before, and the eighteen-year-old midshipman in his blue jacket, white waistcoat, and cocked hat represented an image of freedom and hope. Although Izard left no account of the meeting, he must have told Bainbridge and the other officers about the squadron's activities, and shared social news of their naval friends floating offshore. Back on the *Constitution*, he told Preble that Bainbridge looked gaunt, prompting Preble to write Bainbridge, "Mr. Izard tells me you are grown thin, I fear my friend you let your Misfortunes bear too heavy on your mind by which you may destroy your health." Bainbridge responded that he had indeed grown thin, as he was beset by worries, "sad reflections" on "painful subjects." Well into spring 1804, neither Bainbridge nor any of his officers had heard anything from America, and there was tremendous delay in receiving letters from diplomats posted around the Mediterranean. The lack of news "makes the hours pass heavily with us." He did not know that Preble had enjoined the American diplomats stationed around the Mediterranean not to write Bainbridge in cypher because it would arouse the bashaw's suspicions and perhaps end the officers' mail privileges. Preble, in fact, had temporarily directed the officers in the squadron to not write to their friends in captivity at all, for fear that details of American plans would be disseminated.[17]

Under a white flag the next day, March 28, Preble sent a boat ashore for Beaussier, which brought him aboard the *Constitution*. He stepped on deck between a ceremonial line of marines as cannon boomed out a salute. Preble escorted him down to the great cabin of the *Constitution*. Preble and Beaussier discussed what the bashaw would demand for ransom. Preble impressed upon Beaussier that the campaign season was approaching, he soon expected to receive bomb ketches and gunboats on loan from Naples, and if the bashaw was unreasonable, Preble intended to attack Tripoli. Although Preble authorized the French consul to initiate negotiations on behalf of the United States, he refused to provide Beaussier with the maximum amount Preble would agree to spend to ransom the captives.[18]

The next day, Beaussier returned to the *Constitution* to brief Preble on his initial talks with the bashaw. Yusuf said that he was delighted by Napoleon's interest in arranging a peace and that out of respect for him, he would not use all his leverage over the Americans. However, he would not agree to an exchange of prisoners nor allow the Americans to use their own boats to supply clothing and stores for the captives; he would allow clothing and goods to be landed from a neutral vessel. Yusuf asked Beaussier to arrange for the release of the Tripolitan sailor captured in Decatur's raid to burn the *Philadelphia*, so he might question the sailor as to the "massacre" of combatants on the frigate.

Preble refused to release the Tripolitan sailor. When Beaussier returned to the bashaw's court the next day without the sailor, Yusuf was astonished and Dghies, who had suggested this step as a confidence-building measure, was mystified. To Beaussier, turning over one sailor would not weaken America's negotiating position, and he was confident the gesture would be reciprocated by the Tripolitans. He asked the commodore to reconsider, but Preble refused, seemingly out of sheer stubbornness, but perhaps because he feared what the sailor might say he had witnessed.[19]

Shuttling back to the bashaw, Beaussier told Yusuf that American naval power was massing and that if negotiations failed, Preble intended to send a ship to Alexandria to find Hamet Karamanli and support him in a landward attack on Tripoli. He also advised Yusuf that the United States would not pay for peace or pay an annual tribute but would ransom the captives if the price was not exorbitant. Yet these points made no impression on the bashaw. Beaussier told Preble that he guessed the bashaw would demand $500,000 but ultimately would settle for $250,000. When Beaussier told Yusuf that his "exorbitant pretentions" for money would displease Napoleon, the bashaw answered that whatever the deference he owed to "his Friend Buonaparte," the French leader would not wish him to "divest him of the advantages acquired by the Chances of War." Beaussier warned Preble that even if the squadron battered Tripoli, the bashaw would not release the captives, and in fact, "the more damage you cause to be done to the Country, the higher will be their pretentions, be it from Avarice or from obstinacy." Beaussier again asked Preble to give him a bottom-line figure for his negotiating authority and said he did not want to continue as "arbitrator & conciliator" unless Preble provided him full information. Preble refused, presumably because he thought it was a poor strategy to confide in a foreign consul he did not know and whose integrity he suspected.

In a strange non sequitur, Beaussier also said his continuing services as a negotiator depended on Preble lifting the blockade for neutral merchant vessels. Preble believed that Beaussier, like British Consul Mc-Donogh, was not to be trusted and was working in his own, or the bashaw's, interest. Preble claimed to have intelligence that privately, Beaussier had contracted to supply Tripoli with five hundred barrels of gunpowder and other military stores from Marseilles, which he planned to land in Tunis and transport overland to avoid the American blockade. Besides, Preble divined that the true interest of the French government was for the United States to remain at war with Tripoli and even encourage a war with Tunis because the US Navy's blockades of Barbary ports cut off food from the British garrison and naval base at Malta. Preble was fed up with the Frenchman, and when a gale set in, the squadron sailed off from Tripoli, out of contact for the next two months. Beaussier, who seems to have been legitimately trying to broker a peace, reported to Paris that negotiations would not progress until Preble gave him his ultimate negotiating authority, but even if he did, "the gap will be great between the demands [of the Tripolitans] and the offers [by the Americans], and it will be difficult to reconcile everything."[20]

Even while there were negotiations, the bashaw feverishly built up his defenses. Preble wrote Robert Livingston that fourteen Spanish ship carpenters sent from His Most Catholic Majesty's naval yards were building gunboats for the bashaw on the strand; they wore the red and gold Spanish cockade in their hats and were paid weekly by the Spanish consul in Tripoli, Joseph (Don Gerardo José) de Souza. The bashaw was also forcing the crew of the *Philadelphia* to construct masonry fortifications for gun batteries east and west of the port. He concluded, "We must therefore depend wholly on our own exertions for effecting a peace, which can only be done by an increase of our force, and a Number of Gun & Mortar boats to batter down his Castle and town." Preble wistfully mused that if he had two more frigates, and a few gunboats and bombs, he would be able to subdue Tripoli "directly."[21]

TEN

HARDSHIPS

I N PUNISHMENT FOR THE DESTRUCTION of the *Philadelphia* in February 1804, the American officers were at first prohibited from leaving the consul house, with a guard of twenty heavily armed Tripolitan soldiers placed at the door and on the roof. Nissen was not allowed to visit them, and Dr. Cowdery was not allowed to tend to the sick. The bashaw forbade the officers from sending letters. Incoming letters were broken open and read, and if they contained information about Tripoli, they were destroyed. Bainbridge wrote a note to Dghies protesting that the change in treatment was unwarranted. Decatur's raid was not the captive officers' doing, he argued, and burning the *Philadelphia* was "the fate of War." The numerous guards were "entirely unnecessary. The Walls of the City are sufficient barriers to our making the attempt of getting away," although their parole of honor would be a stronger bind that no American officer would break. But the worst aspect of close confinement was the lack of contact with the outside world. Letters were the captives' "only consolation," and preventing letters from coming in or going out did not help Tripoli because it was "entirely out of our Power to give any information; and could we, prudence would forbid it," which was untruthful, given Bainbridge's efforts to send intelligence to Preble with passages written in "sympathetic" ink—lime juice or a weak solution of silicate mineral water. Dghies came to the consul house to meet with Bainbridge and assured him that "nothing unpleasant would take place" and that the Americans would be treated with "humanity." But conditions were about to get dramatically worse.[1]

On March 1, 1804, the officers were moved, this time permanently, to a newly created prison beneath the courtyard of the bashaw's castle. An early biographer of Bainbridge asserted that the bashaw increased the severity of the officers' confinement because he believed that in burning the *Philadelphia*, Decatur had killed Tripolitan prisoners in cold blood. The officers marched under a strong guard through the yard where the enlisted men were mustering. Although ordered not to talk to them, Bainbridge told his gathered men to be "of good heart," though Ray thought the captain himself looked dejected.[2]

Dr. Ridgely wrote that no description could adequately convey the horrors of their new prison. He called their space a "dungeon," noting the only light or air came through a grated skylight. The air was close, and lizards slithered on the floor. In a letter home, Cowdery called their new prison a dark and smoky cell. He referred to the skylight as "an Iron grating in the top"; noted the doors were kept locked and were strengthened by iron bars; and said they were "guarded by infamous Turkish soldiers, who are ready to plunge their daggers into our hearts." The officers were packed together in what they knew was an unhealthy environment. Thomas Harris, Bainbridge's confidant and early biographer, wrote that the officers felt "entombed." No foreign consuls were allowed in, and there was no mail. Only Nissen's cook could enter, to bring food, but he was prohibited from carrying any letters in or out. The idea that their personal mail was being intercepted and read by the bashaw struck one of the officers as "villainous." Within days, the officers' *dragoman* was relieved of his duties on the suspicion that he had become too friendly with the captives. Months later, Nissen learned that Gaetano Schembri had convinced Yusuf that by "very hard treatment of the Capti[ve] Officers," Tripoli might get better terms for ransoming the Americans. The officers would remain consigned to the castle's dungeon for fifteen months, until June 1805.[3]

Bainbridge wrote another note to Dghies protesting the change in conditions, and the bashaw's minister again "very politely came to our Prison." Dghies told the officers that if the guards insulted the officers, they would be severely punished. Bainbridge responded that the Americans would not be "intimidated by all the guards in his dominions— Inform the Bashaw from me, that the safest way of keeping an American Officer is on a Parole of Honor." Dghies apologized at having to open the officers' letters, an order he said he had protested. He made clear that Yusuf was so enraged about the loss of the *Gift of Allah* that Dghies would have to wait to let the bashaw's anger cool before approaching him to ameliorate the Americans' conditions.[4]

Dghies, regarded by the officers as "our friend," was soon able to revive their mail privileges and even to convince the bashaw to allow small groups of officers to walk out into the countryside under guard.[5] Some letters and packages came through. Midshipman Henry Wadsworth of the *Constitution* corresponded with David Porter. Wadsworth, a talented writer with literary ambitions, had been Porter's shipmate on the *New York* in Morris's squadron. In one surviving letter, written from Syracuse in Sicily during the 1804 carnival, Wadsworth shared that he had met "a bouncing English girl at the masquerade last night. She said she was married, but I might cuckold her husband. Nice bit!" Wadsworth also sent Porter a package with donated books he collected from the officers of the *Constitution*, along with a painting kit, an old flute, and a violin, jesting that Porter was neither a piper nor a fiddler but there must be some officers who could "'dance at the sound of the lute.' But what are you to do for partners?" He whimsically suggested he could send the wife of the *Constitution*'s bosun to preside at their "tea board."[6]

Once they were allowed out again for air, the officers took advantage of that interlude of freedom. One officer wrote home that "we are as much secluded and as closely confined, as any of the Bashaw's women." There were supposedly many sights for a visitor, but "we might remain here 20 years and not know more of them." Another officer wrote that two or three times per week, he went out for walks, "a ramble into the country most commonly to the Bashaw's gardens." The flower garden, he noted acidly, was "not laid out with any taste," but the orchards were delightful, and the officers lolled around in the shade of the trees, enjoying the fresh air and gorging on the oranges. On one walk, Dr. Cowdery went into the bashaw's garden with two fellow officers, guarded by two Turks to prevent an escape attempt, because ships of the squadron were then in sight, cruising off the harbor. A few weeks later, ten officers strolled into the gardens, again with an armed escort, and brought back flowers and apricots, which must have alleviated some of the gloom of their quarters. In mid-May, it was Cowdery's turn again, and with a party of officers, he walked to the edge of the desert, about four miles inland. They climbed a sand bank, and a panorama opened before them: the desert went off to a mountain range, which they could see miles away. Before them lay the sand, "in heaps, like snow drifts in our country. There was not a house nor any other object to be seen; nor a thing growing to interrupt the sight; but it appeared like an ocean of sand." Walking back through the gardens, the officers picked oranges, lemons, apricots, and flowers, and tasted *lagby*, a liquor from the sap of date trees, which tasted like mead.[7]

At that time, Dr. Harwood wrote his father a short, sad letter. Seven months had passed since the *Philadelphia* had surrendered, and Harwood had received no letters from his family. It seemed, he wrote, that "our Ransom appears as far Distant, if not more so, than the first day" when the frigate crashed onto the reef. Noting "[d]espondence appearing in each and every countenance," he wrote that like "stoics," the officers tried to "bare up against misfortune." He confessed that his "misfortunes and unhappy destiny prays so totally on [his] mind," but evidently not one to dwell on his daily struggles, he revealed little. Stating he too had visited the bashaw's garden and fishponds, he wryly commented he had not had an opportunity to tour the bashaw's castle under which he was lodged but believed it was "of the true oriental stile." That was all he could offer up, writing that "Prison affords very little matter for a letter." He signed it, "Yr. Affectionate but Captive Son."[8]

In the first days of their captivity, the bashaw had granted the American officers their parole of honor, an agreement in which they promised not to try to escape in exchange for the privilege of walking about the city. However, according to Midshipman James Renshaw, "not wishing us to have any communication with our crew," Yusuf had almost imme-

diately "put an end to the only pleasure we could derive from being prisoners in Barbary," their freedom of movement. Because the bashaw had
annulled their parole, the officers considered their own promise to be
canceled. With the harsh conditions of confinement beneath the castle,
the officers' thoughts turned to escape.[9]

They faced enormous obstacles in trying to escape. Being Americans,
they looked and dressed differently than Arabs and Turks. Except for
Cowdery, none of them knew Arabic or Turkish. They could not rely on
anyone in the local populace for help or concealment. The nearest Americans were offshore, and communications with the squadron were slow
and intermittent and could be interrupted. But because the castle was
situated on the harbor, they had one thing in their favor. If they could
get to the water, they could steal a boat and make it out to the blockading
ships offshore; or, if they could coordinate with the squadron, under the
cover of darkness, the squadron could send in some small boats to take
them off. Either way, they had to get to the water's edge.

In April 1804, the *Philadelphia*'s officers began digging, and Bainbridge reportedly sent a letter to Preble to inform him of their plans and
to arrange for boats to surreptitiously enter the harbor one night to carry
them away. After four days of tunneling through the castle's floor, the
officers reached a depth of twenty-five feet and found a loose mix of
sand and water. Their digging confronted an insurmountable engineer-
ing problem. As they dug closer to the water, the mix got wetter and
looser, and they had no wood to reinforce the tunnel walls or pumps to
displace the water. They had to abandon the tunnel.[10]

In May, they tried another idea. One of the walls where they were
confined was linked to an underground passage that led to an outer wall
of the castle, on its landward side. If they could open a hole in the outer
wall, they might escape, although what they would do once they were
in the town was unclear. With nothing more than case knives, a dull axe,
and an iron bolt, the officers loosened and removed the stones in the
wall one at a time. They managed to make a hole into a dark passage,
which they followed until it led them to another wall. This wall they also
were able to breach, only to find the dirt of the castle's foundation. The
officers began to dig a tunnel through the dirt large enough for a single
man to crawl through on his hands and knees. The displaced dirt was
scattered throughout the passage. The tunnel cratered under the weight

of the rampart above it, forcing the officers to abandon their second escape route.[11]

The officers continued scheming about how to get away. One night, Bainbridge and Jacob Jones decided to see if they could get into a space next to the dungeon. They picked through a thick plaster wall and opened a hole into the next room. The room was two stories high, the floor of the second story was broken down, and over the second story was a window secured with iron bars. The window was so high that the Tripolitans must have thought it was unreachable. But the imprisoned men, being sailors, were used to climbing and difficult footholds, and the officers were able to reach the window. Looking out, they discovered it overlooked the castle's ramparts, from which they estimated it might have been seventy feet down to the water. The officers devised a plan to whittle away the iron bars on the window, drop down to the rampart, fasten a rope to one of the cannon, fling the rope over the wall, and climb down to the water. From there, each man would swim to a small ship in the harbor. They would surprise the watch on the ship, board and capture her, and sail her out to the squadron.

Like other escape plans, this scheme faced many difficulties. It would take time for all the officers to descend on the rope, and each successive officer would be at increased risk of discovery, imperiling them all. In addition, not all the officers could swim. Only capable swimmers could think of propelling themselves out to the vessel in the harbor, and even so, they would have no weapons to overcome resistance, only their fists. The *Philadelphia* officers who did not know how to swim protested, leading Bainbridge, who could swim, to agree to stay behind with them and remain a prisoner.

The plan was put into operation. Within days, the iron bars were filed down, and ropes were made from strips of blankets sewn together. At the designated hour near midnight on May 21, the escape began. Three lieutenants and three midshipmen crawled into the next room, climbed up the wall, removed the iron bars, "passed through the window, and crawled in single file along the rampart" to the cannon where they were to descend, rope coiled in hand. The Tripolitan relief guard was spotted coming along the rampart, which halted everything. The six officers remained hiding on the rampart for nearly two hours, waiting for an opportunity to go over the wall. But the rampart was covered with guards, and they had no way to get away, so the officers aborted the escape. Unobserved, they retraced their steps back through the window, replaced the iron bars, and descended back to their dungeon. Writing in invisible ink to Preble, Bainbridge noted that "a Vessel laying in the Harbour with a Boat out induced the attempt which was found . . . impracticable from the Vigilance of the Guards on the Top of the Castle. The Officers were fortunate in making good their retreat." They were sorely disappointed, but in fact they were lucky because the vessel they had planned to swim to had sailed earlier that evening, and after reaching the harbor, there would have been no escape.[12]

At the end of June 1804, the officers tried tunneling again, this time through the walls of the castle and the ramparts and ending above the high waterline at the harbor. The plan was to crawl through the tunnel, emerge at the water, and swim out to a British frigate known to be arriving in Tripoli. Apparently, the Americans began their dig, but the route lay directly beneath a heavy cannon mounted on the rampart. Their digging weakened the rampart and caused its floor to sink, resulting in the tunnel starting to cave in. Although the Tripolitans did not discover the tunnel, the Americans gave up the idea of escaping.[13]

In June 1804, the sailors and marines were moved to a newly fashioned prison in the eastern part of the city, abutting the city wall. It is unclear why the Americans were moved, although it is likely that the bashaw wanted greater distance between the enlisted people and their officers, in case of an uprising or escape attempt. Their new prison was more spacious than the old magazine: 150 feet long by 30 feet wide, with a height of 25 feet. Even with 100 Neapolitan slaves confined with more than 250 Americans, their new quarters were a marked upgrade. The men slung their cots in between the columns of the building, one above the other, to the vortex of the arch. Saving a little of the olive oil doled out each day to each man, they were able to illuminate their space at night with two hundred lamps. The poet in Ray thought the lamps cast a romantic, multiform display of light and shadow. A new sick bay was established across the parade yard, beyond a fortified gatehouse, where a dozen soldiers were always on guard at night. Within a few weeks, four warrant officers (Godby, the carpenter; Hodge, the bosun; Fenton, the master's mate; and Douglass, the sailmaker) were moved into their own apartment in the upper story of the sick bay. But with the new venue came a penalty: the bashaw cut off the weekly portion of beef that Bainbridge had provided for his men.[14]

Although Ray later complained in his writings of the special treatment given to Cowdery, Ray also received favored treatment. Bainbridge put in a word for him with Dghies, and to Ray's great joy, in May 1804, he was exempted from hard labor and allowed to serve as a copyist for Nicholas Nissen in the Danish consul house. Nissen gave Ray a holiday on July 4, and enough money for Ray and a few of his shipmates to buy *lagby*. They drank all day under an orange tree, with breezes wafting in from the sea. As the sun went down, several ships of the blockading squadron hove into view, adding to their joy, and Ray returned to the prison with several jugs of *lagby*, a "wholesome and cheering liquor," which must have made him a hero to his friends.[15]

That summer, Yusuf intervened decisively in Cowdery's life, ordering him to attend the bashaw's family and the American sailors as their doctor. In exchange, the bashaw moved Cowdery's bed and possessions to what the surgeon's mate called "a pleasant and well furnished apartment in his palace." In a letter home, he wrote, "The Bashaw has taken me from the prison where my fellow officers were confined and ordered me to attend his sick slaves who are principally Neapolitans, negroes and our unfortunate crew," although he noted that "to relieve the distress of the [slaves] is a pleasure to me." With his new role, Cowdery was given liberties afforded no other American, including the freedom to walk about the town as he pleased—as long as he stayed away from the fortifications and avoided the European consuls—or to ride into the countryside on a mule. Sometimes his *dragoman*, a large, English-speaking Turk, accompanied him, loaded with weapons, to prevent Cowdery from escaping or "meeting with insult," and also to act as his interpreter, although Cowdery had learned to speak Arabic "tolerably well." Removed from confinement with his brother officers, he was forbidden to talk with them, and his letters were "examined with the utmost scrutiny."[16]

Dr. Cowdery's rounds exposed him to the local practice of medicine. The bashaw called on Cowdery to help treat several Tripolitans suffering from burns. Yusuf directed that the injured men be brought into an apartment in the castle where he visited them and gave each man ten dollars. A team of surgeons and Yusuf's bodyguards dressed their wounds. Cowdery was astonished to see Yusuf helping with his own hands. Present also were *marabouts*, Islamic holy men who, Cowdery stated dismissively, were "employed to expel evil spirits, and make intercession with Mahomet their prophet, for their recovery." Burns were treated with a layer of honey to preserve the skin as much as possible and keep the burned area exposed to the air, and then the ulcerated parts were sprinkled with a fine powder of white lead (ceruse) until a scab formed. Cowdery observed that the treatment allowed scabs to be preserved until healing, which, he said, occurred quickly. This treatment did not differ much from contemporary American naval medicine: on board the frigate *New York* on her 1802–03 cruise, the ship's surgeon, Dr. Peter St. Medard, stocked "emplastrum," an adhesive plaster made from olive oil and white lead.[17]

Cowdery also observed Islamic social and legal dynamics. Although later accused by William Ray of being too empathetic with the bashaw and his people, Cowdery wrote that Yusuf was a tyrant, with draconian punishments for crime. The bashaw was "cruel to his subjects, when he finds them guilty of crimes; for murder, treason &c he beheads them; for theft, housebreaking &c he takes off the left hand and right foot, at the Joint and dips the stump Into boiling tar; for less crimes he gives them from five hundred to a thousand bastinadoes" which often caused death.[18]

In the hot summer days, the new British consul, William Wass Langford, wrote Commodore Preble that the American sailors "whom I daily meet in the streets complain heavily of bad living & hard work." Yet Langford, like McDonogh before him, was no help to them. Ray recounted that some of the *Philadelphia*'s tars who were once British subjects were dragging a cart one day when they passed Langford. They called out to him, asking for help. Langford responded that having deserted His Majesty's service, they got what they deserved. When the men "had the spirit to damn both him and his majesty," Langford lifted his walking stick to strike them, and then wisely restrained himself. Cowdery recorded in his diary that "Our men complained of being drove and beat about at an unmerciful rate." A number had fainted and "dropped beneath the weight they were compelled to sustain," and were "brought back half dead to the prison." In August 1804, the crew petitioned the bashaw:

That your humble petitioners, when doing their duty with all their power, as they are commanded, are most cruelly beaten by our wardens, stoned, insulted, and spit upon by the soldiers and others; required to carry burthens impossible for us to sustain, and chased and bruised, until we are, or soon shall be, unable to labour at all. From the many acts of justice, kindness, and generosity we have experienced from your Excellency, we cannot suppose that such conduct is authorized by your commands; or that we should be punished for what is out of our power to perform; or for the actions of others, which we have no agency in, and which we cannot prevent. . . . [R]elying upon your goodness for protection, we therefore most humbly pray, that your Excellency would interpose your royal authority and grant us a speedy relief.

After the petition was explained to the bashaw by Lewis Hacksener, one of the seamen who had "turned Turk," Yusuf forbade the wardens from striking the prisoners, but the command was "insincere," for the very next day, Ray watched as the bashaw stood by and did nothing as overseers *bastinadoed* several sailors.[19]

The wardens were hard men. With typical jack tar insolence, the American sailors gave them nicknames to mock and diminish them, even as they were threatened by them. The chief overseer was a vicious man Ray called a "calm, thinking villain" named Abdullah, whom the sailors nicknamed "Captain Blackbeard" (for obvious reasons). His chief assistant was "Scamping Jack" Soliman, described as irascible, "fierce and cruel when provoked." The other overseers included Toussef, whom they called "Quid" (a dismissive epithet, probably now equivalent to "loser"), of French origin whom Ray described as "captious, querulous and malevolent"; an elderly, humane Greek man whom, because of his deformed legs, they called "Bandy"; a "ferocious" old Algerine nicknamed "Blinkard"; and a mean-spirited man dubbed "Red Jacket." Altogether, Ray said they were so cruel that local people in the street hissed at them, and the crew regarded them with "as much contempt as slave drivers in our own country" or, he could not help adding, "boatswains' mates of a man of war."[20]

Meanwhile, the crew were not only being beaten but were also feeling the effects of malnutrition. Fortunately, in the spring, they had realized they could sell some of their coarse bread in the *souk* and, for the price of one loaf, purchase enough vegetables for three men. They made a soup with the vegetables, bread, salt, and a little olive oil. Some of the messes bought a clay pot in which to cook their soup, their fires made with wood chips the men were allowed to carry from the bashaw's shipyard. Alternatively, they discovered little shops in the *souk* where they could buy a cheap, pulverized mash called *tirsha*, made of cooked carrots or turnips with red pepper, oil, lemon juice, and fennel seed. When Ray first tasted *tirsha*, he thought it was "disagreeable," but it became "palatable" as he got used to it. The coopers and smiths among the crew sometimes were given coins by the bashaw to encourage them to work, and sometimes, the men dragging heavy loads would receive a few coins as a gratuity, money they could use to supplement their diets.[21]

Still, the scanty rations lacked protein, and the tars and marines grew thin and were hungry. In August 1804, they sent a plaintive petition to Captain Bainbridge:

SIR

As all hopes of release for the present are vanished it is our unanimous wish provided it is in your power, that you would grant or procure us a trifling sum of money in daily allowances. There are not any of us paid for our work as heretofore. And the two small black loaves and scanty allowance of oil are scarcely sufficient to afford us subsistence.

We are fully persuaded Sir, that did you know our wants, you would do every thing in your power to relieve them.

We are totally ignorant of your pecuniary resources, and would not by any means willingly trouble you with vain and unreasonable requests, for [if] it is not in your power to assist us we must patiently submit to our sufferings by the keen [g]nawings of hunger.

THE CREW[22]

Bainbridge, of course, had been kept with the other officers in close confinement underneath the castle since March and had almost no interaction with the crew. Despite his iron discipline aboard ship, no sentient captain could be blind to the needs of his men. Not allowed to visit them, he immediately put pen to paper, and responded that he was sorry to learn of their plight. Bainbridge opted not to give the men a monetary allowance because he was afraid of stealing, gambling, or wasting the funds on *aguardiente*. But he promised to pay for whatever additional bread they needed, and he would also order "fresh meat sent twice a week or oftener if our finances will admit." He asked for a response signed by specific petty officers on the crew's behalf so he would know the authors of the request, and he asked the signers to get "the opinion of the whole Crew & not of a part of them so that there may be no misunderstanding."[23]

Two days later, five petty officers replied to Bainbridge on behalf of the crew, thanking their captain "for the anxiety you feel and the pains you are tak[ing] to relieve our necessary wants." They enclosed two lists, one containing the names of those who wanted more food, and the other listing the names who declined because they were "the Cooks and Waiters in the Castle, Painters, Coopers &c. who receive more sustenance than the majority; some few who refuse it from economical motives[;] and some for the same reason which induced them to petition for the meat [which Bainbridge had paid for out of the credits provided by Preble and Davis] on Sundays to be discontinued." The vast majority asked Bainbridge for an "additional allowance of two white or finer loaves of bread every day, and meat twice a week or oftener if convenient." Wary of "confusion & murmuring for the future," they suggested one or more of the warrant officers—or anyone Bainbridge preferred—be directed to arrange the men into messes to ensure "that the provisions be equally & justly divided & distributed."[24]

Bainbridge did his duty by them. For the 224 sailors and marines who wanted more food, he arranged with Nissen to contract for an additional 224 loaves of bread to be sent each day to their prison, as well as 224 pounds of beef and vegetables delivered twice a week, in addition to the bashaw's rations. Bainbridge left it to the crew to choose "proper characters" to dole out the additional rations. Despite excoriating Bainbridge in his memoir for failing to care for the crew, William Ray, whom Bainbridge had exempted from hard labor, was given the job of dividing up the twice-weekly deliveries of beef and vegetables. Ray allotted the food equally among eight-man messes that all the men were required to join. With the additional provisions, the crew's hunger was, for a time, put off.[25]

ELEVEN

ATTACKS AND NEGOTIATIONS

I N MAY 1804, WHILE DINING IN NAPLES with Sir John Acton, the prime minister of the Kingdom of Naples, Commodore Preble asked for the loan of eight gunboats and two bomb vessels, along with powder, shells, and trained bombardiers, for the close combat he anticipated with Tripoli. The king, Ferdinand IV, agreed to support the US Navy's operations against "the Common Enemies." Writing home, Preble apologized for obtaining the ships without authority—he did not know that the March 26, 1804, law gave the navy that authority—pleading that "it has become absolutely necessary to our National and Naval Character in the Eastern World, that we humble that Regency and bring the Bashaw to our own terms [and] this cannot be done without the assistance of Gun Boats and Bomb Vessels."[1]

By the end of the month, Preble arrived at Syracuse with six Neapolitan gunboats: sixty-foot-long, shallow draft, single-masted vessels armed with a long 24-pounder cannon in the bow. The two mortar boats were being outfitted and would not be ready for service for another month. Because the squadron wasn't ready to fight, Preble decided to engage in negotiations first.[2]

He arrived off Tripoli on June 12, and once more, the *Constitution* fired off a gun, the ships of the blockading squadron raised white flags of truce, and the Tripolitans responded with a white flag. Richard O'Brien went ashore with a letter to Dghies announcing O'Brien's authority to ransom the captives. Preble also sought to deliver clothing for the crew, and he was finally willing to set onshore the prisoner taken from the *Philadelphia* for Dghies to interview, provided he was returned or swapped for a captive American sailor, because his orders did not allow him to "freely give him" back. Preble gave O'Brien authority to ransom the officers and crew of the *Philadelphia* for $40,000, an additional $10,000 as a present to the bashaw when a new American consul would be named to Tripoli, and $10,000 more for O'Brien to dispense to Yusuf's ministers to smooth negotiations. But Preble was clear that the United States would not "pay one cent for Peace." O'Brien also carried a letter to Beaussier in which Preble insulted the French diplomat, observing that the "First Consul expected [Beaussier's] mediation would have had more weight with the Bashaw of Tripol[i] than it appears to have had," and that Bonaparte would feel "somewhat mortified" that Beaussier had "not been able even to obtain permission to land the necessary clothing & Stores which the American Prisoners are suffering for want of." He invited Beaussier to assist O'Brien but made clear the "blockade must continue while the negotiation is going on, and forever after, until a treaty of Peace is signed."[3]

Outraged by Preble's letter, Beaussier sputtered in response that he had done as well as he could with Preble's instructions. The commodore's new offer, he said, was "truly ridiculous and offensive abruptly made after an absence of two and a half months." Beaussier could not understand how the Americans conducted negotiations. He would not use Bonaparte's name to propose $40,000 to ransom three hundred sailors and noted Preble must have been unaware that the customary "ransom of a lowly cabin boy is four to five hundred dollars."[4] Beaussier reported to Talleyrand that he had told Preble that ransom and peace might cost $500,000. Preble had replied that he would never pay one-

tenth of that, and he depreciated French mediation. Beaussier was as exasperated with Preble as Preble was with him, concluding his dispatch,
"What opinion can one have of a commander who, without being authorized by his Government, risks committing the arms of his Nation,
and of being dismissed himself, and who risks the lives of 300 prisoners
to the fanatism and despair of these Africans!"[5]

Preble dropped Beaussier as a negotiator. He sent O'Brien ashore, but
he made no progress and was treated disrespectfully. He was kept waiting
for an hour in the scorching sun in the boat that anchored near the castle
and then kept waiting for another hour alone in an anteroom. Dghies
finally met with him and took Preble's proposal to the bashaw. O'Brien
was not allowed to speak to Bainbridge, his officers, the European consuls, or the bashaw. Again, the Americans could not land clothing for
the bereft sailors and marines; the squadron had been trying to provide
new clothes to the enlisted men for months. The bashaw rejected
O'Brien's offer of $40,000 for ransom and was so irritated by the pro-
posal that he demanded $1 million. Preble was not surprised. Signifi-
cantly, Lear had authorized Preble to offer ransom of $600 per man, and
although Preble was confident the bashaw would accept that sum, he
thought offering that much would only "stimulate the avarice of the
other Barbary Powers." When the Neapolitan gunboats and mortar boats
arrived, Preble would begin his attacks, which he hoped would make the
bashaw see matters differently. O'Brien's abrupt departure and their ignorance of the status of negotiations left the American officers "extremely anxious," as Bainbridge put it. But Bainbridge agreed that "a few
shells here would have a good effect." To George Davis, he added, "the
Commodore would do well to get a bomb ketch or two, and every night
heave some shells into the Town, it would drive [out] all the Inhabitants
and greatly tend towards a speedy & reasonable Peace."[6]

In July 1804, at Preble's urging, Bainbridge attempted to initiate negotiations with Dghies, but the bashaw's minister refused to discuss
terms with him because he was a prisoner. Dghies wanted to negotiate
with a diplomat and specifically made clear that Preble was not a proper
negotiator: he continuously threatened Tripoli verbally but had failed to
convince it that the squadron had the force to back up the threats. But
even if the squadron "knock[ed] every house in Tripol[i] down," Dghies
told Bainbridge, the bashaw would not accept an offer of $50,000. Dghies

reminded Bainbridge that Holland had paid $80,000 and Denmark $40,000 to maintain peace with Tripoli, and neither country had a prisoner to ransom; the Americans offered only $50,000, but had three hundred sailors in captivity.[7]

The summer brought hotter and hotter weather. With little air circulating in the underground vault, the officers' close confinement was oppressive. Bainbridge and his officers felt as if they were suffocating. With no relief in sight, the officers picked away at the stone and lime, knocking a small hole in the wall to let in more air. Word leaked to one of the overseers. A Tripolitan officer rushed into the room and demanded to know who had opened the wall. David Porter answered that he had opened the hole, and "[h]e was immediately dragged away." Porter was brought before Dghies, who received him politely, expressed regret at the unpleasant conditions, and immediately released Porter.[8]

As critical as fresh air was access to the foreign consuls, especially Nissen, which was completely denied. Living in such an unhealthy spot contributed to sickness raging through the officers' ranks. Bainbridge was allowed to leave the prison only when he had some business with Dghies, and always under heavy guard. In July 1804, he wrote, "I have seen the Sea four times in 5 months." For an eight-month period, including summer 1804, the officers were not allowed to leave the castle dungeon at all. A half-year after the officers were moved to the castle, Midshipman James Renshaw wrote, "Our Situation . . . is beyond conception, nearly Six Months Solitary imprisonment have elapsed since the doors of our prison have been opened for any other purpose than supplying us with our daily sustenance." Renshaw even mused about crossing the line between being a prisoner and being a slave, reflecting at "how much better would it have been for us to have been put to hard labour, as our crew[;] then we could feel the fresh air, which is so essential to human nature."[9]

The officers left no information about how they coped with some of the basic issues of daily life and personal hygiene. Aboard ship, they had access to a privy in the quarter galleries near the wardroom, but in captivity, they presumably used chamber pots in a corner or in a separate compartment in their dungeon. Aboard ship, the officers used basins with sea water to hand wash themselves, and in Barbary captivity, they presumably did the same thing, although with rain water gathered from the castle's roof and supplied to them. Aboard ship, the officers' clothes would be laundered by stewards and servants, and in Barbary captivity, they retained a few orderlies living with them; they had fewer changes of clothes, but presumably their clothing was still washed, albeit rarely. With forty men sharing a hot, poorly ventilated space and all of them needing to tend to their basic needs, not only was their dungeon dark and shadowy but it also must have been pervaded by an overpowering stench.

Nor is there much information about how the sailors and marines coped with their basic issues of daily life and personal hygiene. At sea, the seamen and marines relieved themselves at the "head," the latrine seats ranged far forward on each side of the bow of the ship, near the bowsprit. In captivity, their sanitary situation is unclear; there may have been latrine holes in the floor, now called "Turkish toilets." After their work details around the port and city were finished for the day, the sailors and marines could wash themselves and their clothes in the sea. William Ray wrote that the men's work day began before sunrise when they were "turned out" and ended at sunset, when they were locked in their quarters, and that they all became "afflicted with vermin, and not having clothes to change, the only way we had to keep ourselves from becoming insufferably filthy, was to go to the beach and strip off our shirts, going naked until we washed and dried them, and then our tro[u]sers, in the like manner."[10]

The clothing of the enlisted men, working outdoors and washed occasionally in sea water, was in tatters. By the middle of 1804, most of the sailors and marines were almost naked, and many had no shoes, their feet bloodied over the rough gravel alleys of Tripoli. Because Preble refused to send the Tripolitan prisoner ashore when he visited early in 1804, the bashaw refused to allow the Americans to send in boats carrying all the clothes and shoes for the crew. Not until June 1804 could Preble arrange for the delivery of fourteen bales of clothes. The Royal Navy put a bomb vessel called *Eliza* at the Americans' disposal to carry the supplies. Preble asked Langford, the British consul, to receive the clothing and some provisions and stores for the American prisoners. Preble noted that he would not have asked for Langford's help "in this business, if they were not almost naked." Preble also enclosed 125 gold doubloons to repay Nicholas Nissen for some of the expenditures he had made for the captives.[11]

When the clothes arrived, the Americans were allowed to store them in the now-abandoned American consul house, with Spence given the key to control the distribution and account for it all. After months of delay and frustration, the seamen and marines finally received clean clothes for summer and winter. In the consignment were 628 shirts, 300 cloth jackets and trousers, 300 duck jackets and trousers, 600 pairs of shoes, and 320 round hats, as well as fresh uniforms for the officers. In addition, Higgins, the naval agent at Malta, thoughtfully packed fifteen baskets of fruit and vegetables; two sacks of melons, onions, and barley; 133 iron puncheons filled with fresh water; tea; sugar; wine; and 288 clay bottles of porter. Bainbridge was so abstemious in the dark, hot prison that he responded, "I hope that Mr. Higgins will not send us anything from Malta [unless] we demand it: We wish to live cheap, as in fact we have lost all relish for dainties, except books." Not everyone agreed. Spence wrote Polly that the provisions had buoyed their spirits. What disappointed them was the lack of news from America or letters from anyone. Spence complained that "we are kept in ignorance in a great measure, of every thing passing." He had heard nothing from his wife and family, but he realized the eight months since he was made prisoner was scarcely enough time for the news to get to America and a letter from Polly to reach him. He had also heard nothing from his son Robert Spence, a midshipman on the *Syren* offshore, because they had no communications with the squadron.[12]

From the first days of their captivity, Bainbridge had taken the precaution when writing to Preble or the diplomats to interline his letters with secret information in "sympathetic" ink that became visible only when the paper was warmed over a fire. Those letters had been passed through Nissen. After the officers were shut into the castle's dungeon, Nissen was not permitted to visit. Yet Nissen continued as the officers' letter carrier through his cook who delivered food to the officers. Nissen and Bainbridge devised an ingenious scheme to smuggle letters into and out of the dungeon. The lime-juiced or "soda water" letters were written on plain paper, which was folded over the books that passed into and out of the prison, ostensibly to protect their leather covers (what now would be called dust jackets). The guards never intercepted these secret-message letters.[13]

In early July 1804, Preble finally learned of the reaction in the United States to the news that the *Philadelphia* had run aground and that her crew was in captivity. Midshipman William Lewis arrived in Malta on July 1, after a five-week passage from Gibraltar, carrying every newspaper he could find, bundles of letters, and dispatches from the secretary of the navy. Lewis reported that the "Intelligence of the loss of the *Philadelphia* arrived before [Midshipman Gadsden, with Preble's dispatches] and ... caused Universal Concern throughout the United States." Lewis brought the news that the frigates were on their way from America as reinforcements.[14]

The seemingly interminable repairs to the bomb vessels in the dockyards at Messina, Sicily, were finished by July 4. Preble planned to sail with them, rendezvous with the Neapolitan-loaned gunboats off Syracuse, and then head to Tripoli. He joked that he had "700 Bomb Shells and plenty of shot to amuse the bashaw." Bainbridge, suffering with the other officers in the heat of the summer, wrote Preble that he "hoped to God" the squadron would "reduce this place," and the sooner the better for the sake of the captives. The bashaw expected an attack and had moved his family inland, into his gardens for their safety, although he returned each night to the castle. Bainbridge placed his hopes on the bomb ketches, which could anchor every night "and heave some bomb shells in[to] the Town." The Tripolitans, he thought, "have dreadful Ideas of bombs," and three months of lobbing shells into the city would leave them "clamorous" and induce the bashaw to moderate his terms. The bomb vessels would have near impunity because, he claimed, the Tripolitans were such bad marksmen that a bomb vessel anchored a half-mile offshore would be impervious to shore-based cannon fire. Richard O'Brien, Preble's diplomatic adviser, agreed that "throwing Bomb shells" into Tripoli would "Bring them to Their Bearings, and would be a terror of a new system of Warfare."[15]

On July 9, the *Constitution* finally set sail from Messina with the two borrowed Neapolitan bombs and the schooner *Enterprize*. They arrived in Syracuse the next day and rendezvoused with the *Nautilus* and the six lent gunboats, but bad weather delayed their departure. Preble's ships finally arrived off Tripoli on July 25; nearly nine months had elapsed since the *Philadelphia* had crashed onto the reef. The commodore made his plans for attack, recognizing that the enemy was in "a city well walled, protected by batteries judiciously constructed, mounting one hundred and fifteen pieces of heavy cannon, and defended by twenty-five thousand Arabs and Turks." In the harbor lay a swarm of gunboats, two galleys, two 8-gun schooners, and a 10-gun brig forming "a strong line of defence, at secure moorings, inside a long range of rocks and shoals, extending more than two miles to the eastward of the town, which ... renders it impossible for a vessel of the *Constitution*'s draught of water to approach near enough to destroy them." [16]

Although distrusted by Preble, at the end of July 1804, Beaussier made one last appeal for a diplomatic resolution to Yusuf. Addressing him as "Illustrious and Magnificent Lord," Beaussier noted that the interest Napoleon, who had been named emperor of France on May 19, "takes in the prosperity of your Reign and the happiness of your Subjects, obliges me to put the following considerations before your eyes." Adroit diplomat that he was, Beaussier argued in the alternative. "If the American attack does not succeed," he observed, the war "will continue to the great disadvantage of your income, and of your country, already impoverished by three years and three months of war." But if the Americans prevailed, the price of peace might be "the deliverance of all the prisoners without any ransom. In this case your expenses would be a complete loss in addition to the damage that the city will have suffered." Continuing the war mattered little to the Americans, he argued, who were more concerned with developing a navy and training their officers and sailors. He suggested the bashaw consider these "reflections," which were "dictated by the interest of your Glory and by Bonaparte's desire to see you at peace with the Americans." [17]

The bashaw thanked Beaussier but stated he would prefer being buried under the ruins of his country rather than cowardly bowing to the will of the enemy. With that answer, Beaussier expected an imminent bombardment. To oppose the Americans, the bashaw only had "eighteen small and large, badly directed, gunboats, and the fire of various forts and batteries from which the gunners are not very skilled." In a timely postscript to his letter to Talleyrand reporting on his conversation with Yusuf, he added, "The Americans are in sight." [18]

The US Navy made five concerted attacks against Tripoli. The first came August 3. Two or three miles offshore, Preble saw Tripolitan gunboats emerge from the harbor to the seaward side of the shoals. At 12:30, he signaled his bomb and gunboat commanders to come within hailing distance and told them they were going to initiate an attack on the enemy gunboats and batteries. Half the crews of the ships of the squadron were taken out to man the gunboats and mortar boats, which had been towed toward the harbor by the larger ships. At 2:30, Preble hoisted the flag signal "attack." Onshore, some of the sailors repairing the Tripolitan fortifications came running back to the prison yard, calling out that the entire coast was "lined with our shipping." The city was, in Ray's words, in an "uproar," the soldiers running to their posts, but "wild disorder rang through every arch."

Mortars firing shells could be more precise than an ordinary cannon firing horizontally because mortar fire was more scientific. The placement of the shells could be corrected for distance by adjusting the amount of gunpowder and by changing the angle of the mortar up and down. And because the mortar was set into a fixed position along the centerline of the anchored bomb vessel, the placement of the shells could be corrected laterally by a few turns of the anchor cables. At 2:45, the two bomb vessels with their Neapolitan bombardiers began to lob shells into the city, each mortar firing off a 196-pound shell every minute or so. One shell burst next to a gun battery. Other shells "were thrown into the town," and a minaret from a mosque toppled. The bomb vessels came under intense fire from shore batteries, Preble noting that "the spray of the sea occasioned by the enemies shot almost covered them." The *Constitution* and some of the other ships closed with the shore, firing broadside after broadside into the gun batteries from three cables lengths (1,800 feet) to help provide cover for the borrowed Neapolitan gunboats, which sallied in with their American crews against the Tripolitan gunboats. Contrary winds allowed only three of the gunboats to come to grips with the Tripolitan gunboats. With "unspeakable pride," the *Philadelphia*'s officers watched the battle from their grated skylight, as those three gunboats bore down on and then boarded nine enemy gunboats. While the officers watched the battle unfold, Tripolitan soldiers ordered the *Philadelphia*'s sailors and marines to run with gunpowder and shot strapped on their backs from the castle's magazine to supply the Tripolitan gun batteries.

In the bloody, hand-to-hand fighting outside the harbor, Lieutenant James Decatur, Stephen Decatur's younger brother, was killed when a Tripolitan sailor shot him in the head while Decatur was boarding a gunboat that had feigned surrender. Stephen Decatur was almost killed, too, spared when a sailor interposed his own body to take a saber slash in a melee on another Tripolitan gunboat. When Preble ordered the recall at 4:45 PM, the Americans had captured three gunboats, sunk another, and taken forty-nine prisoners. As a humanitarian gesture, Preble returned the badly wounded prisoners to Tripoli, but he kept the others to trade off with the bashaw against American sailors in captivity. Two shells had torn into Consul Nissen's house but did not explode. Nissen was the only European consul not to seek refuge from the bombardment in the gardens in the interior; he stayed in the city to ensure food and supplies would reach the captive Americans.[19]

The American attack killed almost fifty Tripolitan sailors on their gunboats, where pistols, swords, pikes, and tomahawks did bloody work. In a letter to Keith Spence, Stephen Decatur wrote that "hand to hand is not childs play, 'tis kill or be killed." But he had always known that Americans would stand up to the legendary, feared "Turks," that "we could lick them their own way and give them two to one [odds]." No one knew how many Tripolitans were killed and wounded ashore, among the gun batteries and in the town. It was not the casualties that would shake the bashaw, Preble surmised, but the ferocity of the American attack and the willingness to fight Barbary corsairs in their own way, close combat.[20]

The next day, the *Philadelphia*'s crew was put to work repairing and recementing the masonry walls of the Tripolitan forts damaged by their brother tars' cannon fire. Where the local population came upon the Americans, they threw stones or spit on them. They could not believe, Ray reported, that the country that surrendered a frigate without a single casualty had men who could fight so staunchly; they assumed the American sailors must all have been drunk to encourage their reckless bravery. Two days after the attack, Dr. Cowdery dressed a mameluke's shattered hand. He amputated the man's fingers with a dull knife and bandaged his hand in a bungling manner, hoping to lose credibility, because otherwise, he "expected to have [his] hands full of wounded Turks in consequence of the exploits of [his] brave countrymen."[21]

On the afternoon of August 7, the Americans attacked again. This time, the mortar boats fired on the town from a small bay to the west, while the gunboats tried to silence a gun battery near that position. In Tripoli, an alarm gun was fired, but before the soldiers manned their guns, they all faced east toward Mecca, kneeling on the ground in prayer, their foreheads touching the ground in unison, with as much precision, Ray joked, as an infantry company going through the manual of arms. After three hours, the squadron had fired forty-eight mortar shells into the town and almost five hundred 24-pounder shot at point-blank range into the batteries, silencing their cannon. A US gunboat blew up, reportedly from a red-hot shot from a Tripolitan battery, although the sailing master of the *Constitution* thought that a flaming piece of wad from an American cannon's discharge caused the explosion. Watching from the top of the castle, Cowdery witnessed "a tremendous cannonading" and the gunboat exploding, "the mangled bodies of [his] countrymen precipitated into the air." The explosion stilled the battle for a few seconds, and then the firing erupted as loud as before. He saw the mortar shells explode, which "set fire to the town in many places; but the houses being principally built of stone, mud and mortar, the fire did but little damage. The shells and shot, however, battered the town very much, and almost destroyed some of the houses." The bashaw sheltered in his bombproof room in the castle, coming out after hearing the gunboat blow up, having taken the precaution of getting a *marabout* to seal a black piece of paper on the top of his head, with a Qur'anic inscription assuring his safety.[22] On August 17, more than a week after the attack, the bashaw told Cowdery that fifteen American bodies had drifted ashore. Although Yusuf at first gave the captive American officers permission to bury the dead, he reneged, and three weeks later, Cowdery recorded in his diary that he "found that our men, who were destroyed by the explosion of the gunboat . . . lay in a state of putrefaction on the beach. They were scattered on the shore for miles, and were torn in pieces by dogs."[23]

On the evening after the second attack, the first reinforcing ship from the United States, the *John Adams*, arrived off Tripoli, and brought news that the four frigates of Samuel Barron's command had sailed just four days after the *John Adams*. Preble decided to wait a few days; if the reinforcements arrived in a timely fashion, "the fate of Tripoli must be decided in a few hours, and the Bashaw completely humbled." Even without them, if the *John Adams* had brought out to the Mediterranean her own gun carriages—she had shipped them on board two of the reinforcing frigates—he would have had her guns mounted and would "not have waited a moment, and can have no doubt but the next attack would make the arrival of more ships unnecessary for the termination of the Tripoli[tan] war."[24]

After the two attacks, the bashaw sent for Cowdery to learn more about the squadron visible offshore. The attacks, which contrasted with Bainbridge's surrender, gave him pause. Still, Yusuf told Cowdery that "for two dollars he could repair all the damages that the bombardment did to his town," that no one had been killed, and that only one person was wounded in the bombardment, all of which was false. He remarked that the Americans had offered him only $50 per man in ransom, which the prisoners were earning for him in captivity every two months. Yusuf asked how much the Americans would be willing to pay for *him*. Cowdery did not know, he said; perhaps fatuously, perhaps to show how much he had come to value him, the bashaw responded that he would not take $20,000 for him. Cowdery replied that if that were so, he would remain a slave for life. Yusuf patted him on the shoulder and said he hoped the doctor would be content to stay in Tripoli.[25]

On the morning of August 9, the French consulate raised a white flag under the tricolor, the agreed-upon signal that the bashaw was interested in opening a negotiation. Preble sent a boat into the harbor with letters for Bainbridge and his officers. The boat returned with the bashaw's demands: $500 ransom for each captive but no money to buy peace or for annual tribute. Isaac Chauncey, the commander of the *John Adams*, told Preble that the Jefferson administration thought that the arrival of four frigates would beat down Tripoli and force the bashaw to release the officers and men without paying any ransom. In fact, the president's own notes from a May 1804 cabinet meeting made clear the administration's more nuanced policy: if Preble's naval campaign was "successful, insist on their deliver[in]g up men without ransom, and reestablishing old treaty without paying any thing. If unsuccessful, rather than have to continue the war, agree to give 500. D. a man, (having first deducted for the prisoners we have taken) and the sum in gross & tribute before agreed on." Following the directive, Secretary of State Madison then authorized Lear to pay up to $500 per man to ransom the net number of American prisoners after an exchange of Tripolitan prisoners in American hands, but Madison's June 6 instructions had not yet arrived.[26]

In light of Chauncey's statement, Preble wrote Beaussier, informing him that the four frigates were *en route* to Tripoli and expected at any moment. Five powerful frigates would enable the American squadron to destroy Tripoli and the towns along the coast. Once Barron and his frigates arrived, Preble would not have it in his "power to offer a single dollar either as ransom or peace." Because he still had authority, Preble proposed $80,000 for the American captives, all the Tripolitan prisoners would be returned, a new peace treaty signed, and the new US consul would make a $10,000 present to the bashaw. Preble sent O'Brien ashore with a letter giving Yusuf a deadline of the next morning. The bashaw did not need that much time. The white flag over the castle was hauled down, a signal there would be no peace. Beaussier informed Preble that according to Dghies, the August 3 attack had intimidated the bashaw "a little," but the August 7 attack "encouraged him against the Efforts" of the American squadron because Yusuf knew he could withstand the worst the Americans could dish out. The bashaw was bent on continuing the war, he had the support of the *divan* and the people, and according to Beaussier, it would be "prejudicial" to even float the idea of $80,000 when the bashaw talked of three or four times that amount. However, Dghies suggested to Beaussier that Yusuf might accept $150,000, which Beaussier thought was realistic. Preble initially declined to raise his offer, although he confided in his journal that the captives could not be freed for anything less.[27]

Preble faced a dilemma. He possessed the negotiating authority to ransom the captives, yet Chauncey had told him that Jefferson and Madison thought he could free them without paying a penny, and Barron was coming with four frigates that might well batter down the walls of Tripoli. Preble did not want to return to his country as an object of scorn of the administration and his naval colleagues, like his predecessor, Commodore Morris. He decided to raise the ante again. He added $20,000 as a present to the bashaw to the $80,000 for ransom, and $10,000 to distribute as presents to Dghies and the other ministers (Preble mentioned these gifts in a separate letter and asked them to be given "privately")—a total of $110,000, as well as a $10,000 present when a new consul arrived. He added again, and therefore not credibly, that he had reached the limit of his authority, that "when the whole Squadron arrives, no such offer will ever again be made," and that with five frigates' massive firepower, "we can reduce Tripol[i] to a heap of Ruins: the destruction of Derna & Bengaz[hi] will follow, and the blockade be constantly cont[in]ued, unless the present terms are accepted."[28]

The bashaw would have none of it. The rumor swept through the squadron that the bashaw increased his demands as a result of Preble's diplomacy, perhaps because the arrival of the *John Adams* seemed to herald peace or positive orders from the administration to make peace; all the talk about the four frigates appearing might have been seen as pure bluster because they had never arrived; and the limited success of the last attack, in which Tripoli did not lose a single gunboat. Preble reacted to the bashaw's refusal of his terms as a personal affront and decided to attack the city that night, the squadron standing in for that purpose, but the wind and weather forced them offshore.[29]

Many residents of Tripoli moved inland, fearing another bombardment. The bashaw ate, drank, and slept in his castle's bombproof room. At the same time, perhaps a thousand desert tribesmen arrived to bolster the defenses of the city, although Cowdery dismissed them as "almost naked, half starved, and without discipline." Cowdery was struck by the defenders' fanaticism, running to and fro and shaking their muskets over their heads, shrieking "Holouet Buoy" ("I am my father's son"), with *marabouts* shouting Qur'anic verses, cursing the American ships, prophesizing success in battle, and singing chants from rooftops in town.[30]

For twelve days, the American ships tried to bombard Tripoli, but adverse winds and bad weather kept them away. The third American attack was a bombardment that began at 2:00 AM on August 24. The *Argus* and *Syren* each towed one of the unwieldy bomb vessels close to the shore, and the mortars began to heave shells into the city. In the dark night, the fall of the shells could not be accurately observed, and most of the shells missed their targets. The Tripolitan gun batteries remained silent and, eerily, not a light was seen in the town or at the batteries. At 4:45 AM, with dawn arriving, Preble, uncertain of their effect, signaled for the bomb vessels to cease firing and withdraw. Beaussier asserted, "No bomb fell on the city, not even in the port, nor on the forts," although as the sun rose, Sailing Master Haraden, four miles offshore on the *Constitution*, thought he saw through his spyglass a forty-foot breach in the wall of the bashaw's castle. Likely he was mistaken. Nissen wrote in his diary that the Americans had fired thirty-three or thirty-four bombs, but "most of them fell in the sea, few came onto the land, none fell in the city, only one blew up, and did so in the air."[31]

The American squadron attacked again on the night of August 27–28. At 4:00 AM, eight gunboats closed to the shore to fire on the town, shipping, castle, and batteries, anchoring within 1,800 feet of the bashaw's castle. Cowdery awoke to "a heavy and incessant fire of cannon, and the whistling and rattling of shot all around me." Every cannon in Tripoli that could be brought to bear returned fire. The bombardment ended a few minutes past sunrise, when the gunboats were towed off, and the *Constitution* moved forward to within point-blank range of the batteries west of the castle, bore down, and fired two broadsides. Haraden saw "showers of stone & dust" bursting from the batteries. The squadron then stood out and anchored off the harbor. The navy had fired off more than seven hundred cannonballs, most into the batteries, as well as grapeshot and cannister, sinking one Tripolitan gunboat and two small vessels, and forcing two other gunboats to beach themselves to avoid sinking. Preble noted laconically that the *Constitution*'s rigging and sails had been cut up by the batteries' firing grapeshot, but "only" nineteen cannonballs struck the ship. The Americans assumed they had killed and wounded many Tripolitan defenders. What they did not know was that they had nearly killed William Bainbridge. A 24-pounder cannonball blasted through a wall into the room where he was lying, missing his head by less than a foot, and knocked out stones and mortar, burying him under the rubble until his officers could dig him out. He was bruised and his right ankle was bashed, which made him walk with a limp for months. Nissen later reported that the "bombardment & cannonade" had little effect on the bashaw, "who don't care much about his Town or his Subjects' [lives]." The Danish consul warned that the bashaw intended to order his artillery to fire red-hot shot when the Americans attacked next, but the Tripolitans had not mastered the technique, and doing so "certainly will blow up his gunners."[32]

In defending against every bombardment, the Tripolitans used the captive American sailors and marines as powder monkeys. As the US Navy's shot and shell whistled overhead or burst around them, the *Philadelphia*'s people carried gunpowder and shot from the magazine in the castle to the various gun batteries around the port. An overseer loaded a small barrel of gunpowder on each sailor's back, and hunched over, the tars were forced to run to the batteries, as far as three-quarters of a mile away, with a warden behind, prodding the runner with a stick, while onlookers hurled insults and rocks. None of the American sailors or marines was killed or wounded in the squadron's attacks.[33]

Ray welcomed the bombardment by his countrymen, even if the shells and cannonballs might kill or wound him or his fellow sailors:

> To free the captive, Preble *wing'd his aid*,
> *And more firm valor never was display'd.*
> *When round our prison's solitary walls*
> *Burst the dread meteor-bomb-shells—shower'd the balls!*
> *Our hearts for liberty or death beat high,*
> *And who for freedom would not wish to die?*
> *To him we look'd, on him our hopes relied—*
> *The friend of seamen, and the seaman's pride;*
> *To him we look'd, and righteous heav'n implored*
> *To speed the vengeance of his slaughtering sword.*[34]

After the four bombardments, Yusuf granted an audience to Beaussier. The bashaw rejected out of hand Preble's suggestion to exchange the forty-two Tripolitans the squadron had captured for a like number of Americans as something unprecedented between Muslims and Christians. To show he was not intimidated by the bombardment or the arrival of four more frigates, Yusuf demanded 400,000 Spanish dollars for ransom and a peace treaty, as well as presents for himself and his ministers. Yusuf said he would accept that sum "merely out of Regard & Respect for his good friend the French Emperor." He added that if the liberation of the American captives could not be agreed on then, they might come to terms the next year.[35]

In fact, the bombardments were not doing much damage. Two of the *Philadelphia*'s warrant officers, Sailmaker Joseph Douglass and Carpenter William Godby, smuggled a letter to Preble offshore. "The last attack you made," they wrote, "Injured a grate Many houses[,] killed several Turcks & drove them entirely out of three of there Batrys [but . . .] the shells that was hove the last night all fell in the Water but verry few of shells that has been hove in Town has Bursted." Beaussier reported the same thing, writing Preble that the effect of the third attack on the night of August 23–24 was "perfectly null—Not a single Bomb was thrown beyond the Forts." The fourth attack, on August 27–28 was "more serious"—one shot "struck the Castle and passed through the apartment of the Prisoners[;] another [went] through the Sail[o]rs' prison, & others struck a number of Houses, especially those of the Spanish, Swedish & Dutch Consuls." Some shot went past the city, killing a camel, and others flew as far as the gardens. A couple of little vessels were sunk in the harbor, and four men on a Tripolitan corsair were killed. But, Beaussier added, Yusuf "seems to care little about the Injury done to the Houses by the Shot, which is easily repaired; the Shells only, which he fears may burn and destroy his Town, give him some uneasiness and revive in him the desire for an Accommodation." Zuchet was not as blasé as the bashaw because he almost died in the bombardment of August 27–28. When the attack began, he leaped out of his bed and started down the stairs as a cannonball hit the wall in his bedroom, skimmed over his bed, and embedded itself in the opposite wall. Had he not moved, he "would have been cut in half." He reported fifteen were killed that night in Tripoli.[36]

Preble conceded the limitations of his squadron in a letter to Sir Alexander Ball, the governor of Malta. Without the reinforcing frigates, he could not overpower Tripoli's defenses, and if the frigates did not arrive immediately, the campaign would be over for that season. Preble's ships were running low on shot and powder, and the weather had started to become difficult for his borrowed gunboats and bombards. "The stern of a frigate," Preble wrote, "affords but a poor shelter for them." Although the mortar boats and gunboats were critical, they needed to be escorted into battle, and given the layout of the harbor and the shoals, Preble could only send them in with a wind from the southeast or the east-southeast.[37]

At three thirty in the afternoon of September 3, the mortar boats again bombarded the town. They sailed to a spot two miles off the eastern side of Tripoli, fired a few ranging shots to get the distance and correct the fall, and then opened a slow, methodical fire. According to Sailing Master Haraden, watching from the *Constitution*, one bomb vessel fired nineteen shells, and he saw fifteen explode in the town; the other bomb vessel fired twenty-two shells, eighteen of which fell into the town. Cowdery watched the shells destroy the house of the chief Spanish ship carpenter and damage other houses. Eight gunboats forced the Tripolitan galleys and gunboats to seek protection under the guns of a battery on the east side of the harbor, but then the battery, as well as the Tripolitan ships, were attacked by the brigs, schooners, and gunboats of the squadron. When the mortar boats came under fire, one being disabled, the *Constitution* ran between them and the shore batteries, and at point-blank range fired eleven broadsides into the batteries, the city, and directly at the castle. At four thirty, the squadron disengaged.[38]

Again, despite reports of severe damage, the cannonade had no effect on the bashaw. Preble, justifiably proud of the bravery of his officers and men, referred to the September 3 battle as "a complete victory." Yet Beaussier wrote, "The little effect of the third attack & the little injury they received from the fourth [on September 3] has entirely changed the State of things[.] The [bashaw] is determined to encounter all your forces in Order that Europe & Africa may conceive a favorable opinion of his strength & courage." Ray reported that shells hit in the city but few exploded. Other shells flew over the prison housing the men and stuck in the sand; a few struck the prison; one shot went through the cookhouse at the end of the prison yard; and others struck the front wall or corners obliquely, without doing any real damage. To show his derision, the bashaw distributed coins to Tripolitans who retrieved unburst shells. Months after the 1804 campaign was over, Bainbridge, who earlier had been the great champion of bomb vessels, depreciated the bombardments because the houses in Tripoli were made of stone and clay and did not catch fire.[39]

The next day, September 4, Preble launched the final attack of the 1804 campaign season. The *Intrepid*, which had borne Decatur and his band into the harbor to burn the *Philadelphia* six months earlier, was tapped to be a "fireship." A fireship was also known as an "infernal," presumably because it was a hellish weapon. Famously, fireships had been used by the English against the Spanish Armada in 1588 and by the Americans against British ships in the Hudson River in 1776, during the Revolutionary War. Loaded with explosives, a fireship sailed into an enemy fleet or a port and then was left by the crew to drift toward her target with a fuse of sufficient length to give the men time to escape before the explosion. A fireship, in other words, was a floating time bomb. In early September, the *Intrepid* was loaded with nearly 100 barrels of gunpowder and 150 mortar shells. For the command, Preble chose Master Commandant Richard Somers, and with Somers went two junior officers and ten sailors. Somers's mission was to sail near the castle, light the fuse, set the *Intrepid* adrift, and escape on two boats the *Intrepid* would tow behind her. The ensuing explosion, Preble hoped, would destroy Tripolitan gunboats, damage the castle, terrorize the population, and scare the bashaw and his *divan* into making peace.

After dark, the *Intrepid* began her mission, from six miles outside the harbor. The *Nautilus* followed the *Intrepid* until the water was five fathoms deep, where she backed her topsails and waited. After the *Intrepid* steered around the shoals and entered the harbor, she was spotted. Alarm guns were fired. A few minutes before 10:00 PM, there was a huge explosion, a tremendous blast seen and heard for many miles. A young officer stationed on the *Nautilus* later recalled that "the flash illumined the whole heavens around, while the terrific concussion shook everything far and near. Then all was hushed again and every object veiled in a darkness of double gloom." After a few moments of utter silence, "the din of kettle-drums beating to arms, with the noise of confusion and alarm, was heard from the inhabitants on shore." From six miles out, the *Constitution* shot off signal rockets every ten minutes until the next morning, when the *Nautilus* came within hail and reported the *Intrepid* had blown up prematurely. Whether her explosive charges were ignited accidentally or by a Tripolitan shot, or whether Somers deliberately blew her up to avoid capture (as he promised to do before setting out) will never be known. All hands were killed, and the fireship, which exploded hundreds of yards from where Somers intended for her to blow up, did not damage Tripoli.[40]

Yusuf ordered the Americans' bodies to be retrieved from where they washed up on shore several days later. According to Zuchet, the bashaw ordered the dead brought to the arsenal, and "from his balcony, he amused himself by watching his people hurl curses and insults at the corpses. He wanted to share this spectacle with Captain Bainbridge under the pretext of letting him see whether he recognized anyone among the dead." He allowed Bainbridge and several officers out of their prison dungeon to view the remains, and although the dead were mutilated and unrecognizable, apparently Bainbridge recognized Somers's uniform. He asked permission to bury them, but Yusuf refused for three days, allowing the greater part of their bodies to be devoured by dogs. Zuchet was appalled by the cruelty and desecration.[41]

With that terrible finale, the 1804 campaign ended. The little squadron had fired off most of its ammunition; the *Constitution* alone shot off 641 cannonballs and 573 strands of grapeshot and cannister. The lent Neapolitan bomb vessels were no longer seaworthy. With the prodigious mortar in the forward part of the ship, the bombards were not stable in anything but the most placid seas. After they had been in combat over the summer, Haraden recorded that one bomb vessel "has been several times reported to the Commodore to be unsafe & unserviceable owing to her leaky state occasioned by the 5 different actions she has been in, & is at present useless," and the bed for the mortar on the second bomb was "so split & shivered that she is totally unserviceable and is at present considered useless." On September 7, the bomb vessels and gunboats were towed back to Syracuse, where they were returned with thanks to the king of Naples. Three days later, too late for the 1804 campaign season, the reinforcing frigates from America finally arrived off Tripoli.[42]

The "ifs" of the 1804 campaign are many. Preble thought if he had those reinforcing frigates two weeks earlier, he could have brought the war to a successful close by flattening Tripoli. Even without the frigates, if the mortars had not fired off so many duds, the bomb vessels might have been able to destroy vast tracts of the city. But it is impossible to know if a heavier bombardment would have forced Yusuf to agree to a smaller ransom or no ransom to free the captives.

Too late for the 1804 campaign, Secretary of State Madison's instructions to Tobias Lear finally arrived on the scene. Madison directed Lear to join oncoming Commodore Barron "at a suitable time" to negotiate peace with Tripoli. While the administration hoped this could be achieved "without any price or pecuniary concession whatever," if the alternative was a continuation of the war, Lear was to pay ransom because a "pecuninary sacrifice" was preferable to a "protraction of the war." Madison authorized Lear to spend up to $500 per prisoner, deducting an amount for a prisoner-for-prisoner swap, the amount the bashaw had suggested to Preble. Madison hoped, however, that the effect of the 1804 campaign and the knowledge that the US Navy would attack Tripoli again in 1805 would moderate the bashaw's demands. Madison depreciated reliance on Hamet Karamanli and made clear that Jefferson and Madison believed that the squadron would be "sufficient for any exercise of coercion which the obstinacy of the Bashaw may demand."[43]

In dispatches sent out with Barron and the frigates, the president and Secretary Smith assured Preble that he had performed splendidly but there were not enough captains junior to him to allow him to continue in command. Preble remained in the Mediterranean for some time, however, assisting Barron with messy prize cases, seeking permission from the king of Naples to borrow gunboats and mortar boats for the next year's campaign, and basking in praise for all he had done with the small means at his disposal.[44]

Yet Preble's conduct of diplomacy left much to be desired. Leaving aside his overt disdain for Beaussier and his disregard for diplomatic forms, his alternating force with increasing offers for ransom was unhelpful. The diplomats gave him a chorus of criticism. Beaussier wrote Preble directly how "impolitic" it was to bombard and then negotiate, raising the bashaw's "pretensions," concluding, "It [would have] been much better *at the beginning* to have threatened, and to have followed up your attacks with energy & effect, *without entering into any negotiations.*" Nissen, whose friendship for the Americans could not be doubted, asked to be excused for the liberty of expressing himself frankly, and wrote George Davis in Tunis that the commodore entered "too often in parlamenting—the Bashaw takes it as a necessity for peace & grows more obstinate.—After every attack, there has been next day a flag of truce—this is no good Policy towards an Enemy as Tripoli." Davis himself wrote home to Madison that a negotiator "[s]hould never offer terms but once; these terms being rejected, no apparent Success of Arms, should induce us to renew them, for when they are to be accepted, the Bashaw will read[il]y devise means to make it known."[45]

TWELVE

PROSPECTS

W HEN SAMUEL BARRON ARRIVED in the Mediterranean to command the squadron in September 1804, the bomb vessels and gunboats had returned to Naples, and bad weather was in the offing. After a few desultory days off Tripoli, Barron ordered a few small ships to maintain the blockade, but he retreated with the balance of the squadron to Malta. Barron was just thirty-nine, but his command of the squadron would be severely limited by chronic illness, supposedly a liver disease secondary to an earlier bout of yellow fever, which left him incapacitated and ashore for much of fall and winter 1804–05.

Barron was a popular and well-connected officer. Born in 1765 and raised at his family's Little England plantation in Hampton, Virginia, Barron received a grammar school education in Petersburg and Williamsburg. At fourteen he entered the Virginia State Navy in the Revolutionary War. When General Lord Cornwallis surrendered at Yorktown in 1781, Barron was said to have been on the field. After the war, he commanded merchant ships sailing from Norfolk to Europe and the West Indies. When the Quasi-War against France erupted, a Norfolk merchant recommended him as "a perfect seaman an Industrious Active Sober man & in all respects a Gentleman." Barron initially commanded the brig *Richmond*, and then several larger ships, and was retained as a captain in the postwar contraction of the navy. Now he was taking over the Mediterranean squadron at a critical time.[1]

The Jefferson administration sent Barron to the Mediterranean to command a squadron double the force that Preble commanded and gave him wide latitude. Secretary Smith's orders to Barron noted that the loss of the *Philadelphia* "subjected a number of our Fellow Citizens to the Condition of Slaves." He authorized Barron to alleviate their suffering by sending Spence money to buy them clothing and food as Bainbridge directed, but Smith did not want Barron providing money directly to the sailors and marines. Nine vessels had been put back into commission and formed the new squadron, and "no doubt whatever can exist," the orders read, that Barron could force Tripoli "to a Treaty upon our own Terms." Given the distance from Washington, the government gave him discretion in using his forces, but he was to maintain the blockade as long as possible, and if Hamet Karamanli would help in the campaign, Smith did not object to Barron using him. Finally, Barron was to cooperate with Colonel Lear on diplomatic measures "best calculated to effectuate a termination of the war with Tripoli."[2]

With the close of the 1804 campaign, Lear wrote Madison that nothing had been heard from Tripoli after the last attack. Lear did not know whether the bombardments had made an impression on the bashaw, but he did not expect Yusuf to be interested in negotiations until spring 1805, nine months distant. In the meantime, in Tripoli, the sailors and marines from the *Philadelphia* were put to work repairing the damage done to the buildings, forts, and batteries in the five attacks, laying new gun platforms, building gun carriages, and hauling timber to build gunboats and stone to erect new fortifications.[3]

The American diplomats were confronted by a moral hazard. Secretary of State Madison had authorized Lear to pay ransom of $500 per man, although his instructions anticipated that another campaign would lessen the cost of freeing the captives. Lear was not eager to begin negotiations until the bashaw showed a willingness to come to terms on a more reasonable basis, and that, he thought, could only be expected after renewed American naval cannonading. But that strategy was problematic. The 1804 campaign, which had achieved modest success as a diplomatic matter by reducing the bashaw's demands, had resulted in thirty American sailors and marines being killed in action and twenty-four wounded. Even if the 1805 campaign would result in a successful negotiation to free the captives, it still would cost blood. Closing the gap between the bashaw's demands and the Americans' offers would cost an unknown number of lives of sailors and marines, probably dozens of casualties.

And the nine-month delay presented other risks. No one knew what might happen to the sailors and marines in captivity ashore, who might die of deprivation or disease. The risk of contagion, such as the plague, was the very reason ports like Naples and Livorno insisted on long quarantines for ships that had touched on the Barbary coast. There was no way the American diplomats in 1804 could know if some, even hundreds, of their countrymen held in captivity might succumb to disease before the next naval campaign had even begun. Another risk was that the more successful the 1805 campaign might be, the greater the possibility that the bashaw would kill the captives. All told, the human costs of getting a lowered financial demand for ransom were potentially enormous. As a matter of policy, the United States implicitly believed those risks were worth taking, when weighed against the cost of not deterring Tripoli and the other Barbary regimes from seizing American sailors in the future. Perhaps Sir Alexander Ball put the calculation best. He wrote Preble that he had "done well in not purchasing a peace with money— A few brave men have been sacrificed; but they could not have fallen in a better cause: and I even conceive it better to risk more lives than submit to terms which might encourage the Barbary States to add fresh demands & insults." Whether that calculation was correct depends on the value placed on human lives on the one hand, and on national honor and deterrence on the other.[4]

At the time, some Americans criticized the navy and the diplomats for taking those risks. A leading Southern newspaper, the *Charleston Courier*, wrote that to leave American sailors in slavery, "to await the issue of 'a base bargain, a huckstry' about a few dollars," was "inglorious, nay ignominious to a nation. . . . If three hundred Americans are to be left to perish in the dungeons of the Barbarians, let it not be for the vile peculium of so many dollars, as on calculation would be exactly seven cents a head to the population of the Union." A Philadelphia newspaper, the *True American*, decried the refusal to pay ransom and instead to maintain a war. Not only had fifty men been killed or wounded, but also "three times the necessary cost to purchase the captives' freedom has already been expended in the war." The writer hoped the captives would be freed, but "the means employed" were "the reverse of what they should be."[5]

All the talk about slaves and ransom struck a nerve with other Americans, who marveled at the irony of the United States sending its navy thousands of miles to batter an African regime to free, or at least to lower the cost of ransoming, its slaves, while Americans were still importing seized Africans as slaves. Writing in a rural Pennsylvania newspaper, "JANUS" observed that the importation of black slaves into South Carolina was "full proof of the inconsistency of Mankind." The African regime that made slaves of its prisoners only wanted $150,000 to ransom them. JANUS wondered, "What would the task-masters of Carolina demand as the ransom of those slaves, whom they have imported in the course of the last year, to the amount of several thousands, and who have been brought by force into captivity and bondage, from their native country of Africa?" Raising the connection between the redemption of their fellow (white) citizens in Africa and the redemption of black Africans in America was a connection lost on most Americans, starting with President Jefferson.[6]

A widely reprinted poem went further. "American Captives in Tripoli," first published in an upstate New York newspaper, questioned whether the United States, dominated on the federal level by the Southern slave-owning interest, really cared about relieving the fate of American sailor-slaves held by the bashaw. In verse, the poet connected the slavery of the *Philadelphia*'s mostly white crew with the black slavery in the American South:

> *Ah, hapless day! That I should live to hear*
> *A Brother's moan from Afric's torrid shore;*
> *In bitterness of soul to shed a tear*
> *For that sweet freedom he enjoy'd before.*

Must those brave men be doom'd to slav'ry's chain,
Who, for our trade's support, have bravely fought?
With cruel labor must they strife maintain
Who, to protect us, distant seas have sought?
. . .
Is there no prospect then, their fate to change?
Must our dear countrymen in slav'ry lie?
Whilst they, in tho't, o'er our vast country range—
Can they no where a ray of comfort spy?

The proud Virginian, who by slaves grows great;
The Carolinian, rich in ricy fields;
The Georgian too that rides in ample state—
No men or treasure for your ransom yields.
. . .
From these, who to our country's councils come,
And have their suffrage from their numbered slaves,
Ye've nought to hope but slavery for your doom,
They'll neither ransom, fight, nor tempt the seas.[7]

The poet was wrong about "proud Virginians" like Jefferson and Madison. Despite owning slaves, they assumed that American seamen deserved freedom from the yoke of Islamic slavery because, as white Americans, they were born (or naturalized as) freemen. At the same time, they thought their black slaves, some of whom were Muslim, were not entitled to freedom, and since they were enslaved, it was too dangerous to white society to set them free. The facts that some sailors on the *Philadelphia* were free black men and that much of the crew was not actually American did not confound their analysis. Jefferson was periodically troubled by slavery in his own country, though he was not troubled enough to expend political capital to act on it. Yet he believed Barbary "piracy" and slave taking was a scourge the United States had to battle.[8]

Commodore Samuel Barron's first priority on taking command of the Mediterranean squadron was to get the bomb vessels and mortar boats reloaned for the 1805 campaign, but he was shocked to learn that Naples would not agree to provide them again. Ostensibly, Naples needed to keep all its ships in home waters because Sicily and southern Italy were at risk from raids by Barbary corsairs. Preble smelled a lie and assumed that "Some Interest more powerful than ours, has been working against us," suspecting both the French and the English. The denial of the boats was a "severe Disappointment," and without gunboats and bombs, Barron feared that the coming 1805 campaign would be "ineffectual." Barron appealed to the king of Naples, but he refused to reconsider. Barron then sent officers to Trieste and Ancona seeking to borrow gunboats and bomb vessels, but they initially sent discouraging reports. The inability to muster gunboats and mortar boats "Extinguished all hope," Barron wrote, of obtaining the essential naval force for "ensur[ing] the complete success" of the expected 1805 campaign.[9]

With that option closing, Barron launched William Eaton on what seemed a quixotic mission to find Hamet Karamanli somewhere in lower Egypt, raise or hire soldiers, and attack Tripoli from the east, across hundreds of miles of desert. In November 1804, the *Argus* set sail for Alexandria with Eaton on board. The son of a Connecticut farmer, Eaton had joined the army at sixteen in 1780, then attended Dartmouth College, taught school, and rejoined the army, where he rose to captain. A protégé of Secretary of State Timothy Pickering, Eaton resigned his army commission in 1797 to accept the appointment as consul to Tunis. There he learned to speak several Arabic dialects, but after the bey forced him out, he returned to America in 1803 to rally support for Hamet. Ambitious and charismatic, Eaton pressed the administration for military action with himself as generalissimo.[10]

Eaton regarded Hamet as the legitimate ruler of Tripoli. The conventional thinking about Hamet, however, was that he was weak and indecisive, even "stupidly insolent; in adversity the most abject and degraded of beings." In Washington, Eaton had spoken to Jefferson, Madison, and Smith about a military expedition with Hamet to topple Yusuf. Eaton sailed on Barron's ship back to the Mediterranean and urged the new commodore to support Hamet. If the administration was at best lukewarm to the idea of regime change, and Barron uncertain, Colonel Lear, a fierce enemy of Eaton, plainly disapproved of any ties to Hamet, a man without "any force or influence." In fact, Lear preferred "a peace with the present Bashaw, if he is well beaten into it" than a Tripoli with Hamet "placed on the throne by our means." But at the end of 1804, Eaton landed in Egypt. For months, he was out of touch, searching up the Nile for Hamet.[11]

By the end of October 1804, the blockade of Tripoli was beginning to bite, aided by a poor harvest, despite Bainbridge's earlier assumption that a blockade could not be effective as a weapon against Tripoli because of the abundant local grain. According to Captain John Rodgers, who had charge of the ships offshore, in fall 1804, only four small ships were able to slip through the American blockade into Tripoli. Richard Farquhar, a Scottish merchant resident at Malta, wrote Commodore Barron that his correspondents reported "the People [are] displeased with the Bashaw as they are distressed for Grain." The eastern areas of Tripolitania near Derne and Benghazi were said to be in a state of famine because of the failed harvest. The bashaw ordered that grain in the *souk* in Tripoli could be sold only to his household. Ray reported, "No bread to be had," and, "Money would not command bread, and starvation was whetting her teeth to devour us." Bainbridge learned that the bashaw "scarcely allows our Crew the subsistence" he had provided. For three days the captive Americans had no bread, and for eleven days they were allowed little, subsisting on dates pressed flat into cakes and some vegetables. By November, the bashaw discontinued the meat allowance Bainbridge paid for on American credits. The crew then knew real hunger. They resorted to selling their clothes, stealing money from a distiller of *aguardiente* while he was absent from his shop for the Jewish sabbath, and even trying to counterfeit Tripolitan coins. None of these expedients could work for long. Two of the *Philadelphia*'s sailors came to Zuchet, asserted they were Dutch, and begged for his help; he gave each man a loaf of bread on the days the bashaw gave nothing. By December, the crew was nearing actual starvation. Cowdery recorded in his diary, "Our men suffer for the want of provisions. The Bashaw does not allow them either victuals or cash. They get but a small allowance of bread" despite their onerous labor every day. Even so, there were those on the spot who doubted that the populace's hunger, caused in part by the blockade, would make a difference in the bashaw's calculus. Bainbridge was one of the doubters: "Tripoli can never be starved by the most rigid blockade[;] ... the block-

ade affects the town considerably, and I hope it will be continued thro'
the winter—every distress will assist towards a desire for peace, but we
must not calculate too largely on the distresses of the inhabitants in
bring[ing] the Bashaw to terms. He is [an] absolute [ruler] and feel[s]
but little regard for the interest of his Subjects."[12]

Driven to extremities, the American tars decided to respond by going
on strike. Sailors had a history of striking. Indeed, the word "strike" (in
the sense of a collective refusal to work) derives from English sailors
who, in 1768, "struck" down the yardarms of their ships to prevent them
from sailing, to force owners to listen to their demands. In Tripoli, at
dawn on December 10, when the overseers unlocked the prison doors
and demanded the crew fall out for the day's labors, not one of the
American sailors or marines moved. "Our men," Cowdery recorded, "all
agreed not to work unless they were fed, and accordingly when the wardens went to the prison and ordered them out, they all refused." The
overseers began to beat them. Whether they became frustrated by the
difficulty of attacking men lying on cots stacked high up along the wall,
as Ray asserted, or whether they grew tired of beating haggard men, as
Cowdery believed, the guards stopped the beatings. Not one American
broke. The sailors then told their guards that they would not work if
they were not fed. The guards threatened to call in soldiers to shoot
them. No American moved. Some of the guards left to tell the bashaw
what had happened, and they returned with the bashaw's promise that
if they went to work, the sailors and marines would all be fed at noon.
The Americans agreed to end their strike. The bashaw fulfilled his promise. Collective action broke the bashaw. The bread ration, meager as it
was, was back.[13]

In fall 1804, the officers still suffered in their prison dungeon. Spence
wrote his wife that of the thirty-seven officers and stewards imprisoned
together below the castle, thirty, including Spence himself, had been
down with fevers since mid-September. He depreciated the seriousness
of his illness, noting that in ten or twelve days, he was better. "Our confinement," wrote Spence, "for some months back, has been very close
and strict, insomuch that we have not been outside our prison doors

since the latter part of May." Outwardly sanguine about their health, Spence tried to keep an optimistic tone in writing Polly, "Hope, however, has not yet forsaken us." Yet the other officers suffered from illness and worries. Midshipman Renshaw wrote that "most of us [have] been afflicted with the fall fever which prevails in this horrid climate." Bainbridge was sick for four months and was so ill for a time that the British consul appealed to the bashaw to allow him to be moved back into the airy and comfortable premises of the American consul house. Yusuf refused. Bainbridge never complained. "Not a word from America, or the Commodore do we hear," he wrote, "perfectly in the dark as to all movements, and harassed in mind with dreadful anxiety."[14]

A few weeks later, Cowdery wrote his father that the sailors were at "hard labor, without mercy, and have suffered much, for the necessities of life." If not for the letters of credit that Bainbridge drew on to help feed the crew, "perhaps they would perish with hunger." Cowdery himself had been lucky that when he was ill twice, with dysentery and ophthalmia, Yusuf had paid him "every attention." While he yearned for freedom and a return to America, he wanted liberation to come "in a manner that will do honour to our country." He remained in good spirits, but added, "[h]ow long we are to remain here, God only knows; I am in hopes of once more seeing my Parents."[15]

Cowdery, whom the bashaw had moved from the castle to the subterranean prison with the other officers and ordered to take care of all the sick slaves, had a chance to assess the health of the crew. He had seen some of the crew "chained to a cart loaded with stones which they were dragging through the town to repair the fortifications. They complain much of hunger, cold, hard labor and the lash of the whip. I confess I never saw anything that wounded my feelings equal to the sight of those poor fellows," he wrote a friend in New York. "Our crew are not very healthy," Cowdery concluded, and Bainbridge's efforts "to relieve the wants of his crew are often countermanded by our new masters." Two weeks later, Cowdery wrote in his journal that the bashaw had given orders "to treat the American prisoners with the utmost cruelty, in order to induce the United States the sooner to make peace. He was impatient for his money."[16]

President Jefferson's November 8, 1804, Annual Message to Congress contained just two sentences about the war against Tripoli:

The activity and success of the small force employed in the Mediterranean in the early part of the present year, the reinforcement sent into that sea, and the energy of the officers having command in the several vessels, will, I trust, by the sufferings of war, reduce the barbarians of Tripoli to the desire of peace on proper terms. Great injury, however, ensues to ourselves as well as to others interested, from the distance to which prizes must be brought for adjudication, and from the impracticability of bringing hither such as are not sea-worthy.[17]

Perhaps because he did not want to raise expectations about three hundred Americans held in captivity when diplomatic efforts to free them had been fruitless, or perhaps because he had no recent news of their well-being, Jefferson said nothing about them. But the newspapers realized there was not "a single word respecting our unfortunate fellow-citizens." The president had gone on at length about things like the Delaware Indians and speculations in mines, yet "not a syllable is given to the sufferings of our gallant seamen, not a ray of comfort is extended to the afflicted relatives" of the captives.[18]

And with the arrival of the winter season with its gales on the African lee shore, the blockade waned. The small ships of the squadron retreated to Malta; there was no continuing naval or economic pressure on the bashaw. Yusuf remained steadfast in his demands for ransom. The British consul predicted that with the abundant rain of the season, there would be a good crop in 1805, which would buttress the regime, because the expense "of every article of life is at the present incredible."[19]

Just before Christmas, the Tripolitan overseers disrupted a plot, hatched by the warrant officers, for a mass revolt by the crew. The plan was undeveloped, but the idea was that when the prison gates were first opened in the morning, the crew would rush the guards, overcome them, and, having fashioned some bladed weapons beforehand, force their way into the castle, free their officers, seize the armory and magazine, overcome the bashaw's janissaries, and hold Yusuf and his family hostage. Cannon loaded with grapeshot would be planted at each gate to the castle, and the bashaw would be persuaded to furnish vessels for the Americans to sail out of Tripoli. Ray thought the plan was preposterous. While it might succeed initially, Ray believed the Tripolitans would regroup after the initial surprise, mass their cannon, and batter the castle down. In response to learning of the plot, the overseers searched for arms (none were found), the guard over the crew was doubled, and the same warrant officers who had been moved into the crew's prison (Godby, the carpenter; Hodge, the bosun; Fenton, the master's mate; and Douglass, the sailmaker) were moved back into the officers' dungeon and into close confinement.[20]

A few days later, on Christmas, the crew, now used to petitioning the bashaw, asked to be excused from labor for the holiday, and Yusuf rather graciously agreed. The crew asked Bainbridge for money for a special meal, and the captain asked Nissen to buy meat and vegetables, as well as an entire cask of wine, which netted each sailor and marine about a quart. One might think that drinking a quart of wine on Christmas was profane, but according to Ray, they celebrated the holiday with "decent propriety" and then sang songs and carols together.[21] The crew thanked Bainbridge, and he returned the favor by ordering more food and wine for them for New Year's Day. Ray and eight shipmates were sent to the Danish consul house to get the wine for the crew. When they tapped the cask, Nissen urged the shipmates to drink as much as they wanted, and the sailors "accepted of his liberal invitation with such unreserved cordiality" that by the time they finished their sampling, they could not carry the cask. More sailors were called for, and they too accepted Nissen's invitation until they became nearly as drunk as the first set, but somehow, the whole group was able to wheel or carry the cask back to their prison. As they departed, Nissen gave each man a handful of coins. "Our tars," Ray reported, "pronounced him the best fellow they had ever met with, and swore he must have been a sailor, or he would not be so generous with his cash and his grog."[22]

The new year of 1805 showed no signs of relief for the beleaguered officers and men. Bainbridge wrote Secretary Smith that "our situation in this place, is the same as it has been for twelve months past; the Officers are kept in close confinement, and the crew at labour. We bear our captivity with the firmness of Americans, and have the fullest confidence that our Government will take such measures as will soon restore us to the *arms* of our Country."[23] For ten months, the officers had lived in confinement in the bowels of the bashaw's palace, packed into three rooms. Although they had their books and daily instruction in mathematics, navigation, and tactics, their lives were meager. They ate reasonably well, on what Nissen was able to procure for them, but they never saw the sun or felt fresh air, they had no place to walk, they had nothing to see, and they were cut off from the crew. The close confinement had one advantage: it drew some of them closer. Bainbridge wrote Biddle that he not only respected him as an officer but esteemed him, suggesting that Biddle should treat him as if he were his father, and he put his "purse and services" at his disposal until he could "consign" Biddle "to the arms of [his] family." Although stiff with formality, it was a warm sentiment, and it was telling that Bainbridge, who was only ten years older than Biddle, wanted to be treated as a father figure.[24]

In a letter home, one officer wrote:

Our days drag heavily on, we are still closely confined, not having enjoyed a sight of the Heavens (but once) excepting through a small grated hole in the Terrace since May last. We are secluded in a loathsome prison, surrounded by vermin, without the enjoyment of pure air, and debarred from holding converse with any person outside the walls of our prison—the policy of concealing the operations of the fleet from the enemy cuts off the intercourse with our countrymen and keeps us in ignorance and constant suspense—the letters from our friends in America are intercepted, opened, and sometimes never reach us—after spending a tedious day, sleep, the solace of the wretched, comes to ease the burden of our minds, and sometimes transports us by a visionary flight to our beloved friends, but the return of light awakens us to the dreary realities of our prison. Even hope has now almost deserted us, and though we struggle to support with fortitude the horrors of our situation, yet human nature is scarcely equal to the conflict.[25]

There were occasional lighter moments in the dungeon's gloom. Even before his naval service, Midshipman Richard B. Jones was James Biddle's friend. In 1801, Jones had left Princeton on a gambling spree with his father's money in Baltimore, where he "lost every farthing he had." Jones's father collected him from a boardinghouse, and on their return to Philadelphia, the father and prodigal son breakfasted with the Biddles.

Perhaps that was the key for Jones's father to allow Richard to go to sea; he received a midshipman warrant in 1802.[26] Richard Jones, James Biddle, and Nicholas Biddle (Jones's friend at Princeton) were in a circle of friends with Midshipmen Bernard Henry, Robert Gamble, and James Gibbon, and Lieutenant Theodore Hunt. Biddle, Jones, Henry, and Gibbon had all served together as midshipmen on the *Constellation* in Morris's squadron.[27] While on that cruise, Biddle had written to Vice President Burr about the friendships and harmony among the officers of the ship.[28] Captivity in a Tripoli dungeon drew them into closer friendship. In April 1805, a boat from the squadron delivered mail and supplies to the imprisoned Americans. James Biddle received letters from friends in America and one from his brother Nicholas, who was in Paris serving as secretary to the US minister to France. For men in captivity, mail was a Godsend, and James pleaded with Nicholas to send him frequent letters. From Malta, disregarding Bainbridge's dour statement a year before about not needing "dainties," Sir Alexander Ball had sent Biddle "no small quantity" of porter, cheese, tea, coffee, and sugar, "so that for the few months to come at least I shall <u>live</u>."[29]

Richard Jones also received a letter from Nicholas Biddle, written eleven months before. Despite what he termed "the dull uniformity of a prison" and the bad health he had suffered due to "the severity of our confinement," Jones responded that James Biddle was sharing Ball's gifts with his friends. Theodore Hunt took over writing the letter from Jones, noting that Jones joked that he (Hunt) took "better care of James's Porter than I do of his Person." Jones had asked him, Hunt concluded conspiratorially, not to mention "the situation some of my Friends were in last night, all I can say is that Jones complained very much that his hand shakes, I won't say whether James's head Aches or not." James Biddle then took up the pen, complaining that Hunt had left him little space on the paper, putting "it out of my power to abuse him much." But he got in a dig, noting that Hunt claimed not to have been drunk the night before, "but he forgot to tell you his situation yesterday morning."[30]

The enlisted men's lives had little levity. Rousted out of bed every morning at sunrise, the sailors and marines were worked like beasts of burden, always prodded and sometimes beaten by their wardens. As slaves, they hauled materials and cargo from and around the port, and carried stones for building houses, fortifications, and gun batteries. The

Tripolitans did not use pack animals within the city; they packed slaves. Cowdery recorded an incident in May 1805 in which twenty-five members of the crew were forced to pull a cart into the surrounding country to gather timber. The wind, a *sirocco*, enveloped them with suffocating hot air and heaps of sand. At some point, the work detail stopped near a well, and the exhausted tars asked their overseer if they could drink. He exploded that they were all *romo kelps*, Christian dogs, refused their plea for water, and hit them, again and again, with his large *bastinado*. He forced them back to the cart, "which the poor fellows had to drag, loaded with timber, through the burning sands. They returned towards night almost [having] perished."[31]

Yet being struck by a baton-wielding overseer may have not been too different or more painful than getting flogged on board ship. What differentiated their Barbary slavery from service aboard ship was the men's slow decline in malnutrition and the deprivation of their sense of liberty. Although they never had enough to eat, and most had grown thin, their diet in Tripoli had fresh vegetables, grain, oil, occasional meat, and some fruit, which at least was wholesome. Those lucky enough to work in the mechanics' gangs or who ran small favors received coins to buy *aguardiente*. In February 1805, when the crew realized their bread was made lighter than before, they finally persuaded Bainbridge to provide them with money to buy food. Bainbridge arranged for Nissen to provide each sailor and marine with a *bukhamseen* per day, the equivalent of $10.75 for the entire crew per day. As Ray acted as Nissen's secretary, he received the money and divided it among the crew, and he also distributed coins provided to the men pulling carts and to those working as masons on the castle, although some of that was stolen by the guards.[32]

As their captivity dragged on, at home, public interest in the captives may have waned. An essayist in one newspaper feared "the state of the captives seems to be lost to the public sight," and over time, the people "grow reconciled to the loss and captivity of their countrymen." The column called on the people to maintain support for their countrymen working "like the meanest beasts of burden," while the government refused to either pay for their release or provide enough force to destroy Tripoli, leaving the poor captives "to sink, to rot, [and] to perish." The writer cautioned readers not to think that over time, the crew had grown accustomed to their suffering, and might be living "easy under it."[33]

The outlook for the Americans' release seemed poor. Toward the end of 1804, some of Bainbridge's officers received letters indicating that the Jefferson administration intended to support Hamet with an expedition to overthrow his brother, Yusuf. Aghast at the notion that his freedom would depend on Hamet and Eaton, Bainbridge suggested that the United States should just "abandon us to our unfortunate fate & save treasures which will [be] uselessly spent." He could not imagine that Hamet, whom he called a "poor effeminate fugitive," could help bring about their freedom. After the squadron would make its attacks in summer 1805, which he knew would not bring the bashaw to terms, Bainbridge hoped the United States would "make peace on the best terms attainable; for a continuation of the War would be attended with considerable Expence without reducing much the demand."[34]

As winter turned to spring, Spence, who had still not received a single letter from his wife, wrote Polly that he could not guess when they might be freed. The officers all hoped that that the coming summer would see the end of their captivity, but no one knew what the government, or the navy offshore, had in mind, so that "our hopes are founded on nothing but our wishes." Since Barron's arrival "he has been as silent as the grave; and we as much in the dark as if we were buried in it." Spence assured her he was healthy, and "excepting our confinement, we are as well treated as prisoners would be in any part of Europe," which was meant to bolster Polly's confidence rather than provide the truth about the officers' prison. Three weeks later, Spence reported that Bainbridge had asked the bashaw to move the officers back to the American consul's house, and Spence hoped they could move because, he finally disclosed, "we suffered much last summer from the heat and unwholesome air." Although the bashaw initially agreed, he kept the officers in the underground castle prison.[35]

THIRTEEN

PEACE AND THE RETURN

O PINIONS WERE MIXED AT THE PROSPECT of the coming campaign. From his perch in Tunis, George Davis wrote in late March 1805 that the bashaw "has made considerable preparations for a vigorous defence; but he is much str[a]ightened—he has to contend against civil com[m]otions, Famine, and an enterprising enemy—the rumour is spread of the arrival of his Brother Achmet Bashaw; and [Y]ussuph has actually sent a [flying] Camp against Derna—thus far every thing favours, our approaching Campaign." Yet Hugh Campbell, the captain of the frigate *Constellation*, wrote Secretary Smith three weeks later that "at present I see no prospect of the desired success against Tripoli, nor have I since the aid of Gun Boats, were refused, by the Court of Naples; which has left us the only alternative of Battering their Walls, until our Shot & Powder are expended; & then resume our former Station." Campbell depreciated the expedition in the desert, which he called

Eaton's "peregrination," and expected to hear that Eaton and his marines and mercenaries had been taken prisoner at Derne, if he was lucky enough to get that far, unless the navy arrived in time to rescue him.[1]

The man whose view counted most about what would happen in 1805 was President Jefferson. If Barron's squadron could not produce peace that summer, Jefferson wrote his old William & Mary classmate, John Tyler, "we shall recall our force, except one frigate and two small vessels, which will keep up a perpetual blockade. Such a blockade will cost us no more than a state of peace, and will save us from increased tributes, and the disgrace attached to them. There is reason to believe the example we have set, begins, already to work on the dispositions of the powers of Europe to emancipate themselves from that degrading yoke." Although Jefferson said nothing about how the captives might be freed from their degrading yoke if the 1805 campaign failed to resolve the war, in notes he drew up in January he stated, "if the enterprise in the spring does not produce peace & delivery of prisoners, ransom them."[2]

At the same time, the slow march of Eaton's little army across the desert toward Tripoli got the bashaw's attention. Dr. Cowdery, as the *de facto* court physician, had access to Yusuf and liberty to walk around the city. On March 1, he learned that the bashaw was preparing an army (what George Davis called a flying camp) to march against what was bandied about as "refractory tribes" on his Egyptian border. Three days later, a commander was named for the bashaw's forces, and Cowdery recorded that the crew of the *Philadelphia* packed their ammunition and stores. A panic started in Tripoli, as wealthy families began to move into country homes, expecting a siege by the Americans. On March 17, Cowdery walked by the US consul house, now jammed with women and boys, and learned they were the families of the bashaw's military officers, who were being held to ensure the officers' loyalty to Yusuf. A false rumor swept through the city that Hamet and four thousand soldiers had sailed from Alexandria to Sicily and were poised to launch an amphibious attack on Tripoli with American naval support. The bashaw's son-in-law made a four-day sweep of the countryside for troops to protect Tripoli, but, according to Cowdery, he returned empty-handed. Ten thousand soldiers had been expected to muster on the beach outside the city wall, but "not one of them appeared."[3]

Beyond the warlike signs, the bashaw was tired of fighting the pesky Americans. The US Navy offshore showed surprising tenacity; 1805 would be the fifth year of naval campaigns and a renewed blockade. His people, cowed as they were, showed signs of discontent, and food was scarce. Tripoli and the surrounding countryside were filled with soldiers he had raised to fight the Americans, but he had to feed them, and his treasury was running low. Although Yusuf had long denigrated Hamet, his brother's approach represented an existential threat. Yusuf wanted to exit an unprofitable war.[4]

Back in December 1804, the bashaw had met with Joseph de Souza, the Spanish consul. When he mentioned in passing that he wanted to end the war with the Americans, de Souza responded that the Americans would end the war if they could achieve honorable terms. De Souza understood that Yusuf had mentioned peace with the Americans as a signal for him to write Lear, and so he did. But Lear did not respond. In spring 1805, Dghies, who had opposed the war from the beginning, asked Nissen to provide Lear with his comments that the time was advantageous to begin negotiations:

The situation [. . .] of your unfortunate Countrymen here . . . [is] such that they & their relations in America cannot but look upon it as an act of Humanity to accelerate the conclusion of a peace that again can restore them to their Country. Sidi M Dghies is desirous of a peace, and he wishes that a Negotiation should be renew'd before the commencement of any direct hostilities against this place. His health & particularly the state of his Eyes will oblige him to retire with his family in a short time to the Country, & will not permit him again to return to Town at any future overture or Negotiation of Peace, & he is afraid that being absent he shall not be able so easily to suscitate in the mind of the Bashaw equal peaceful sentiments with his own. . . . He proposes therefore as the most effectual manner of conducting a Negotiation of Peace to send to Tripoli a person properly authorized & furnished with Instructions. . . . Sidi M. Dghhies . . . don't believe it necessary to observe that a sincere & lasting peace is at any time preferable even to a successful War, that War has many chances & that often unforeseen accidents occasion losses.[5]

Finally, in late March 1805, Lear wrote de Souza from Malta, reminding him that the bashaw had rejected Preble's proposals the past year.

"We must now await Proposals from him," Lear confided, "for we cannot again hazard a rejection." He emphasized that "Altho' our Force in this sea is Considerable, and will act with decided Vigour," the United States would negotiate if there was an assurance that the bashaw would conclude an honorable peace. Yet de Souza was hardly a friendly intermediary; he was paying the Spanish carpenters to build gunboats in Tripoli at the dockyard and along the strand, and Cowdery learned that de Souza presented Yusuf with three hundred stands of arms and advised him to keep up the war, to force the Americans to pay his demand.[6]

Nevertheless, through de Souza, the bashaw responded to Lear, demanding $200,000 for peace and ransom, and the return of all the captured Tripolitans. De Souza added that the bashaw's demand was intended as an opening bid in negotiations and Yusuf did not expect the Americans to accept it. At the bashaw's behest, Dghies sent a letter to Bainbridge stating that Yusuf knew the US Navy was providing support to Hamet and he resented it. "As long as the war was a war between America and him," Dghies reported Yusuf saying, "it was a war of interest, that easily might be brought to a conclusion by a lesser or greater sacrifice upon one side or the other, but now it was a war directed against his personal safety, the view of which was his dethronation. He w[oul]d therefore act in a manner that the feelings of the U[nited] States sh[oul]d be hurt in the most tender part, it was in his power to hurt them (meaning the prisoners)." Dghies echoed an earlier warning from Nissen, who wrote Davis that if Eaton and Hamet successfully mounted an attack through the desert, the Americans would "sacrifice your prisoner's life here." Zuchet believed the same thing, writing the Dutch foreign ministry, "If the Bashaw is forced to leave the city, the American prisoners will be killed."[7]

Nissen reported to the foreign ministry in Copenhagen that the bashaw was now "perfectly informed" of the American government's agreement with his brother Hamet and that he knew Eaton had gone off up the Nile to find Hamet. The bashaw understood immediately that Eaton and Hamet meant to attack overland while the American squadron attacked from the sea. Echoing what Dghies must have told him, Nissen wrote, "This gives the war a completely different appearance from what it had previously; the war becomes more personal; formerly, a peace could have been easily brought about by a greater or lesser sacrifice of money on one of the sides, with it seeming now more difficult to perceive how the Americans, after having once made a common cause with Sidi Hamet, will be able to abandon him later."[8]

Lear received the bashaw's $200,000 demand in late April but deemed the terms "inadmissible" because the United States would "never pay a Cent for peace," and ransom would be paid only for the difference between Americans in captivity and Tripolitan prisoners. He decided not to respond. A week later, he wrote Captain John Rodgers that he had received Yusuf's terms "proposed as the *Ground Work* of a nego[t]iation." The letter was "the first direct overture which has been officially made," Lear observed, "& altho much less extravagant than I should have expected; yet is totally inadmissible." De Souza and Dghies had both suggested that if Lear came in person, he could make a deal with Yusuf, but Lear did not think so.[9]

Information about the Eaton campaign in the desert came to Lear, the squadron, and the captives, but it was fragmentary and incomplete. Eaton's army consisted of eight US marines and two midshipmen, forty Christian mercenaries (mostly ethnic Greeks), and several hundred mounted Arab tribesmen, held together by American money and Eaton's charismatic leadership. With this scratch force, and little water and food, Eaton and Hamet made the nearly five-hundred-mile trek from Alexandria to Derne, a coastal city more than five-hundred miles from the city of Tripoli. By the time Eaton's army had reached the Gulf of Bomba, forty miles east of Derne, they had eaten their last rations and his Arab soldiers were about to mutiny, threatening to kill the Americans. The timely arrival of the *Argus* off Bomba in mid-April with supplies saved the expedition, and they continued their trek. On April 27, 1805, Eaton's force attacked and took control of Derne, with gunfire support from three navy ships offshore. A marine lieutenant named Presley O'Bannon planted the Stars and Stripes on the city's battlements, commemorated forever in the Marine Corps hymn, "From the halls of Montezuma to the shores of Tripoli." One marine was killed and two were wounded in the assault; Eaton himself was shot through his wrist. The forces loyal to Yusuf then laid siege to Derne, but Eaton's army managed to hold the city.[10]

The irony of Eaton's expedition is that it was the perception of its failure, not of its actual success, that spurred the United States to negotiate.

As Eaton's little army trudged across the desert, Commodore Barron gleaned from Eaton's dispatches that Hamet lacked "energy and Military talents," and the expedition did not have "sufficient means to move on with firm steps towards [Tripoli]." He inferred that Hamet was "no longer a fit subject for our support and Cooperation." Percival Farquhar, the brother of Richard Farquhar and an adventurer who had returned from the desert march, told Lear, a willing listener, that Eaton was a "madman." That sense of failure suggested to Barron the moment was ripe to initiate negotiations, with Lear in charge. Noting the "Value of such a man as Captain Bainbridge and of his Officers"—Barron said nothing about the value of the sailors and marines laboring as slaves—he asserted that "the liberty and perhaps the lives of so many valuable & estimable Americans ought not to be sacrificed to points of honor, taken in the abstract." Lear finally agreed to negotiate, and on May 22, he sailed from Malta to Tripoli on the frigate *Essex*. That same day, Barron, whose illness still incapacitated him, signed over the squadron command to the next senior captain, John Rodgers. Barron wrote that "if any thing could restore me to Health as by a Charm, it would be the sight of Capt. Bainbridge and his fellow-sufferers restored at length to freedom."[11]

Although Barron saw the Eaton-Hamet expedition as likely to fail, Yusuf saw his regime in increasing danger. He first told Cowdery that "if the Americans drove him to extremities, or attacked his town, he would put every American prisoner to death." Later, he "swore by the prophet of Mecca, that if the Americans brought his brother against him, he would burn to death all the American prisoners," except Cowdery himself, because the doctor had saved his child's life. Yet Cowdery reported that, fearing an internal collapse if the Hamet-Eaton expedition prevailed, the bashaw decided to keep his family—his wives and their many children—in the castle over the coming warm season because "if they must be taken, they would rather fall into the hands of the Americans than the Arabs." On April 19, Yusuf summoned Cowdery to question him about the strength of his American foe. The bashaw asked how many marines the United States had under arms, perhaps the first time a foreign enemy recognized the corps' elite status. Cowdery responded that there were ten thousand, although in fact, the entire Marine Corps in 1805, from the commandant to the lowest drummer boy, contained fewer than five hundred men. Yusuf then asked how many soldiers

America could field, and Cowdery responded there were eighty thousand men (the US Army actually had about three thousand officers and
men), backed by a militia of one million. Confronted by these numbers,
Yusuf "assumed a very serious look."[12]

In the middle of May, a spy in the bashaw's pay arrived in Tripoli from
Malta—proof that the blockade was not as tight as the Americans might
have thought—bearing the (faulty) intelligence that the American fleet
had sailed for Alexandra, where they were to take on board Hamet and
his soldiers and proceed along the coast, taking each town from the sea,
and then assault Tripoli, placing Hamet on the throne. The news spread
like wildfire throughout the city, and Cowdery wrote that Yusuf and his
followers seemed "much agitated."[13] On May 22, the same day that Lear
sailed from Malta bound to Tripoli, the bashaw received a letter by camel
announcing that three weeks earlier, Hamet and the Americans had
taken Derne. Zuchet wrote to Amsterdam that the news was "devastat-
ing" to Yusuf and "produced alarm in the Regency and in the whole
country, although the Bashaw deludes himself that his enemies will soon
be destroyed by his troops." Yusuf called a meeting of the *divan* to discuss
whether the American captives should be put to death, but the *divan* decided to postpone a decision. Two days later, assuming that Eaton's army
was inexorably approaching, Yusuf told Cowdery that if he could have
peace by giving up his American prisoners, he "would gladly do it, without the consideration of money." That was an enormous admission for
a bashaw to make, since the foundation of his regime's treasury was tribute. Yusuf was running out of money and could afford to feed his court
and janissaries just one meal per day, depending on what he called his
"wealthy Turks" to feed his troops.[14]

On May 26, the frigates *Essex*, *Constitution*, and *President*, and the
brig *Vixen*, sailed close inshore to Tripoli, fired two guns, and hoisted a
white flag, indicating a desire to parley. The castle raised a white flag and
sent off a boat to the *Essex*. On board were several Tripolitan leaders,
Spanish Consul de Souza, and Leon Farfara, the merchant who acted as
interpreter. After the negotiators were on the *Essex* two hours, the boat
took them to the *Constitution*, where Colonel Lear awaited. Lear told de
Souza that the bashaw's last offer of $200,000 for peace and ransom, and
the return of all the captured Tripolitans, was "totally out of the question, and must be relinquished before I w[oul]d consent to move one

step in the business." Lear demanded "unequivocal evidence that they would be put a side" before he would agree to go ashore and told de Souza he should come back the next day only "if the Bashaw was desireous of having peace on terms which we could admit." De Souza left the ship and went ashore.

Rumors swirled. Cowdery wrote that de Souza "returned at evening with the joyful news of a prospect of peace. There was a visible change, from gloominess to joy, in the countenance of all the Turks." They were not the only ones. Ray exulted that "[o]ur men were in paroxisms of joy." The next day, Cowdery wrote "[w]e were all agitated alternately by hope and despair. The terraces and every eminence in town, were covered with people of all classes and ages, who were looking for" Lear to land in the city, to continue negotiations. According to Cowdery, the bashaw showed the greatest eagerness for peace, aware that his treasury was nearly empty and his people were dissatisfied by the lack of bread.[15]

On May 29, de Souza returned to the *Constitution* with new terms: no payment for peace per se, but the bashaw demanded $130,000 to ransom the American captives, and the return of all his subjects *gratis*. Through de Souza, Yusuf sent a message to Lear and Rodgers:

I know that the exertions of your squadron this summer will be sufficient to reduce my capital; but recollect that I have upwards of three hundred of your countrymen in my hands; and I candidly tell you that, if you persevere in driving me to the last extremity, I shall retire with them to a castle about ninety miles in the interior of the country, which I have prepared for their confinement and my own security. Money is not my object at present, but a peace on terms that will not disgrace me hereafter.

The reduction in Yusuf's demands, and his clear suggestion of a willingness to deal, encouraged Lear, who laid down in writing the American terms, as an ultimatum: (1) there should be an exchange of prisoners, man for man, (2) the bashaw would send all the American captives to the squadron, (3) the Tripolitans held as prisoners would be brought over from Syracuse and delivered as soon as possible, (4) because the bashaw held about three hundred Americans, and as the United States held about one hundred Tripolitans, the United States would pay "the balance in his favour 60,000 Dollars," almost exactly $200 per captive, and agree to a treaty of peace on mutually beneficial terms. De Souza returned to Tripoli that evening. Days passed with the *divan* meeting nearly continuously. On May 31, the bashaw sent a messenger to Cowdery that the negotiators had reached basic terms for peace, and asked Cowdery to tell Bainbridge, which he did "to the great joy of the officers."[16]

However, there was a hitch. The next day, June 1, Dghies sent for Nissen, and when he arrived at court told him that the negotiations with the Americans were confused because Lear had demanded the freeing of all the American prisoners before Yusuf received money or the return of his subjects. Dghies then summoned Bainbridge to explain that position. Bainbridge offered to bridge the divide between the parties if he were allowed to go offshore to talk to Lear. He gave his word of honor that he would return. Yusuf and his *divan* could not credit the notion that the captain's word would bind him. But in an act of moral courage, Dghies and Nissen declared themselves jointly responsible for Bainbridge's good faith, Dghies even pledging his own life that Bainbridge would return. No captive had ever been allowed to leave on parole, and the bashaw is said to have muttered that it was inconceivable that a Christian would keep his word and return to captivity, but he gave his permission.[17]

The brig *Vixen* stood in under the bashaw's batteries and lay to, waiting for a boat coming from shore. At noon, the boat came off. According to the *Vixen*'s steward, Hezekiah Loomis, "to our joy," there was Bainbridge, and when he came aboard, he "exhibited a spirit of joy and gladness, mixed with humiliation which I never saw before." Loomis was struck by his "pale meagre countenance." Bainbridge went from the *Vixen* to the *Constitution* to see Lear and Rodgers. To one American, "it was the most affecting thing I ever beheld to see him and Commodore Rodgers meet," but before sunset, it was just as distressing to see Bainbridge leave the ship to begin the return trip to the castle for another night in prison. His return, in Nissen's telling, "was probably not a little to the astonishment of the [bashaw] himself." While aboard the *Constitution*, Bainbridge told Lear that the bashaw desired to end the war more than exacting more money for the captives, and Lear should not insist on the delivery of the captives to the squadron before concluding a treaty. Lear made clear to Bainbridge that the demand for a prior release of the prisoners was not an absolute, and when Bainbridge told that to Yusuf and Dghies, they became enraged at de Souza, thinking he had lied to them. The bashaw asked Nissen to negotiate on his behalf instead of de Souza, even giving him a power of attorney with his seal to deliver to Lear.[18]

Having Nissen negotiate with Lear made it clear to everyone that Yusuf wanted peace; the bashaw knew that Nissen had supported the Americans throughout their captivity. Nissen and Lear hashed out the terms. The bashaw and his *divan* accepted $60,000 (which Lear did not have at hand; he had to draw the money, in silver and gold, from Higgins in Malta) for ransom. The Americans insisted that nothing in the treaty would suggest that the money was for peace or for annual tribute, an important principle that would guide American policy with the Barbary powers in the future. The three hundred captive Americans would be swapped for the Tripolitans the squadron had captured (there were eighty-three), whom a ship from the squadron fetched from Sicily. The Americans agreed to evacuate Derne. The final sticking point was Hamet. Yusuf was anxious about his brother and wanted leverage over him, refusing to allow Hamet's family to leave Tripoli to join him. Lear reached a secret side deal with Yusuf that, when it was revealed in 1807, caused a small explosion in Congress: Lear agreed to allow Yusuf to hold Hamet's family for four years, as security against Hamet trying to overturn the regime. The *divan* agreed to the treaty's terms, and the bashaw used his personal signet on the articles to show his assent.[19]

On June 2, Bainbridge wrote Cowdery that the parties had agreed on peace terms and that every officer, sailor, and marine would soon be allowed to board the ships of the squadron. Cowdery gathered the sailors and marines around him and read Bainbridge's letter aloud. Then the bashaw released Bainbridge so he could go among his men. With emotions that can only be guessed at, he told them the treaty had been agreed on but not yet signed, and they should not exult too much in case it should all come to naught. In fact, Cowdery noted in his diary that the overseers still insisted the crew be put "to hard work, and many of them [were] flogged."[20]

But June 2 was their last day as slaves. On June 3, Lear went ashore. Hundreds, perhaps thousands, of people packed the streets, including the *Philadelphia*'s officers. The sight of them, Lear wrote, "was grateful to my soul." In the bashaw's castle, Lear and Yusuf signed the peace treaty, signified by "royal salutes" of twenty-one guns thundering from the ships of the squadron and the Tripolitan batteries. It was, perhaps, the best possible deal the United States could have negotiated. Still, having abandoned Hamet and not allowed Eaton's army to march on Tripoli to try to topple Yusuf, many then and later questioned the deal. Eaton was the first. Writing Secretary Smith, he said he thought the deal was "precipitate." How could it be, he asked rhetorically, that the United States would send such a formidable squadron into the Mediterranean, "to *negotiate* without *showing itself* before the enemy's port?" Eaton thought that the navy need only have "appeared off the place, [and] I have no doubt the effect would have been a peace *without money.*" He upbraided "Aunt Lear," Barron, and everyone else who supported the treaty. Many claimed that if Eaton had been allowed to continue his trek across the Sahara and Rodgers's squadron been allowed a season to bombard Tripoli, Yusuf would have been forced to free the captives without a penny of tribute and sign any peace treaty that Lear put before him.[21]

That was not the opinion of Nissen or Zuchet nor was it the captives' own view. Months later, Secretary Smith wrote that he had talked with many of the *Philadelphia*'s officers when they reported to him on their return, "all [of whom] say positively that if Lear had persisted in refusing paying a ransom for them peace would not have been made and they would all have been certainly massacred—The Bashaw said again & again that having killed a father & brother he would not have any scruples in killing a few infidels." After nineteen months' captivity, Ray reported that the men were "sickly, and emaciated," and called their condition at the moment of their freedom to be "weak, palid, and broken with toils." President Jefferson's view on first learning of the treaty was that "Eaton's fire was all spent at Derne," and "the peace is a subject of satisfaction." Although there was criticism of the $60,000 ransom, the US Senate ratified the treaty on April 17, 1806, by a 21-8 vote.[22]

What finally persuaded the bashaw to seek peace? Samuel Barron's secretary, probably speaking for the ailing commodore, gave credit to the navy, writing that "[t]he blockade of the Enemy's Harbor has been kept up closely & without intermission—so as almost to preclude the possibility of his receiving any sort of Supplies and there is every reason to believe that great distress is felt by the Inhabitants." Wallace Wormeley, a midshipman in Tripoli captivity who, oddly enough, later became a Marine Corps officer, wrote that the news of Eaton's defeat of Yusuf's army at Derne caused "the greatest terror and consternation . . . throughout the whole town of Tripoli." The bashaw knew his treasury and his people were both exhausted, and he "dared not levy new contributions for fear of their revolting and joining Hamet." Were it not for Eaton's capture of Derne, he concluded, "we should have been to this day prisoners in Tripoli." Thomas Jefferson certainly agreed that Eaton's capture of Derne was decisive, telling Congress, "[A]n operation by land, by a small band of our countrymen, & others engaged for the occasion, in conjunction with the troops of the Ex-Bashaw of that country, gallantly conducted by our late Consul Eaton, and their successful enterprise on the city of Derne, contributed doubtless to the impression which produced peace."[23]

Despite the heroics of men like Preble, Decatur, and Somers, the blockade and bombardments of Tripoli in 1804 did not force Yusuf to terms. The loss of Derne to Eaton's small army unsettled the bashaw, and when his own forces could not retake the city, he wisely shut down the war and preserved his reign by returning the captives for the modest ransom payment of $60,000. Although Lear and by extension the Jefferson administration would soon be attacked for "selling out" Hamet, regime change was never the goal of American policy. Tripoli was too far from America and relatively unimportant for Jefferson and Madison to care who ruled there. The goals of the United States were to free the captives and not pay annual tribute, as part of a broader vision of establishing freedom of the seas. Once the *Philadelphia* went aground and three hundred Americans were taken captive, almost every American understood that to redeem them would require money. Rather than risk the bashaw's murdering the captives, or their dying of malnutrition and disease, Lear was right to make the peace he made. The very first newspaper report on the treaty captured this dynamic nicely, observing the bashaw

was heard to declare, that if [Eaton] should approach nearer to Tripoli, he would massacre every American and every Christian in his power. Mr. Lear has been blamed for making a treaty precipitately and before the appearance of the fleet, but as the danger of the prisoners was imminent, and their release the principle object of the war, it would appear that no moment that could obtain this desirable end was to be wasted in calculations of future success, and that in embracing the very first opening to release them from the cruelty of the bashaw, and shutting the door forever on the return of his caprice or the chance of future events, he acted with the wisdom and precision of a politician and patriot.[24]

In 1806, when the ink on the treaty was barely dry, the first book written about the war concluded, "We must wink at arrangements which reason resists as an insult, and subscribe to smaller evils to avoid greater." The treaty was admittedly no great victory for principle. Paying money for freeing captives was the opposite of Jefferson's vision and the opposite of what would become a stated fixture of American policy. It was expedient but lacked honor. The ransom money allowed Yusuf to save face with his *divan* and soldiers, and Tripoli never tested American mettle again. The four naval campaigns, and particularly the 1804 effort under Preble, had provided the navy with a showcase for its bravery and professionalism, but the failure to provide a decisive victory against the weakest of the Barbary powers only confirmed for Jefferson and his Republicans the limitations and expense of navies; Jefferson, who had already begun to build a fleet of gunboats to provide coastal and harbor defense, expanded that effort enormously and dismantled much of the high seas navy. A decade later, when the US Navy would return to fight another Barbary war in 1815, to try to end slave taking and paying tribute forever, the opponent was the most powerful Barbary power, Algiers, not Tripoli.[25]

All that lay in the future. An unidentified officer wrote home that as soon as the bashaw accepted Lear's terms, the "bolts and bars" of their prison doors were unlocked, and the overseers, who had looked on them with "morose insulting looks," which the *Philadelphia*'s officers returned with feelings of "equal contempt and indignation," were now gone. The officers walked to the American consul house for their last night ashore. The cannon from the US squadron and the Tripolitan shore batteries were "now roaring in mutual joy and congratulation," and Spence looked forward to going on board the next day, although he expected to be the last man to embark, because he had to settle accounts with Nissen. Some of his brother officers were "almost frantic with joy" as the iron discipline of the past nineteen months broke down and the officers were drinking large amounts of *aguardiente*. Lear went ashore and raised the Stars and Stripes at the US consul house, which the castle saluted with another twenty-one guns, answered with twenty-one guns by the *Constitution*. The next day, Rodgers dashed off a note to Commodore Barron, announcing that peace was at hand, and "Our business here is so far finished as not to leave me a hope of receiving a Button for my services, much [less] a Medal."[26]

On June 4, the day all the American captives were released, they could not take the boats and barges out to their friends in the squadron offshore until the late afternoon because they all had got drunk the night before. Lear informed Rodgers that "the intoxication of Liberty & Liquor has deranged the faculties" of the newly freed sailors. The next day, officers from the squadron went ashore to sightsee, and they sat down to a feast, courtesy of Yusuf. The batteries fired periodic salutes in honor of the peace, answered by the ships of the squadron. Over the next days, Cowdery took his final leave from Yusuf, who seemed distraught at his departure, and Dr. Ridgely, who bravely agreed to stay as the acting consul of the United States, went back ashore. The *Vixen* ventured inside the treacherous rocks off the harbor and anchored off the bashaw's castle. An hour before sunset, the bashaw and his cavalry escort rode onto the beach, and the horsemen put on a demonstration of wheeling in formation, and firing and reloading while riding in a circle at full speed, with the riders jumping off their horses at the same spot they had started from. Loomis was impressed by the spectacle.[27]

The Americans had one last contretemps with Beaussier. After peace was proclaimed, two seamen, John Green and David Nichols, asserted they were French and sought protection from the consul. Presumably, these were two of the four men whom Beaussier had identified in November 1803 as Frenchmen who should be released to him. Still, it was odd that Green and Nichols waited until their captivity was over to contact Beaussier. He gave them French protection and had the audacity to ask Rodgers for their back pay. Instead, Rodgers asked him to return the men, and not knowing of the French consul's earlier approach to Yusuf, asserted that Beaussier had never claimed them for the nineteen months they were in slavery, when doing so "might have aided the cause of humanity." Beaussier refused to produce the two men. Rodgers then blasted

Green and Nichols as deserters who broke their oath of allegiance to the United States, writing that affording protection to them made Beaussier an "instrument of a perjury," offending God, honor, and truth. But Green and Nichols remained under the protection of the tricolor and did not return to America.[28]

The sailors of the *Philadelphia* had one final surprise before departing Tripoli. The crew wrote Bainbridge about an unnamed Neapolitan slave who was one of their wardens but had treated them well. They wanted to free the man, whom they called "a poor fellow sufferer," and asked Bainbridge to deduct from their accrued pay $300, a little more than one dollar each, the price the Tripolitans demanded for his ransoming. Spence advanced the money, the enslaved man was redeemed, and one of the American ships conveyed him to Naples. It was a magnificent, altruistic gesture that demonstrated the tars' essential decency and humanity, which was not lost on American newspapers when they learned of it.[29]

Five Americans converted to Islam during the nineteen-month captivity—Thomas Prince, John Wilson, Peter West, one of the Thomas Smiths, and Lewis Hacksener. On June 3, the bashaw called the five "renegades" before his *divan*, announced that peace had been concluded, and said the captive sailors were about to be freed and leave Tripoli. He said that if any of the five converts wished, they could leave with the squadron. All except Wilson told Yusuf they wanted to return to America. Wilson, more suspicious or cynical than the others, thanked the bashaw but assured him he preferred Tripoli to America and Islam to Christianity, and wished to stay and serve him. Yusuf welcomed Wilson. He then ordered the other four driven into the desert under guard. As they passed by, Ray saw their faces filled with "horror and despair." There is no further record of them.[30]

Seven of the *Philadelphia*'s sailors died in, or immediately after, their Barbary captivity. John Hilliard died in January 1804 of dysentery. James Anderson, who also died that month, had been sick since the time the Americans were captured, but it is unclear what caused his death.[31] John Morrison died in April 1804 from a work accident, while loading timber onto a wagon, when the load collapsed on him. Morrison, who had been captain of the foretop, lingered for a few days in great pain, but Dr. Ridgely was allowed to see him only the night before he died. As Morrison lay on his deathbed, he was beaten by an overseer, who thought he was feigning injury and called him an infidel. In September 1804, John McDonald, whom Cowdery referred to as "M'Donah," died of consumption (tuberculosis). Edward Gorman died in October 1804 of an unknown cause. Jacob Dowdesher died in February 1805 in a construction accident when part of a wall fell on him. Cowdery noted sardonically that the "only consolation we received from the Turks, was, that he was *amak deric* and *sansafedah*—that is D—n his mother, he has got no faith, *Romo Kelfi*—He is a Christian dog." After their liberation, John Garrabant died at sea on June 14, and James Ingerson died at sea on June 19, perhaps of the effects of malnutrition. Ingerson had come aboard the *Philadelphia* at Gibraltar, and Bainbridge essentially had impressed him into the navy.[32]

None of the Americans died of the plague, the contagion that all the European ports feared from the Barbary world, and none died of typhus, the lice-borne "gaol fever" that killed thousands of Americans on prison ship hulks in Wallabout Bay off Brooklyn during the Revolution. In the face of malnutrition, the infestation of lice, the rarity of bathing, and the absence of clean clothes, the low mortality rate of the sailors and marines is remarkable. In contrast, in an eleven-month cruise the frigate *Essex* took to the East Indies and back, from January through November 1800, fifteen of her crew died of fevers, dysentery, accidents, and unknown causes, although the *Essex* saw no combat nor did any epidemic range through her people. On a sixteen-month cruise to the Mediterranean in 1802–03, the frigate *New York*, which saw only slight combat, had thirty men die, mostly of fevers, dysentery, and accidents. Based solely on mortality rates, it is hard not to conclude that serving in the navy in the age of sail could be as dangerous as the brutalized treatment of a slave in Barbary.[33]

Before they left Tripoli, Bainbridge and his officers wrote a note to Nicholas Nissen. Thanking him for his kindness, they said they would never forget him. The officers contributed more than $700 to commission a silver urn for him, to be fashioned in London. Eighteen months later, David Porter delivered the urn in Livorno, as Nissen was making his way home to Denmark. In a note he handed to Porter for Bainbridge, Nissen depreciated what he had done for the Americans and asked Bainbridge to thank all the officers for the gift, which would serve to recall the friends he expected never to see again.[34]

The *Constitution* sailed from what Spence called "the land of bondage" on June 6, first stopping at Malta, though no one was allowed ashore for fear of disease. Navy agent Higgins hired a boat and sent out to Spence a package containing ten shirts and cravats, which Polly had sent him nearly two years earlier. But to his disappointment, Spence found no letters awaiting him; he had not received a single line from Polly or any friend since he had left America.[35]

A few days later, the *Constitution* arrived in Syracuse, where Bainbridge faced a naval court of inquiry into the loss of the *Philadelphia*. All the commissioned and warrant officers from the *Philadelphia* testified that the frigate ran aground despite Bainbridge having leadsmen sounding the depth, and there was ample evidence that the ship lacked an accurate chart of the area. Their testimony was clear that Bainbridge displayed coolness and professionalism during the disaster and tried everything to get the ship off the rocks. He emerged from the trial with his reputation undamaged: the court was "decidedly of opinion, that Captain William Bainbridge acted with fortitude and conduct in the loss of his ship" and that "no degree of censure should attach itself to him from that event."[36]

On July 4, the newly freed officers and crew celebrated Independence Day in Sicily. Ray composed a poem, "Independence," for the occasion, which was sung by the collected officers of the squadron to the tune of "Mason's Daughter." A few days later, Bainbridge, most of the *Philadelphia*'s officers, and ninety of her crew sailed for America on the frigate *President*, the officers as passengers and the crew working as part of the ship's company. The *Philadelphia* sailors and marines not going home on the *President* (including Ray) were scattered among the other ships in the squadron, but all of them eventually made it safely to America.[37]

The first word of the peace came to America by way of the merchant brig *Eliza*, under a Captain Taylor, which arrived in Charleston, South Carolina, on August 22, thirty days from Gibraltar. Taylor reported that a month earlier, a Portuguese warship had hailed the *Eliza*, reporting that Tripoli had made peace with the Americans.[38]

Captain Bainbridge, along with Lieutenant Jacob Jones, Surgeon's Mates Cowdery and Harwood, Purser Spence, and about one hundred other officers and sailors from the *Philadelphia*, landed at Hampton, Virginia, in early September. Their trip north was slowed, Spence wrote, by "the hospitality of the towns through which we passed; the inhabitants of which gave us every proof of the sincere pleasure they feel at our deliverance from captivity." In Richmond on September 16, Bainbridge and his officers were the guests at a gala dinner at the Eagle Tavern, and the company enjoyed "unfeigned hilarity," no doubt aided by seventeen toasts, including to the "officers and crew of the *Philadelphia*—Magnanimous in Captivity, they supported the dignity of the American character." Before they reached Fredericksburg, Virginia, local civic and military leaders and the Spotsylvania Troop of Cavalry went on the road to greet them. The local militia fired off a seventeen-gun salute on Bainbridge's arrival, and such was the cheering and joy on every face in the crowd as the procession entered the town that Bainbridge was overcome, and tears rolled down his cheeks as he returned their salute. The next day, Fredericksburg hosted another public dinner in honor of Bainbridge. The officers arrived in Washington on September 19, where Bainbridge reported to Secretary Smith. Bainbridge spoke about the generosity of Nicholas Nissen, which resulted in Congress passing a resolution formally thanking the Danish consul. The citizens of Washington turned out for yet another public dinner for Bainbridge and his officers, where the Marine Corps band played and the guests joined in patriotic songs in between seventeen toasts, including encomiums to the navy, to "Men in Captivity," to "Captivity Triumphant," and to Lear, to Eaton, and to Nissen.[39]

Spence was kept busy settling accounts, which was a nightmare because most of the ship's papers were lost when she was captured, and over the nineteen months of captivity, food, clothes, and credit had come from Preble, Barron, Pulis, Nissen, Higgins, Davis, and Lear. A letter Secretary Smith wrote while Spence was still in captivity provides an understanding of how onerous Spence's task must have been. Smith assumed Spence had "the accounts of the crew," and that he knew "what is due each individual, and the component parts of the ration." While they all were in captivity, Spence was forbidden to issue food and slops beyond the "rations allowed by Law, and in the purchase and issues of Clothing he must be governed entirely by Captain Bainbridge or in his absence by Lt. Porter." For clothing, he was required to "keep the original Bills of purchase, upon which he may charge for his Trouble and responsibility 10 per Cent," but those "Bills must be signed by Capt. Bainbridge or Lieut. Porter, and must be exhibited to this department in the settlement of The Accounts;" but for provisions, which also had to be signed and submitted, "he is to charge nothing for his Trouble."[40]

As he made his way home to see his wife, Susan, and baby daughter, Bainbridge wrote a report about his officers. He was generous with praise. Porter was "one of the best Officers, I ever knew," and Jacob Jones was "a brave good Officer and a correct man." He recommended two of his midshipmen, James Gibbon and Daniel Patterson, for promotion. James Biddle had already been promoted to lieutenant, and Bainbridge wrote that from his "high sense of honor and talents [he] must one day be conspicuous in the service of his Country." Bainbridge saved his greatest accolade for Midshipman Robert Gamble, who "will make a second DECATUR." On the other hand, perhaps the school for officers had been taken to an extreme in the case of Midshipman William Cutbush, whose "head is always too much engrossed (to make a good Sailor) with the works of Sir Isaac Newton—he is an excellent mathematician." In a postscript, Bainbridge noted that when next called to duty, he wanted Gibbon, Patterson, Biddle, or Gamble to serve with him, but added that "he should feel pleasure in having any of the others."[41]

One might think that once they arrived home, the *Philadelphia*'s sailors and marines would be given an enormous celebration. After all, they had been slaves in Barbary for nineteen months, and they had captured the country's imagination. Now, except for the seven who had died, the five who had converted to Islam and stayed, and the two who decided they were French, 250 sailors and marines were coming home safe.[42] There were, of course, joyous private reunions with family and friends, and some public turnout for the returning captives. In Annapolis, Maryland, welcoming home Nicholas Harwood, there was, one newspaper reported, "general rejoicing," a discharge of eighteen guns, a parade, and a drill of militia on College Green. At social events, such as dinners after militia musters, toasts were made to the returning captives.[43] The theater also marked the captives' return. In Baltimore, there were several performances of a children's dance, "The Sailors' Return from Tripoli," which, an advertisement stated, was "Founded on the Favorite Ballet of 'The Sailor's Landlady; Or, Jack in Distress.'"[44] At a theater in Philadelphia, a new song was sung, "The American Captives Emancipation." After expressing joy that they were no longer slaves and could be "jovial tars" again, one verse rang out:

> *The blessings of Peace, let us hail in loud chorus,*
> *Which to Freedom and plenty again does restore us,*
> *Whilst to sweethearts and wives, & our dear native shore,*
> *We haste with delight, for the war is now o'er.*[45]

Yet there was no massive national celebration, no day of thanksgiving, and no reception at the White House.[46] Jefferson was at Monticello when the returning captives arrived in Washington, but he apparently felt no urgency to return to the capital to greet them. For all the love of man Jefferson professed, he was a Virginia aristocrat, and there was a gaping social divide between him and uncouth and boisterous sailors. Inviting the crew into the White House would have meant having hundreds of rough jack tars as his guests. It is difficult to imagine the slave-owning president lauding the free black sailors among the crew, had he feted them at the White House. Although Robert Smith greeted the *Philadelphia*'s officers as they passed through Washington, there is no evidence that Jefferson met any of the captives returning from Tripoli.[47]

The crew of the *Philadelphia* was not treated so warmly by Congress either. In December 1805, James Hogg, a quartermaster, and five sailors (William Jones, Charles Simmons, Jacob Farmer, Henry McClaskey, and Jonathan Butler) presented a petition to the House of Representatives on behalf of the crew, asking for compensation for the clothing they received during their captivity, and a small sum for tobacco and other articles, which they characterized as "jail money," that Spence had deducted from their accumulated pay. One congressman anonymously wrote that he was "grieved" to hear the petition "from our brave fellows who fell into the hands of the Barbarians of Tripoli" read on the House floor, complaining the "small pittance" had been withheld. What the petitioners called "the comfort of sailors"—their stipend to buy tobacco—was unpaid, and if deserving under the law, it was "abominable neglect." But the Navy Department made clear there was no such thing as "jail money," the House Committee on Claims reported unfavorably, and the crew withdrew the petition before a vote was taken. From the day they entered the service to the day they were discharged on arrival in the United States, the sailors and marines were paid only what the law required, their accumulated back pay and unused rations, which for the petitioners ranged as high as $502.73 for Hogg to a low of $216.89 for Farmer. Congress was not interested in giving them any special compensation for having been slaves in Barbary. Charles Simmons tried again, presenting another petition to the House two months later, signed by himself on behalf of the rest of the crew, "praying [for] relief in consideration of [their] present distress, occasioned by sufferings sustained while in captivity in Tripoli," but Congress refused to award the crew any additional money.[48]

The nineteen-month captivity of three hundred Americans, in which the officers were placed in a dark, fetid dungeon for more than a year and the enlisted people were treated as slaves and beaten by their overseers, may have caused them psychological issues. Each man had the benefit of the months-long sail back to the United States with the camaraderie of their shipmates, free to drink their grog and swap their stories, to try to set themselves to rights. But if they had lingering fears or anxiety about their experience when they arrived home, the period of the early republic was not an era of psychologists or social workers. There is no record of how many of the crew turned their backs on the sea or decided to remain in the navy or ship out on merchant vessels. Just as the backgrounds of most of the sailors and marines of the *Philadelphia* are obscure, so too is it unclear what happened to them after they returned to freedom.[49]

In reporting on the return of the captives, President Jefferson congratulated Congress "on the liberation of our fellow-citizens who were stranded on the coast of Tripoli and made prisoners of war. In a government bottomed on the will of all the life and liberty of every individual citizen become interesting to all. In the treaty, therefore, which has concluded our warfare with that State an article for the ransom of our citizens has been agreed to." It was odd phrasing for the deal Lear made, still odder that Jefferson thought it needed to be bottomed on democratic theory. People living under monarchs cared about the lives and liberty of their countrymen in Barbary slavery as much as people living in republics. The "will of all" Americans in the liberty of the *Philadelphia* crew made no difference in the timing or result of the negotiations; in fact, the initial popular ardor to ransom the prisoners had been cooled by the government. Still, William Ray was moved by the words of his hero Jefferson, using the sentence, "In a government bottomed on the will of all the life and liberty of every individual citizen become interesting to all," in the introductory passage of his memoir *Horrors of Slavery.*[50]

The 1805 treaty with Tripoli allowed American trade to flow relatively unscathed into the Mediterranean, but only briefly, as Jefferson's embargo of December 1807, and then the War of 1812, curtailed most American international trade. But the essential aspect of the treaty—peace without annual tribute—was an important milestone in American foreign policy. The Tripolitan War showed the European world that the United States could project a modest power overseas and that it would not limit itself to the accepted international norms of dutifully paying tribute to "piratical" regimes. After the War of 1812 ended in 1815, the United States would send squadrons under Decatur and Bainbridge to deal with the largest Barbary power, Algiers, to end the slave-taking-and-ransom business.

The experience of three hundred American captives in Tripoli more than two centuries ago still resonates, in part because the United States finds itself entangled in the Arab and Muslim world and has faced situations where its citizens have been held captive by foreign states and terrorist groups. Never have so many Americans been held as prisoners in a Muslim country as when the *Philadelphia* went aground, however, and yet almost all of them survived and made it home safely. Even though two centuries ago, Americans referred to their Islamic captors as barbarians, and were appalled by the mercenary aspect of slavery in Barbary, other wars, before and after the Tripolitan War, show much more barbarity toward prisoners of war, some inflicted by Americans on Americans. During the Revolution, thousands of Americans, prisoners of war to the British, died of malnutrition, typhus, and willful neglect in so-called "sugar houses" in Manhattan and on prison ship hulks in the East River. During the Civil War, forty-five thousand Union soldiers, prisoners of war to the Confederacy, suffered from hunger, filthy water, exposure, and disease just at Andersonville Prison, Georgia, killing thirteen thousand through starvation, scurvy, typhoid, and dysentery. During

World War II, about 30 percent of American GIs, sailors, and marines who were prisoners of war to the Japanese died of malnutrition or untreated tropical diseases, or by summary execution. While much of the low mortality experienced by the *Philadelphia*'s sailors and marines represented the fortuitous absence of diseases that often ravaged the populations of the Maghreb, it also is true that because of the mercenary aspect of slavery in North Africa—it was a cash business—the bashaw had an incentive to keep the Americans alive, since each one represented a monetary reward.

The moral from the *Philadelphia* captives' saga is that if the United States had refused to pay ransom and continued with force, more Americans would have died. Even if Eaton's motley army had the cohesion and strength to reach Tripoli, hundreds of miles of desert from Derne, and then was able to beat the bashaw's army—both questionable propositions—there would have been American casualties. Those who thought deposing Yusuf and rescuing the hundreds of captive Americans would be easy or even bloodless were unrealistic. If Yusuf had been pushed to the last extremity, few on the spot doubted that he would kill the captive crew. It would have been a pyrrhic victory if Eaton were able to take Tripoli and establish Hamet on the throne if, in doing so, the three hundred American sailors and marines were slaughtered in cold blood.

"Send in the marines" has been the stuff of American legend and glamorized by Hollywood. Negotiating with hostage takers seems weak and unprincipled, succumbing to blackmail that only invites more. But force does not always work. On April 24, 1980, President Jimmy Carter sent in the army's Delta Force to attempt to end the Iran hostage crisis by rescuing fifty-two US embassy staff held captive in Tehran. The plan called for a direct assault on the embassy building, with the extraordinary risks such an assault entails to the attackers and the hostages. The operation was aborted when several of the helicopters failed at the landing site, and an accident resulted in the deaths of eight airmen and marines. The mission failed, the debacle damaged American prestige throughout the world, and the failure was a substantial reason Carter lost reelection in 1980.[51] The true lesson of the *Philadelphia* captives is that every foreign hostage situation differs; that using force has risks and costs; that typically, diplomacy and force must be used together; and that in some circumstances, ransom must not be removed as an option.

PEACE AND THE RETURN

But the saga of the American sailors in Tripoli is not just about lessons to be drawn in dealing with foreign hostage taking. In broad strokes, the experience of the *Philadelphia* sailors is a timeless story of American honor and endurance in adversity. For the officers, honor meant that each man refused to accept private ransoming until they all could leave together. It meant repeated attempts to escape, even though they knew that success was nearly impossible. Leaving aside the five sailors who "turned Turk," the sailors and marines displayed their honor through resilience. There they were, stranded in Barbary, thousands of miles from home, in an intensely alien world, underfed and sometimes beaten. Yet they remained unbowed. They drank wine and sang carols on Christmas Eve, mocked their guards despite the beatings, danced and cut capers even though they were hungry, built furnaces for hot-shot designed to crack and fail, engaged in collective protest, struck for better conditions, and pooled their pay to free a hapless Neapolitan slave. Their guards claimed the Americans "were the most difficult to manage of any people they had ever seen," obstreperous and contrarian. The *Philadelphia*'s people set an example of endurance for subsequent generations of American prisoners of war in other foreign wars to follow. They may have been treated as slaves, but they did not lose their humanity. If they did not have a chance to fight for their freedom when the *Philadelphia* went aground, they showed their mettle for the nineteen months they were prisoners to the bashaw.[52]

~ EPILOGUE ~

AFTER 1816, WHEN A BRITISH NAVAL EXPEDITION bombarded Algiers and forced the dey of Algiers to free all his captives, the Barbary powers, including Tripoli, slowly abandoned corsair activities. Without ransom or tribute, however, Yusuf Karamanli was unable to find a new basis for Tripoli's economy. As he aged and his power waned, his three sons vied to succeed him. In 1832, Yusuf abdicated in favor of his son Ali, but civil war soon began. In 1835, the sultan sent troops, who deposed and exiled Ali, ended the Karamanli dynasty, and made Tripoli a province of the Ottoman Empire. Yusuf died in 1838. In 1911, the Italians invaded and seized the coastal regions of Tripolitania, which they called Libya.

Mohammed Dghies, the cultivated minister to the bashaw and friend to the captives, died in Smyrna in 1837, reportedly blind or nearly so, after filling diplomatic roles for the sultan.

Edward Preble returned to America as a national hero. He was lionized and feted throughout the country. A rumor, false but widely bruited about, was that Jefferson asked him to be the secretary of the navy. Preble stayed in uniform, supervising the building of gunboats in Portland, Maine, near his home. His health sharply declined, and he died in 1807 at age 46.

On William Bainbridge's return to America, after a shore command, the navy granted his request for a furlough. As the master of a merchant ship sailing to the Baltic, he had a reunion with Nicholas Nissen in Copenhagen. His crews continued to regard him as a harsh disciplinarian. During the change-of-command ceremony aboard the frigate *Constitution* in 1812, the crew broke ranks, begging their affable captain, Isaac Hull, to stay. Humiliated, Bainbridge called out, demanding to know if any man who had sailed with him before would refuse now; several voices piped up that they *had* sailed under him before and would refuse now. Nevertheless, as captain of the *Constitution*, Bainbridge finally met with success, sinking the British frigate *Java* off the coast of Brazil. When war loomed with Algiers in 1815, Bainbridge longed for the command, but Stephen Decatur arrived with another squadron first, won the war, and negotiated peace before Bainbridge arrived. Bainbridge never forgave Decatur for what he took to be a humiliation. Five years later, he encouraged Decatur into a duel with a fellow commodore, which mortally wounded Decatur and appalled the nation. As he aged, Bainbridge became addicted to alcohol and opiates. He died in 1833.

Upon his return to Denmark in 1807, Nicholas Nissen was appointed to a new office: third director of the Bank and Exchange Office in Copenhagen. In 1815, he was sent back to Tripoli to negotiate a new treaty with Yusuf Karamanli. Nissen, who never married, was promoted to councillor of state, and then named a royal councillor to King Frederick VI. He died in Copenhagen in 1836.

In the War of 1812, David Porter commanded the frigate *Essex*, which he sailed into the Pacific in 1813, destroying the British whaling fleet. But Porter surrendered the *Essex* after she was cornered and pummeled by British warships off Valparaiso, Chile, in March 1814. After the war, Porter served as a navy commissioner and then commanded the West Indies squadron, but he was court-martialed in 1826 for landing an assault force at Fajardo, Puerto Rico (a Spanish colony), to exact an apology for the jailing of one of his officers. Porter resigned and then served, unhappily, as the commander of the Mexican navy (1826–29). President Andrew Jackson appointed him consul general to the Barbary powers (Lear's old job), and later Porter was chargé d'affaires and minister to the sultan in Constantinople, where he died in 1843. His son, David Dixon Porter, and his foster son, David Glascow Farragut, were Union admirals in the Civil War.

Dr. Jonathan Cowdery stayed in the navy. His letters and diary entries from Tripoli were widely published in newspapers, and his diary was published as a pamphlet in 1806. Promoted to surgeon in 1807, Cowdery remarried, had five children with his new wife, and became a devout Christian. Cowdery remained on the navy's rolls, rising to become its senior surgeon in the 1830s. He died in 1852, at age 85.

Keith Spence went to Havana in 1806 on a business venture and then served as the navy agent in New Orleans, where he died in 1810. One of Spence's daughters, Harriet Brackett Spence, married into the Lowell family of Massachusetts, and her son (Keith Spence's grandson) was James Russell Lowell (1819–91), the poet, abolitionist, editor of *Atlantic Monthly*, and US minister to Spain and Britain. One of Keith Spence's direct descendants was Robert Lowell (Robert Traill Spence Lowell IV, 1917–77), one of America's great poets, who suffered from profound mental illness, which also affected Robert Traill Spence, Harriet Brackett Spence, and perhaps Keith Spence as well.

James Leander Cathcart served as consul in the Madeira Islands (1807–15) and then at Cadiz (1815–16). On his return to America, he was appointed navy agent in Louisiana to survey timber, and then (after appealing to ex-President Madison for a federal job) served for twenty years as a clerk in the Treasury Department. Cathcart died in 1843, age 76. More than a half-century later, a daughter published two books containing his detailed and colorful letters, both official and private, about his life in the Maghreb and his diplomacy with the bashaw.

Tobias Lear received strident criticism for negotiating the Tripolitan treaty because the United States paid ransom. After the secret article "selling out" Hamet was discovered, Lear was widely excoriated, and his reputation never recovered. Lear remained consul general in Algiers until 1812, when he returned to the United States. President Madison kept him on the federal payroll as an accountant in the War Department. In October 1816, Lear committed suicide. He was 54. He did not leave a note.

On his return to America, William Ray left the marines and wrote *Horrors of Slavery* (1808). He sent the book to Jefferson and Madison, asking them for money, but they wisely did not respond. Ray spent the rest of his life editing newspapers in upstate New York, publishing his poems, and writing a novel. When he died in July 1826, obituaries lauded him as a poet, although he gradually fell into obscurity.

In June 1805, as Lear negotiated the treaty that freed the American tars, Ray wrote a poem that covers the whole range of the captives' emotional experience, and that allows him the last word here:

> How fearful lour'd the gloomy day,
> When stranded on the shoals we lay
> Expos'd, our foremast cut away,
> To the rough dashing sea;
> When the hostile gun-boats thunder'd round,
> And no relief, nor hopes were found,
> These mournful words swell'd ev'ry sound,
> Adieu, blest Liberty!
>
> In helpless servitude, forlorn,
> From country, friends, and freedom torn,
> Alike we dread each night and mourn,
> For naught but grief we see;
> When burthens press—the lash we bear,
> And all around is black despair,
> We breathe the silent, fervent pray'r,
> O come, blest Liberty!
> . . .
> And when invading cannons roar,
> And life, their blood, from hundreds pour,
> And mangled bodies float ashore,
> And ruins strew the sea;
> The thoughts of death, or freedom, near,
> Create alternate hope and fear;
> Oh! When will that blest day appear,
> That brings sweet Liberty!
>
> When rear'd on yonder castle's height,
> That now bare flagstaff's drest in white,
> We gaze, enraptur'd at the sight;
> How happy shall we be!
> When thund'ring guns proclaim a peace,
> Our toils all o'er, our woes shall cease,
> We'll bless the pow'r that brings release,
> And hail sweet liberty![1]

NOTES

ABBREVIATIONS

Beaussier Letters	Archives Diplomatiques, Ministère des Affaires. Etrangères, Correspondence Consulaire, vol. 32, Tripoli de Barbarie, Paris, France.
Biddle Family Papers	Letters of Commodore James Biddle. Biddle Family Papers. Box 1. Andalusia Historic House and Gardens, Andalusia, PA.
Founders Online	Founders Online. National Archives, Washington, DC, https://founders.archives.gov.
MCHC	Maryland Center for History and Culture, Baltimore.
NA	National Archives and Records Administration, Washington, DC.
NDBW	*Naval Documents Related to the United States Wars with the Barbary Powers.* Edited by Dudley W. Knox. 7 vols. Washington, DC: Government Printing Office, 1939–45.
NDQW	*Naval Documents Related to the Quasi-War between the United States and France.* Edited by Dudley W. Knox. 7 vols. Washington, DC: Government Printing Office, 1935–38.
Nissen Letters	Letter Book and Correspondence of Nicolai Christian Nissen, in Tripoli, konsulaer representation and konsulaer retsprotokol, 2-2215 in Korrespondancesager 1752–1834, Rigsarkivet, Copenhagen, Denmark.
RG	Record Group.

| Spence Papers | Letters of Keith Spence. Papers of the Spence and Lowell Families, 1740–1958. Huntington Library, San Marino, CA. |
| Zuchet Letters | Victor Enthoven, "'From the Halls of Montezuma, to the Shores of Tripoli': Antoine Zuchet and the First Barbary War, 1801–1805." In Research in Maritime History No. 44, *Rough Waters: American Involvement with the Mediterranean in the Eighteenth and Nineteenth Centuries.* Edited by Silvia Marzagalli, James R. Sofka, and John J. McCusker. St. John's, Newfoundland: International Maritime Economic History Association, 2010 (reprinting in translation Zuchet's letters from National Archief, The Netherlands, Archief van het Ministrie van Buitenlandse Zaken, 1795–1813). |

INTRODUCTION

1. Victor Enthoven explains that Arabic lacks a "p," and the Turkish word *paşa* (in English, pasha) was pronounced bashaw in North Africa. "'From the Halls of Montezuma, to the Shores of Tripoli': Antoine Zuchet and the First Barbary War, 1801–1805" (hereafter cited as Zuchet Letters), in Research in Maritime History No. 44, *Rough Waters: American Involvement with the Mediterranean in the Eighteenth and Nineteenth Centuries*, ed. Silvia Marzagalli, James R. Sofka, and John J. McCusker (St. John's, Newfoundland: International Maritime Economic History Association, 2010), 118n4.

2. One commentator, for example, explained on National Public Radio, "Once you start down that road [of paying ransom for hostages] it's very difficult to turn back." Confusing association with causation, he added, "I know it's an almost ancient comparison but for a long time we did pay money to the Barbary pirates, and they wound up taking an entire crew of a U.S. naval vessel hostage." The commentator, George J. Terwilliger III, a former US deputy attorney general, thought paying money makes no sense. "All you're doing is condemning other Americans to future captivity when people realize that it could be a source of funding for them." Brian Naylor, "Should the US Pay Ransom for ISIS Hostages?," NPR, Sept. 19, 2014, https://www.npr.org/2014/09/19/349883335/should-the-u-s-pay-ransom-for-isis-hostages.

PROLOGUE

1. William Bainbridge to Secretary of the Navy Robert Smith, Nov. 1, 1803, and Bainbridge to Smith, Nov. 25, 1803, in *Naval Documents Related to the United States Wars with the Barbary Powers* (hereafter cited as *NDBW*), ed. Dudley W. Knox (Washington, DC: Government Printing Office, 1939–45), 3:171-73 and 3:175-76; *The Oxford Companion to Ships and the Sea*, ed. Peter Kemp (Oxford: Oxford University Press, rev. ed. 1988), 946 (xebec); Dudley Pope, *Life in Nelson's Navy* (London: Unwin Hyman, 1987), 205 (range).

2. Bainbridge to Smith, Nov. 1, 1803, Bainbridge to Smith, Nov. 25, 1803, Bainbridge to Consul General Tobias Lear, Feb. 8, 1804, Proceedings of Court of Inquiry into the Loss of the U.S. Frigate *Philadelphia*, June 29, 1805 (testimony of Lt. David Porter and statement of Captain William Bainbridge), and Porter to Midshipman Henry Wadsworth, March 5, 1804, in

NDBW, 3:171-73, 3:175-76, 3:176-78, 3:189-93, and 3:475-76; David F. Long, *Nothing Too Daring: A Biography of Commodore David Porter, 1780–1843* (Annapolis, MD: Naval Institute Press, 1970), 21; Ian W. Toll, *Six Frigates: The Epic History of the Founding of the U.S. Navy* (New York: W.W. Norton, 2006), 190; William Ray, *Poems, on various subjects, religious, moral, sentimental and humorous, To which is added, a brief sketch of the author's life, and of his captivity and sufferings among the Turks and barbarians of Tripoli on the coast of Africa* (Auburn, NY: U. F. Doubleday, 1821), 226; Thomas Wilson, *The Biography of the Principal American Military and Naval Heroes*, 2 vols. (New York: John Low, 1817, 1819), 2:157. The Kaliusa reef was not on the charts, a strange omission because it stretched several miles off the coast, broken in several places by channels, and because historic nautical charts indicate its existence. Had Bainbridge either kept on his course a little longer before bearing up or maintained his course toward Tripoli pursuing the xebec, the *Philadelphia* would not have grounded. Glenn Tucker, *Dawn Like Thunder: The Barbary Wars and the Birth of the U.S. Navy* (Indianapolis: Bobbs-Merrill, 1963), 214.

3. Bainbridge to Smith, Nov. 1, 1803, Bainbridge to Lear, Feb. 8, 1804, Proceedings of Court of Inquiry into the Loss of the U.S. Frigate *Philadelphia*, June 29, 1805 (Lieutenant Porter testified about Bainbridge's "great coolness and deliberation" and that Bainbridge first tried to free the ship by ordering all sail set to force her over the reef), and Porter to Wadsworth, March 5, 1804, in *NDBW*, 3:171-73, 3:176-78, 3:189-93, and 3:475-76. The prescribed weight of a British 18-pounder cannon was 37 hundredweight, and given that the English hundredweight was 112 pounds, each cannon weighed 4,144 pounds. Brian Lavery, *Life in Nelson's Navy: The Ships, Men and Organisation 1793–1815* (Annapolis, MD: Naval Institute Press, 1997), 80. Although the *Philadelphia*'s guns were cast in American foundries and may have been slightly lighter, they were of the same scale.

4. Bainbridge to Smith, Nov. 1, 1803, and Bainbridge to Commodore Edward Preble, Nov. 12, 1803, in *NDBW*, 3:171-73 and 3:173-74; Ray, *Poems*, 226-27; Wilson, *Biography*, 2:158.

5. William Ray, *Horrors of Slavery: Or, The American Tars in Tripoli* (Troy, NY, 1808), 54; Proceedings of Court of Inquiry into the Loss of the U.S. Frigate *Philadelphia*, June 29, 1805 (testimony of Lts. Porter and Hunt), in *NDBW*, 3:189-90; Long, *Nothing Too Daring*, 23. In response to questions from the court of inquiry, Lt. Theodore Hunt testified that before the *Philadelphia* left America, he had experimented in the Delaware River with carrying an anchor out in the *Philadelphia*'s launch, but the anchor was so heavy that the launch needed to be buoyed by casks to stay afloat.

6. Ray, *Poems*, 227; Tucker, *Dawn Like Thunder*, 233-34.

7. Bainbridge to Smith, Nov. 1, 1803, Bainbridge to Preble, Nov. 12, 1803, Bainbridge to Lear, Feb. 8, 1804, Proceedings of Court of Inquiry into the Loss of the U.S. Frigate *Philadelphia*, June 29, 1805 (testimony of Porter), Porter to Wadsworth, March 5, 1804, and Bainbridge to Preble, Nov. 25, 1803, in *NDBW*, 3.171-73, 3:173-74, 3:176-78, 3:189-90, 3:475-76, and 3:175-76; Ray, *Poems*, 227-28.

8. Porter to Wadsworth, March 5, 1804, in *NDBW*, 3:475; Ray, *Horrors of Slavery*, 82.

9. Ray, *Poems*, 228; Porter to Wadsworth, March 5, 1804, in *NDBW*, 3:475-76; Wilson, *Biography*, 2:158-59 (an unidentified officer); *Philadelphia Evening Post*, May 9, 1804, reprinting a letter from an unidentified officer, Nov. 11, 1803. That officer is identified as James Biddle in David F. Long, *Sailor-Diplomat: A Biography of Commodore James Biddle, 1783–1848* (Boston: Northeastern University Press, 1983), 20-21. A. B. C. Whipple states that Midshipman Henry Wadsworth was sent to announce the surrender, but Wadsworth did not serve on the *Philadelphia*. *Shores of Tripoli: The Birth of the U.S. Navy and Marines* (New York: William Morrow, 1991), 118,

10. Bainbridge to Preble, Nov. 12, 1803, and Proceedings of Court of Inquiry into the Loss

of the U.S. Frigate *Philadelphia*, June 29, 1805 (testimony of Porter), in *NDBW*, 3:173-74 and 3:189-91. The Tripolitans seized Bainbridge's papers, and probably the *Philadelphia*'s log and muster books as well, because within a few days, the French consul, Bonaventure Beaussier, gained access to them, as he reported to the Foreign Ministry in Paris. The papers revealed the size and composition of Commodore Edward Preble's oncoming squadron, including the ships' names, some of their movements in the Mediterranean, the size of the US Navy under the Naval Peace Establishment Act of 1801, and even the low monthly pay of American sailors compared to seamen on merchant ships. Beaussier reported to Paris that when Bainbridge raised the question of pay with Robert Smith, the secretary of the navy, Smith replied that by "limiting the Salaries, the United States would be able to maintain one more warship in the Mediterranean." ("Sur les representations d'un capitaine de frégate, Robert Smith, Secretaire du Département de la Marine repondit qu'il limitant ainsi les Salaires, les États-Unis seraient a menus de s'entretenir un batiment de guerre de plus dans la Mediterranee."). Beaussier reported to Foreign Minster Charles Maurice de Talleyrand-Périgord that he "took all these details, Citizen Minister, from the papers of the frigate that fell into the hands of the Bashaw, which I knew how to obtain and translate" ("J'ai puise tous ces details Citoyen Ministre, dans le papiers de la frégate tombés dans les mains du Pacha, que j'ai su me procurer et traduire"), suggesting that he bribed the bashaw or a high-ranking officer. Beaussier promised to send the naval information to the French minister of the marine, Admiral Denis Decrès. Beaussier to Talleyrand, Nov. 7, 1803, Correspondence Consulaire, Tripoli de Barbarie, Letters and Memoranda of Bonaventure Beaussier, Archives du Ministère des Affaires Etrangères, Paris, France (hereafter cited as Beaussier Letters). Bainbridge never acknowledged that his letter book and papers were seized, although it is possible he delegated the destruction of his papers to a junior officer and did not know his order was not obeyed. The papers would have been important to the French government; France had recently fought the so-called Quasi-War (1798–1800) against the United States.
11. Bainbridge to Smith, Nov. 12, 1803, in *NDBW*, 3:173-74; Ray, *Poems*, 228; Ray, *Horrors of Slavery*, 55.

CHAPTER ONE: BARBARY

1. Paul Baepler, ed., *White Slaves, African Masters: An Anthology of American Barbary Captivity Narratives* (Chicago: University of Chicago Press, 1999), 6, 44-48; Robert C. Davis, *Christian Slaves, Muslim Masters: White Slavery in the Mediterranean, the Barbary Coast, and Italy, 1500–1800* (Basingstoke, UK: Palgrave Macmillan, 2004), 191; Frederick C. Leiner, *Millions for Defense: The Subscription Warships of 1798* (Annapolis, MD: Naval Institute Press, 2000), 18.
2. "Sublime Porte" literally refers to the gate leading to the outermost courtyard of the Topkapi Palace, the sultan's residence in Istanbul, where the imperial Ottoman government did much of its business. The term took on the meaning of the Ottoman government itself, particularly its foreign affairs. The Topkapi Palace is now a museum. Directorate of National Palaces Administration, Istanbul, Turkey, https://www.millisaraylar.gov.tr/saraylar/topkapi-sarayi/.
3. Fuad Sha´ban, *Islam and Arabs in Early American Thought: The Roots of Orientalism in America* (Durham, NC: Acorn Press, 1990), 66-67; Robert Greenhow, *The History and Present Condition of Tripoli With Some Accounts of the Other Barbary States* (Richmond, VA: T. H. White, 1835), 8-9; Ray W. Irwin, *The Diplomatic Relations of the United States with the Barbary Powers 1776–1816* (Chapel Hill: University of North Carolina Press, 1931), 9n32, 12-13; Davis, *Christian Slaves*, 45; Richard B. Parker, *Uncle Sam in Barbary: A Diplomatic History* (Gainesville: University Press of Florida, 2004), 8-9; Kola Folayan, *Tripoli during the Reign of Yūsuf Pāshā Qaramānlī.* (Ife, Nigeria: University of Ife Press, 1979), 29.

4. Seaton Dearden, *A Nest of Corsairs: The Fighting Karamanlis of the Barbary Coast* (London: John Murray, 1976), 22; Denise A. Spellberg, *Thomas Jefferson's Qur'an: Islam and the Founders* (New York: Vintage Books, 2013), 127.

5. Folayan, *Tripoli during the Reign*, 7-9; Greenhow, *History and Present Condition*, 11-12; Dearden, *Nest of Corsairs*, 117-18, 141-43.

6. Parker, *Uncle Sam in Barbary*, 134; Tucker, *Dawn Like Thunder*, 234; Ray, *Poems*, 228-30; Jonathan Cowdery, *American Captives in Tripoli* (Boston: Belcher & Armstrong, 1806), diary entry for Oct. 31, 1803; Mordecai M. Noah, *Travels in England, France, Spain, and the Barbary States in the Years 1813–14 and 15* (New York: Kirk and Mercein, 1819), 357.

7. Ray, *Horrors of Slavery*, 110-15; Tucker, *Dawn Like Thunder*, 221-24; Richard Zacks, *The Pirate Coast: Thomas Jefferson, the First Marines, and the Secret Mission of 1805* (New York: Hyperion, 2005), 50.

8. Europeans and Americans used the word "Moors" to apply to all North African Muslims, sometimes with a contemptuous connotation. Yet "Moors" also had a more specialized meaning, referring to the descendants of Muslims who, centuries before, had retreated from Spain, as opposed to the indigenous Arabs of the Maghreb or the Berbers. Parker, *Uncle Sam in Barbary*, 16. Americans and Europeans (such as Shakespeare, with his title character in *Othello*) used the word "Moor" imprecisely. In a given context, it might mean dark-skinned people, but as used in regard to people in the Maghreb, it did not mean sub-Saharan black Africans.

9. Dearden, *Nest of Corsairs*, 37; Folayan, *Tripoli during the Reign*, 10.

10. Noah, *Travels*, 355-57; Ray, *Horrors of Slavery*, 110-15; Tucker, *Dawn Like Thunder*, 234.

11. David J. Dzurec III, *Our Suffering Brethren: Foreign Captivity and Nationalism in the Early United States* (Amherst: University of Massachusetts Press, 2019), 83; Irwin, *Diplomatic Relations*, 18, 72; Sha´ban, *Islam and Arabs*, 71; James Leander Cathcart, *The Captives: Eleven Years a Prisoner in Algiers*, comp. J. B. Newkirk (LaPorte, IN: Herald Print, 1899), 158-95; Parker, *Uncle Sam in Barbary*, 103-4. The ransom payment to Algiers was $585,000, and the United States gave $40,000 in presents, and agreed to pay approximately $22,000 in annual tribute in the form of naval stores. Treaty of Peace and Amity, signed at Algiers September 5, 1795, The Avalon Project; Documents in History, Law and Diplomacy, Yale Law School, New Haven, CT, https://avalon.law.yale.edu/18th_century/bar1795t.asp; Parker, *Uncle Sam in Barbary*, appendix 4, 208-16, identifies each American captive and ship seized, and the fate of each captive.

12. Irwin, *Diplomatic Relations*, 84-86; Folayan, *Tripoli during the Reign*, 31. The treaty, signed in Tripoli November 4, 1796, and ratified by the US Senate unanimously June 7, 1797, took effect June 10, 1797, when President Adams signed it. The treaty has become known for article 11, which provides, "As the government of the United States of America is not in any sense founded on the Christian Religion, as it has in itself no character of enmity against the laws, religion or tranquility of Musselmen, and as the said States never have entered into any war or act of hostility against any Mehomitan nation, it is declared by the parties that no pretext arising from religious opinions shall ever produce an interruption of the harmony existing between the two countries." Treaty of Peace and Friendship, Signed at Tripoli November 4, 1796, Avalon Project, https://avalon.law.yale.edu/18th_century/bar1796t.asp. However, there is no equivalent language in the Arabic version of the treaty. Parker, *Uncle Sam in Barbary*, 257n2.

13. Whipple, *Shores of Tripoli*, 51-53; Cathcart to Secretary of State John Marshall, Jan. 3, 1801, in Cathcart, *Tripoli*, 232; Parker, *Uncle Sam in Barbary*, 134, 166; Jefferson to Senator Abraham Baldwin, Feb. 10, 1802, in Founders Online, National Archives, Washington, DC, https://founders.archives.gov/documents/Jefferson/01-36-02-0361. There is important information about Cathcart in Brett Goodin, *From Captives to Consuls: Three Sailors in Barbary*

and Their Self-Making Across the Early American Republic, 1770–1840 (Baltimore: Johns Hopkins University Press, 2020).

14. Folayan, *Tripoli during the Reign*, 25-27; Dearden, *Nest of Corsairs*, 38-39n2, 142n1; Caitlin M. Gale, "The Role of the Barbary Regencies during Nelson's Command of the Mediterranean Fleet, 1803–1805" (paper submitted to Oxford University faculty of History, n.d.), 6-7; J. W. Hirschberg, *A History of the Jews in North Africa*, vol. 2, *From the Ottoman Conquests to the Present Time* (Leiden, Netherlands: Brill Academic, 1981), 167-68; Ray, *Horrors of Slavery*, 117.

15. Cathcart to William Eaton, Aug. 27, 1800, 168, notation, April 8, 1799, 11, Cathcart to Consul Richard O'Brien, April 13, 1799, 21-22, Cathcart to Eaton, May 10, 1799, 32-33, Cathcart to Eaton, Nov. 9, 1799, 97, Cathcart to Eaton, [undated but Nov. or Dec.], 1800, 215-20, Cathcart to Eaton, Nov. 17, 1800, 208-9, Cathcart to Eaton, Nov. 5, 1799, 88, and Cathcart to Eaton, Feb. 17, 1800, 125-26, in Cathcart, *Tripoli*; Hirschberg, *Jews in North Africa*, 34; Irwin, *Diplomatic Relations*, 75; Parker, *Uncle Sam in Barbary*, 117; Ray, *Horrors of Slavery*, 113-14.

16. Cathcart to Secretary of State Timothy Pickering, May 12, 1800, 149, Cathcart to Minister to Spain David Humphreys, Dec. 14, 1799, 105, and Cathcart to Pickering, Dec. 30, 1799, 111-12, in Cathcart, *Tripoli*; Folayan, *Tripoli during the Reign*, 29-30, 33-34.

17. Cathcart to Pickering, April 18, 1800, 136, Cathcart to O'Brien, May 25, 1800, 144, and Cathcart to Pickering, May 15 and 27, 1800, 152-55, in Cathcart, *Tripoli*.

18. Karamanli to Adams, May 25, 1800, Founders Online, https://founders.archives.gov/documents/Adams/99-02-02-4372.

19. Cathcart to Acting Secretary of State Charles Lee, Nov. 1, 1800, and Cathcart to O'Brien and Eaton, Jan 7, 1801, in Cathcart, *Tripoli*, 194, 227; *New-York Gazette*, April 22, 1801, reprinting letter, Cathcart to Consul Thomas Appleton, Jan. 3, 1801.

20. Cathcart to Lee, Oct. 18, 1800, and Diplomatic Note, Feb. 5, 1801, in Cathcart, *Tripoli*, 182-86, 264-65; Irwin, *Diplomatic Relations*, 9; Eaton to Secretary of State [James Madison], April 10, 1801, in *The Life of the Late Gen. William Eaton*, comp. Charles Prentiss (Brookfield, MA: E. Merriam, printers, 1813), 191-92. Some modern historians suggest the looming war was the fault of the United States, that, as Denise Spellberg puts it, "hostilities first arose on the [American] side, the first American peace treaty with Tripoli having sown the seeds of a military conflict." She concludes that "American diplomats seem to have misread Tripoli's grievances," and that Yusuf's annoyance at not receiving the same amount of tribute as Tunis or Algiers was justified. *Thomas Jefferson's Qur'an*, 214. Paul Baepler believes "some of the blame [for the war] must rest with John Adams's dilatory response to Tripoli's diplomatic overtures" (*White Slaves*, 9n26), suggesting that somehow, a faster and more conciliatory response to those demands would have prevented war. Kola Folayan argues that because Tripoli had seized only one American merchant vessel during this tense period, which it returned without demanding ransom, any American claim that the war was about "piracy" was false, and that, in reality, the war was due to America's failure to recognize Tripoli's sovereignty, a view shared by Robert Allison, who denies that the United States went to war "to suppress piracy or stop outrageous demands from an avaricious pasha." Folayan asserts that America prompted the war by not treating Tripoli as a fully sovereign state, for instance, by suggesting that the bey of Algiers would arbitrate any disputes and that the US consul general in Algiers had supervisory power over the US consul in Tripoli. *Tripoli during the Reign*, 31-35; Robert J. Allison, *The Crescent Obscured: The United States and the Muslim World, 1776–1815* (Chicago: University of Chicago Press, 1995), 230-31n49. Folayan is correct that in October 1800, after a Tripolitan corsair captured the American merchant brig *Catherine* and brought her into Tripoli, Yusuf ordered the ship and crew released. Dghies, the bashaw's foreign min-

ister, told Cathcart that Yusuf was awaiting the president's response and in the interim would not "take any measures whatsoever against the United States." Folayan fails to mention that the bashaw did not take action because he presumed the president would agree to pay annual tribute. Cathcart responded that the bashaw should "erase" that idea from his mind. Cathcart to Lee, Oct. 18, 1800, in Cathcart, *Tripoli,* 182-84. More generally, these rationales ignore the fact that Yusuf's desire for enhanced tribute had been foresworn by treaty, and they ignore the long history of piratical threats by the bashaw, to which the United States had to respond or jeopardize its trade in the Mediterranean.

21. Circular Letter, Nov. 12, 1800, and Cathcart to O'Brien and Eaton, April 17, 1801, in Cathcart, *Tripoli,* 197-99, 315; Circular Letter, Jan. 3, 1801, in *NDBW,* 1:404-5; *New-York Gazette,* Aug. 7, 1801, printing a letter from twenty-three American masters and supercargoes, May 15, 1801. Years later, Cathcart wrote former President Madison that he had "temporized" with the bashaw "a sufficient length of time, to alarm our Commerce, and, a thing unprecedented in the Annals of Barbary, not one of our Vessels was captured by his Cruisers, altho' the Mediterranean was crowded with them." Cathcart to Madison, Sept. 18, 1821, Founders Online, https://founders.archives.gov/documents/Madison/04-02-02-0323.

22. Dearden, *Nest of Corsairs,* 133-34, 220; Zacks, *Pirate Coast,* 46 (spelling his name "Lyle"); H. G. Barnby, *The Prisoners of Algiers: An Account of the Forgotten American Algerian War 1785–1797* (Oxford: Oxford University Press, 1966), 296. Kola Folayan mistakenly identifies Murad's former name as "Peter Leslie." *Tripoli during the Reign,* 28. Paul Baepler refers to the long history of Barbary rulers appointing Christian renegades as the *rais* of their corsairs. *White Slaves,* 42.

23. Christopher McKee, *Edward Preble: A Naval Biography, 1761–1807* (Annapolis, MD: Naval Institute Press, 1972), 87; Jefferson to Senator Wilson Cary Nicholas, June 11, 1801, Founders Online, https://founders.archives.gov/documents/Jefferson/01-34-02-0250; *Vermont Gazette* (Burlington), May 4, 1801.

24. *Norwich (CT) Packet,* Feb. 9, 1802. In 1801, the Baptist congregation in Cheshire, Massachusetts, manufactured a "mammoth cheese" to honor Jefferson for his republicanism and support of religious liberty. The cheese used the milk of nine hundred cows, measured six feet in diameter, weighed 1,230 pounds, and was delivered to Jefferson at the White House. Federalist newspapers responded with derision at the ludicrous nature of the enormous cheese and used it as a metaphor for visionary projects of the Jefferson administration. Apparently, most of the cheese was never eaten, but was kept at the White House for years, and may finally have been dumped into the Potomac River. Thomas Jefferson's Monticello, "Mammoth Cheese," https://www.monticello.org/site/research-and-collections/mammoth-cheese.

25. *Newburyport (MA) Herald,* May 12, 1801.

26. O'Brien to Humphreys, April 6, 1801, *National Intelligencer* (Washington), May 29, 1801; Cathcart to Agents and Consuls, May 15, 1801, *Gazette of the United States* (Philadelphia), Sept. 3, 1801; Stephen Cleveland Blyth, *History of the War between the United States and Tripoli, and Other Barbary Powers. To which is prefixed, A Geographical, Religious and Political History of the Barbary States in General* (Salem, MA: Printed at the Salem Gazette Office, 1806), 87-88; Gardner W. Allen, *Our Navy and the Barbary Corsairs* (Boston: Houghton Mifflin, 1905), 91; Michael L. S. Kitzen, *Tripoli and the United States at War: A History of American Relations with the Barbary States, 1785–1805* (Jefferson, NC: McFarland, 1993), 47.

CHAPTER TWO: THE MEN

1. Jefferson to Gouverneur Morris, June 6, 1801, Founders Online, https://founders.archives. gov/documents/Jefferson/01-34-02-0226. Joseph Wheelan makes the important point that in 1801, with Congress in recess, Jefferson acted on his own initiative and without consulting

or informing Congress, which set an important precedent for a president in using force to protect American interests and foreshadowed an enduring issue for American government. *Jefferson's War: America's First War on Terror 1801–1805* (New York: Carroll & Graf, 2003), 105. One representative, John Stanly, a Federalist from New Bern, North Carolina, wrote his constituents that Jefferson's executive decision to send Dale's squadron to protect American commerce was "seasonable and efficacious." Commenting on the president's instructions, Stanly thought that when the United States had been attacked and was already in a state of war, it was "extremely absurd" to think that the president needed Congress to declare war before taking action; consequently, Stanly was "at a loss to comprehend the existence of a state of things" in which the navy could fire on and kill Tripolitans or sink their ships if attacked but not capture their seamen or make prizes of their ships if they were found entering Tripoli. John Stanly to constituents, May 1, 1802, in *Circular Letters of Congressmen to Their Constituents, 1789–1829*, ed. Noble E. Cunningham, Jr. (Chapel Hill: University of North Carolina Press, 1978), 287-88.

2. Acting Secretary of the Navy Samuel Smith to Capt. Richard Dale, May 20, 1801, Samuel Smith to Thomas Fitzsimons, June 4, 1801, and William Eaton to U.S. Agents and Consuls in Europe, July 23, 1801, in *NDBW*, 1:465-69, 1:486-87, and 1:528; Charles W. Goldsborough, *The United States Naval Chronicle* (Washington, DC: James Wilson, 1824), 190-93; Toll, *Six Frigates*, 169; Kitzen, *Tripoli*, 46; Druzec, *Our Suffering Brethren*, 92.

3. Jefferson to Karamanli, May 21, 1801, *NDBW*, 1:470. Historian Robert Allison asserts that Jefferson was "predisposed to go to war" and Yusuf's belligerency gave Jefferson the war he had wanted against Barbary since his days as a diplomat in Paris fifteen years before. *Crescent Obscured*, 230-31n49. It would be odd for a president supposedly predisposed to war to apologize if the very presence of a squadron in international waters caused "umbrage." Jefferson was not a pacifist, but in coming into office he wanted peace, because war was the great corrupter of republican institutions, and by nature he was opposed to the cost and entanglement of naval force. Robert W. Tucker and David C. Hendrickson aptly write that for Jefferson, war was "the great nemesis" in that it led to debt, taxes, standing armies, corrupt patronage, and the enlargement of the executive branch, ending in monarchy. The war with Tripoli might appear to be a contradiction to "[t]he commitment to peace that dominated Jefferson's diplomacy," but they note that Jefferson sent Dale's squadron to try to prevent Tripoli from breaking the peace. Although in the 1780s Jefferson had espoused the use of naval power against the Barbary regencies, in the 1790s, as the Republican Party formed, he abandoned the idea of a high seas navy. Tucker and Hendrickson conclude, "In deciding to employ force in the Mediterranean, Jefferson's consistent goal was simply to restrain the demands of Tripoli and the other Barbary states," and he used the navy to attempt to do that. *Empire of Liberty: The Statecraft of Thomas Jefferson* (New York: Oxford University Press, 1990), 16-17, 294-95n80. As Jefferson once wrote his secretary of the navy, "nothing but the warring on them at times will keep the demand of presents within bounds." Jefferson to Robert Smith, March 29, 1803, Founders Online, https://founders.archives.gov/documents/Jefferson/01-40-02-0095.

4. *Bee* (New London, CT), Sept. 16, 1801; *New York Daily Advertiser*, Nov. 20, 1801; *American* (Baltimore), Nov. 23, 1801; Consul John Gavino to Secretary of State, Aug. 3, 1801, and Gavino to Capt. Samuel Barron, Aug. 8, 1801, in *NDBW*, 1:541-42 and 1:543.

5. On August 1, 1801, under the command of Lt. Andrew Sterrett, the schooner *Enterprise* defeated a 14-gun Tripolitan polacre called *Tripoli*. (A polacre was a two- or three-masted vessel with a lateen sail on the forward-sloping foremast.) After the *Tripoli* twice feigned surrender, the *Enterprise* pummeled her into submission, with no one hurt on the *Enterprise*. After dumping the *Tripoli*'s cannon, anchors, and rigging overboard and cutting down her

masts, Sterrett allowed her to limp away because his orders did not allow him to capture a Tripolitan ship. Yusuf attributed the defeat to cowardice, and when Mahomet Sous, the *rais* (commander) of the polacre, returned to Tripoli, he was paraded through the streets on a jackass, jostled by a jeering mob, and then beaten with the *bastinado*, a three-foot wooden bat, applied to the soles of his feet. Blyth, *History of the War*, 91-92; Goldsborough, *Naval Chronicle*, 197-98; Tucker, *Dawn Like Thunder*, 141-44; Whipple, *Shores of Tripoli*, 79-80; Wheelan, *Jefferson's War*, 118-19; Greenhow, *History and Present Condition*, 14.

6. *New York Evening Post*, Nov. 23, 1801; Blyth, *History of the War*, 89, 93; Greenhow, *History and Present Condition*, 14; Benjamin Armstrong, *Small Boats and Daring Men: Maritime Raiding, Irregular Warfare, and the Early American Navy* (Norman: University of Oklahoma Press, 2019), 55; Kitzen, *Tripoli*, 51, 55-57; Allen, *Our Navy*, 97; McKee, *Edward Preble*, 91; Jeff Seiken, "The Reluctant Warrior: Thomas Jefferson and the Tripolitan War, 1801–1805," in *Rough Waters: American Involvement with the Mediterranean in the Eighteenth and Nineteenth Centuries*, ed. Silvia Marzagalli, James R. Sofka, and John J. McCusker (St. John's, Newfoundland: International Maritime Economic History Association, 2010), 193-94; Tucker, *Dawn Like Thunder*, 148-49. Given the nonperformance of the Tripolitan navy, it is hard to understand the claim that "[b]etween 1801 and 1802 the American blockade of Tripoli was rendered ineffective by the naval efforts of Tripoli under the general direction of Admiral Murad Rais." Folayan, *Tripoli during the Reign*, 35.

7. Jefferson, First Annual Message, Dec. 8, 1801, Founders Online, https://founders.archives. gov/documents/Jefferson/01-36-02-0034-0003; "An act for the protection of the Commerce and Seamen of the United States, against the Tripolitan Cruisers," 7th Cong., 1st Sess., stat. I, chap. 4, *Public Statutes at Large*, ed. Richard Peters (Boston: Charles C. Little and James Brown, 1845–50), 3:132-33; Druzec, *Our Suffering Brethren*, 96.

8. John Stratton to constituents, April 22, 1802, in *Circular Letters*, 281.

9. William Dickson to constituents, April 5, 1802, in ibid., 280.

10. Smith to Morris, April 1, 1802, and Madison to Cathcart, April 18, 1802, in *NDBW*, 2:99-100 and 2:126-27; Tucker, *Dawn Like Thunder*, 152-55, 179-81, 186-87; Parker, *Uncle Sam in Barbary*, 136; Kitzen, *Tripoli*, 60-61, 67, 73; Goldsborough, *Naval Chronicle*, 203-4; Seiken, "Reluctant Warrior," 195-96, 199; John H. Schroeder, *Commodore John Rodgers: Paragon of the Early American Navy* (Gainesville: University Press of Florida, 2006), 33-34; Irwin, *Diplomatic Relations*, 126-27; Parker, *Uncle Sam in Barbary*, 137; Allen to father, Dec. 13, 1802, "Letters of William Henry Allen, 1803–1813, Part One: 1800–1806," ed. Edward H. Tatum Jr. and Marion Tinling, *Huntington Library Quarterly* 1, no. 1 (Oct. 1937): 110; Jefferson to Smith, June 16, 1803, Founders Online, https://founders.archives.gov/documents/ Jefferson/01-40-02-0412; Eaton to Speaker of the House [Nathaniel Macon], [undated, but Jan. 1804], *Life of Eaton*, 244; Report of the Court of Inquiry into Commodore Richard V. Morris, April 13, 1804, *NDBW*, 4:38-39; Tucker, *Dawn Like Thunder*, 159-60, 171-86; Whipple, *Shores of Tripoli*, 86-89, 95-101.

11. O'Brien to Lear, April 24, 1804, Capt. Alexander Murray to Smith, and Cathcart to Secretary of State [Madison], July 30, 1802, in *NDBW*, 4:59-61, 2:191, and 2:217-19; Jefferson to Madison, March 22, 1803, Founders Online, https://founders.archives.gov/documents/ Madison/02-04-02-0531 ("Our misfortune has been that our vessels have been employed in particular convoys, instead of a close blockade."); Richard Valentine Morris, *A Defence of the Conduct of Commodore Morris During His Command in the Mediterranean: With Strictures on the Report of the Court of Enquiry Held at Washington* (New York: I. Riley, 1804), 36-38, quoting Morris to Smith, Aug. 17, 1802; Irwin, *Diplomatic Relations*, 117.

12. Second Annual Message, Dec. 15, 1802, Founders Online, https://founders.archives.gov/ documents/Jefferson/01-39-02-0148.

13. Gallatin to Jefferson, Aug. 16, 1802, Library of Congress, The Thomas Jefferson Papers at the Library of Congress: Series 1: General Correspondence. 1651 to 1827, https://www.loc.gov/resource/mtj1.026_1002_1007/?st=grid.

14. Jefferson to Smith, March 29, 1803, Founders Online, https://founders.archives.gov/documents/Jefferson/01-40-02-0095; Notes on a Cabinet Meeting, April 8, 1803, Founders Online, https://founders.archives.gov/documents/Jefferson/01-40-02-0119; Madison to Cathcart, April 9, 1803, Founders Online, https://founders.archives.gov/documents/Madison/02-04-02-0599; Druzec, *Our Suffering Brethren*, 101; Irwin, *Diplomatic Relations*, 126-28; McKee, *Edward Preble*, 129; Parker, *Uncle Sam in Barbary*, 137.

15. Eaton to Madison, Jan. 21, 1803, Founders Online, https://founders.archives.gov/documents/Madison/02-04-02-0322. Ship passports were engraved certificates a consul could provide for merchant ships. The ship passport was cut in half. A corsair would carry the bottom half, and if it matched the top half of a merchant ship stopped at sea, the corsair was to allow the merchant vessel safe passage. In addition, a consul could issue a passport to a corsair captain, which allowed him to operate if stopped by a warship of the country that issued the passport. Dearden, *Nest of Corsairs*, 16-17; Greenhow, *History and Present Condition*, 17-18; Abigail G. Mullen, "'Good Neighbourhood With All': Conflict and Cooperation in the First Barbary War, 1801–1805," PhD diss. (Northeastern University, 2017), 41-43.

16. Jefferson to Rep. Joseph H. Nicholson, Feb. 23, 1803, Founders Online, https://founders.archives.gov/documents/Jefferson/01-39-02-0480.

17. McKee, *Edward Preble*; Tyrone G. Martin, *A Most Fortunate Ship: A Narrative History of Old Ironsides* (Annapolis, MD: Naval Institute Press, 1997), 86-88; Allen, *Barbary Corsairs*, 139-40; Higginson to Pickering, June 6, 1798, and Stoddert to Adams, May 25, 1799, in *Naval Documents Related to the Quasi-War between the United States and France* (hereafter cited as *NDQW*), ed. Dudley W. Knox, 7 vols. (Washington, DC: Government Printing Office, 1935–38), 1:106-7 and 3:252-53.

18. The *Argus* was launched on August 20, 1803. *Commercial Gazette* (Boston), Aug. 22, 1803; *Gazetteer* (Boston), Aug. 24, 1803. The *Vixen* was launched on June 25, 1803, and "hauled off from [Price's] wharf, into the stream" on August 2, 1803. *NDBW*, 7:80; *Telegraphe and Daily Advertiser* (Baltimore), Aug. 3, 1803. The *Syren* was launched from Hutton's shipyard in Southwark, Philadelphia, and "coppered to the bends" on August 6, 1803. *Independent Chronicle* (Boston), Aug. 11, 1803. Details about the design of these ships are in Howard I. Chapelle, *The History of the American Sailing Navy* (New York: W. W. Norton, 1949), 184-88, and Geoffrey M. Footner, *Tidewater Triumph: The Development and Worldwide Success of the Chesapeake Bay Pilot Schooner* (Mystic, CT: Mystic Seaport Museum Press, 1998), 94-95.

19. Smith to Bainbridge, May 21, 1803, in *NDBW*, 2:412; Kennard R.Wiggins, Jr., *America's Anchor: A Naval History of the Delaware River and Bay, Cradle of the United States Navy* (Jefferson, NC: McFarland, 2019), 58.

20. In his standing orders on the *George Washington*, Bainbridge provided, "Should any person quit his station before he is regularly relieved, or ordered to do so, he is to ride the spanker boom for three hours." In addition, if "there be any so base as to sleep on their station he is immediately to be put in Irons." Bainbridge's Orders for Relieving Watches, June 1, 1801, *NDBW*, 1:483. While such punishment may seem harsh, during the Civil War, at least two thousand Union soldiers were court-martialed for sleeping at their posts, of whom ninety were sentenced to death. Senior officers believed that sleeping on guard duty (watch) put the entire garrison (or ship) at risk, and an example needed to be made of offenders. President Abraham Lincoln commuted the death sentences of all ninety soldiers. Jonathan W. White, *Midnight in America: Darkness, Sleep, and Dreams during the Civil War* (Chapel Hill: University of North Carolina Press, 2017), 3-7.

21. Christopher McKee, "Fantasies of Mutiny and Murder: A Suggested Psycho-History of the Seaman in the United States Navy, 1798–1815," *Armed Forces & Society*, 4 (1978), 301; John Rea, *A letter to William Bainbridge, Esqr. formerly commander of the United States Ship George Washington relative to some transactions, on board said ship, during a voyage to Algiers, Constantinople, &c* (Philadelphia: privately printed, 1802), 4, 10-12, 15-18, 23.

22. Allen to father, June 26, 1800, in "Letters of William Henry Allen," 104; Eaton to Pickering, Nov. 10, 1800, in *NDBW*, 1:397-98; Blyth, *History of the War*, 82-87. The biographies of Bainbridge are David F. Long, *Ready to Hazard: A Biography of Commodore William Bainbridge, 1772–1833* (Lebanon, NH: University Press of New England, 1981); H. A. S. Dearborn, *The Life of William Bainbridge, Esq.*, ed. James Barnes (Princeton, NJ: Princeton University Press, 1931); and Thomas Harris, *Life and Services of Commodore William Bainbridge, United States Navy* (Philadelphia: Carey, Lea & Blanchard, 1837). Excellent shorter profiles are in Tucker, *Dawn Like Thunder*, 28-35, and Craig Symonds, "William S. Bainbridge: Bad Luck or Fatal Flaw?" in *Command Under Sail: Makers of the American Naval Tradition, 1775–1850*, ed. James C. Bradford (Annapolis, MD: Naval Institute Press, 1985), 97-125.

23. Leiner, *Millions for Defense*, 53-71, 187-89. The frigate measured 157 feet between perpendiculars (the length from the stem, the main bow perpendicular timber, to the sternpost, the main stern perpendicular timber) and 1,240 tons (by "carpenters' measure," an indicator of volume). Chapelle, *American Sailing Navy*, 161, 549.

24. An "able seaman" was a sailor experienced in all the critical tasks expected at sea, able to go aloft in all weathers, and skilled enough to take the helm to steer the ship; in the parlance of the time, an able seaman could "hand, reef, and steer." An "ordinary seaman" had been to sea before and had working knowledge of the ropes but lacked some critical skills. Newcomers were "landsmen" or "boys." Stephen Taylor, *Sons of the Waves: The Common Seamen in the Heroic Age of Sail* (New Haven, CT: Yale University Press, 2020), 24.

25. Martin, *Most Fortunate Ship*, 81; Gerard T. Altoff, *Amongst My Best Men: African-Americans and the War of 1812* (Put-in-Bay, OH: Perry Group, 1996), 20; Eric Brown, "A Sailor's Favorite Elixir: The Spirit Ration and the United States Navy, 1794–1862," *Journal of the War of 1812* 12 (Summer 2009): 20-21; Harold D. Langley, *Social Reform in the United States Navy 1798–1862* (Annapolis, MD: Naval Institute Press, 2015), 75; Paul A. Gilje, *Liberty on the Waterfront: American Maritime Culture in the Age of Revolution* (Philadelphia: University of Pennsylvania Press, 2004), 16-19. Crimps were not unique to the US Navy. For instance, the Dutch navy relied on crimps, "commonly known as *zielverkopers* (sellers-of-souls), [who] preyed on the destitute and desperate, offered them an advance on room and board, and then forced them into the first available warship. The navy then paid the man's wages to the crimp until all his accumulated debts had been cleared." Niklas Frykman, "Seamen on Late Eighteenth-Century European Warships," *International Review of Social History* 54 (2009): 70.

26. Smith to Bainbridge, June 19, 1803, Preble to Smith, July 5, 1803, and Preble to Smith, July 21, 1803, in *NDBW*, 2:455, 2:467, and 2:494.

27. *Oxford Companion*, 698; Langley, *Social Reform*, 74-75; William T. Fowler, *Jack Tars & Commodores: The American Navy 1783–1815* (Boston: Houghton Mifflin, 1984), 128; Gilje, *Liberty on the Waterfront*, 19, 112. In Baltimore, advertisements for a rendezvous at David Moss's tavern in Fells Point appeared in the *Telegraphe and Daily Advertiser*, Aug. 21, 1802. A news article from New York reported, "A rendezvous is open in this city for recruits for the navy. The recruiting officer was very successful yesterday—a number of hearty fellows were seen following the enlivening drum and fife—happy at the prospect of again serving their country." *Federal Gazette & Baltimore Daily Advertiser*, Sept. 4, 1802.

28. Martin, *Most Fortunate Ship*, 81; Herman Melville, *White-Jacket* (Oxford: Oxford University Press, 1996) (orig. pub. 1850), 76; *New York Daily Advertiser*, June 8, 1803; James Du-

rand, *An Able Seaman of 1812: His Adventures on "Old Ironsides" and as an Impressed Sailor in the British Navy*, ed. George S. Brooks (New Haven, CT: Yale University Press, 1926), 17.

29. *Albany Gazette*, Aug. 1, 1803; *New England Palladium* (Boston), Aug. 16, 1803; *New York Evening Post*, Aug. 17, 1803. The Fly Market was New York's oldest market (1728), selling meat, produce, and fish under a covered roof, situated at the foot of Maiden Lane, where it ended at Front Street facing the East River. It was demolished in 1823. Wikipedia, "Maiden Lane (Manhattan)," https://en.wikipedia.org/wiki/Maiden_Lane_(Manhattan).

30. Spence, "Abstract of Balances due to sundry persons, part of the Crew of the United States late frigate *Philadelphia*," Sept. 30, 1805, *NDBW*, 3:184-88; Niklas Frykman, "Connections between Mutinies in European Navies," *International Review of Social History* 58 (2013): 99; Dan Hicks, "True Born Columbians: The Promises and Perils of National Identity for American Seafarers of the Early Republican Period," PhD diss. (Pennsylvania State University, 2007), 66-67. A few years after the *Philadelphia* recruited her crew in 1803, correspondence with the secretary of the navy reveals the cosmopolitan nature of the early US Navy. The captain of one frigate reported, "More than four fifths of [the marines] are foreigners." Not a single man on that ship would admit to being a British subject or deserter from the Royal Navy, although her captain wrote that it was "a well known fact" that "a vast majority of our Seamen have, at some period of their lives, been impressed into the British service." Another captain wrote from Connecticut that it was difficult to find seamen, and "a number cannot speak one word of English." Decatur to Smith, Aug. 25, 1807, Decatur to Smith, Nov. 17, 1807, and Hull to Smith, Sept. 18, 1807, in National Archives, Washington, DC (hereafter cited as NA), Record Group 45 (hereafter cited as RG), M125, "Letters Received by the Secretary of the Navy: Captains Letters 1805-61."

31. *Public Statutes at Large*, "An Act for the Relief and Protection of American Seamen," May 28, 1796, 4th Cong., ch. 31, 477-78; Ira Dye, "Early American Merchant Seafarers" *Proceedings of the American Philosophical Society* 120, no. 5 (Oct. 15, 1976): 331-360; Ira Dye, "The Philadelphia Seamen's Protection Certificate Applications," *Prologue-Quarterly of the National Archives* 18, no. 1 (1986): 46-55; "Proofs of Citizenships Used to Apply for Seamen's Protection Certificates for the Port of Philadelphia, 1792–1861," NA, RG 36, Records of the US Customs Service, microcopy 1880, rolls 1 (1792–98), 2 (1798–1801), and 3 (1801–04). It is not certain that the men identified in the seamen's protection certificate registers were, in fact, the men listed in the crew of the *Philadelphia* with the same name, but the less common the name, the more likely the positive identification.

32. Taylor, *Sons of the Waves*, 31.

33. Stoddert to Lt. Henry Kenyon, Aug. 8, 1798, and Preble to Lt. William C. Jenckes, July 13, 1803, in *NDQW*, 1:281 and 2:479; "Proofs of Citizenships Used to Apply for Seamen's Protection Certificates for the Port of Philadelphia, 1792–1861," NA, RG 36, Records of the US Customs Service, microcopy 1880, rolls 1-3.

34. Fowler, *Jack Tars*, 129. An advertisement, "Runaway Negroes," placed in the newspaper by the marshal of the District of Columbia, mentioned that he was holding two men, including

> James Frazier, who says he was raised in Carlisle county Pennsylvania, and was set free by Wm. Frazier of that place about the year 1798 that the year following he went to sea; and has been either in the British or American navy mostly ever since. He was a hand on board the frigate President, when she lately returned from the Mediterranean. Frazier is about 35 years of age, 5 feet 5 inches high, has a large angular scar on his right side, and wears a blue round jacket, nankeen trousers striped vest &c.

The advertisement ominously concluded that anyone who claimed the fugitive slaves should make "legal application and take them away; otherwise they will be disposed of as the law allows." *National Intelligencer*, Nov. 8, 1805. Thus, a few fugitive slaves may have gotten past recruiting officers, or perhaps the officers, needing a crew, did not examine too carefully some of the men seeking to enlist, who sought refuge in the navy.

35. *Republican* (Baltimore), Aug. 5, 1803; Dye, "Early American Merchant Seafarers," 349-51; W. Jeffrey Bolster, *Black Jacks: African American Seamen in the Age of Sail* (Cambridge, MA: Harvard University Press, 1997), 70-82, 88-91, 93-101; Harold D. Langley, "The Negro in the Navy and Merchant Service, 1789–1860," *Journal of Negro History* 52 (Oct. 1967): 273-286; Altoff, *Among My Best Men*, 20-21.

36. David McCullough, *John Adams* (New York: Simon & Schuster, 2001),141-42; Dye, "Early American Merchant Seafarers," 340, 347, 357; Myra C. Glenn notes that most historians who have reviewed records such as seamen's protections conclude that "most mariners had trouble reading and writing," most seamen signing their protections wrote their names "with some difficulty," and 80 percent of sailors were barely literate. *Jack Tar's Story: The Autobiographies and Memoirs of Sailors in Antebellum America* (New York: Cambridge University Press, 2010), 18n48. The historians who posit a higher literacy rate—some as high as 75 percent of American seamen—assume that the ability to sign one's name indicates a functional degree of literacy. Hester Blum, "Pirated Tars, Piratical Texts: Barbary Captivity and American Sea Narratives," *Early American Studies* 1 (Fall 2003): 142-43 and 143n14. Charles E. Brodine Jr. notes that the first documented record of women serving aboard a US Navy warship was in 1813, when two women were entered as "supernumeraries" aboard the frigate *United States.* "'Children of the Storm': Life at Sea in the First Six Frigates," *Naval History* 23 (Aug. 2009): 18. Christopher McKee points out that the wives of warrant and petty officers sometimes accompanied their husbands to sea, but that practice was not followed on the *Philadelphia. Edward Preble*, 216n*.

37. Ray, *Poems*, 201, 208-11, 215, 218-22; Ray, *Horrors of Slavery*, xii-xv. Underneath one of Ray's poems, the *Balance* (Hudson, NY), Dec. 18, 1804, wrote, "If we mistake not (says the Troy Budget), this is the same Ray who was a confined debtor within the limits of the jail of this county in the year '98."

38. *Philadelphia Gazette*, July 22, 1803; *New York Evening Post*, July 25, 1803.

39. *New York Evening Post*, July 28, 1803; Biographical Note and Spence to Polly Spence, July 26, 1803, in Letters of Keith Spence, Papers of the Spence and Lowell Families, 1740–1958, Huntington Library, San Marino, CA (hereafter cited as Spence Letters); Kay Redfield Jamison, *Robert Lowell, Setting the River on Fire: A Study of Genius, Mania, and Character* (New York: Vintage, 2018), 40-43; *Naval Regulations Issued by Command of the President of the United States of America., Jan. 25, 1802* (Annapolis, MD: Naval Institute Press, 1970), 26-28; Langley, *Social Reform*, 82; Ray, *Horrors of Slavery*, 47.

40. Melville, *White-Jacket*, 23; Langley, *Social Reform*, 141; Brodine, "Children of the Storm," 16-17; Samuel Leech, *Thirty Years from Home, or a Voice from the Main Deck* (Boston: Tappan & Dennet, 1843), 44.

41. Leech, *Thirty Years*, 39-42 (emphasis in original); Peter Linebaugh and Marcus Rediker, *The Many-Headed Hydra: Sailors, Slaves, Commoners, and the Hidden History of the Revolutionary Atlantic* (London: Verso, rev. ed. 2012), 150-51, 160-61, 332-33; Niklas Erik Frykman, "The Wooden World Turned Upside Down: Naval Mutinies in the Age of Atlantic Revolution," Ph.D. diss. (University of Pittsburgh, 2010), 14, 30; Gilje, *Liberty on the Waterfront*, 12-13, 28-30; Taylor, *Sons of the Waves*, xvii-xviii.

42. Jefferson to Elbridge Gerry, Jan. 26, 1799, Founders Online, https://founders.archives.gov/documents/Jefferson/01-30-02-0451. Joseph Wheelan errs in asserting that Jefferson had a "staunch belief in the navy's utility," and his belief "evolved into a philosophy of perpetual naval preparedness." *Jefferson's War*, 129. In October 1803, the very month the *Philadelphia*

went aground, Jefferson personally worked through the numbers to reduce naval expenditures for the coming year from $780,000 to $599,061; Congress eventually appropriated $650,000. Notes on Reducing Navy Expenses, Oct. 10, 1803, Founders Online, https://founders.archives.gov/documents/Jefferson/01-41-02-0373.

43. *Augusta (GA) Chronicle*, May 2, 1801; Charles Oscar Paullin, *Paullin's History of Naval Administration 1775–1911* (Annapolis, MD: Naval Institute Press, 1968), 121-32; George E. Davies, "Robert Smith and the Navy," *Maryland Historical Magazine* 14, no. 4 (Dec. 1919): 301-22; Goldsborough, *Naval Chronicle*, 212-13; Alexander S. Balinky, "Albert Gallatin, Naval Foe," *Pennsylvania Magazine of History and Biography* 82, no. 3 (July 1958): passim.

44. Smith to Bainbridge, July 13, 1803, in *NDBW*, 2:477-78.

CHAPTER THREE: THE CRUISE

1. *Gazette of the United States*, Aug. 4, 1803; Ray, *Poems*, 223; Ray, *Horrors of Slavery*, 17, 40-41.

2. Brown, "A Sailor's Favorite Elixir," pt. 1: 17, 19, pt. 2: 7-12; Pope, *Life in Nelson's Navy*, 153; Melville, *White-Jacket*, 54. Tokay is a Hungarian sweet white wine. Another theory as to why jack tars welcomed their tots comes from a sailor-historian who wrote, "[A]nyone who has made long voyages under sail knows . . . a monotonous diet produces a powerful craving for a sharp, violent taste which is eased by rum." Pope, *Life in Nelson's Navy*, 146.

3. Langley, *Social Reform*, 14-41; Leech, *Thirty Years*, 48-51; Pope, *Life in Nelson's Navy*, 219-21, 226; Frykman, "The Wooden World Turned Upside Down," 39; Brown, "A Sailor's Favorite Elixir," pt. 1: 23.

4. Fowler, *Jack Tars*, 138; Taylor, *Sons of the Waves*, 223-24.

5. Court-Martial of William Johnson, Nov. 24, 1804, Stewart to Preble, Aug. 12, 1804, Preble to Stewart, Aug. 12, 1804, in *NDBW*, 5:158-59 and 4:405; Rea, *A letter to William Bainbridge*, 13.

6. Langley, "The Negro in the Navy," 281; Langley, *Social Reform*, 140-41; Ray, *Horrors of Slavery*, 17, 40-41, 44, 47; Long, *Sailor-Diplomat*, 18. Daniel Mendoza (1764–1836) was the boxing champion of England from 1792 to 1795. He introduced the "scientific style" of boxing, including side-stepping, ducking, blocking, raising the guard, and the straight left. Wikipedia, "Daniel Mendoza," https://en.wikipedia.org/wiki/Daniel_Mendoza.

7. Long, *Sailor-Diplomat*, 13-19.

8. Ray, *Poems*, 69-70, "A Voyage;" Ray, *Horrors of Slavery*, 50; Ray, *Poems*, 70-72, "Exercising Ship."

9. *Philadelphia Gazette*, Oct. 17, 1803; *Commercial Advertiser* (New York), Oct. 6, 1803, reprinting letter, O'Brien to Joseph Yznardi, Aug. 2, 1803. What O'Brien called a "galoeta" was properly known as a galliot, a small galley used as a commerce raider, typically rowed by sixteen to twenty oars, with a single mast and sail. *Oxford Companion*, 336.

10. Bainbridge to Consul James Simpson, Aug. 29, 1803, and Bainbridge to Simpson, Aug. 29, 1803, in *NDBW*, 2:518-19 and 3:1-2; Goldsborough, *Naval Chronicle*, 214-15; Spence to Polly Spence, Sept. 1, 1803, in Spence Papers.

11. Irwin, *Diplomatic Relations*, 83-84; Parker, *Uncle Sam in Barbary*, 156-57. Salvage was a doctrine of admiralty law by which a court ordered the owner of a rescued ship to compensate the rescuer for actual services rendered in saving the vessel from an enemy in wartime. The Supreme Court case defining salvage was *Talbot v. Seeman*. John Marshall and Supreme Court of the United States, *U.S. Reports: Talbot v. Seeman*, 5 U.S. (1 Cranch) 1 (1801), https://www.loc.gov/item/usrep005001/. A survey of the *Mirboka* valued her at $10,000. Preble to Bainbridge, Dec. 19, 1803, in *NDBW*, 3:280.

12. *Oracle Post* (Portsmouth, NH), Nov. 15, 1803, reprinting circular letter, Gavino to Consul William Jarvis, Sept. 1, 1803; Bainbridge to Preble, Sept. 12, 1803, in *NDBW*, 2:520; Spence to Polly Spence, Sept. 15, 1803, in Spence Papers.

13. In a letter to an Italian friend, Philip Mazzei, which had been published in foreign news-papers and then republished in English in the United States, Jefferson wrote, "In place of that noble love of liberty and republican government which carried us triumphantly thro' the war, an Anglican, monarchical and aristocratical party has sprung up. . . . It would give you a fever were I to name to you the apostates who have gone over to these heresies, men who were Samsons in the field and Solomons in the council, but who have had their heads shorn by the harlot England." Jefferson to Philip Mazzei, April 24, 1796, Founders Online, https://founders.archives.gov/documents/Jefferson/01-29-02-0054-0002.

14. Noah, *Travels*, 352; Ray Brighton, *The Checkered Career of Tobias Lear* (Portsmouth, NH: Portsmouth Marine Society, 1985), passim; Parker, *Uncle Sam in Barbary*, 165.

15. Stewart to Gore, Oct. 7, 1803, Gore to Stewart, Oct. 8, 1803, Stewart to Gore, Oct. 9, 1803, Preble to Gore, Oct. 17, 1803, and Preble to Smith, Oct. 23, 1803, in *NDBW*, 3:112, 3:113, 3:120, 3:143-44, and 3:160-62; *Telegraphe and Daily Advertiser*, Feb. 6, 1804, reprinting letter, Preble to Smith, Oct. 31, 1803; Ray, *Horrors of Slavery*, 46; Taylor, *Sons of the Waves*, 100.

16. *Newburyport Herald*, Oct. 28, 1803; *Columbian Centinel* (Boston), Nov. 2, 1803; *Salem (MA) Register*, Nov. 3, 1803; *New York Evening Post*, Nov. 3, 1803; *Telegraphe and Daily Advertiser*, Nov. 7, 1803; *Philadelphia Gazette*, Nov. 2, 1803, reprinting extract from a letter dated Gibraltar, Sept. 1, 1803.

17. Smith to squadron commander, Nov. 8, 1803, in *NDBW*, 3:207; *Annals of Congress*, 13:74, Presidential Message of Nov. 4, 1803; *Newburyport Herald*, Nov. 15, 1803.

18. Suleiman (1766–1822) was the king of Morocco from 1792 to 1822. One of five sons of Mohammed III, Suleiman fought a civil war against his brothers for control of the kingdom. Morocco remained largely passive for the subsequent decades of his rule. He is described as an essayist and man of letters. Wikipedia, "Slimane of Morocco," https://en.wikipedia.org/wiki/ Slimane_of_Morocco.

19. Preble to Smith, Sept. 22, 1803, in *NDBW*, 3:69-70.

20. McKee, *Edward Preble*, 141-45, 155-72; Irwin, *Diplomatic Relations*, 131-33; Toll, *Six Frigates*, 182-84; Blyth, *History of the War*, 105-6; *Telegraphe and Daily Advertiser*, Feb. 6, 1804, reprinting letter, Preble to Smith, Oct. 31, 1804; Preble to Smith, Oct. 1, 1803, and Imperial edicts, Oct. 11, 1803, in *NDBW*, 3:95-96 and 3:124-26; *City Gazette* (Charleston, SC), Dec. 17, 1803, reprinting extract from an Oct. 18, 1803, letter from an officer on board the *Syren*; *New-York Herald*, Feb. 8, 1804, reprinting an Oct. 11, 1803, letter from an officer serving in the Mediterranean squadron.

21. *Salem Gazette*, Nov. 25, 1803.

22. *Telegraphe*, Dec. 10, 1803, reprinting letter, Rodgers to Smith, Dec. 6, 1803.

23. The law passed by Congress also awarded $5,000 to Captain John Rodgers's ship *John Adams* for capturing the Tripolitan polacre *Meshouda* in June 1803. The *Meshouda* was the same ship Dale's squadron had trapped at Gibraltar in 1801, and which the Tripolitans had sold to Morocco. Rodgers secured a declaration from her crew that Morocco had transferred the *Meshouda* back to Tripoli and that she was acting under the bashaw's orders in trying to bring into Tripoli a cargo of munitions and naval stores. Presidential Message of Dec. 5, 1803, and "An act for the relief of the captors of the Moorish ships Meshouda and Mirboha [*sic*]," March 19, 1804, in *Annals of Congress*, 8th Cong,1st Sess., 13:210-11 and 13:1280-81; Wheelan, *Jefferson's War*, 149; McKee, *Edward Preble*, 143; Goldsborough, *Naval Chronicle*, 217. A statute provided for the distribution of prize money. An Act for the Better Government of the Navy of the United States, April 23, 1800, chap. 33, § 6, *Public Statutes at Large*, 2:45-53.

24. Long, *Nothing Too Daring*, passim; Long, *Ready to Hazard*, 173-75; David Dixon Porter, *Memoir of Commodore David Porter; of the United States Navy* (Albany, NY: J. Munsell, 1875), 9-28, 56; Wilson, *Biography*, 2:123-25; Langley, *Social Reform*, 136; John M. Niles, *The Life*

of Oliver Hazard Perry with an Appendix, Comprising a Biographical Memoir of the late Captain James Lawrence; With Brief Sketches of the Most Prominent Events in the Lives of Commodores Bainbridge, Decatur, Porter, and Macdonough (Hartford, CT: Oliver D. Cooke, 1821), 338-39; extract from Midshipman Henry Wadsworth journal, June 2, 1803, in *NDBW*, 2:435-37; Ray, *Horrors of Slavery*, 53.

25. Hicks, "True Born Columbians," 64-65; Bainbridge to Preble, March 4, 1804, and Preble to Bainbridge, June 12, 1804, in *NDBW*, 3:467 and 4:179-80; Ray, *Horrors of Slavery*, 52.

26. Smith to Preble, July 13, 1803, and Preble to Minister to France James Monroe, Nov. 12, 1803, in *NDBW*, 2:474-77 and 3:215-16. Preble sent the same letter announcing the blockade to the US ministers in London, Madrid, and Paris, and to the US consuls at Marseilles, Barcelona, Cadiz, Alicante, Malaga, Livorno, Naples, Lisbon, Gibraltar, and Tangier. Preble belatedly mentioned the blockade in a letter to the US consul at Malta, the port closest to Tripoli. Preble to Consul Joseph Pulis, Dec. 10, 1803, Preble to Bainbridge, Sept. 16, 1803, and Preble to Smith, Sept. 22, 1803, in *NDBW*, 3:261, 3:50, and 3:69-70; McKee, *Edward Preble*, 148; Morris, *A Defence of the Conduct*, 5; Schroeder, *Commodore John Rodgers*, 31. As a legal matter, Preble had instituted a blockade with insufficient force to make it effective, which drew a French protest. Under the law of nations, no place would be considered as under a blockade that was not "actually besieged." The Jefferson administration privately recognized that the French were right. Frederick C. Leiner, "Preble's Blockade of the Barbary Coast," *The Northern Mariner/le marin du nord* 25 (April 2015): 126-27.

27. Nissen to Cathcart, Sept. 19, 1803, in *NDBW*, 3:61-62; *Guardian or New Brunswick (NJ) Advertiser*, Sept. 10, 1801, reprinting Cathcart to Appleton, June 2, 1801.

28. Spence to Polly Spence, Sept. 15, 1803, in Spence Papers; Bainbridge to Preble, Oct. 4, 1803, in *NDBW*, 3:103-4; Porter, *Memoir*, 56-57; Ray, *Horrors of Slavery*, 53.

29. Bainbridge to Preble, Oct. 22, 1803, and Proceedings of Court of Inquiry into the Loss of the U.S. Frigate *Philadelphia*, June 29, 1805 (statement of Bainbridge), in *NDBW*, 3:159 and 3:192-94. Chipp Reid states that Preble ordered Bainbridge to keep the *Vixen* close to the *Philadelphia*, but Bainbridge ignored these orders. *Intrepid Sailors: The Legacy of Preble's Boys and the Tripoli Campaign* (Annapolis, MD: Naval Institute Press, 2012), 51. In fact, Preble's orders gave Bainbridge discretion to use the *Vixen* as he did. But the decision to send the *Vixen* to Cape Bon has justly been criticized as demonstrating poor judgment. It was not just a question of mutual assistance in case of accident. By sending the brig away, Bainbridge could not prevent small craft hugging the shoreline from entering and leaving Tripoli, the very purpose of the blockade. At sea, as on land, a division of forces in the face of the enemy is problematic. Tucker, *Dawn Like Thunder*, 212-13.

CHAPTER FOUR: CAPTIVITY

1. Philip MacDougall, *Islamic Seapower during the Age of Fighting Sail* (Woodbridge, Suffolk, UK: Boydell Press, 2017), 142.

2. Cowdery, *American Captives*, diary entry for October 31, 1803.

3. Cowdery, *American Captives*, diary entry for October 31, 1803; Bainbridge to Preble, Feb. 16, 1804, and Sailing Master William Knight to Thomas L. Bristoll, Nov. 1, 1803, in *NDBW*, 3:408-10 and 3:179-80.

4. Ray, *Poems*, 228; Wilson, *Biography*, 159-60.

5. Cowdery, *American Captives*, diary entry for Oct. 31, 1803; James Biddle to Vice President Aaron Burr, Nov. 29, 1803, in Letters of Commodore James Biddle, Biddle Family Papers, Box 1, Andalusia Historic House and Gardens, Andalusia, PA; Wilson, *Biography*, 2:159-60; Jon. Cowdery to Jabez Cowdery, Nov. 7, 1804, in F. L. Pleadwell and W. M. Kerr, "Jonathan Cowdery, Surgeon in the United States Navy, 1767–1852," *United States Naval Medical Bul-*

letin 17 (July 1922 and Aug. 1922): 71-72. Bainbridge provided the number of captives as 307 (43 officers and their attendants at the consul house and 264 enlisted people) in his first letter to the department. The letter and list were later printed in newspapers across the United States, beginning with the *National Intelligencer*, March 21, 1804, printing Bainbridge to Smith, Nov. 1, 1803. The list is also in *NDBW*, 3:183. The forty-three officers and men quartered at the American consul house were Captain William Bainbridge; Lieutenants David Porter, Jacob Jones, Theodore Hunt, and Benjamin Smith; William S. Osborne, lieutenant of marines; John Ridgely, surgeon; Keith Spence, purser; William Knight, sailing master; Jonathan Cowdery and Nicholas Harwood, surgeon's mates; George Hodge, bosun; Midshipmen Bernard Henry, Daniel T. Patterson, James Gibbon, Benjamin F. Read, William Cutbush, Wallace Wormeley, Robert Gamble, Richard B. Jones, James Renshaw, James Biddle, and Simon Smith; Joseph Douglass, sailmaker; Richard Stevenson, gunner's mate; William Godby, carpenter; William Anderson, captain's clerk; Minor Forenten, master's mate; James C. Morris, ships' steward; Otis Hunt and David Irvine, sergeants of marines; William Leith, cook; Peter Williams, corporal of marines; James Casey, master of arms; and sailors John Babtist, Lewis Hecksener, Frederick Lewis, Charles Mitchell, Peter Cook, Leonard Foster, William James, William Gardner, and William Kemprefill (the last name is Temperfelt in *NDBW*). The nine sailors served as stewards to the officers. No newspaper listed by name the 264 captive enlisted men and marines in any of the hundreds of articles published about the Americans' captivity.

6. Ray, *Horrors of Slavery*, 57-58.

7. Ray, *Horrors of Slavery*, 58. Ray's reference is the only one to a black sailor among the crew.

8. Ray, *Poems*, 231-32; Ray, *Horrors of Slavery*, 58-60, 62. Joseph Wheelan refers to the crew being lodged in the dungeon of the bashaw's castle, but the crew was not lodged there. *Jefferson's War*, 174 75, 177, 270.

9. Bainbridge to Officers, Nov. 1, 1803, and Officers to Bainbridge, Nov. 1, 1803, in *NDBW*, 3:169 and 3:169-70. For reasons that are unclear, Danish Consul Nicholas Nissen attested to a copy of the letter, signed by all the officers, that was copied into his chancery book. Letter book and Correspondence of Nicolai Christian Nissen in Tripoli, konsulaer representation and konsulaer retsprotokol, 2-2215 in Korrespondancesager 1752–1834, Rigsarkivet, Copenhagen, Denmark (hereafter cited as Nissen Letters). The officers' letter was later printed in newspapers across the United States, including the *Philadelphia Gazette*, March 26, 1804, the *National Intelligencer*, March 28, 1804, and the *Telegraphe and Daily Advertiser*, March 29, 1804.

10. Biddle to Burr, Nov. 29, 1803, in Biddle Family Papers; Harris, *Life and Services*, 82; Bainbridge to Susan Bainbridge, Nov. 1, 1803, in *NDBW*, 3:178-79. Harris was a surgeon in the navy who rose to become the chief of the navy's Bureau of Medicine and Surgery.

11. Bainbridge to Smith, Nov. 1, 1803, in *NDBW*, 3:171-73. The phrase in Bainbridge's letter that "the Crew will be supported by this Regency" outraged William Ray. In his memoir, he railed against Bainbridge, asking how he could know that the bashaw would feed the men, although he conceded that Bainbridge understood that Yusuf would feed them as *quid pro quo* for their laboring as his slaves. Ray took the phrase as Bainbridge's indication that the government and charitable private Americans need not support the crew. Ray claimed that during their captivity, when the men applied to Bainbridge for help, he "invariably" replied that "it was entirely out of his power to do any thing for us," which to Ray "evince[d] a total disregard and dereliction" of his duty and showed that he thought his men were "totally unworthy." Ray, *Horrors of Slavery*, 60-61. Ray's indictment of Bainbridge was largely if not completely false.

12. Bainbridge to Preble, Nov. 1, 1803, and Richard Farquhar to President Thomas Jefferson, Nov. 15, 1803, in *NDBW*, 3:171 and 3:272.

13. Pulis to Preble, Nov. 26, 1803, Preble to Pulis, Dec. 10, 1803, and Bainbridge to Preble, Dec. 13, 1803, in *NDBW*, 3:236-37, 3:261, and 3:269.

14. *Portsmouth (NH) Oracle*, March 24, 1804, reprinting letter, Cathcart to Capt. Orne, December 16, 1803.

15. Cathcart to Nissen, Dec. 12, 1803, Cathcart to Madison, Dec. 15, 1803, Cathcart to Madison, Oct. 15, 1804, and Preble to Mackenzie & Glennie, Dec. 22, 1804, in *NDBW*, 3:266-67, 3:272-73, 5:86, and 5:207. Lear complained that the "style of Mr. Cathcart's letter to me was arrogant & dictatorial, and carrying with it the idea that he was the person empower[e]d to do these things. . . . Mr. C should consider that he is now but a private Citizen; & further, he should remember, that his conduct has given disgust (whether right or wrong) to the Barbary powers; and therefore it could do no good to our affairs for him to assume an agency in them." Lear to Bainbridge, Feb. 12, 1804, in ibid., 3:403-5.

16. Lear to Consul George Davis, Dec. 15, 1803, Lear to Bainbridge, Dec. 16, 1803, and Bainbridge to Lear, Jan. 14, 1804, in ibid., 3:271-72, 3:274-75, and 3:329-30.

17. Carl Frederik Bricka, *Dansk biografik Lexikon Dansk* (Copenhagen: Gyldendalske Boghandels Forlag, 1887–1905) (runeberg.org/dbl/12/0301.html), 12:299; Harald Holck, "Kommandør Carl Christian Holcks Dagbøger som Konsul i Tunis. Af kontorchef" (Commander Carl Christian Holcks' Diaries as Consul in Tunis. Head of Office), PersonalHistorik Tidsskrift, 82 (1962), 124.

18. Cowdery, *American Captives*, diary entries for Nov. 1–6, 1803; Bainbridge to Preble, Nov. 15, 1803, in *NDBW*, 3:223-24; *Pennsylvania Correspondent, and Farmers' Advertiser* (Doylestown), July 7, 1804, printing extract of a letter from a *Philadelphia* midshipman, Feb. 11, 1804.

19. Knight to Bristoll, Nov. 1, 1803, in *NDBW*, 3:179-80.

20. Spence to Polly Spence, Nov. 1, 1803, in Spence Papers; Cowdery, *American Captives*, diary entries for Nov. 6 and 8, 1803; Biddle to Burr, Nov. 29, 1803, in Biddle Family Papers.

21. Harwood may have been studying medicine in Annapolis with or under John Ridgely (1778–1843), also a St. John's College graduate, who was appointed the surgeon of the *Philadelphia* in 1803 and may have asked Harwood if he wanted to come along. "Harriet Callahan Ridgely," Hammond-Harwood House Museum, https://hammondharwoodhouse. org/harriet-callahan-ridgely/.

22. Edith Rossiter Bevan, "Letters from Nicholas Harwood, M.D., U.S.N.: Prisoner of War in Tripoli, 1803–'05," *Maryland Historical Magazine* 40, no. 1 (Spring 1945): 67-68, quoting Harwood to brother-in-law Lewis Duvall, Nov. 3, 1803, in Hammond-Harwood House Collection, MS 1303, Maryland Center for History and Culture (hereafter cited as MCHC).

23. *Aurora and General Advertiser* (Philadelphia), March 20, 1804.

24. Zuchet to Foreign Ministry, Nov. 16, 1803, letter no. 356, 1804/19, in Zuchet Letters, 121; Nissen to Danish consul in Marseilles, Nov. 2, 1803, in *NDBW*, 3:182.

25. Phineas Bond to Simon Lucas, April 24, 1804, in Correspondence to and from London and Malta, Benghazi etc. 1800–1815, in Correspondence to and Letter Books, 1700 to 1948, Consulate, Tripoli, Libya (formerly Ottoman Empire): FO 160/35 Foreign Office and predecessor, British National Archives, Kew, England; Davis to Biddle, Sept. 10, 1804, in Biddle Family Letters; Nissen to Davis, Sept. 30, 1804, in *NDBW*, 5:58-59; "Biographical Notice of Captain James Biddle," *Analectic Magazine* 6, Nov. 1815, 383-99; Long, *Sailor-Diplomat*, 19. A copy of Bond's letter but dated March 14, 1804, is in the Biddle Family Papers.

26. Bainbridge to Susan Bainbridge, Nov. 1, 1803, in *NDBW*, 3:178-79.

27. Smith to Preble, Nov. 19, 1803, in *NDBW*, 3:230.

28. Dearborn, *Life of William Bainbridge*, 60; Bainbridge to Smith, Nov. 25, 1803, in *NDBW*, 3:175-76; Ray, *Poems*, 232; Porter, *Memoir*, 62; Ray, *Horrors of Slavery*, 58, 61-63, 66-67, 121.

29. Leech, *Thirty Years*, 65-66; Dearborn, *Life of William Bainbridge*, 60; Bainbridge to Smith, Nov. 25, 1803, in *NDBW*, 3:175-76; Ray, *Poems*, 232; Ray, *Horrors of Slavery*, 58, 61-63.

30. Dearborn, *Life of William Bainbridge*, 60; Bainbridge to Smith, Nov. 25, 1803, in *NDBW*, 3:175-76; Leech, *Thirty Years*, 65; Ray, *Poems*, 232; Ray, *Horrors of Slavery*, 58, 61-63, 67.

31. Zuchet to Foreign Ministry, Nov. 1, 1803, letter no. 356, 1804/17, in Zuchet Letters, 117, 120; McDonogh to Yorke, Nov. 9, 1803, in General Correspondence before 1906, Tripoli, Consuls Richard Tully, Simon Lucas, Proconsul B. McDonogh, Consul William Wass Langford 1793–1804, FO 76, Foreign Office and predecessors: Political and Other Departments, British National Archives, Kew, England.

32. Bainbridge to Preble, Nov. 6, 1803, and Bainbridge to Smith, Nov. 25, 1803, in *NDBW*, 3:173 and 3:175-76; Allen, *Barbary Corsairs*, 152; Cowdery, *American Captives*, diary entry for Nov. 3, 1803; Toll, *Six Frigates*, 205 (giving the Tripolitan name of the *Philadelphia* as *Gift of Allah*); Zuchet to Foreign Ministry, Nov. 5, 1803, letter no. 356, 1804/18, in Zuchet Letters, 121 (translating the name as *God's Present*). Although Bainbridge wrote he "surrendered to the rocks," Folayan asserts that the Tripolitan navy "inflicted" the capture, a claim that is hard to understand. *Tripoli during the Reign*, 36. There is a factual dispute about when the *Philadelphia* refloated. Ray insisted that the *Philadelphia* came off the rocks "the very next morning after she was captured," likely to insinuate that Bainbridge had misjudged the situation. *Horrors of Slavery*, 60-62. The Dutch chargé, Zuchet, wrote in his diary that "the ship during *the same night* floated free without any rescue efforts." Zuchet to Foreign Ministry, Nov. 1, 1803, letter no. 356, 1804/17, in Zuchet Letters, 120 (emphasis added). Some of the historical literature, accepts those accounts. Baepler, *White Slaves*, 19, and Zacks, *Pirate Coast*, 46-47. However, the weight of the evidence, including the unpublished letters of Spence, Harwood, and Knight, is that the frigate came off the reef nearly two days after she went aground. Porter asserted the ship came off forty-eight hours after grounding. Porter to Wadsworth, March 5, 1804, in *NDBW*, 3:475-76. Danish Consul Nissen wrote his foreign ministry, "A west-wind and the sea lifted the frigate from the reef 48 hours after it ran aground." Nissen to Board of Directors [*pro memoria*], Nov. 25, 1803, Nissen Letters ("En Vesten Vind og Søegang lættede Fregatten af Banken 48 Timer efter den kom paa Grund"). As to the examples Bainbridge cited, *Hannibal* was a 74-gun British ship-of-the-line that ran aground off Algeciras, Spain, during a battle against the French fleet on July 5, 1801. Despite running aground, the *Hannibal* kept fighting until she was abandoned by the British squadron and surrendered with 140 dead and wounded. *Jason* was a 38-gun British frigate wrecked on blockade duty off Brest (not St. Malo) on October 13, 1798.

33. Zuchet to Foreign Ministry, Nov. 16, 1803, and Jan. 20, 1804, letter nos. 356, 1804/19 and 356, 1804/22, in Zuchet Letters, 121-22; Nissen to Board of Directors [*pro memoria*], Nov. 25, 1803, Nissen Letters ("Paschaen har forlangt en Fokkemast fra Malta, da den blev kappet af Amerika=nerne for at lette Skibet"). Some of the historical literature suggests that the Tripolitans could not have used the *Philadelphia* after her capture, either because the harbor was too shallow or because Tripoli lacked sufficient seamen to repair or man her. Nissen's letter belies those assertions. The Spanish shipwrights working for the bashaw or the captured American sailors could have mounted and rigged a new foremast; moreover, as shown by their having sailed the *Mirboka* and *Meshuda*, the Tripolitans had sufficient expertise to have sailed what they called the *Gift of Allah*.

34. Spence to Aunt Brackett, Nov. 5, 1803, in Spence Papers.

35. Ray, *Horrors of Slavery*, 51-52; Harris, *Life and Services*, 86-87; *Aurora and General Advertiser*, May 9, 1804, reprinting letter of an unidentified officer, Dec. 6, 1803; Cowdery, *American Captives*, diary entries for Nov. 10–14, 1803; Biddle to Burr, Nov. 29, 1803, in Biddle Family Papers. Ray, having read Cowdery's account after it was published in 1806, depreci-

ated his "whining" and corrected his "misrepresentations." First, Ray stated, their prison was not in the castle, and second, the men offered the officers bread and boiled salt beef, brought from the *Philadelphia*, from which several officers "made a hearty repast." Ray, *Horrors of Slavery*, 67. Spence also believed the men were housed in the castle, writing his wife, "The Men are at the Castle prison." Spence to Polly Spence, Nov. 27, 1803, in Spence Papers. This is a curious discrepancy because the officers marched to the magazine. Perhaps the Tripolitan officers told them they were being sent to the castle prison but meant it was the prison for the castle's prisoners.

36. Bainbridge to Preble, Nov. 15, 1803, and Preble to Bainbridge, Dec. 10, 1803, in *NDBW*, 3:223-24 and 3:260; Nissen to Board of Directors [*pro memoria*], Nov. 25, 1803, Nissen Letters ("Paschaen lod sig ilfredsstille med at Capt Bainbridge gav Rapport om Sagen til Commandør Prebble. Det er umuligt at Tripolinnerne som er i Amerikanernes Magt, uagtet den fortrinlig gode Behandling de nyde, skrive det modsatte, for engang ved deres Tilbagekomst at erholde Erstatning af Paschaen, eller for at tilsende deres Familie Gaver . . .").

37. Nissen to Board of Directors [*pro memoria*], Nov. 25, 1803, in Nissen Letters ("Blandt Besætningen fandtes naturligviis Folk af alle Slag og Nationer. . ."); Christopher McKee, "Foreign Seamen in the United States Navy: A Census of 1808," *William and Mary Quarterly*, 3d series, 42 (July 1985): 383-93.

38. James Gambier to William Jarvis, Jan. 15, 1805, in *NDBW*, 5:281.

39. Bainbridge to Preble, Dec. 5, 1803, in ibid., 3:253.

40. *Morning Chronicle* (New York), Jan. 6, 1803, reprinting letter, O'Brien to Madison, June 26, 1802; *Alexandria (VA) Daily Advertiser*, Oct. 4, 1802, reprinting letter, O'Brien to Consul at Malaga William Kirkpatrick, June 30, 1802; Capt. Andrew Morris to Cathcart, July 22, 1802, and Cathcart to Consul at Marseilles Stephen Cathalan, Aug. 28, 1802, in *NDBW*, 2:176-77 and 2:259; Dzurec, *Our Suffering Brethren*, 97-100; Lawrence A. Peskin, *Captives and Countrymen: Barbary Slavery and the American Public, 1785–1816* (Baltimore: Johns Hopkins University Press, 2009), 145; Irwin, *Diplomatic Relations*, 117-18. For the help he provided to the *Franklin* crew before they were ransomed, Danish Consul Nissen received the gift of a snuff box as a symbol of the United States' thanks. Lear to Nissen, June 4, 1804, in *NDBW*, 4:18-49.

41. Taylor, *Sons of the Waves*, 33, 223-25; Thomas Malcolmson, *Order and Disorder in the British Navy, 1793–1815: Control, Resistance, Flogging and Hanging* (Woodbridge, Suffolk, UK: Boydell Press, 2016), 207-8, 211, 255; Lavery, *Life in Nelson's Navy*, 144. US Navy regulations provided that any person who deserted "shall suffer death, or such other punishment as a court martial shall adjudge," albeit at the time, the punishment was often remitted to a flogging. An Act for the Better Government of the Navy of the United States, April 23, 1800, chap. 33, § 1, art. 27, *Public Statutes at Large*, 2:45-53; James E. Valle, *Rocks and Shoals: Naval Discipline in the Age of Fighting Sail* (Annapolis, MD: Naval Institute Press, 1986), 127-28.

42. Preble to Smith, July 21, 1803, in *NDBW*, 2:494; Ray, *Horrors of Slavery*, 46; Toll, *Six Frigates*, 185-86.

43. *Vermont Centinel* (Burlington), March 22, 1804, reprinting an extract from the purser of the *Argus*, Timothy Winn, Jan. 23, 1804; Lt. John Johnson to Lt. Col. William Burrows, Jan. 24, 1804, in *NDBW*, 3:357. According to Ray, most of the British-born sailors in the *Philadelphia*'s crew had genuinely "adopted America as their country, laughed at their [fellow sailors'] credulity and hissed at their project, positively declaring that they would not be released by a government which they detested, on account of its tolerating the impressment of seamen, and swearing they would sooner remain under the Bashaw than George the third." Ray, *Horrors of Slavery*, 64.

44. It is unclear how the bashaw knew there were 170 Britons in the crew, but that figure

seems accurate. Beaussier to Talleyrand, 15 Brumaire an douze (Nov. 7, 1803), and Beaussier to Talleyrand, 4 Frimaire an douze (Nov. 26, 1803) ("la délivrance de quelques Deserteurs, laquelle devra nécessairement entrainer celle de plus de la moitié de l'équipage de la frégate Américaine, c'est à dire de 170 hommes qui sont anglais et le priver par la plusieurs centaines de milliers de francs qu'il se propose de retirer des Etats-Unis pour leur rançon."), in Beaussier Letters.

45. Nissen to Board of Directors [*pro memoria*], Nov. 25, 1803 ("Blandt Fregattens Mandskab har jeg hidindtil kun forefundet [. . .] Danske der har meldt sig, nemlig: Knud Knudsen fra Bergen, Matros Jens Andersen fra Cronborg Amt [. . .] Denne sidste er sygelig, jeg gav ham derfor lidt Hjælp; men da samtlige Besætnings [. . .] Hyre vil vedblive at vorde betalt uagtet Fange=skabet, har jeg saa meget mindre troet mig betroet Ret til at give nogen Understøttelse for Hr Majestæts Regning, som de deruden ingen Ret havde dertil."), in Nissen Letters.

46. Ray, *Horrors of Slavery*, 65-67; Cowdery, *American Captives*, diary entry for Nov. 8, 1803; Bainbridge to Preble, Nov. 15, 1803, Preble to Swedish consul [Burstrom], Dec. 19, 1803, and Bainbridge to Preble, Feb. 16, 1804, in *NDBW*, 3:223-24, 3:280-81, and 3:409-19.

47. Ray, *Horrors of Slavery*, 67. Cowdery, *American Captives*, diary entry for Jan. 28, 1804; Spencer C. Tucker, *Arming the Fleet: U.S. Navy Ordnance in the Muzzle-Loading Era* (Annapolis, MD: Naval Institute Press, 1989), 93-94. The British use of red-hot shot at Gibraltar is in Roy Adkins and Lesley Adkins, *Gibraltar: The Greatest Siege in British History* (New York: Viking, 2017), 280-81, 286-87, 324-42.

48. Bainbridge to Preble, Nov. 15, 1803, and Bainbridge to Preble, Dec. 13, 1803, in *NDBW*, 3:223-24 and 3:269; Cowdery, *American Captives*, diary entries for Jan. 12 and 24, 1804; Ray, *Horrors of Slavery*, 67-68; *Philadelphia Gazette*, May 15, 1804, reprinting an extract of a letter from a midshipman, Nov. 22, 1803.

49. Cowdery, *American Captives*, diary entry for Feb. 1, 1805; Ray, *Horrors of Slavery*, 102.

50. Cowdery, *American Captives*, diary entry for Nov. 27, 1803; Ray, *Horrors of Slavery*, 68.

51. Cowdery, *American Captives*, diary entry for Nov. 30, 1803; Ray, *Horrors of Slavery*, 68, 71-72.

52. Taylor, *Sons of the Waves*, 288; Leech, *Thirty Years*, 74.

53. Gilje, *Liberty on the Waterfront*, 125, 180-81; Ray, *Horrors of Slavery*, 78, 113; Brodine, "Children of the Storm," 18; Trevor James, *Prisoners of War at Dartmoor: American and French Soldiers and Sailors in an English Prison during the Napoleonic Wars and the War of 1812* (Jefferson, NC: McFarland, 2013), 102-3.

54. William Spencer, *Algiers in the Age of the Corsairs* (Norman: University of Oklahoma Press, 1976), 33; Dearden, *Nest of Corsairs*, 21; Ray, *Horrors of Slavery*, 72, 112; Taylor, *Sons of the Waves*, 179, 313.

55. Stephen Budiansky, "A Half-Pint of Rum, Hard Biscuit, and 20 Lashes," *New York Post*, Jan. 16, 2011; Ray, *Horrors of Slavery*, 70; *Philadelphia Gazette*, June 2, 1804, reprinting extract from an officer of the *Philadelphia*, Dec. 2, 1803.

56. Harold D. Langley, *A History of Medicine in the Early U.S. Navy* (Baltimore: Johns Hopkins University Press, 1995), 38; Pleadwell and Kerr, "Jonathan Cowdery," 62-88.

57. Cowdery, *American Captives*, diary entries for Nov. 17-Dec. 12, 1803; Ray, *Horrors of Slavery*, 67.

58. Biddle to Burr, Nov. 29, 1803, in Biddle Family Papers.

59. Spence to Polly Spence, Nov. 20 and 27, 1803, in Spence Papers; *Philadelphia Evening Post*, May 9, 1804, reprinting a letter from an unidentified officer, Nov. 11, 1803; *Philadelphia Gazette*, May 15, 1804, reprinting an extract of a letter from a midshipman, Nov. 22, 1803; Cowdery, *American Captives*, diary entry for Nov. 10, 1803.

60. Spence to Polly Spence, Nov. 20 and 27, 1803, in Spence Papers.

61. Harris, *Life and Services*, 84-85; Dearborn, *Life of William Bainbridge*, 90.

62. Circular Letter from Smith to unemployed midshipmen, July 28, 1803, and Smith to Bainbridge, July 12, 1803, in *NDBW*, 2:500-501 and 2:473; Christopher McKee, *A Gentlemanly and Honorable Profession: The Creation of the U.S. Naval Officer Corps, 1794–1815* (Annapolis, MD: Naval Institute Press, 1991), 203.

63. Dearborn, *Life of William Bainbridge*, 58; Harris, *Life and Services*, 85; Porter, *Memoir*, 64; Allen, *Barbary Corsairs*, 154; *Poulson's American Daily Advertiser* (Philadelphia), May 16, 1804, reprinting Bainbridge to Porter, Nov. 5, 1803. Bainbridge's letter was reprinted in many newspapers, including the *New York Evening Post*, May 17, 1804, *National Intelligencer*, May 21, 1804, *Repertory* (Boston), May 22, 1804, and *Enquirer* (Richmond, VA), May 23, 1804.

64. "Biography of Captain Jacob Jones," *Analectic Magazine* 2, July 1813, 70-78; Wilson, *Biography*, 2:89-92; J. Worth Estes, "Commodore Jacob Jones: A Doctor Goes to Sea," *Delaware History Journal* 24, no. 2 (Fall-Winter 1990), 109-22; Mark M. Cleaver, *The Life, Character, and Public Services of Commodore Jacob Jones* (Wilmington: Historical Society of Delaware, 1906), 3-6, 29-31; Ray, *Poems*, 222.

65. Porter, *Memoir*, 63; Niles, *Life of Perry*, 340; Wilson, *Biography*, 2:165; Midshipman James Renshaw to Rodgers, Oct. 15, 1804, in *NDBW*, 5:87-88. *The Port Folio*, 3rd ser., vol. 5, no. 2 (Feb. 1815), a national magazine, contained extracts from Porter's journal of the cruise on the frigate *Essex* into the Pacific during the War of 1812, illustrated with Porter's drawings of a native warrior chief and a war canoe, both engraved by William Strickland.

66. Philip K. Allan, "Navigating to the Sextant," *Naval History*, June 2020, 6-7; Stanford J. Shaw, *Between Old and New: The Ottoman Empire under Sultan Selim III, 1789–1807* (Cambridge, MA: Harvard University Press, 1971), 152; MacDougall, *Islamic Seapower*, 58.

67. Long, *Nothing Too Daring*, 25-26; Bainbridge to Preble, July 7, 1804, in *NDBW*, 4:255-56; Long, *Sailor-Diplomat*, 23; Porter, *Memoir*, 63. Wargaming in the US Navy is typically regarded as a late-nineteenth-century development, beginning at the Naval War College in Newport, Rhode Island. Peter P. Perla, *Art of Wargaming: A Guide for Professionals and Hobbyists* (Annapolis, MD: Naval Institute Press, 1990), 61-70. Although abstract war games like chess have existed for a millennium, the first naval war game was created in 1779 by John Clerk, a Scottish intellectual who had never been to sea but who recoiled at the tactics British admirals used in the American Revolution. In January 1780, Clerk demonstrated his tactical theories with small wood and wax ship models in meetings with leading British naval officers. Clerk privately published and distributed *An Essay on Naval Tactics, Systemic and Historical*, in 1782, and three commercially published editions followed, starting in 1790. Clerk's ideas had immediate effect. Admiral Lord Rodney, whose fleet broke the French line at the Battle of the Saintes in April 1782, credited Clerk's ideas, as did other British officers, including Nelson. Jim Tildesley, "The Influence of the Theories of John Clerk of Eldin on British Fleet Tactics, 1782–1805," *Mariner's Mirror* 106 (May 2020): 162-74. It is unclear whether US naval officers of that era knew about or had a copy of Clerk's work, the only "original work on naval tactics in English during the eighteenth century." Ibid., 172. If the captive officers consulted a book for their floor problems, it was more likely David Steel's *A System of Naval Tactics*, one of his volumes of The Elements and Practice of Rigging, Seamanship, and Naval Tactics, first published in 1794. Steel, an English civilian, sold nautical books, charts, and instruments from his Navigation Warehouse at Little Tower Hill in London. Steel's books were widely read by naval officers. Pope, *Life in Nelson's Navy*, 33, 77. Commodore Preble had a copy of Steel's book. McKee, *Edward Preble*, 219.

68. Ron Chernow, *Washington: A Life* (New York: Penguin, 2010), 331; Michael Schulman, "G.I. Jive, *The New Yorker*, Jan. 9, 2017, 9; Wilson, *Biography*, 2:165 (identifying the plays the officers performed); Wikipedia, "The Castle Spectre," https://en.wikipedia.org/wiki/

The_Castle_Spectre; Wikipedia, "The Heir at Law," https://en.wikipedia.org/wiki/The_Heir_ at_Law; Wikipedia, "August von Kotzebue," author of *The Stranger*, https://en.wikipedia.org/ wiki/August _von_Kotzebue; Wikipedia, "Thomas Morton (playwright)," author of *Secrets Worth Knowing*, https://en.wikipedia.org/wiki/Thomas_Morton_(playwright). In December 1804, Baltimore printers Warner and Hanna published a six-volume anthology of plays; the first volume contained the four plays staged in Tripoli. *Telegraphe and Daily Advertiser*, Dec. 5, 1804 (advertisement). Warner and Hanna likely plagiarized a London printing used by the officers in Tripoli.

CHAPTER FIVE: REACTION

1. Extract from Preble diary, Nov. 24, 1803, extract from *Constitution* log book, Nov. 24, 1803, and Preble to Smith, Dec. 10, 1803, in *NDBW*, 3:175, 3:236, and 3:256.

2. Preble to Smith, Dec. 10, 1803, in *NDBW*, 3:256-60.

3. Lear to Davis, Dec. 12, 1803, in *NDBW*, 3:263-66. In fact, the news had reached Tunis by November 13, when the Danish consul, Carl Christian Holck, wrote in his diary that "the American frigate *Philadelphia* began chasing a Tripolitan corsair, but was grounded outside Tripoli and struck her flag, whereafter the officers and the crew (307 persons) went ashore and were enslaved." ("D. 13. giorde den amerikanske Fregat "Philadelphia" Jagt paa en tripoli-tansk Korsar, men stødte paa Grund ud for Tripolis og strog Flaget, hvorefter Officerer og Mandskab (307 Personer) gik i Land og blev gjort til Slaver.") Holck, "Kommandør Carl Christian Holcks Dagbøger," 91, diary entry of Nov. 13, 1803. George Davis must have known as well but neglected to inform Lear.

4. Preble to Smith, Dec. 10, 1803, Gavino to Madison, Jan. 4, 1804, extract from log book of the *Constitution*, Dec. 15, 1803, and Preble to Smith, Jan. 17, 1804, in *NDBW*, 3:256-60, 3:313-14, 3:273-74, and 3:337-40.

5. *Boston Commercial Gazette*, March 8, 1804.

6. *Democrat* (Boston), March 10, 1804; *Connecticut Courant* (Hartford), March 14, 1804; *Philadelphia Evening Post*, March 15, 1804; *Charleston (SC) Courier*, March 21, 1804.

7. Preble to Bainbridge, Dec. 19, 1803 (emphasis in original), in *NDBW*, 3:280; McKee, *Edward Preble*, 182, citing Preble to Mary Preble, Dec. 10, 1803; Harris, *Life and Services*, 93-96 (reprinting letter).

8. Preble to Smith, Dec. 10, 1803, Preble to Decatur, Dec. 10, 1803, extract from log book of the *Constitution*, Dec. 16, 1803 (entry of Sailing Master Nathaniel Haraden), and extract from log book of the *Constitution*, Dec. 17, 1803 (entry of Haraden), in *NDBW*, 3:256-60, 3:260-61, 3:276, and 3:278.

9. Preble to Dent, Dec. 19, 1803, Preble to Smith, Dec. 10, 1803, extract from Preble diary, Dec. 20, 1803, and Wadsworth to unknown, Jan. 10, 1804, in *NDBW*, 3:281, 3:256-60, 3:282, and 3:322-24; McKee, *Edward Preble*, 184.

10. Preble to Bainbridge, Jan. 16, 1804, Preble to Lear, Jan. 17, 1804, extract from log book of *Constitution*, Dec. 23, 1803, extract of Preble diary, Dec. 24, 1803, and Preble to Reed, Dec. 23, 1803, in *NDBW*, 3:334-35, 3:340, 3:288, 3:294, and 3:288-89; Armstrong, *Small Boats*, 58-59; McKee, *Edward Preble*, 183-84; Long, *Nothing Too Daring*, 24. Albert Gleaves states that the *Mastico* was originally a French vessel that was captured by the British navy at the Battle of Aboukir Bay in 1798 and given to the bashaw as a gift. *James Lawrence: Captain, United States Navy* (New York: G.P. Putnam's Sons, 1904), 48.

11. Extract from *Constitution* log book, Dec. 25, 1803, extract from *Constitution* log book, Dec. 30, 1803, extract from Preble memorandum book, Dec. 26, 1803, and Preble to Bainbridge, Jan. 4, 1804, in *NDBW*, 3:295-96, 3:302-3, 3:298, and 3:310-11.

12. Bainbridge to Preble, Jan. 9, 1804, in *NDBW*, 3:319-20; Spence to Polly Spence, Jan. 8,

1804, in Spence Papers. The reason the captives received no letters from Preble or anyone else was Joseph Pulis. As consul in Malta, he gathered all the letters meant for the captives, but instead of forwarding them to Tripoli (in a ship with a passport or via Tunis and then overland), he put the letters (and outbound letters from the captives) in four parcels to ship to the United States. Preble discovered his wrongdoing. Pulis had not rifled through the mail, and Preble never understood his motivation, although Pulis had once been the bashaw's consul, and Preble derided him as having "no respectability." Preble appointed Higgins as the US naval agent at Malta and asked that he be made consul, to replace Pulis. Preble to Smith, Feb. 3, 1804, in *NDBW*, 3:384-86; Tucker, *Dawn Like Thunder*, 258-59. Joseph Whee-lan errs in attributing to Pulis the five months' time the news of the loss of the *Philadelphia* took to reach America; Preble sent Gadsden with dispatches on December 15, and Pulis did not delay him. *Jefferson's War*, 168.

13. Ray, *Horrors of Slavery*, 70-71; Bainbridge to Preble, Dec. 13, 1803, and Bainbridge to Preble, Feb. 16, 1804, in *NDBW*, 3:269 and 3:408-410. Godby complained to the bashaw that three men had beaten him. As a result, the three men were punished with 150 strokes of the *bastinado*, a punishment John Wilson prescribed. Ray, *Horrors of Slavery*, 72-73; Blyth, *History of the War*, 109. None of the names of the three men identified by Ray appear on the list of the crew compiled by Spence at the end of their captivity. *NDBW*, 3:184-88.

14. Preble to Warrant and Petty Officers, Seamen and Marines of the late U.S. Frigate Philadelphia, Jan. 4, 1804, in *NDBW*, 3:312.

15. Preble to D'Guise (*sic*), Jan. 4, 1804, Preble to Bainbridge, Jan. 4, 1804, Bainbridge to Preble, Feb. 16, 1804, Dghies to Bainbridge, March 5, 1804, and Bainbridge to Preble, July 8, 1804, in *NDBW*, 3:312-13, 3:310-11, 3:408-9, 3:474, and 4:258-59. Some historians believe, incorrectly, that Preble's letter was delivered to the crew. Allison, *Crescent Obscured*, 115; Mullen, "Good Neighbourhood," 141; and Peskin, *Captives and Countrymen*, 154. Robert Allison has misconstrued Preble's letter, claiming it meant that it was in the sailors' "power, even when their situation seemed to deprive them of any choice to refuse to be slaves." From that premise, he concludes that "[s]lavery was not a life of toil; . . . rather, slavery and freedom were defined by a man's attitude toward work and ease." *Crescent Obscured*, 115.

16. Lear to Preble, Dec. 21, 1803, Lear to Davis, Dec. 17, 1803, and O'Brien to Preble, Dec. 21, 1803, in *NDBW*, 3:285-86, 3:276-78, and 3:283-84; Gary E. Wilson, "American Hostages in Moslem Nations, 1784–1796: The Public Response," *Journal of the Early Republic* 2 (Summer 1982): 138-39.

17. *True American and Commercial Daily Advertiser* (Philadelphia), July 24, 1804, reprinting an extract from a letter of a *Philadelphia* officer, Feb. 24, 1804.

18. Parker, *Uncle Sam in Barbary*, 138; McKee, *Edward Preble*, 202; Preble to Smith, Jan. 17, 1804, in *NDBW*, 3:337-40. Wilkie must have been unsure what the proposed annual tribute would be because Preble left blank spaces in his letter to Secretary Smith as to the amount.

19. Preble to Lear, Jan. 31, 1804, Preble to Smith, Feb. 3, 1804, and Preble to Smith, March 11, 1804, in *NDBW*, 3:377-79, 3:384-86, and 3:485-88; David F. Long, *Gold Braid and Foreign Relations: Diplomatic Activities of U.S. Naval Officers, 1798–1883* (Annapolis, MD: Naval Institute Press, 1988), 30.

20. Preble to Bainbridge, Jan. 4, 1804, in *NDBW*, 3:310-11.

21. Livingston to Talleyrand, Jan. 2, 1804, in *NDBW*, 3:308-9; Leiner, *Millions for Defense*, 15-17.

22. Talleyrand to Beaussier, 25 Nivose an douze [Jan. 15], 1804, and Bainbridge to Preble, Dec. 5, 1803, in *NDBW*, 3:332 and 3:253-54. Beaussier, born in 1748, was a career diplomat. He served as chancellor at Tripoli and at Alexandria in the 1770s; vice consul at Aleppo, Naf-plio, and Koroni (in Greece), at Sidon (modern Lebanon), and at Constantinople in the

1780s and 1790s; and as consul in Smyrna, Tunis, and Tripoli from 1797 until his death in 1814. Napoleon awarded him the Legion of Honor. *Correspondance des beys de Tunis et des consuls de France avec la cour, 1577–1830*, ed. Eugène Plantet (Paris: F. Alcan, 1899), 279.

23. Harris to Preble, Jan. 26/Feb.7, 1804, and Livingston to Talleyrand, April 14, 1804, in *NDBW*, 3:397 and 4:24-25; Mullen, "Good Neighbourhood," 146-47. A year later, Commodore Samuel Barron, who succeeded Preble in command of the squadron, wrote Harris that the Russian ambassador at Constantinople, d'Italinsky, had informed him that he was still awaiting instructions from St. Petersburg regarding a mediation with the bashaw for the release of the American captives. Barron to Harris, Jan. 16, 1805, in *NDBW*, 5:283-86. Had the sultan issued a *firman*, the bashaw may well have disobeyed; a few years before, when the Danish consul handed Yusuf a *firman* ordering the release of Danish shipping and slaves from captivity, the bashaw is reputed to have responded, "You think a firman is something big. I can tell you that in Constantinople, you can obtain one for 40 Levantine piastres. It is nothing but a piece of paper!" Dearden, *Nest of Corsairs*, 150.

24. de Konig to Wallen, Feb. 28, 1804, in *NDBW*, 3:462.

25. Jefferson to Smith, April 27, 1804, Library of Congress, Thomas Jefferson Papers at the Library of Congress: Series 1: General Correspondence, http://hdl.loc.gov/loc.mss/mtj.mtj bib013398.

CHAPTER SIX: PRISONERS OR SLAVES

1. Cowdery, *American Captives*, diary entry for Dec. 15, 1803.

2. Ibid., diary entry for Jan. 16, 1804; Long, *Nothing Too Daring*, 26; Dearborn, *Life of William Bainbridge*, 65-67.

3. Cathcart to O'Brien and Eaton, Feb. 20, 1801, and Cathcart to Marshall, Feb. 25, 1801, in Cathcart, *Tripoli*, 266-67 and 290-91; Bainbridge to Lear, April 30, 1804, in *NDBW*, 4:76; *True American and Commercial Daily Advertiser*, July 24, 1804, reprinting an extract from a letter of a *Philadelphia* officer, Feb. 26, 1804.

4. Ray, *Horrors of Slavery*, 72.

5. Cowdery, *American Captives*, diary entries for Dec. 16, 1803–Jan. 3, and Jan. 18, 1804; Melanie Randolph Miller, *Envoy to the Terror: Gouverneur Morris and the French Revolution* (Washington, DC: Potomac Books, 2004), 180.

6. Ray, *Poems*, 73-74n; Cowdery, *American Captives*, diary entry for Jan. 4, 1804; Ray, *Horrors of Slavery*, 75.

7. Ray referred to Ridgely (whom he called "Ridgby," suggesting he was not much of a presence) visiting sick sailors at least once. No one mentioned Harwood treating anyone. Ray, *Horrors of Slavery*, 79; Bainbridge to Barron, March 16, 1805, in *NDBW*, 5:416-17; Cowdery, *American Captives*, diary entry for March 28 April 13, 1804; Cowdery to Mitchill, Nov. 24, 1804, in Pleadwell and Kerr, "Jonathan Cowdery," 72-73. Detailed records exist of how one naval surgeon treated dysentery in that era. Dr. Peter St. Medard, surgeon on the frigate *New York* during her sixteen-month cruise to the Mediterranean in 1802–03, began treatment for dysentery with emetics (drugs that induce vomiting) or cathartics (drugs that accelerate defecation, to flush out "unbalanced humors") such as calomel, followed occasionally with Peruvian bark (from the cinchona tree, a drug containing quinine, which was administered to treat stomach problems), and absorbents (containing kaolin) for about half of his patients starting on the third day of treatment. The average duration of a case of dysentery was sixteen days. Of all those who contracted dysentery on the cruise of the *New York*, 18.4% died of it. The medical historian of that cruise concluded, "Dr. St. Medard's remedies cannot have contributed much to his patient's recoveries." J. Worth Estes, *Naval Surgeon: Life and Death at Sea in the Age of Sail* (Canton, MA: Science History Publications, 1998), 74-75, 174, 184-85,

191. Another medical historian concluded that Cowdery's use of natron fit within accepted contemporary medical thinking. Natron would not be regarded as an appropriate or effective therapeutic in modern medicine, but it would do something to replace electrolyte losses from diarrhea. Natron also would help metabolic acidosis caused by diarrhea and would help defend against infection because most bacteria do not grow well in an alkaline environment. Dr. Seth LeJacq, email communication with the author, June 13, 2020.

8. *Alexandria Advertiser*, Oct. 16, 1804, reprinting an extract from a letter by "G," March 28, 1804. Ray's "Elegy on the Death of John Hilliard" was published in *The Port Folio* and reprinted in far-flung newspapers, including the *New-York Herald*, Oct. 13, 1804, *New England Palladium*, Oct. 16, 1804, *Patriot* (Utica, NY), Oct. 22, 1804, and *Kentucky Gazette* (Lexington), Nov. 27, 1804. Ray included it in Ray, *Poems*, 74. Faud Sha´ban views the last stanza as showing the contrast of "the helplessness of the captive and the inhumanity of the captors," part of an American creation of the Oriental character of Muslims as barbarous and alien people. More generally, Sha´ban claims that Ray's poems emphasize the character of the "Oriental" as "[t]yranny, cruelty, despotism, inhumanity, and barbarism." *Islam and Arabs*, 78. Perhaps. But Ray's poems express his lived experience. If he engaged in poetic license, his image of Muslims and the conditions to which he was exposed was shared by the other captives, as their writings demonstrate.

There is substantial disagreement among literary scholars as to Ray's and Cowdery's treatment of the bashaw and his people. Riche and Zerar believe that "reshuffling" the conventions of the captivity narrative, Cowdery deemphasized the theme of suffering and regarded Yusuf as a "sympathetic figure." Because Cowdery was impressed by the orchards and gardens he toured, a veritable "botanical republic," they see him as "re-imagining" the Arab as "industrious as the Jeffersonian ideal man, the yeoman." This view seems far-fetched. At the same time, they believe that based on his lower social class and ardent republicanism, Ray portrayed the bashaw as despicable and emphasized the crew's sufferings. They argue that Ray and Cowdery shared one characteristic, "a pre-imperial orientalism." Bouteldja Riche and Sabrina Zerar, "William Ray and Dr. Jonathan Cowdery Captivity Narratives: A Case of Political Partisanship in the Early American Republic," *International Journal of Arts and Sciences* 11 (2018): 362-71. "Orientalism" is a term made popular by Edward Said, who, in his seminal book *Orientalism*, observed and critiqued the Western world's historic representations of the Islamic world, finding persistent prejudice against Arabs and Muslims in false and romanticized images drawn by Europeans and Americans. In contrast with Riche and Zerar, Jacob Rama Berman asserts that Americans inherited from European literature and history a sense of Arabs and Muslims representing "the middle ground between savagery and civilization" and finds that both Cowdery and Ray sought to "marginalize" Tripolitans, Cowdery by describing the backwardness of the bashaw's soldiers and Ray by describing the bashaw's decadence, a combination of a splendid appearance and inhumanity. "The Barbarous Voice of Democracy: American Captivity in Barbary and the Multicultural Specter," *American Literature* 79 (March 2007): 5-7.

9. Preble to McDonogh, Jan. 16, 1804, in *NDBW*, 3:333-34. In 1799, Cathcart paid McDonogh a "douceur"—literally, a "sweetener," i.e., a bribe—to secure his help because earlier, McDonogh had used his influence to frustrate American diplomacy. Cathcart warned that it "would be very improper to intrust our affairs again to his guidance." Cathcart to David Humphreys, Dec. 14, 1799, in Cathcart, *Tripoli*, 103. The charge that McDonogh had undermined American interests was raised at the Court of St. James's in November 1801, but the British government responded that if true, his conduct was unauthorized, and anyway, he would soon be replaced. Irwin, *Diplomatic Relations*, 121-22.

10. McDonogh to Preble, March 19, 1804, in *NDBW*, 3:504-5; *Aurora and General Advertiser*,

Sept. 28, 1804, reprinting extract from letter from an unidentified American officer, May 4, 1804; Cowdery, *American Captives*, diary entry for Nov. 6, 1803. Yusuf ordered McDonogh out of Tripoli after the *Syren* stopped a British merchant vessel with McDonogh's passport carrying Tripolitan goods for Malta, which McDonogh had assured the bashaw the American naval commanders would respect. *Philadelphia Gazette*, Sept. 24, 1804, reprinting extract of a letter from an imprisoned officer, April 7, 1804. French consul Beaussier thought Mc-Donogh was a "wicked, vindictive man, an enemy of peace, who especially suspecting the intervention of France [as a mediator], will have sought vengeance over the Regency, the Americans and us by means of advice and perfidious insinuations." Beaussier to Talleyrand, 25 Prairial XII [14 June 1804] ("C'est un homme méchant, vindicatif, ennemi de la paix, qui soupconnant surtout l'intervention de la France, aura cherché à se vent à la fois de la Régence, des américains et de nous par des conseils et des insinuations perfides"), in Beaussier Letters.

11. Spence to Polly Spence, Jan. 8, 1804, in Spence Papers. Seizing on the tension between regarding oneself as a slave, who was forced to work, and a prisoner of war, who was confined, Lawrence Peskin suggested that the slavery in Barbary was self-actualized, as if each American could control how he was treated. *Captives and Countrymen*, 153-54. Rather, it was because the Tripolitans recognized the officers were "gentlemen" that they were regarded as prisoners of war who did not have to work; the Tripolitans understood the common sailors and marines could be compelled to work as slaves. Despite eyewitness accounts of the enlisted people punished with the *bastinado* and their meager rations resulting in deprivation and malnutrition, some historians depreciate the severity of their captivity. Because the officers called themselves slaves but acknowledged they were not treated badly, Robert Allison concluded that "[s]lavery did not necessarily mean harsh treatment" but rather denoted a life of boredom and indignity. Davis, *Christian Slaves*, 106; Peskin, *Captives and Countrymen*, 153-54; Allison, *Crescent Obscured*, 112-13. These historians, however, do not consider the 260 sailors and marines when they depreciate the harshness of Barbary slavery.

12. Spence to Polly Spence, Feb. 12/16, 1804, in Spence Papers. Preble's first five letters to Bainbridge (December 19 and 20, 1803; January 4, 16, and 24, 1804) all arrived February 16, 1804. Bainbridge to Preble, Feb. 16, 1804, in *NDBW*, 3:408. While Spence worried about the effect of his imprisonment on his psychology, he did not know that his son, Midshipman Robert Traill Spence, an officer on the *Syren*, had become temporarily incapacitated by mental illness. Stewart to Preble, Jan. 1, 1804, in *NDBW*, 3:307 ("I left at Leghorn [Livorno] Robert T. Spence Midshipman, whose mind had been for some time deranged.").

13. *True American and Commercial Daily Advertiser*, July 24, 1804, reprinting an extract from a letter of a *Philadelphia* officer, Feb. 28, 1804. A. B. C. Whipple incorrectly asserts that European slaves served the officers; the seamen from the crew served the officers, *Shores of Tripoli*, 127.

14. Cowdery, *American Captives*, diary entries for Jan. 19 and Feb. 10, 1804; Dearborn, *Life of William Bainbridge*, 67-68; Renshaw to Rodgers, Oct. 15, 1804, in *NDBW*, 5:87-88.

15. Spence to Polly Spence, Jan. 25, 1804, in Spence Papers.

16. Deidre Barrett, Zach Sogolow, Angela Oh, Jasmine Panton, Malcolm Grayson, and Melanie Justiniano, "Content of Dreams from WWII POWs," *Imagination, Cognition and Personality* 33 (2013): 193-204. There is also scholarship that touches on the dreams of prisoners of war during the American Civil War. Their dreams centered on food, home, freedom, escape, and death. White, *Midnight in America*, 37-41. Of course, the Civil War soldiers were much closer in time and demographics to the *Philadelphia* captives than the British World War II officers, though they lived more than a half-century later, in a country that had undergone enormous social transformation. However, the dreams of Civil War prisoners of

war were highly influenced by battle as well as their camp conditions of squalor and starvation, such as at Andersonville prison in Georgia. The dreams of the British officers resemble those of inmates more than battlefield soldiers precisely because (like the *Philadelphia*'s officers and crew) they were captured before seeing much, if any, combat, and because (again, like the American officers in Tripoli) they lived with better material conditions than Civil War prisoners of war.

17. Davis, *Christian Slaves*, 127; Ray, *Horrors of Slavery*, 63.

18. Charlene M. Boyer Lewis, *Elizabeth Patterson Bonaparte: An American Aristocrat in the Early Republic* (Philadelphia: University of Pennsylvania Press, 2012), 17-20; Helen Jean Burn, *Betsy Bonaparte* (Baltimore: Maryland Historical Society, 2010), 61-63; Alexandra Deutsch, *A Woman of Two Worlds: Elizabeth Patterson Bonaparte* (Baltimore: Maryland Historical Society, 2016), 14-15. As Myra Glenn observes about sailors' narratives, "[n]o doubt there were times when they padded their life stories, exaggerating or minimizing certain experiences," but their memoirs reveal, "sometimes unintentionally, widespread concerns about manhood" in their recollections. Glenn, *Jack Tar's Story*, 10-11.

19. Valle, *Rocks and Shoals*, 166-75; Langley, *Social Reform*, 172-74; B. R. Burg, *Boys at Sea: Sodomy, Indecency, and Courts Martial in Nelson's Navy* (Basingstoke, UK: Palgrave Macmillan, 2007); N. A. M. Rodger, *The Command of the Ocean: A Naval History of Britain, 1649–1815* (New York: W. W. Norton, 2005), 407; Taylor, *Sons of the Waves*, 47-48; Melville, *White-Jacket*, 379; Gilje, *Liberty on the Waterfront*, 38-39, quoting Josiah Cobb, *A Greenhand's First Cruise, Roughed Out From the Log-Book of Memory, of Twenty-Five Years Standing*, 2 vols. (Boston, 1841), 2:246; Malcolmson, *Order and Disorder*, 157-63, 231-32.

CHAPTER SEVEN: THE RAID

1. Zuchet to Foreign Ministry, Nov. 16, 1803, letter no. 356, 1804/19, in Zuchet Letters, 121. The last word in the published version is translated as "victimized," which does not seem to be what Zuchet meant to convey.

2. Bainbridge to Lear, Jan. 14, 1804, in *NDBW*, 3:329-30.

3. Greenhow, *History and Present Condition*, 19; Armstrong, *Small Boats*, 57.

4. E. H. Jenkins, *A History of the French Navy, from its Beginnings to the Present Day* (London: Macdonald and Jane's, 1973), 65-66; Lavery, *Life in Nelson's Navy*, 54; Tucker, *Arming the Fleet*, 109; Preble to Cathcart, Jan. 4, 1804, Preble to Degen, Purviance & Co., Jan. 9, 1804, and Preble to Dent, Feb. 10, 1804, in *NDBW*, 3:311-12, 3:319, and 3:401-2. The idea of using mortar boats was first raised by Dale in 1801-02. McKee, *Edward Preble*, 92. The *Argus* brought out a mortar when she joined Preble's squadron, but that mortar was not mounted on any boat until nearly three years later. Rodgers to Smith, May 23, 1806, in *NDBW*, 6:431.

5. Preble to Bainbridge, Jan. 4, 1804, extract from Preble diary, Jan. 21, 1804, extract from *Constitution* log book, Jan. 28, 1804, and Preble to Lear, Jan. 31, 1804, in *NDBW*, 3:310-11, 3:351, 3:371, and 3:377-78. There was, of course, no US court nearby to consider the evidence and condemn the *Mastico* as "good prize," with a subsequent public auction to determine the market price of the vessel. Instead, Preble ordered three of his officers to survey the *Mastico* and assess her value, much as in the twenty-first century, a real estate appraiser might value a house that could not be put on the market. The surveyors estimated the *Mastico* to be worth $1,800. Stewart and others to Preble, Jan. 31, 1804, in *NDBW*, 3:377. Under settled prize law, Preble needed a court decree formally declaring her a "good prize" to be entitled to prize money upon her sale. Because the *Mastico* was too small for a winter voyage across the Atlantic, Preble decided to send just her papers to the United States, hoping that would suffice. Preble to Smith, Feb. 3, 1804, in *NDBW*, 3:384-86. Chipp Reid asserts that, violating his orders, Preble used a local court to declare the *Mastico* a good prize. *Intrepid Sailors*, 75.

There seems scant evidence for this: if a Neapolitan court condemned the *Mastico*, Preble would have had no reason to send her papers to the United States or to have asked surveyors to assess her value.

6. Preble to Lear, Jan. 31, 1804, in *NDBW*, 3:377-78.

7. Extract from Preble diary, Jan. 29, 1804, in ibid., 3:371.

8. James Tertius De Kay, *A Rage for Glory: The Life of Commodore Stephen Decatur, USN* (New York: Free Press, 2004), 21, 36, and 221-22; Tucker, *Dawn Like Thunder*, 265-68; S. Putnam Waldo, *The Life and Character of Stephen Decatur* (Hartford, CT: P. B. Goodsell, 1821), 73. Decatur's leadership qualities are assessed in Spencer C. Tucker, *Stephen Decatur: A Life Most Bold and Daring* (Annapolis, MD: Naval Institute Press, 2004), 30-32; Robert J. Allison, *Stephen Decatur: American Naval Hero, 1779–1820* (Amherst: University of Massachusetts Press, 2005), 30; Charles Lee Lewis, *The Romantic Decatur* (Philadelphia: University of Pennsylvania Press, 1937), 234-36; and Reid, *Intrepid Sailors*, 42-43.

9. Preble to Smith, Nov. 9, 1803, and Stewart to Susan Decatur, Dec. 12, 1826, in *NDBW*, 3:209 and 3:426-27.

10. Preble to Decatur, Jan. 31, 1804, in *NDBW*, 3:376-77. From Tripoli, Bainbridge sent Preble many letters written in "sympathetic" ink (using lime juice as ink, which made the writing visible only after being warmed over a fire), in which he suggested how to destroy the frigate. In a December 5, 1803, letter, Bainbridge thought "six or Eight good Boats well manned" could enter the harbor and destroy the frigate "if the thing was attempted without giving them much warning." In another letter, Bainbridge suggested that Preble charter a merchant vessel, "[send] her into the Harbour, with the men secreted and steering directly on board the Frigate." Bainbridge warned that it would be impossible to try to seize the *Philadelphia* and sail her out, "owing to the difficulty of the Channel," and, he might have added, the difficulties of sailing at night a ship that was unbalanced, having had her foremast chopped down. Bainbridge to Preble, Dec. 5, 1803, in ibid., 3:253-54. Bainbridge wrote two more letters urging a raid to burn the *Philadelphia*, but Preble did not receive either before he sent off the mission. Lawrence Peskin states the destruction of the *Philadelphia* was "more or less the way Bainbridge planned it," but Preble did not need any prompting, and Bainbridge did not plan it. *Captives and Countrymen*, 155.

11. Certificate of Salvadore Catalano, Dec. 19, 1825, in *NDBW*, 3:421.

12. Preble diary, Feb. 3, 1804, in *NDBW*, 3:388. The intelligence is mentioned in the same diary entry that refers to the *Intrepid* and *Syren* sailing off to Tripoli, and it is unclear whether Preble received this information in time to share it with Decatur and Stewart. Although he cited Preble's diary entry, historian W. M. P. Dunne noted that Preble had received various reports about the number of Tripolitans guarding the frigate, and "[u]ntil the Americans swung over the captured frigate's bulwarks, they would live in fearful anticipation." "Stephen Decatur, 1779–1820: A Critical Biography," 1995 typescript manuscript in the possession of the author, 267-68.

13. Extract from the *Constitution* log, Jan. 31, 1804, extract from Haraden log book, Feb. 3, 1804, and Izard to Alice Izard, Feb. 2, 1804, in *NDBW*, 3:380, 3:388, and 3:381-82. In using the phrase "more lucky than the rest may reach his heart," Izard quoted Sempronius's speech to the Roman Senate, with Caesar approaching, from Joseph Addison's play *Cato*: "Can a Roman senate long debate/Which of the two to choose, slavery or death!/No, let us rise at once, gird on our swords,/And, at the head of our remaining troops,/Attack the foe, break through the thick array/Of his throng'd legions, and charge home upon him./Perhaps some arm, more lucky than the rest,/May reach his heart, and free the world from bondage." Joseph Addison, *Cato, a Tragedy* (1712), act 2, scene 1.

14. Extract from the journal of Midshipman F. Cornelius deKrafft, Feb. 6, 1804, and Izard

to Alice Izard, Feb. 20, 1804, in *NDBW*, 3:391 and 3:416-17; Morris, *Autobiography*, 25; Frederick C. Leiner, "Decatur and Naval Leadership," *Naval History* 15 (Oct. 2001): 33.

15. Extract from deKrafft journal, Feb. 8, 1804, in *NDBW*, 3:399.

16. Morris, *Autobiography*, 25-27; Leiner, "Decatur and Naval Leadership," 33.

17. Morris, *Autobiography*, 29-30; Heermann Affidavit, April 26, 1828, in *NDBW*, 3:418-20; Goldsborough, *Naval Chronicle*, 257n.

18. Bainbridge to Preble, Feb. 15, 1804, and Stewart to Preble, Feb. 19, 1804, in *NDBW*, 3:408 and 3:415-16.

19. Morris, *Autobiography*, 26.

20. Izard to Alice Izard, Feb. 20, 1804, in *NDBW*, 3:416-17; Cowdery, *American Captives*, diary entry for Feb. 16, 1804; Ray, *Horrors of Slavery*, 76.

21. Heermann Affidavit, April 26, 1828, in *NDBW*, 3:418-20; Morris, *Autobiography*, 26-27. In Shakespeare's *Henry V*, act 4, scene 3, the king tells his soldiers, "If we are mark'd to die, we are enow/To do our country loss; and if to live,/The fewer men, the greater share of honor./God's will! I pray thee wish not one man more."

22. Morris, *Autobiography*, 27.

23. Izard to Alice Izard, Feb. 20, 1804, in *NDBW*, 3:416-17; Morris, *Autobiography*, 28.

24. Gleaves, *James Lawrence*, 49; Morris, *Autobiography*, 28; Izard to Alice Izard, Feb. 20, 1804, in *NDBW*, 3:416-17.

25. Morris, *Autobiography*, 30; Izard to Alice Izard, Feb. 20, 1804, and Heermann Affidavit, April 26, 1828, in *NDBW*, 3:416-17 and 3:419; House Committee on Naval Affairs, Claims (HR 23A-D13.1, bundle 3), Claim of Susan Decatur, "Reminiscences of Lewis Heermann Surgeon U.S. Navy—1826," 23rd Cong., NA, RG 23, 8. Beaussier reported that the Tripolitans had posted only seven men to guard the *Philadelphia*, what he termed "Barbary carelessness" ("l'incurie barbaresque"). Beaussier to Talleyrand, 26 Ventose XII [17 March 1804], in Beaussier Letters. If this was true, the Americans who took part in the mission exaggerated the opposition. On the other hand, in the aftermath of the raid, the Tripolitans had an incentive to downplay their defensive precautions.

26. Preble to Cathcart, Feb. 19, 1804, and Heermann Affidavit, April 26, 1828, *NDBW*, 3:437-38 and 3:419; Goldsborough, *Naval Chronicle*, 258n; Toll, *Six Frigates*, 213-14; Leiner, "Killing the Prisoners," 29-30.

27. Morris, *Autobiography*, 30.

28. Izard to Alice Izard, Feb. 20, 1804, Preble to Cathcart, Feb. 19, 1804, and extract from deKrafft journal, Feb. 17, 1804, in *NDBW*, 3:416-17, 3:437-38, and 3:431-32; Morris, *Autobiography*, 29.

29. *True American and Commercial Daily Advertiser*, July 2, 1804, reprinting an extract of a letter from a *Philadelphia* midshipman, Feb. 24, 1804.

30. Cowdery, *American Captives*, diary entry for Feb. 16, 1804; *True American and Commercial Daily Advertiser*, July 24, 1804, reprinting an extract of a letter from a *Philadelphia* officer to his friend in New York, March 4, 1804.

31. Ray, *Horrors of Slavery*, 76.

32. Extract from Haraden log book, Feb. 19, 1804, in *NDBW*, 3:443-44.

33. *City Gazette*, June 2, 1804, reprinting undated letter "from a gentleman in Tripoli to his friend in Paris"; extract of a letter, Nissen to Danish consul at Marseilles, Feb. 29, 1804, in *NDBW*, 3:421-22; Ray, *Horrors of Slavery*, 76.

34. Dunne, "Decatur," 281-82; Preble to Smith, Feb. 19, 1804, in *NDBW*, 3:413.

35. Zuchet to Foreign Ministry, Feb. 28, 1804, letter no. 356, 1804/23, in Zuchet Letters, 123; *City Gazette*, June 2, 1804, reprinting undated letter "from a gentleman in Tripoli to his friend in Paris"; *Commercial Advertiser*, July 18, 1804, printing extract of a letter from Tripoli, March

4, 1804; Ray, *Horrors of Slavery*, 76-77.

36. Beaussier wrote, "Le Pacha ne doute pas qu'ils n'ayent été massacrès a près leur enleve-ment, et jettés ensuite à la mer. Si le fait est vrai, il ne dont pas en accuser les Amèricains, mais plutôt les chefs de l'expedition incendiaire." Beaussier to Talleyrand, 10 Ventose an douze [1 March 1804], in Beaussier Letters; Cowdery, *American Captives*, diary entry of March 4, 1804; Dghies to Bainbridge, March 5, 1804, and Preble to Bainbridge, March 12, 1804, in *NDBW*, 3:474 and 3:489-90.

37. Preble to Smith, Feb. 19, 1804, and Preble to Livingston, March 18, 1804, in *NDBW*, 3:438-39 and 3:498-99.

CHAPTER EIGHT: REINFORCEMENTS

1. *Annals of Congress*, 13:1200, March 19, 1804.

2. Wilson, "American Hostages," 131, 133-37; Dzurec, *Our Suffering Brethren*, 63, 67-83.

3. Madison to Thomas Fitzsimmons, April 13, 1804, in *NDBW*, 4:23.

4. *Charleston Courier*, Jan. 7, 1805.

5. *National Intelligencer*, March 21, 1804; *Public Statutes at Large*, Act of March 26, 1804, 8th Cong., 1st Sess., chap. 46, 2:291-92; *Republican Advocate* (Frederick, MD), March 30, 1804; *New-York Herald*, April 18, 1804.

6. John Fowler to constituents, March 27, 1804, in *Circular Letters*, 375.

7. Smith to Lt. John Cassin, March 21, 1804, Smith to Lt. Isaac Chauncey, March 21, 1804, Smith to Lt. George Cox, March 21, 1804, and Smith to Lt. Samuel Evans, March 21, 1804, in *NDBW*, 3:509-10; *United States Gazette* (Philadelphia), April 26, 1804.

8. *National Aegis* (Worcester, MA), March 14, 1804; *Aurora and General Advertiser*, March 28, 1804; *New Hampshire Sentinel* (Keene, NH), March 31, 1804.

9. *True American and Commercial Daily Advertiser*, March 30, 1804.

10. *Repertory*, April 3, 1804 (reprinting a *New York Evening Post* column). A modern historian has taken up the "smallest force competent" argument, noting that Jefferson's priority as president was eliminating the accumulated federal debt and that the squadrons dispatched under Dale, Morris, and Preble were incapable of achieving their military goals. In this view, fiscal economy was the determining factor in decisions regarding the administration's policy toward Tripoli. Seiken, "Reluctant Warrior," 186, 191-92, 197-98, 201-3.

11. *Columbian Centinel*, April 4, 1804.

12. *Aurora and General Advertiser*, April 9, 1804; *National Aegis*, April 11, 1804; *Salem Register*, April 26, 1804.

13. Smith to Barron, June 6, 1804, and Barron to Rodgers, July 1, 1804, in *NDBW*, 4:152 54 and 4:241. One ship, the *John Adams*, carrying stores for the Mediterranean squadron and her own guns stored as ballast in the hold, had departed a few days earlier. Chauncey to Smith, June 26, 1804, in ibid., 4:227.

14. *Philadelphia Gazette*, July 6, 1804 (advertisement); *Providence Gazette*, Sept. 16, 1804 (advertisement); *Political Observatory* (Walpole, NH), May 26, 1804; *Sun* (Dover, NH), June 2, 1804.

15. *Aurora and General Advertiser*, March 26, 1805 (advertisement); *New York Daily Advertiser*, July 23 and Aug. 6, 1805 (advertisements); *Herald of the United States* (Warren, RI), June 5, 1804 (advertisement).

CHAPTER NINE: BLOCKADE AND DIPLOMACY

1. Preble to Lt. John Smith, Feb. 3, 1804, Preble to Cathcart, Feb. 19, 1804, and Preble to Robert Smith, June 14, 1804, in *NDBW*, 3:387, 3:437-38, and 4:187-90.

2. Bainbridge to Preble, Dec. 5, 1803, and Preble to Lear, Jan. 31, 1804, in *NDBW*, 3:253-54 and 3:377-79.

3. Extract from Preble diary, Feb. 21, 1804, Somers to Preble, Feb. 16, 1804, and Somers to Preble, March 7, 1804, in *NDBW*, 3:449 and 3:411; Barbara E. Koedel, *Glory, at Last!: A Narrative of the Naval Career of Master Commandant Richard Somers: 1778–1804* (Somers Point, NJ: Atlantic County Historical Society, 1993), 112-15, 121-22.

4. Stewart to Preble, March 17, 1804, extract from Preble diary, April 17, 1804, Preble to O'Brien and others [undated], O'Brien and others to Preble, April 16, 1804, extract from Preble diary, April 17, 1804, and Preble to Robert Smith, April 19, 1804, in *NDBW*, 3:495-96, 4:35, 3:496, 3:496, 3:496-97, 4:35, and 4:40-44. A Baltimore-built, pilot-boat type schooner, the *Transfer* had been captured from her American owners in the 1790s and became the French privateer *Quatre Freres*, and then was captured by the British navy in 1797 and sold in 1802 to a Maltese owner. Footner, *Tidewater Triumph*, 76.

5. Stewart to Preble, March 22, 1804, and Preble to Smith, April 19, 1804, in *NDBW*, 3:511 and 4:40-44.

6. Stewart to Preble, June 13, 1804, Isaac Hull to William Higgins, May 31, 1804, Preble to George Davis, June 19, 1804, Spanish Consul Don Joseph Noguera to Davis, June 22, 1804, Davis to Noguera, June 22, 1804, Hull to George Dyson, June 4, 1804, Beaussier to Preble, June 3, 1804, and Preble to Beaussier, June 26, 1804, in *NDBW*, 4:182-83, 4:137, 4:204-5, 4:216, 4:204-5, 4:149, 4:146, and 4:227-28; Linda M. Maloney, *Captain from Connecticut: The Life and Naval Times of Isaac Hull* (Boston: Northeastern University Press, 1986), 93; Bruce Grant, *Isaac Hull, Captain of Old Ironsides* (Chicago: Pellegrini and Cudahy, 1947), 97. Liguria is the coastal region of northwestern Italy, the principal port of which is Genoa.

7. Beaussier to Talleyrand, 4 Prairial an douze [24 May 1804], in Beaussier Letters; Zuchet to Foreign Ministry, Aug. 4, 1804, letter no. 356, 1804/29, in Zuchet Letters, 127; Nissen to Davis, Sept. 30, 1804, in *NDBW*, 5:58-59; Allen to father, Aug. 31, 1805 (emphases in original), in "Letters of William Henry Allen," 129.

8. Extract from de Krafft journal, April 29, 1804, in *NDBW*, 4:75.

9. Wadsworth to Jack [—], June 28, 1804, in ibid., 4:233-34.

10. Tucker, *Dawn Like Thunder*, 11-13; Preble to Gen. Guillaume Brune, March 4, 1804, Preble to "Captain Pacha," March 7, 1804, and Preble to Bainbridge, March 12, 1804, in *NDBW*, 3:469, 3:480-81, and 3:490.

11. Preble to Lear, Feb. 19, 1804, Lear to Preble, March 23, 1804, and Cathcart to Preble, April 17, 1804, in *NDBW*, 3:442, 3:516-18, and 4:31-33; Mullen, "Good Neighbourhood," 175; Wilson, "American Hostages," 132n18. Biographical details about O'Brien are scattered in Goodin, *From Captives to Consuls*.

12. Beaussier to Talleyrand, 6 Ventose an douze [26 Feb. 1804] ("Le Commodore Preble ne pouvait pas choisir un négociateur plus inept, moins adroit, et plus capable d'avancer des absurdités, des contradictions et des faussetés."), in Beaussier Letters.

13. Dghies to Bainbridge, March 5, 1804, Preble to Bainbridge, March 12, 1804, Farquhar to Preble, April 11, 1804, Bainbridge to Preble, March 26, 1804, and Bainbridge to Dghies, March 27, 1804, in *NDBW*, 3:474, 3:489-90, 4:19-20, 3:525-27, and 3:537-38. Despite Preble's explicit denial that he did not know who Schembri was and had never seen or spoken to him, some historians assume the opposite is true. Abigail Mullen writes that "[s]omehow [Schembri] made the leap from commercial agent for the bashaw to negotiator for the Americans. After overhearing conversations between Preble and the commissary for the British fleet at Malta, Patrick Wilkie, Schembri took it upon himself to go to the bashaw and put out feelers for a peace settlement." "Good Neighbourhood," 165-66. It is unrealistic to think that Schembri would have had his ear at the door of a conversation that likely occurred between Wilkie and Preble on board the *Constitution*. It seems far more likely that, if anything, Wilkie came to Preble as Schembri's agent to provide him with the bashaw's initial demand,

and Preble laid out the basic American position, which Wilkie relayed to Schembri. Christopher McKee first states that Schembri contacted Preble "indirectly" but then refers to supposed personal discussions about potential treaty terms and ultimately states that Preble "was aware of Schembri's mission." *Edward Preble*, 188-89, 203-4. That assertion also seems unlikely, given Preble's reaction to Schembri's negotiation, which not only would have been utter hypocrisy but also a falsehood Schembri would have disputed. Without attribution, Spencer Tucker states that Preble spoke directly with Schembri and negotiated a deal with him by which the United States would provide a schooner and $100,000 and receive in return the damaged *Philadelphia* and all the American captives, but that the deal was not "finalized." *Stephen Decatur*, 44. I have found no support in the documents for this assertion. Chipp Reid merely states that Schembri sailed to Tripoli to negotiate "after Preble seemed amenable to the idea," which also seems unsupported. *Intrepid Sailors*, 116. My skepticism for these accounts mirrors Nissen's contemporary view. Schembri, whom Nissen called the bashaw's *vekil* (Arabic for "deputy" or "representative") "fled onboard" ("flygtet ombard") a ship to return to Malta. "There has been much astonishment," Nissen wrote, "over this man's personal fear of the Americans, who by his account had sent him here [to Tripoli] in order to make peace for them." Nissen to Board of Directors, April 3, 1804 ["Man har meget forundret sig over denne Mands personlige Frygt for Nord Amerikanerne der dog efter hans Sigende havde sendt ham hertil for at mægle Fred for dem."], in Nissen Letters. Schembri apparently feared being discovered as a fraud.

14. Schembri to Preble [undated but after March 22, 1804], in *NDBW*, 3:511-13.

15. Preble to Schembri, Sept. 19, 1804 (this date must be incorrect; the letter likely was written in April), in *NDBW*, 3:513-14. Schembri called in diplomatic support because the *Madonna di Catapaliani* sailed under the Russian flag. The Russian consul at Naples demanded the return of the ship and her cargo, claiming she had been seized against the law of prize, and his protest was soon followed by that of the Russian chargé in Naples. Soon after, Preble learned of the Russian government's offer to mediate for the release of the captive Americans. This gesture of good will caught Preble's attention. He wrote the Russian ambassador at Constantinople that although the capture of the *Madonna di Catapaliani* was valid, he was "so deeply . . . impressed by the generous interposition" of the tsar's government that he had decided to release the ship, which he did on June 7, 1804. That same day, he negotiated the return of the *Santissimo Crocifisso* to Schembri upon his payment of $300 and Schembri's promise not to pursue a claim against the Americans and to indemnify the Americans if other claimants were awarded damages. The *Transfer*, however, was deemed a good prize by a US court. Russian Councilor at Naples N. de Manzo to U.S. Consul to Naples John S. M. Matthiew, May 3, 1804, Matthiew to Preble, May 5, 1804, Russian charge d'affaires P. d'Karpow to Preble, May 18, 1804, Preble to d'Karpow, May 19, 1804, Preble to Ambassador Andrei d'Italinsky, June 6, 1804, extract from Preble diary, June 7, 1804, and Preble to Consul Levett Harris, June 7, 1804, in ibid., 4:83-84, 4:86, 4:107-8, 4:110, 4:158-59, 4:163, and 4:161.

16. Livingston to Preble, Jan. 17, 1804, Preble to Livingston, March 18, 1804, extract from Preble diary, March 27, 1804, Preble to Smith, April 19, 1804, Preble to Dghies, March 26, 1804, Dghies to Preble, March 26, 1804, Preble to Dghies, March 27, 1804, and Preble to Bainbridge, March 27, 1804, in ibid., 3:337-38, 3:498-99, 3:538-39, 4:40-44, 3:527, 3:527, 3:535-36, and 3:536-37.

17. Extract from Preble's diary, March 27, 1804, Preble to Bainbridge, March 27, 1804, Bainbridge to Preble, March 29, 1804, Preble to Cathcart, June 1, 1804, and Bainbridge to Lear, June 4, 1804, in ibid., 3:538-39, 3:536-37, 3:545-46, 4:141-42, and 4:149.

18. Beaussier to Preble, March 27, 1804, and Beaussier to Preble, March 28, 1804, in ibid.,

3:535 and 3:542-44. Seaton Dearden wrongly calls Beaussier a "self-appointed mediator." *Nest of Corsairs*, 165.

19. Beaussier to Preble, May 24, 1804, in *NDBW*, 4:117-18.

20. Beaussier to Preble, March 28, 1804, extract from Preble's diary, March 28, 1804, Preble to Smith, April 19, 1804, Preble to Lear, May 3, 1804, and Beaussier to Preble, May 24, 1804, in ibid., 3:542-44, 3:544-45, 4:40-44, 4:117-18, 5:82; Beaussier to Talleyrand, 13 Germinal an douze [3 April 1804] ("la disparate sera grande entre les prétentions et les offres, et qu'il serait difficile de tout concilier"), in Beaussier Letters.

21. Preble to Livingston, June 29, 1804, in *NDBW*, 4:237-38.

CHAPTER 10: HARDSHIPS

1. Bainbridge to Dghies, Feb. 20, 1804, in *NDBW*, 3:445-46; Cowdery, *American Captives*, diary entries for Feb. 17-24, 1804.

2. Ray, *Horrors of Slavery*, 77; *Weekly Museum* (New York), July 28, 1804, reprinting an extract of a letter from a midshipman to friends in Philadelphia, March 5, 1804; Wilson, *Biography*, 2:162. Chipp Reid incorrectly states that the officers were moved to their new prison the morning after Decatur's expedition burned the *Philadelphia*. *Intrepid Sailors*, 113.

3. *True American and Commercial Daily Advertiser*, July 24, 1804, reprinting an extract from a letter of a *Philadelphia* officer, March 2, 1804; Harris, *Life and Services*, 104; Nissen to Davis, Feb. 18, 1805, in *NDBW*, 5:359-60.

4. Bainbridge to Preble, Feb. 22, 1804, in *NDBW*, 3:449. Bainbridge's second note to Dghies is referenced in a letter later printed in American newspapers but does not appear elsewhere. *True American*, July 24, 1804, reprinting an extract from a letter of a *Philadelphia* officer, Feb. 26, 1804. A March 5 letter from Dghies, however, refers to a March 4 letter to him from Bainbridge. Dghies to Bainbridge, March 5, 1804, in *NDBW*, 3:474.

5. After the American officers had spent four days in the dungeon prison, Dghies was able to prevail upon Yusuf to renew their mail privileges and allow them to "walk in the Town & Country." Dghies to Bainbridge, March 5, 1804, in *NDBW*, 3:474.

6. McKee, *Edward Preble*, 164, 186, 216. As historian W. M. P Dunne noted, Wadsworth's rendezvous with the "bouncing English girl" was "a costly liaison" as it resulted in Wadsworth getting a sexually transmitted disease that prevented him from taking part in the raid that burned the *Philadelphia*. Dunne, "Decatur," 256-57; Extract from Haraden log book, March 4, 1804 (noting Wadsworth as one of three cases "of the Venerial"), in *NDBW*, 3:472.

7. *Aurora and General Advertiser*, Sept. 28, 1804, reprinting a letter from "one of our captive fellow citizens," May 4, 1804; *United States Gazette*, Oct. 1, 1804, reprinting an extract from an officer of the *Philadelphia*, April 20, 1804; Cowdery, *American Captives*, diary entries for April 24, May 16, and May 20, 1804.

8. Bevan, "Letters of Nicholas Harwood," 68-69, quoting Harwood to father [Nicholas Harwood], May 21, 1804, in Hammond-Harwood House Collection, MS 1303, MCHC.

9. Renshaw to Rodgers, Oct. 15, 1804, in *NDBW*, 5:87-88.

10. Dearborn, *Life of William Bainbridge*, 69-70; Wilson, *Biography*, 2:166-67; Harris, *Life and Services*, 104.

11. Wilson, *Biography*, 2:167.

12. Dearborn, *Life of William Bainbridge*, 70-72; Harris, *Life and Services*, 105-6; Wilson, *Biography*, 2:168-69 (with differing details); Bainbridge to Preble, June 14, 1804, in *NDBW*, 4:186-87.

13. Dearborn, *Life of William Bainbridge*, 72; Harris, *Life and Services*, 106-7.

14. Ray, *Horrors of Slavery*, 79-80, 108.

15. Ray, *Horrors of Slavery*, 79-80, 199n2.

16. Cowdery, *American Captives*, diary entry for July 31, 1804; Jon. Cowdery to Jabez Cowdery, Nov. 7, 1804, and Cowdery to Mitchill, Nov. 24, 1804, in Pleadwell and Kerr, "Jonathan Cowdery," 71-73.

17. Cowdery to Mitchill, Nov. 24, 1804, in Pleadwell and Kerr, "Jonathan Cowdery," 72-73; Estes, *Naval Surgeon*, 216. It is now known that ceruse causes lead poisoning, but it was "not until well into the 19th century that significant advances in the understanding of lead poisoning and descriptions of its clinical picture began to appear in the literature." Sven Hernberg, "Lead Poisoning in a Historical Perspective," *American Journal of Industrial Medicine* 38 (2000): 244-54.

18. Jon. Cowdery to Jabez Cowdery, Nov. 7, 1804, in Pleadwell and Kerr, "Jonathan Cowdery," 71-72. Ray witnessed the "shocking" operation of a criminal having his left hand and right foot chopped off with an axe, the stumps dipped in boiling pitch, with the poor man then dragged to the city gates and left to the "mercy of mankind." Ray, *Horrors of Slavery*, 75.

19. Langford to Preble, July 7, 1804, in *NDBW*, 4:255; Ray, *Horrors of Slavery*, 86-87, 112-13; Cowdery, *American Captives*, diary entry for Aug. 10, 1804. Confusingly, Ray listed Hacksener's last name as "Heximer" and Bainbridge called him "Lewis Hickshaw."

20. Tucker, *Dawn Like Thunder*, 426-27; Ray, *Horrors of Slavery*, 107-8.

21. Ray, *Horrors of Slavery*, 78.

22. Crew of *Philadelphia* to Bainbridge, Aug. 21, 1804, in *NDBW*, 5:241.

23. Bainbridge to the crew, Aug. 21, 1804, in ibid., 5:242.

24. James Hogg and others to Bainbridge, Aug. 23, 1804, in ibid., 5:242-43. The respective lists of the seamen have not survived.

25. Bainbridge to Hogg, Aug. 27, 1804, in ibid., 5:243; Ray, *Horrors of Slavery*, 90-91.

CHAPTER ELEVEN: ATTACKS AND NEGOTIATIONS

1. Preble to Acton, May 10, 1804, Acton to Preble, May 13, 1804, and Preble to Smith, May 15, 1804, in *NDBW*, 4:90-91, 4:97-98, and 4:103.

2. Preble to Cathcart, June 1, 1804, in ibid., 4:141-42.

3. Preble to Dghies, June 12, 1804, Preble to O'Brien, June 13, 1804, and Preble to Beaussier, June 12, 1804, in ibid., 4:179, 4:183-84, and 4:180-81.

4. Beaussier to Preble, 24 Prairial an douze [13 June 1804] ("l'offre vraiment mesquire et injurieuse faite *ex abrupto* après une absence de deux mois et demi . . . Vous ignories sans doute, Monsieur le Commodore, que la rançon d'usage d'un simple mousse de quatre a cinq cens piastres fortes . . ."), in Beaussier Letters. *NDBW*, 4:184-85, has the same letter in a rougher English translation.

5. Beaussier to Talleyrand, 15 Thermidor an douze [3 Aug. 1804] ("J'avais marqué au Commodore que cette rançon et la conclusion de la paix seraient peutêtre portées à 500,000 piastres fortes, et je lui en alléquai les motifs, mais je ne lui ai jamais dit que la Régence exigeait cette somme. À cela il me répond qu'il n'en accordera jamais le dixieme parties, et que la Médiation de la France ne produira rien d'avantageaux . . . Quelle opinion peut on avoir d'ailleurs d'un Commandant qui, sans être autôrisé par son Gouvernment, risque de commettre les armes de sa Nation, et d'être destitué lui même, et qui expose la vie de 300 prisonniers au fantatisme et au désespoir de ces afriquains!"), in Beaussier Letters.

6. Preble to Smith, June 14–July 5, 1804, Bainbridge to Davis, June 15, 1804, Davis to Bainbridge, June 23, 1804, Bainbridge to Preble, July 10, 1804, Bainbridge to Preble, June 14, 1804, and Bainbridge to Davis, June 17, 1804, in *NDBW*, 4:187-90, 4:195, 4:222, 4:263-64, 4:186-87, and 4:199-200; Zuchet to Foreign Ministry, June 30, 1804, letter no. 356, 1804/26, in Zuchet Letters, 124.

7. Bainbridge to Preble, July 10, 1804, in *NDBW*, 4:263-64.

8. Dearborn, *Life of William Bainbridge*, 73; *American Naval Biography*, comp. Isaac Bailey (Providence, RI: H. Mann, 1815), 181-82; Wilson, *Biography*, 2:125-26.

9. Renshaw's comment that the officers' miserable situation was "beyond conception" stands in stark contrast to historians who conclude the officers were "very well treated." Baepler, *White Slaves*, 159. Lawrence Peskin believes that the officers were "relatively well treated," and, although he recognizes that "[c]onditions did occasionally deteriorate," mistakenly asserts that the officers' transfer to the castle dungeon was "temporary." Peskin, *Captives and Countrymen*, 154. The conditions in the dungeon are described in many letters, including: Dearborn, *Life of William Bainbridge*, 69; Harris, *Life and Services*, 104; Wilson, *Biography*, 2:162; Ridgely to Susan Decatur, Nov. 10, 1826, Bainbridge to Lear, April 3, 1804, Bainbridge to Preble, June 22, 1804, Bainbridge to Preble, July 7, 1804, Bainbridge to Preble, July 8, 1804, and Renshaw to Rodgers, Nov. 6, 1804, in *NDBW*, 3:425, 4:4-5, 4:213-14, 4:255-56, 4:258-59, and 5:124-25.

10. Ray, *Horrors of Slavery*, 77-78.

11. Preble to Langford, June 23, 1804, and Ball to Langford, July 3, 1804, in NA, RG 45, Subject Files 1775-1910, "American Prisoners in Tripoli," Box 614, folder 3.

12. Preble to Dghies, June 27, 1804, Preble to Bainbridge, June 27, 1804, Preble to Higgins, June 27, 1804, list of stores shipped on *Eliza*, July 3, 1804, Beaussier to Preble, July 6, 1804, Langford to Preble, July 7, 1804, invoice for clothing prepared for Tripol[i], May 15, 1804, and Bainbridge to Preble, July 8, 1804, in *NDBW*, 4:229-30, 4:230, 4:230-31, 4:246, 4:251-52, 4:255, 4:101, and 4:255-56; Spence to Polly Spence, July 7, 1804, in Spence Papers.

13. Nissen to Davis, Sept. 30, 1804, and Nissen to Barron, Nov. 9, 1804, in *NDBW*, 5:58-59 and 5:129-30.

14. Lewis to Preble, July 1, 1804, in *NDBW*, 4:242.

15. Preble to Cathcart, July 5, 1804, Bainbridge to Preble, July 8, 1804, and O'Brien to Madison, Aug. 1, 1804, in ibid., 4:248-49, 4:258-59, and 4:331-32.

16. Preble to commanders of US ships, July 12, 1804, and Preble to Smith, Sept. 18, 1804, in ibid., 4:267-68 and 4:293-308.

17. Beaussier to Karamanli, 8 Thermidor an douze [27 July 1804] ("l'intérêt que l'Empereur de France prend a la prospèrité de votre Regne et au bonheur de vos Sujets, m'oblige a mettre sous vos yeux les considérations suivantes. Si l'attaque des Américaines ne réussit pas . . . la guerre se prolongera encore au grand desavantage de vos revenues, et de votre pays dèja bien appauvri depuis trois ans et trois mois qu'elle dure. Si elle réussit, il est possible que le Commodore exige, pour vous accorder la paix, la déliverance de tous les prisonniers sans aucune rançons. C'est pour lors que vos dépenses auront été en pure parte, indépendament des dommages que la Ville aura souffrent. Il est certain que la continuation de la guerre importe peu aux Etats-Unis de l'Amérique, parce que cette Nation nouvelle est forcée d'armer des escadres pour former des officiers et des Matelots. Ces reflexions, illustre et Magnifique Seigneur, soit dictées par l'interêt de votre Gloire et par le desir qu'a Bonaparte de vous voir en paix avec les Americains.") (underlined in original), in Beaussier Letters.

18. Beaussier to Talleyrand, 15 Thermidor an douze [3 Aug. 1804] ("il a répond verbalement qu'il me remenereiail infiniment de me leur sollicitude, mais qu'il préferait de s'ensevelir sous les Ruines de son pays, plutôt que decider aussi lâchement aux volontes de l'Ennemi. Au reste je ne vois pas comment l'on pourra empêcher le bombardement de Ville . . . Le Pacha n'a à opposer aux progrès des Américains que dix huit chaloupes Cannonieres petites at grandes, mal dirigées, et le feu de divers fortes et batteries dont les Cannoniers ne sont pas bien habiles . . . . P.S. Les Américains sont en vue."), in ibid.

19. Preble to Smith, Sept. 18, 1804, extract from Preble's journal, Aug. 3, 1804, and Preble to Higgins, Aug. 15, 1804, in *NDBW*, 4:293-308, 4:336-38, and 4:417; McKee, *Edward Preble*,

253-65; Cowdery, *American Captives*, diary entry for Aug. 3, 1804; Harris, *Life and Services*, 108; Dearborn, *Life of William Bainbridge*, 69; Ray, *Horrors of Slavery*, 82-84.

20. Extract from Preble's journal, Aug. 3, 1804, and Decatur to Spence, Jan. 9, 1805, in *NDBW*, 4:336-38 and 4:346.

21. Ray, *Horrors of Slavery*, 85; Cowdery, *American Captives*, diary entry for Aug. 5, 1804.

22. McKee, *Edward Preble*, 272-76; Preble to Smith, Sept. 18, 1804, and extract from Haraden log book, Aug. 8, 1804, in *NDBW*, 4:293-308 and 4:378-79; Harris, *Life and Services*, 113; Ray, *Horrors of Slavery*, 85-86; Cowdery, *American Captives*, diary entry for Aug. 9, 1804.

23. Cowdery, *American Captives*, diary entries for Aug. 17–30, 1804.

24. Preble to Smith, Sept. 18, 1804, in *NDBW*, 4:293-308.

25. Cowdery, *American Captives*, diary entries for Aug. 11–15, 1804.

26. Notes on a Cabinet Meeting, May 26, 1804, Founders Online, https://founders.archives. gov/documents/Jefferson/01-43-02-0381.

27. Madison to Lear, June 6, 1804, Preble to Smith, Sept. 18, 1804, Preble to Beaussier, Aug. 9, 1804, extract from Midshipman Charles Morris journal, Aug. 9, 1804, extract from Purser John Darby journal, Aug. 9, 1804, Beaussier to Preble, Aug. 10, 1804, and extract from Preble journal, Aug. 10, 1804, in *NDBW*, 4:155-57, 4:293-308, 4:389, 4:388, 4:391, 4:393, and 4:394.

28. Preble to Beaussier, Aug. 11, 1804, and extract from Midshipman Charles Morris journal, Aug. 11, 1804, in ibid., 4:397-98 and 4:400. David F. Long states incorrectly that Preble's best offer to ransom the captives was $40,000. *Gold Braid*, 30.

29. Extract from Purser John Darby journal, Aug. 11, 1804, in *NDBW*, 4:401.

30. Preble to Higgins, Aug. 21, 1804, in ibid., 4:443; Cowdery, *American Captives*, diary entry for Aug 17, 1804. Jacob Rama Berman asserts that Cowdery's language pushed the Arabs "into the literal and figurative back country," on the "fringe of the modern world," with their backward weapons, and their chants signifying a "regressive" worldview, part of a "discursive strateg[y] for containing Barbary identity." "Barbarous Voice," 6.

31. McKee, *Edward Preble*, 285-89; Preble to Smith, Sept. 18, 1804, and extract from Haraden log book, Aug. 24, 1804, in *NDBW*, 4:293-308 and 4:455-56; Beaussier to Talleyrand, 14 Fructidor an douze [1 Sept. 1804] ("Aucune bombe ne tombe sur la ville, pas même dans le port, ni sur les forts . . ."), in Beaussier Letters; Nissen diary entry, Aug. 24, 1804 ("I Nat kastedes Bomber, der siiges 33 eller 34 Stks, de fleeste faldt i Søen, faae kom i Land, ingen faldt i Byen, kun en sprang og i Luften."), in Nissen Letters.

32. Preble to Smith, Sept. 18, 1804, Preble to Ball, Aug. 29, 1804, extract from Haraden log book, Aug. 28, 1804, and Nissen to Davis, Sept. 1, 1804, in *NDBW*, 4:293-308, 4:474-75, 4:472-74, and 4:495; Cowdery, *American Captives*, diary entry for Aug. 28, 1804; Goldsborough, *Naval Chronicle*, 231n.; Harris, *Life and Services*, 113.

33. Ray, *Horrors of Slavery*, 83, 85, 96.

34. Ray, *Poems*, 83-86, "To the Memory of Commodore Preble."

35. Preble to Beaussier, Aug. 29, 1804, and Beaussier to Preble, Aug. 29, 1804, in *NDBW*, 4:480-81 and 4:481-83.

36. Joseph Douglass and William Godby to Preble, Aug. 19, 1804, and Beaussier to Preble, Aug. 29, 1804, in *NDBW*, 4:479-80 and 4:481-83; Zuchet to Foreign Ministry, Aug. 27, 1804, letter no. 356, 1804/30, in Zuchet Letters, 127.

37. Preble to Ball, Aug. 29, 1804, in *NDBW*, 4:474-75.

38. Cowdery, *American Captives*, diary entry for Sept. 2 (*sic*), 1804; extract from Haraden log book, Sept. 3, 1804, in *NDBW*, 4:503-5.

39. Beaussier to Preble, Sept. 1, 1804, Preble to Sir John Acton, Sept. 6, 1804, and Bainbridge to Barron, March 16, 1805, in *NDBW*, 4:496-97, 4:523-24, and 5:416-17; Ray, *Horrors of Slavery*, 92, 96. A rumor later swept through the squadron that French agents in Naples had sab-

otaged the stock of mortar shells, which accounted for the high number of duds. Tucker, *Dawn Like Thunder*, 312. Christopher McKee attributed the failure of the shells to American inexperience with mortars, by which he presumably meant a widespread failure to cut fuses properly, although Naples had supplied some experienced bombardiers. *Edward Preble*, 295.

40. Preble to Smith, Sept. 18, 1804, and extract from Haraden log book, Sept. 4, 1804, in *NDBW*, 4: 293-308 and 4:506-7; Zuchet to Foreign Ministry, Oct. 12, 1804, letter no. 356, 1805/32, in Zuchet Letters, 128; Rick Atkinson, *The British Are Coming: The War for America, Lexington to Princeton, 1775—1777* (New York: Henry Holt, 2019), 359-60; Tucker, *Dawn Like Thunder*, 323-32; Koedel, *Glory, At Last!*; Livingston Hunt, "Commodore Ridgely's Account of the Last of Somers," U.S. Naval Institute *Proceedings* (June 1928). The squadron's officers who died in the 1804 campaign are commemorated by the Tripoli Monument, a thirty-foot-high marble column, sculpted in Livorno in 1806, which stands on the US Naval Academy grounds. Officers of the squadron funded the monument, which was America's first military monument. One of those killed in the *Intrepid* explosion was Henry Wadsworth, whose married sister, Zilpah Longfellow, named her son, born in 1807, Henry Wadsworth Longfellow. Wheelan, *Jefferson's War*, 229-30.

41. Zuchet to Foreign Ministry, Oct. 12, 1804, letter no. 356, 1805/32, in Zuchet Letters, 129; Harris, *Life and Services*, 115-16.

42. Extract from Haraden log book, Sept. 5, 1804, extract of Purser John Darby journal, Sept. 7, 1804, extract from Haraden log book, Sept. 8, 1804, and Preble to Lt. George W. Reed, Sept. 7, 1804, in *NDBW*, 4:519-20, 5:4, 5:5, and 5:3.

43. Madison to Lear, June 6, 1804, in *NDBW*, 4:155-56. Madison was not the only one to depreciate Hamet, who is described as having "none of the ability of Yusuf," and "[e]ndowed with very little understanding," apparently fonder of women and alcohol than in attempting to address the grave problems confronting Tripoli in the few months he reigned as bashaw. Folayan, *Tripoli during the Reign*, 21.

44. Preble to Barron, Sept. 10, 1804, Preble to Barron, Oct. 8, 1804, Barron to Preble, Nov. 15, 1804, and Preble to Gen. Forteguerra, Dec. 15, 1804, in *NDBW*, 5:13, 5:79-80, 5:143, and 5:194.

45. Beaussier to Preble, Aug. 29, 1804 (emphasis in original), Nissen to Davis, Sept. 1, 1804, and Davis to Madison, Sept. 26, 1804, in *NDBW*, 4:481-83, 4:495, and 5:51-53.

CHAPTER TWELVE: PROSPECTS

1. Leiner, *Millions for Defense*, 129-30, 138.

2. Smith to Barron, June 6, 1804, in *NDBW*, 4:152-54.

3. Lear to Madison, Nov. 3, 1804, in ibid., 5:114-16; Ray, *Horrors of Slavery*, 98.

4. Goldsborough, *Naval Chronicle*, 240-41; Cowdery, *American Captives*, diary entry for April 13, 1805; Ball to Preble, Sept. 20, 1804, in *NDBW*, 5:43. Regarding the fifty-four casualties in the 1804 attacks, Glenn Tucker wrote "[r]arely was more accomplished at so low a cost." *Dawn Like Thunder*, 333. Ian W. Toll pointed out that the United States was a new nation, on the far side of the ocean, and an "enigma" to the Barbary rulers; a "large peace settlement would be interpreted by Tunis and Algiers as a fatal sign of weakness." *Six Frigates*, 203. However, Richard B. Parker (a former US ambassador) believed that Preble might have ransomed the captives even before the five attacks over summer 1804, and "[b]y stubbornly ignoring the authorization that would have permitted him to pay the going price, . . . [he] prolonged the conflict a year at a cost of thirty lives and . . . $500,000 in additional expense. [American] honor was intact, and politically it was worth the price at home, but this was not an example of effective diplomacy on the ground." *Uncle Sam in Barbary*, 169.

5. *Charleston Courier*, Jan. 7, 1805; *True American and Commercial Daily Advertiser*, Aug. 26, 1805.

6. JANUS, "A Short Retrospect of the Year 1804," *Pennsylvania Correspondent, and Farmers' Advertiser*, Jan. 22, 1805; Spellberg, *Thomas Jefferson's Qur'an*, 125. Article I, Section 9 of the Constitution allowed Congress to prohibit the slave trade as of January 1, 1808, which it did. Although other states had outlawed the international slave trade, South Carolina still allowed the importation of slaves in 1804.

7. "American Captives in Tripoli," which is unattributed, was originally published in the *Balance*, Aug. 6, 1805, and was then reprinted in various newspapers, including the *Commercial Advertiser*, Aug. 9, 1805; *Newburyport Herald*, Aug. 16, 1805; and *Federal Gazette & Baltimore Daily Advertiser*, Aug. 21, 1805. No newspaper south of Baltimore seems to have reprinted the poem.

8. Spellberg, *Thomas Jefferson's Qur'an*, 128-30. There is a vast literature on Jefferson's views on slavery, but Spellberg is one of the few historians to draw out the inconsistency of his views on domestic slavery and Barbary slavery. A classic if too sympathetic (to Jefferson) treatment is John Chester Miller, *The Wolf by the Ears: Thomas Jefferson and Slavery* (Charlottesville: University of Virginia Press, 1991). A more critical view about Jefferson and slavery is Alan Taylor, "Hero or Villain, Both and Neither: Appraising Thomas Jefferson, 200 Years Later," *University of Virginia Magazine* 107 (Winter 2018): 48-51.

9. Forteguerra to Preble, Dec. 21, 1804, Preble to Lear, Dec. 23, 1804, Barron to Acton, Jan. 10, 1805, Master Comm. Thomas Robinson to Barron, May 1, 1805, and Barron to Lear, May 18, 1805, in *NDBW*, 5:205, 5:207-9, 5:270-72, 6:2-3, 6:22-23. In spring 1805, the navy contracted to buy vessels to convert into gunboats at Ancona, hoping they might be ready for a summer campaign; the first arrived at Syracuse in July 1805. Mullen, "Good Neighbourhood," 245, 252. In addition, the navy sent nine gunboats built in America to the Mediterranean for the expected 1805 campaign. Gunboat No. 7 was lost at sea with all hands in attempting the Atlantic crossing; the others arrived too late to help the squadron. Chapelle, *American Sailing Navy*, 194-98. When Barron wrote Lear that the failure to borrow gunboats "Extinguished all hope" of obtaining gunboats, he was unaware that gunboats from Ancona and America were soon to be on their way.

10. Eaton is profiled in Reid, *To the Walls of Derne*, 7-15; Wheelan, *Jefferson's War*, 87-90, 239-40; and Tucker, *Dawn Like Thunder*, 347-49, 364-65. Many of his colorful letters are in *The Life of the Late Gen. William Eaton.*

11. Barron's verbal orders to Hull, Sept. 15, 1804, and Lear to Madison, Nov. 3, 1804, in *NDBW*, 5:20 and 5:114-16; Schroeder, *Commodore John Rodgers*, 43-44; Greenhow, *History and Present Condition*, 11; Kitzen, *Tripoli*, 136-37; Wheelan, *Jefferson's War*, 232-36.

12. Bainbridge to Davis, Oct. 31, 1804, Richard Farquhar to Barron, Oct. 15, 1804, and Bainbridge to Davis, Dec. 19, 1804, in *NDBW*, 5:83-84, 5:85-86, and 5:199-201; Ray, *Horrors of Slavery*, 98-99; Schroeder, *Commodore John Rodgers*, 41; Cowdery, *American Captives*, diary entries for Oct. 26 and Dec. 6, 1804; Zuchet to Foreign Ministry, Nov. 24, 1804, and Oct. 12, 1804, letter nos. 356, 1805/32 and 1805/34, in Zuchet Letters, 129-30.

13. Gilje, *Liberty on the Waterfront*, 252; Niklas Frykman, *The Bloody Flag: Mutiny in the Age of Atlantic Revolution* (Oakland: University of California Press, 2020), 6; Frykman, "Seamen," 87-88; Zacks, *Pirate Coast*, 146; Ray, *Horrors of Slavery*, 99-100; Cowdery, *American Captives*, diary entry for Dec. 10, 1804.

14. Spence to Polly Spence, Oct. 16, 1804, in Spence Papers; Nissen to Davis, Sept. 30, 1804, Renshaw to Rodgers, Oct. 15, 1804, and Bainbridge to Davis, Oct. 31, 1804, in *NDBW*, 5:58-59, 5:87-88, and 5:83-84. Fall fever, also known as swamp fever, is a bacteria-caused infection resulting from contact with the urine of diseased animals. The disease can range from mild and symptomless to a more serious, life-threatening form that may be associated with kidney

failure. Free Medical Dictionary, "Leptospirosis," https://medical-dictionary.thefreedictionary.com/leptospirosis.

15. Jon. Cowdery to Jabez Cowdery, Nov. 7, 1804, in Pleadwell and Kerr, "Jonathan Cowdery," 71-72.

16. Cowdery to Mitchill, Nov. 24, 1804, in Pleadwell and Kerr, "Jonathan Cowdery," 72-73; Cowdery, *American Captives*, diary entry for Dec. 7, 1804. Cowdery's letter to Mitchill was reprinted in many newspapers, including the *American and Commercial Daily Advertiser* (Baltimore), July 30, 1805, *True American and Commercial Daily Advertiser* (Philadelphia), July 30, 1805, and *Spectator* (New York), July 31, 1805.

17. Jefferson's Fourth Annual Message, November 8, 1804, Founders Online, https://founders.archives.gov/documents/Jefferson/01-44-02-0592-0012.

18. *Political and Commercial Register* (Philadelphia), Nov. 12, 1804.

19. Langford to Home Secretary Robert Jenkinson, Dec. 15, 1804, in General Correspondence before 1906, Tripoli, Consuls Richard Tully, Simon Lucas, Proconsul B. McDonogh, Consul William Wass Langford 1793–1804, FO 76, Foreign Office and predecessors: Political and Other Departments, British National Archives, Kew, England.

20. Dearborn, *Life of William Bainbridge*, 75; Harris, *Life and Services*, 116-17; Cowdery, *American Captives*, diary entry for Dec. 21, 1804; Ray, *Horrors of Slavery*, 100.

21. Ray, *Horrors of Slavery*, 100.

22. Ibid., 102.

23. Bainbridge to Smith, Feb. 4, 1805, in *NDBW*, 5:327 (emphasis in original).

24. Long, *Sailor-Diplomat*, 24.

25. *True American and Commercial Daily Advertiser* (Philadelphia), July 30, 1805, reprinting an undated extract from an American officer's letter.

26. James Biddle to Nicholas Biddle, April 10, 1801, June [ ], 1801, and June 21, 1801, in Biddle Family Letters.

27. Richard B. Jones received his midshipman warrant on March 29, 1802, and served with James Biddle on the *Constellation* in the Mediterranean in 1802. Bernard Henry, who received his midshipman warrant on November 12, 1800, served on the *Connecticut* during the Quasi-War, and on the *Essex* and *Constellation* (with Biddle and Jones). Robert Gamble received his midshipman warrant only on May 9, 1803, and his first service was on the *Philadelphia*. James Gibbon received his midshipman warrant on June 24, 1799, and served on the *Constellation*, *Insurgente*, and *Enterprize* during the Quasi-War, and on the *Constellation* with Biddle, Jones, and Henry, in the Mediterranean in 1802. Theodore Hunt received his midshipman warrant in September 1798 but was furloughed for eighteen months in June 1801. Promoted to lieutenant on April 4, 1802, he was third lieutenant of the *Philadelphia*. *NDBW*, 7: 19, 20, 25, 27, 29.

28. Biddle to Burr, May 8, 1802, in Biddle Family Letters. Biddle's view of a brotherhood among the *Constellation*'s officers is belied by the record. One of the lieutenants shot and killed the marine lieutenant in a duel; another lieutenant (Jacob Jones) was placed under arrest for acting as second in the duel; and another officer commented that "Captain Murray (being hard of hearing) had no idea of the Dissentions there were on board his ship." Mullen, "Good Neighbourhood," 90; Estes, "Commodore Jacob Jones," 114.

29. James Biddle to Nicholas Biddle, April 10, 1805 (underlined in original), in Biddle Family Letters.

30. Jones/Hunt/James Biddle to Nicholas Biddle, April 14, 1805 (emphases in original), in Biddle Family Letters. Nicholas Biddle (1786–1844) was appointed in 1816 a director of the Second Bank of the United States, for which he became the president in 1822. He is famous for his contentious dispute with President Andrew Jackson in the battle to recharter the bank in 1832.

31. Cowdery, *American Captives*, diary entry for May 23, 1805.

32. Ray, *Horrors of Slavery*, 102-3.

33. *Charleston Courier*, Jan. 7, 1805.

34. Bainbridge to Lear, Nov. 11, 1804, and Bainbridge to Davis, Nov. 22, 1804, in *NDBW*, 5:135-37 and 5:155-56. By disparaging Hamet as "effeminate," Bainbridge clearly meant to invoke the close cultural association between effeminacy and homosexuality. Burg, *Boys at Sea*, 16; Seth Stein LeJacq, "Buggery's Travels: Royal Navy Sodomy on Ship and Shore in the Long Eighteenth Century," *Journal for Maritime Research* 17 (2015): 104.

35. Spence to Polly Spence, March 14, 1805, and April 10, 1805, in Spence Papers.

CHAPTER THIRTEEN: PEACE AND THE RETURN

1. Davis to Preble, March 20, 1805, and Campbell to Smith, April 11, 1805, in *NDBW*, 5:431-32 and 5:502-3.

2. Jefferson to Tyler, March 29, 1805, in *NDBW*, 5:465; Jefferson's Notes on Indian Affairs, Tripoli, Louisiana, Great Britain, Jan. 8, 1805, Founders Online, https://founders.archives.gov/documents/Jefferson/99-01-02-0975.

3. Cowdery, *American Captives*, diary entries of March 1–22, 1805.

4. Toll, *Six Frigates*, 259; Zuchet to Foreign Ministry, March 22 and April 16, 1805, letter nos. 356, 1805/02 and 1805/03, in Zuchet Letters, 131.

5. Nissen to Lear, March 18, 1805, in *NDBW*, 5:421-23. "Sidi" is an honorific or term of respect in Arab cultures, perhaps best translated as "master."

6. Lear to de Souza, March 28, 1805, and Lear to Madison, July 5, 1805, in *NDBW*, 5:463 and 6:159-63; Cowdery, *American Captives*, diary entry for April 12, 1805.

7. Bainbridge to Barron, April 12, 1805, and Nissen to Davis, Feb. 18, 1805, in *NDBW*, 5:505 and 5:359-60; Zuchet to Foreign Ministry, April 16, 1805, letter no. 356, 1805/03, in Zuchet Letters, 131. Glenn Tucker depreciates the risk that the captives would be killed, erroneously claiming, "About the only person in Tripoli who feared the Americans would be slaughtered if Hamet approached appears to have been Bainbridge." *Dawn Like Thunder*, 421.

8. Nissen to Board of Directors, May 16, 1805 ("Paschaen er nu fuldkommen underrettet om den Nord Amerikanske Regierings Overeenskomst med hans Broder Sidi Hamid i Egypten, i hvilken Anledning den forhenværende N: Am: Consul i Tunis Mr Eaton har været afsendt til Rosetta og hvor man troer han endnu opholder sig. Paschaens Broder haaber ved Hjælp han [. . .] fra den N: Am: Regiering og ved sammes Understøttelse at kunne fra Egypten trænge ind i det Tripolinske Gebet og bemægtige sig Landet indtil Tripolis, som han agter at indslutte fra Land Siiden, medens den N: Am: Escadre angribe Staden fra Søe Siden."); Nissen to Board of Directors, April 13, 1805 ("Dette giver Krigen et ganske forskelligt Udseende frem for hidtil; Krigen bliver mere personal; tilforn kunde en Fred letteligen tilveiebringes ved en større eller mindre Penge Opoffrelse paa en af Siderne, med det synes nu vanskeligere at indsee hvorledes Nord Amerika efter en gang at have giort fælleds Sag med Sidi Hamid siden vil kunne forlade ham."), in Nissen Letters.

9. Lear to Davis, April 24, 1805, and Lear to Madison, July 5, 1805, in *NDBW*, 5:136 and 6:159-63.

10. McKee, *Edward Preble*, 330-31; *Life of the Late Gen. William Eaton*, 301-66; Irwin, *Diplomatic Relations*, 147-48; Louis B. Wright and Julia H. Macleod, *The First Americans in North Africa: William Eaton's Struggle for a Vigorous Policy against the Barbary Pirates, 1799–1805* (Princeton, NJ: Princeton University Press, 1945), 151-79; Toll, *Six Frigates*, 260-61; Reid, *To the Walls of Derne*, passim.

11. S. Barron to Lear, May 18, 1805, Lear to Rodgers, May 1, 1805, Lear to S. Barron, May 19, 1805, S. Barron to J. Barron, May 22, 1805, and S. Barron to Rodgers, May 22, 1805, in

NDBW, 6:22-23, 6:1-2, 6:24, 6:31, and 6:31-32. Richard Zacks observes that Barron learned of the victory at Derne, which "snapped him out of his lethargy" and, counterintuitively, suggests that intelligence led to the decision to cut off support for Hamet and begin negotiations for peace. *Pirate Coast*, 246-47.

12. Cowdery, *American Captives*, diary entries for April 12–19, and May 14, 1805. Of course, in the immediate aftermath of the capture of the *Philadelphia*, the bashaw gained access to the ships's and Bainbridge's papers, with information about America's naval strength, and he would have learned more from the newspapers sent to the captives that were intercepted and translated for him. By assuming "a very serious look," perhaps Yusuf displayed his cunning, wishing to give Cowdery (and through him, Bainbridge and Barron) a false impression.

13. Cowdery, *American Captives*, diary entry for May 19, 1805.

14. Cowdery, *American Captives*, diary entries for May 21–24, 1805; Zuchet to Foreign Ministry, May 23, 1805, letter no. 356, 1805/05, in Zuchet Letters, 132.

15. Cowdery, *American Captives*, diary entries for May 26–28, 1805; Ray, *Horrors of Slavery*, 105; Rodgers to Barron, May [ ], 1805, and Lear to Madison, July 5, 1805, in *NDBW*, 6:52-53 and 6:159-63. At this very time, in Algiers, the Turkish garrison blamed local grain shortages on the Bacri & Busnach firm's exports to France; on June 29, 1805, Naphtali Busnach was murdered outside the dey's palace. The dey pardoned the killer; the militia stormed around the city, killing Jews on the streets and pillaging Busnach's property; and then the "plunder became general; they were encouraged by the cries of joy of the women in the streets on the terraces." *American and Commercial Daily Advertiser* (Baltimore), Sept. 27, 1805. Six months later, Farfara, whom Bainbridge called "the chief of the Jews in Tripoli," was assassinated in the bashaw's castle. Bainbridge to Smith, Feb. 12, 1806, in *NDBW*, 6:369. Richard Zacks states that the bashaw arranged for his killing because Farfara had accepted a large (secret) payment for his services from Lear. *Pirate Coast*, 309.

16. McKee, *Edward Preble*, 333; Rodgers to Barron, May [ ], 1805, and Lear to Madison, July 5, 1805, in *NDBW*, 6:52-53 and 6:159-63; Hezekiah Loomis, *Journal of Hezekiah Lewis, Steward on the U.S. Brig "Vixen," Captain John Smith, U.S.N.: War with Tripoli 1804*, ed. Louis F. Middlebrook (Salem, MA: Essex Institute, 1928), 46-47, entries for May 29–31, 1805; Cowdery, *American Captives*, diary entries for May 29–30, 1805.

17. Diplomatic Note, May 31, 1805, and Nissen Report to [Danish foreign office?], June 10, 1805, in *NDBW*, 6:68 and 6:103-5; Dearborn, *Life of William Bainbridge*, 82-83.

18. Loomis, *Journal of Hezekiah Lewis*, 47, diary entry for June 1, 1805; *Norwich (CT) Courier*, Sept. 25, 1805, printing extract of a letter from an officer on the *Constitution*, June 24, 1805; Bashaw's authority given to Nissen, June 1, 1805, Nissen Report to [Danish foreign office?], June 10, 1805, and Lear to Madison, July 5, 1805, in *NDBW*, 6:71, 6:103-5, and 6:159-63.

19. Extract from Capt. Rodgers's journal, June 2, 1805, Lear to Barron, June 6, 1805, and Nissen Report to [Danish foreign office?], June 10, 1805, in *NDBW*, 6:77, 6:94-95, and 6:103-5; Dearborn, *Life of William Bainbridge*, 83-84; Cowdery, *American Captives*, diary entry for June 1, 1805. Denise Spellberg wrongly states that "the only Tripolitan prisoners ever captured" ended up as "spectacles on the New York stage" and "none were ever ransomed to free American captives." *Thomas Jefferson's Qur'an*, 200. According to Richard Zacks, Lear bowed to local Barbary custom, and in addition to the $60,000 ransom, paid a $10 "tax" on each freed captive, a total of $2,950, to be divided among the bashaw's officers and functionaries, as well as $150 in presents to Yusuf's personal servants and slaves. *Pirate Coast*, 309.

20. Cowdery, *American Captives*, diary entry for June 2, 1805; Ray, *Horrors of Slavery*, 106.

21. Wheelan, *Jefferson's War*, 299; Schroeder, *Commodore John Rodgers*, 46; *Life of Eaton*, 366, Eaton to Secretary of the Navy [Smith], July 6, 1805 (emphases in original); Toll, *Six Frigates*, 262. Historian David Long called Lear, Bainbridge, and Barron "appeasers," a his-

torically fraught term. Long, *Sailor-Diplomat*, 26. Long derided the treaty as "a disadvanta-geous pact" and a "mistake" rendered acceptable only because of the "high price" Americans were willing to pay for the lives of the captives, but, paradoxically, Long acknowledged that discounted by the possibility that the bashaw would have killed the hostages if he thought he was on the verge of defeat, the terms of the treaty were "about as good as could be real-istically expected." Long, *Gold Braid*, 32. Glenn Tucker claims Lear "would not hear of delay" and called the treaty "illy conceived and impetuously concluded." *Dawn Like Thunder*, 427.

22. Smith to Preble, Sept. 18, 1805, in *NDBW*, 6:284; Tucker, *Dawn Like Thunder*, 427; Ray, *Horrors of Slavery*, 45; Jefferson to Smith, Sept. 18, 1805, Founders Online, https://founders.archives.gov/documents/Jefferson/99-01-02-2394; The Avalon Project; Doc-uments in History, Law and Diplomacy, Yale Law School, New Haven, CT, Treaty of Peace and Amity between the United States of America and the Bashaw, Bey and Subjects of Tripoli in Barbary, June 4, 1805, https://avalon.law.yale.edu/19th_century/bar1805t.asp.

23. Robert Dennison to Smith, May 22, 1805, and Wormeley to Senator Stephen Bradley, Feb. 19, 1806, in *NDBW*, 6:33-34 and 6:373-74; Jefferson's Fifth Annual Message to Congress, Dec. 3, 1805, Founders Online, https://founders.archives.gov/documents/Jefferson/99-01-02-2746. Kola Folayan inaccurately states that over the course of the war, Tripoli's export of cattle and sheep to feed the British garrison at Malta "maintained a steady rise," which gave Tripoli "a steady source of revenue." Even less credible is his notion that "Tripoli's success [*sic*] was due to its navy." With no discernible basis, he insisted that "[w]ith its size, equip-ment, swift manoeuvrability and the dedicated direction of its officers, the navy made a mockery of the American blockade throughout the war" and "thwarted American strategy." *Tripoli during the Reign*, 41.

24. *Federal Gazette & Baltimore Daily Advertiser*, Sept. 18, 1805. The article was widely reprinted throughout the country, but a Federalist paper called that analysis "ridiculous," depreciating the risk that the bashaw would have killed the prisoners, because the bashaw realized the lives of the captives "were the best guarantee of his [own] life." Had Eaton been allowed two more months, the prisoners would have been freed without paying ransom, Hamet would rule over Tripoli, and "THE AMERICAN FLAG WOULD NOW BE TRI-UMPHANTLY FLYING OVER THAT CITY." *Columbian Centinel*, Sept. 25, 1805 (emphasis in original).

25. Blyth, *History of the War*, 127; McKee, *Edward Preble*, 334; Tucker and Hendrickson, *Em-pire of Liberty*, 294-99n80.

26. *National Intelligencer*, Sept. 25, 1805, reprinting an extract from a letter written by a *Philadelphia* officer; Loomis, *Journal of Hezekiah Lewis*, 48 (entry of June 3, 1805); Lear to Rodgers, June 4, 1805, extract from Capt. Rodgers's journal, June 4, 1805, and Rodgers to Barron, June 3, 1805, in *NDBW*, 6:82, 6:86, and 6:78.

27. Extract from Capt. Rodgers's journal, June 5, 1805, Lear to Rodgers, June 4, 1805, and Lear to Ridgely, June 6, 1805, in *NDBW*, 6:90, 6:82, and 6:93-94; Loomis, *Journal of Hezekiah Lewis*, 48, entries of June 4-7, 1805; Cowdery, *American Captives*, diary entry of June 6, 1805.

28. Rodgers to Beaussier, June 5, 1805, and Rodgers to Beaussier, June 20, 1805, in *NDBW*, 6:88 and 6:128. Green and Nichols were each identified as "claimed as a French citizen in Tripoli" by Keith Spence in "Abstract of Balances due to sundry persons, part of the Crew of the United States late frigate *Philadelphia*," Sept. 30, 1805, in *NDBW*, 3:184-88.

29. In a June 2, 1805, letter to Bainbridge, four sailors—Stephen Howell, Henry Johnson, James Freise, and John Smith—informed their captain that they had conceived the plan to free the Neapolitan slave twelve months earlier because he had "shewed our people many kindnesses," but their long captivity had made the plan impossible. But now, with their own freedom, a majority of the crew subscribed to redeem him. When Bainbridge arrived home,

he placed the crew's letter, as well as his own June 4, 1805, letter to Spence directing him to withhold the money from the crew's pay, in the *Political and Commercial Register*, Oct. 4, 1805, with a cover letter commending "the generosity of those American Tars." The news spread around the country, with some newspapers lauding the "noble example of generosity" and others gushing that "these honest tars merit a wreath more brilliant than ever adorned the brow of a conqueror." *Commercial Advertiser*, Oct. 5, 1805; *National Intelligencer*, Oct. 9, 1805; *New England Palladium*, Oct. 11, 1805; *Enquirer*, Oct. 15, 1805; *Federal Gazette & Baltimore Daily Advertiser*, Oct. 24, 1805. No one named James Freise appeared on the roll Spence prepared of the crew of the *Philadelphia* returning from the Mediterranean in 1805.

30. Enclosure to letter, Bainbridge to Smith, Feb. 5, 1805, in *NDBW*, 5:327-28; Ray, *Horrors of Slavery*, 106-7, Cowdery, *American Captives*, diary entry for April 7, 1805.

31. It is likely that "James Anderson" was in fact a Dane, Jens Andersen from Kronborg, Denmark, who was ill in November 1803, when Nissen gave him some coins.

32. Ray, *Horrors of Slavery*, 75, 78; Cowdery, *American Captives*, diary entries for Jan. 3-4, 1804, April 24, 1804, Sept. 7, 1804, Feb. 5, 1805; Spence, "Abstract of Balances due to sundry persons, part of the Crew of the United States late frigate *Philadelphia*," Sept. 30, 1805, in *NDBW*, 3:184-88.

33. Dearden, *Nest of Corsairs*, 108-9 (the 1785–86 plague may have killed twenty-seven thousand people in Tripolitania, including almost all of the Christian slaves, half of the Jewish community, two-fifths of the Muslim population, and many members of the Karamanli family); Mullen, "Good Neighbourhood," 59-62, 199-200 (smallpox infected men on the *Argus*); Frykman, *Bloody Flag*, 84 (more than eight thousand men died of typhus at the French navy port of Brest in 1793–94); Zachary B. Friedenberg, *Medicine under Sail* (Annapolis, MD: Naval Institute Press, 2002), 75-80; Philip Ranlet, "Typhus and American Prisoners in the War of Independence," *Mariner's Mirror* 96 (Nov. 2010): 443-54; Leiner, *Millions for Defense*, 174; Estes, *Naval Surgeon*, 84, 122, 171, 180, 223-54 (App. 2). By contrast, over the course of two years (1803–05) in the British Mediterranean fleet, which contained 6,500 men, only 110 men died and 141 were sent to hospitals; Nelson kept his ships almost constantly at sea and made sure his men had orange or lemon juice and fresh vegetables. Pope, *Life in Nelson's Navy*, 142.

34. Bainbridge to Nissen, June 3, 1805, Bainbridge to Gavino, July 27, 1805, and Nissen to Bainbridge, Jan. 13, 1807, in *NDBW*, 6:79 and 6:500.

35. Spence to Polly Spence, July 1, 1805, in Spence Papers.

36. Proceedings of Court of Inquiry into the Loss of the U.S. Frigate *Philadelphia*, June 29, 1805, in *NDBW*, 3:189-94. The court's proceedings were reprinted in many newspapers, beginning with the *National Intelligencer*, Sept. 25, 1805.

37. *Federal Spy* (Springfield, MA), Oct. 22, 1805. The poem is not reprinted in Ray, *Poems*.

38. *National Intelligencer*, Sept. 6, 1805, reprinting article from Charleston, Aug. 23, 1805.

39. *Centinel of Freedom* (Newark, NJ), Sept. 24, 1805; "Officers Who Returned as Passengers in the *President*," [undated], and Bainbridge to Smith, Feb. 12, 1806, in *NDBW*, 5:10-11 and 5:39-40; Spence to Polly Spence, Sept. 20, 1805, in Spence Papers; *Republican Watch-Tower* (New York), Sept. 25, 1805; Harris, *Life and Services*, 127n., quoting a letter from Hugh Mercer to Thomas Harris, undated; *American & Commercial Daily Advertiser* (Baltimore), Sept. 27, 1805, reprinting article from a Fredericksburg newspaper; Joint Resolution of Congress, April 10, 1806, reprinted in *Public Statutes at Large*, 9th Cong., 1st Sess., 2:410; *National Intelligencer*, Sept. 25, 1805. Although some accounts state that Bainbridge met with the president, Jefferson was at Monticello throughout September, and Bainbridge could not have met with him upon his arrival in Washington.

40. Spence to Polly Spence, Sept. 26, 1805, in Spence Papers; Smith to Barron, May 31, 1804, in *NDBW*, 4:134-35.

41. Report from Capt. William Bainbridge, Sept. 23, 1805, in *NDBW*, 6:285-86.

42. One historian of the Barbary world has stated poignantly that there were several instances in which black American sailors were captured and treated as slaves in the Maghreb but they were "never allowed, so far as I know, to return to the United States." Baepler, *White Slaves*, 27n65. In fact, the US government paid a stiff ransom in 1802 to redeem some of the crew of the *Franklin*, which included two black sailors. In addition, although it is unclear how many black sailors served on the *Philadelphia*, upon the signing of the treaty and the paying of ransom, all of them returned to the United States in summer 1805. There is no evidence that any of the five "renegades" was black.

43. Bevan, "Letters of Nicholas Harwood," 66; *Telegraphe*, Oct. 10, 1805; *Balance*, Oct. 15, 1805; *Aurora and General Advertiser*, Nov. 6, 1805.

44. *Telegraphe and Daily Advertiser*, Oct. 10, 1805.

45. "The American captives emancipation/writen [*sic*] by A Tar; composed by Mr. R[aynor] Taylor," musical score (Philadelphia: 1806), Rare Books and Manuscripts, Kislak Center for Special Collections, Keffer Collection of Sheet Music, University of Pennsylvania Library, Philadelphia.

46. David J. Druzec III incorrectly states that the "news that the imprisoned crew of the Philadelphia had safely returned home elicited a massive celebration." In fact, the only celebration to which he refers was the dinner at the Eagle Tavern in Richmond for the officers. *Our Suffering Brethren*, 106. Paul A. Gilje writes that the crew was "recognized and rewarded," noting that the men received new clothes and their accumulated pay, and were "feted" and received by President Jefferson. *Liberty on the Waterfront*, 153. Although they did receive their pay, which was no more than what they were entitled to, the crew was not feted nor were they received by the president. Gilje based his statement on a fraudulent sailor memoir purportedly written by an old sailor named Elijah Shaw. Other historians, such as Paul Baepler, have also accepted Shaw's account at face value, including his fictions about Tripoli captivity. *White Slaves*, 19.

47. Smith to Preble, Sept. 18, 1805, in *NDBW*, 6:284. In 1798, President John Adams dined in the President's House in Philadelphia with the representative of the Saint-Domingue government, who was a "mulatto," along with his black wife. There were isolated instances thereafter where black people might enter the White House on personal business, such as to reclaim a coat or recover cargo seized by customs inspectors. In 1844, a black minister went to the White House to eulogize a black servant who had been killed, and he briefly met President John Tyler. In 1860, a black child musical prodigy was invited to perform for President James Buchanan and his guests. But the first president after John Adams to socially receive a black guest was Abraham Lincoln. Jonathan W. White, *A House Built by Slaves: African American Visitors to the Lincoln White House* (Lanham, MD: Rowman & Littlefield, 2022), xxi.

48. *Annals of Congress*, 15:268, 15:313-14; Smith to Rep. John C. Smith, Dec. 12, 1805, in *NDBW*, 6:318-19; *United States Gazette*, Dec. 13, 1805, quoting an extract from a letter by an anonymous congressman; *Annals of Congress*, 15:428. No one named Jonathan Butler appeared on the roll Spence prepared of the crew of the *Philadelphia* returning from the Mediterranean in 1805, and Spence lists a Christopher Simmons, but not a Charles Simmons.

49. At least one ex-*Philadelphia* sailor returned to the Mediterranean a decade later, when the United States fought Algiers in 1815. After two quick battles that forced the dey of Algiers into a treaty, the US squadron arrived off Tripoli on August 6, 1815. At the railing of the brig *Spitfire*, the captain's clerk, Peter M. Potter, talked to a quartermaster named Albright, who

told Potter that he had been captured when the *Philadelphia* ran aground, gestured toward the location of the Kaliusa reef, and pointed out two Tripolitan forts he had helped build when he was a slave. Diary of Peter M. Potter, 128-29, NA RG 45. No one named Albright appeared on the roll Spence prepared of the crew of the *Philadelphia* returning from the Mediterranean in 1805.

50. Jefferson's Fifth Annual Message to Congress, Dec. 3, 1805, Founders Online, https://founders.archives.gov/documents/Jefferson/99-01-02-2746.

51. Mark Bowden, "The Desert One Debacle," *Atlantic*, May 2006; Parker, *Uncle Sam in Barbary*, 158-59. Many other examples of the failed use of force or the need to consider ransom exist. For instance, in 2014, the Iranian government seized three Americans as they hiked in Iraqi Kurdistan near the Iranian border. One was Joshua Fattal, who was held for twenty-six months, charged with spying. His release came after the sultan of Oman paid Iran more than $400,000 in ransom (the Iranians called the payment "bail"). The United States took the position that the government does not pay ransom to gain the release of Americans held hostage; presumably, if ransom is paid by a family or a third party, it is palatable. Naylor, "Should the US Pay Ransom?" Of course, this flips the historic American practice on its head.

52. Wilson, *Biography*, 2:169; Atkinson, *British Are Coming*, 562-63 (referring to timeless attributes of heroic endurance).

EPILOGUE

1. Anonymous [William Ray], "Ode to Liberty," *Morning Chronicle*, Sept. 4, 1805, later published in Ray, *Poems*, titled "Song," 94-96.

⁓ BIBLIOGRAPHY ⁓

A NOTE ON SOURCES

Three men purportedly wrote accounts about their captivity in Tripoli. The first was Jonathan Cowdery, whose Tripoli diary was published in newspapers across the United States. In 1806, a Boston printer, Belcher & Armstrong, brought out the diary in a pamphlet called *American Captives in Tripoli*. In 1922, Cowdery's diary and several letters were published in the *United States Naval Medical Bulletin*. In the 1940s, the US Navy's multivolume *Naval Documents of the Barbary Wars* reprinted Cowdery's diary entries, but unfortunately, they do not appear in chronological sequence with other documents. In 1999, Paul Baepler compiled *White Slaves, African Masters: An Anthology of American Barbary Captivity Narratives,* which included Dr. Cowdrey's diary. Last, in 2007, Robert J. Allison edited a small book, *Narratives of Barbary Captivity*, which again reproduced the diary. All my citations to Cowdery's diary are to the dates of his entries, not to pages in a specified text.

William Ray wrote *Horrors of Slavery: Or, The American Tars in Tripoli*, published in Troy, New York, in 1808. An excerpt from *Horrors of Slavery* appeared in Baepler's *White Slaves, African Masters* in 1999. Allison's *Narratives of Barbary Captivity* contains Ray's book, and in 2008, Rutgers University Press republished it with notes and an introduction about Ray's life, poems, and place in American letters, by Hester Blum. Because it is likely to be more accessible to readers, my citations are to the 2008 (Blum's) publication. Blum aptly observes that Ray's "voice is distinct: prickly, humorous, and always provocative." In 1809, after William Bainbridge came upon *Horrors of Slavery*, he wrote Robert Smith how offended he was by Ray's "calumny & falsehood," not only for Ray's account of the surrender of the *Philadelphia* but also for how he dealt with Bainbridge's supposed "total disregard and dereliction of the unfortunate Crew." Bainbridge presumed Ray's malignity owed to his not supporting Ray when he floated the idea of a book, not providing him with documents, and not subscribing for a copy.

Ray, however, was not done. In 1821, he published *Poems, on various subjects, religious, moral, sentimental and humorous, To which is added, a brief sketch of the author's life, and of his captivity and sufferings among the Turks and barbarians of Tripoli on the coast of Africa*. Ray's scarcely known *Poems* add much to his account of Barbary captivity. It is unclear if Bainbridge ever saw or commented on that book.

In 1843, a man claiming to be an old sailor named Elijah Shaw published *A short sketch of the life of Elijah Shaw, who served for twenty-two years in the Navy of the United States, taking an active part in four different wars between the United States & foreign powers; namely, first—with France, in 1798; second—with Tripoli, from 1802 to 1805; third—with England from 1812 to 1815; fourth—with Algiers, from 1815 to 1816: and assisted in subduing the pirates from 1822 to 1826, and in 1843 entered on board the old ship Zion, under a new commander, being in the 73d year of his age* (Rochester, NY: Shaw & Dawson, 1843). Although some historians have cited Shaw's book, it is a complete fraud, identified by Myra Glenn in *Jack Tar's Story* as part of a genre of nineteenth century fake seafarers' memoirs. Shaw claimed to be the *Philadelphia*'s carpenter, but he was not; the actual carpenter was William Godby. There was no Elijah Shaw listed among the frigate's crew. Like the title character of Zelig in the Woody Allen movie, Shaw purportedly showed up at and took part in many of the navy's famous battles over four wars, but the documents do not bear this out, and it is also virtually impossible that any one man would be so (un)fortunate as to be in so many of the major battles of the US Navy in the age of sail. His claims about the *Philadelphia* and his supposed captivity in Tripoli are clearly imaginary. Among the most outlandish of Shaw's many fictitious claims were that the *Philadelphia* sailed to the Mediterranean from New Brunswick, New Jersey; that when she went aground, the frigate was surrounded by "one hundred or more" gunboats and galleys; that in captivity, the crew was initially locked in iron chains; and that when Decatur's expedition burned the ship, there were nine hundred Tripolitan guards aboard, of whom only sixty or seventy survived.

Finally, the dust jacket of this book contains an image of the *Philadelphia* aground and under attack by Tripolitan gunboats on October 31, 1804, which shows the angle of the frigate on the reef and her inability to get a single gun to bear on her attackers. According to a contemporary advertisement for the original engraving, Charles Denoon, a sailor on the *Philadelphia*, was the artist. Denoon also drew or painted an image of the gunboats' August 3 attack, although that picture and its engraving are now apparently lost or unknown. In November 1805, copies of both of Denoon's "Views of Tripoli" were on display for would-be subscribers at the office of the *Enquirer* (Richmond, VA); the cost of the two engravings was two dollars. In a November 8, 1805, advertisement in the *Enquirer* seeking subscribers, Denoon pledged that his "Views of Tripoli" were accurate and "were taken at the risk of his life, or having dragged out a miserable existence in perpetual slavery." Two of the *Philadelphia*'s officers, Benjamin Read and James Gibbon, certified in the advertisement that Denoon had been a captive in Tripoli and that his "Views" were correct.

OFFICIAL RECORDS AND DOCUMENT COLLECTIONS

Annals of Congress. Vols. 13-15. Eighth Congress: 1st Session to Ninth Congress: 2d Session. Washington, DC: Gales and Seaton, 1852.

Cathcart, James Leander. *The Captives: Eleven Years a Prisoner in Algiers*. Compiled by J. B. Newkirk. LaPorte, IN: Herald Print, 1899.

————. *Tripoli, First War With the United States. [The] Letter Book [of] James Leander Cathcart, First Consul to Tripoli and Last Letters from Tunis*. Compiled by J. B. Newkirk. LaPorte, IN: Herald Print, 1901.

Circular Letters of Congressmen to Their Constituents, 1789–1829. Edited by Noble E. Cunningham, Jr. Chapel Hill: University of North Carolina Press, 1978.

Correspondance des beys de Tunis et des consuls de France avec la cour, 1577-1830. Edited by Eugène Plantet. Paris: F. Alcan, 1899.

Correspondence to and from London and Malta, Benghazi etc. 1800—
    1815, in Correspondence to and Letter Books, 1700 to 1948, Consulate,
    Tripoli, Libya (formerly Ottoman Empire): FO 160/35 Foreign Office
    and predecessor. British National Archives, Kew, England.

Enthoven, Victor. "'From the Halls of Montezuma, to the Shores of
    Tripoli': Antoine Zuchet and the First Barbary War, 1801–1805." In
    Research in Maritime History No.44, *Rough Waters: American Involve-
    ment with the Mediterranean in the Eighteenth and Nineteenth Cen-
    turies.* Edited by Silvia Marzagalli, James R. Sofka, and John J.
    McCusker. St. John's, Newfoundland: International Maritime Eco-
    nomic History Association, 2010, 117-34 (reprinting in translation the
    letters of Dutch Consul Antoine Zuchet).

General Correspondence and Letter Books, 1700 to 1948, Consulate,
    Tripoli, Libya (formerly Ottoman Empire): FO 160/35 Foreign Office
    and predecessor. British National Archives, Kew, England.

General Correspondence before 1906, Tripoli, Consuls Richard Tully,
    Simon Lucas, Proconsul B. McDonogh, Consul William Wass Lang-
    ford 1793—1804: FO 76 Foreign Office and predecessors: Political and
    Other Departments: Series I, FO 76/5. British National Archives, Kew,
    England.

Holck, Harald. "Kommandør Carl Christian Holcks Dagbøger som Kon-
    sul i Tunis. Af kontorchef" (Commander Carl Christian Holcks' Di-
    aries as Consul in Tunis. Head of Office). *PersonalHistorik Tidsskrift,*
    82:61-129 (1962).

Letter book and Correspondence of Nicolai Christian Nissen, in Tripoli,
    konsulaer represenation and konsulaer retsprotokol, 2-2215 in Kor-
    respondancesager 1752-1834. Rigsarkivet, Copenhagen, Denmark.

Letters and Memoranda of Bonaventure Beaussier. Archives du Min-
    istère des Affaires Etrangères: Correspondence Consulaire, Tripoli de
    Barbarie. Paris, France.

Letters and Papers of Richard Somers. Edited by Frank H. Stewart. Wood-
    bury, NJ: Gloucester County Historical Society, 1942.

Letters of Commodore James Biddle. 16 vols. Biddle Family Papers, Box 1.
    Andalusia Historic House and Gardens, Andalusia, PA.

Letters of Nicholas Harwood. Hammond-Harwood House Collection,
    MS 1303. Maryland Center for History and Culture, Baltimore.

"Letters of William Henry Allen, 1803–1813, Part One: 1800–1806." Edited by Edward H. Tatum, Jr. and Marion Tinling. *Huntington Library Quarterly* 1, no. 1 (Oct. 1937): 101-32.

Loomis, Hezekiah. *Journal of Hezekiah Lewis, Steward on the U.S. Brig "Vixen," Captain John Smith, U.S.N.: War with Tripoli 1804.* Edited by Louis F. Middlebrook. Salem, MA: Essex Institute, 1928.

Naval Documents Related to the Quasi-War between the United States and France. Edited by Dudley W. Knox. 7 vols. Washington, DC: Government Printing Office, 1935–38. http://www.ibiblio.org/anrs/quasi.html.

Naval Documents Related to the United States Wars with the Barbary Powers. Edited by Dudley W. Knox. 7 vols. Washington, DC: Government Printing Office, 1939-45. http://www.ibiblio.org/anrs/barbary.html.

Naval Regulations Issued by Command of the President of the United States of America. Jan. 25, 1802. Annapolis, MD: Naval Institute Press, 1970.

Pleadwell, F. L., and W. M. Kerr. "Jonathan Cowdery, Surgeon in the United States Navy, 1767–1852." *United States Naval Medical Bulletin* 17 (July 1922): 63-88 and (Aug. 1922): 243-68. https://ia800109.us.archive.org/24/items/NavalMedicalBulletin171922/ Naval%20Medical%20Bulletin%2017%201922.pdf.

Public Statutes at Large. Edited by Richard Peters. Boston: Charles C. Little and James Brown, 1845–50.

Record Group 23. 23rd Congress, House Committee on Naval Affairs, Claims (HR 23A-D13.1, bundle 3). Claim of Susan Decatur, "Reminiscences of Lewis Heermann Surgeon U.S. Navy—1826." National Archives and Records Administration, Washington, DC.

Record Group 36. Records of the US Customs Service, microcopy 1880. "Proofs of Citizenships Used to Apply for Seamen's Protection Certificates for the Port of Philadelphia, 1792–1861," rolls 1-3. National Archives and Records Administration, Washington, DC.

Record Group 45, M125. "Letters Received by the Secretary of the Navy: Captains Letters 1805–61." National Archives and Records Administration, Washington, DC.

Record Group 45. Entry 392, appendix D #31. Diary of Peter M. Potter, USS *Spitfire*, May 20, 1815–November 23, 1815 (photostat copy). National Archives and Records Administration, Washington, DC.

Record Group 45. Subject Files 1775–1910, "American Prisoners in Tripoli," Box 614, folder 3. National Archives and Records Administration, Washington, DC.

Spence, Purser Keith. Letters. Papers of the Spence and Lowell Families, MSS SL 1-3117. Huntington Library, San Marino, CA.

United States Reports. John Marshall and Supreme Court of the United States, *Talbot v. Seeman,* 5 U.S. (1 Cranch) 1 (1801), 1-45. https://www.loc./gov/item/usrep005001/.

CONTEMPORARY WORKS

Allison, Robert J., ed. *Narratives of Barbary Captivity.* Chicago: R. R. Donnelly & Sons, 2007.

American Naval Biography. Compiled by Isaac Bailey. Providence, RI: H. Mann, 1815.

Baepler, Paul, ed. *White Slaves, African Masters: An Anthology of American Barbary Captivity Narratives.* Chicago: University of Chicago Press, 1999.

Blyth, Stephen Cleveland. *History of the war between the United States and Tripoli, and Other Barbary Powers. To which is prefixed, A Geographical, Religious and Political History of the Barbary States in General.* Salem, MA: Printed at the Salem Gazette Office, 1806.

Cowdery, Jonathan. *American Captives in Tripoli.* Boston: Belcher & Armstrong, 1806.

Durand, James. *An Able Seaman of 1812: His Adventures on "Old Ironsides" and as an Impressed Sailor in the British Navy.* Edited by George S. Brooks. New Haven, CT: Yale University Press, 1926.

Goldsborough, Charles W. *The United States Naval Chronicle.* Washington, DC: James Wilson, 1824.

Greenhow, Robert. *The History and Present Condition of Tripoli With Some Accounts of the Other Barbary States.* Richmond, VA: T. H. White, 1835.

Leech, Samuel. *Thirty Years From Home, or A Voice From the Main Deck.* Boston: Tappan & Dennet, 1843.

The Life of the Late Gen. William Eaton. Compiled by Charles Prentiss. Brookfield, MA: E. Merriam, printers, 1813.

Morris, Richard Valentine. *A Defence of the Conduct of Commodore Morris During His Command in the Mediterranean: With Strictures on the*

Report of the Court of Enquiry Held at Washington. New York: I. Riley, 1804.

Noah, Mordecai M. *Travels in England, France, Spain, and the Barbary States in the Years 1813–14 and 15.* New York: Kirk and Mercein, 1819.

Ray, William. *Horrors of Slavery, or American Tars in Tripoli.* Troy, NY, 1808.

———. *Horrors of Slavery, or American Tars in Tripoli.* Edited by Hester Blum. New Brunswick, NJ: Rutgers University Press, 2008.

———. *Poems on Various Subjects, Religious, Moral, Sentimental and Humorous.* Auburn, NY: U. F. Doubleday, 1821.

Rea, John. *A letter to William Bainbridge, Esqr. formerly commander of the United States Ship George Washington relative to some transactions, on board said ship, during a voyage to Algiers, Constantinople, &c.* Philadelphia: Printed by the author, 1802.

CONTEMPORARY NEWSPAPERS AND MAGAZINES

Albany Gazette
Alexandria (VA) Daily Advertiser
American and Commercial Daily Advertiser (Baltimore)
Analectic Magazine
Augusta (GA) Chronicle
Aurora and General Advertiser (Philadelphia)
Balance (Hudson, NY)
Boston Commercial Gazette
Boston Courier
Carolina Gazette (Charleston, SC)
Centinel of Freedom (Newark, NJ)
Charleston (SC) Courier
City Gazette (Charleston, SC)
Columbian Centinel (Boston)
Commercial Advertiser (New York)
Connecticut Courant (Hartford)
Democrat (Boston)
Enquirer (Richmond, VA)
Federal Gazette & Baltimore Daily Advertiser
Federal Spy (Springfield, MA)
Gazette of the United States (Philadelphia),
Guardian or New Brunswick (NJ) Advertiser

Herald of the United States (Warren, RI)
Kentucky Gazette (Lexington)
Morning Chronicle (New York)
National Aegis (Worcester, MA)
National Intelligencer (Washington)
Newburyport (MA) Herald
New England Palladium (Boston)
New Hampshire Sentinel (Keene)
New York Daily Advertiser
New York Evening Post
New-York Gazette and General Advertiser
New-York Herald
Norwich (CT) Courier
Norwich (CT) Packet
Oracle (Portsmouth, NH)
Oracle Post (Portsmouth, NH)
Patriot (Utica, NY)
Pennsylvania Correspondent, and Farmers' Advertiser (Doylestown)
Philadelphia Evening Post
Philadelphia Gazette and Daily Advertiser
Political and Commercial Register (Philadelphia)
Political Calendar (Newburyport, MA)
Political Observatory (Walpole, NH)
The Port Folio
Poulson's American Daily Advertiser (Philadelphia)
Repertory (Boston)
Republican (Baltimore)
Republican Advocate (Frederick, MD)
Republican Watch-Tower (New York)
Salem (MA) Gazette
Salem (MA) Register
Spectator (New York)
Telegraphe and Daily Advertiser (Baltimore)
True American and Commercial Daily Advertiser (Philadelphia)
United States Gazette (Philadelphia)
Virginia Argus (Richmond)
Weekly Museum (New York)

SECONDARY SOURCES

Books

Adkins, Roy, and Lesley Adkins. *Gibraltar: The Greatest Siege in British History.* New York: Viking, 2017.

Allen, Gardner W. *Our Navy and the Barbary Corsairs.* Boston: Houghton Mifflin, 1905.

Allison, Robert J. *The Crescent Obscured: The United States and the Muslim World, 1776–1815.* Chicago: University of Chicago Press, 1995.

———. *Stephen Decatur: American Naval Hero, 1779–1820.* Amherst: University of Massachusetts Press, 2005.

Altoff, Gerard T. *Amongst My Best Men: African-Americans and the War of 1812.* Put-in-Bay, OH: Perry Group, 1996.

Anthony, Irvin. *Decatur.* New York: Charles Scribner's Sons, 1931.

Armstrong, Benjamin. "'Against the Common Enemies': American Allies and Partners in the First Barbary War." In *The Trafalgar Chronicle: Dedicated to Naval History in the Nelson Era* (new ser. 2), edited by Peter Hore, 48-60. Barnsley, UK: Seaforth, 2017.

———. *Small Boats and Daring Men: Maritime Raiding, Irregular Warfare, and the Early American Navy.* Norman: University of Oklahoma Press, 2019.

Atkinson, Rick. *The British Are Coming: The War for America, Lexington to Princeton, 1775–1777.* New York: Henry Holt, 2019.

Barnby, H. G. *The Prisoners of Algiers: An Account of the Forgotten American Algerian War 1785–1797.* Oxford: Oxford University Press, 1966.

Berube, Claude, and John Rodgaard. *A Call to the Sea: Captain Charles Stewart of the USS Constitution.* Washington, DC: Potomac Books, 2005.

Bolster, W. Jeffrey. *Black Jacks: African American Seamen in the Age of Sail.* Cambridge, MA: Harvard University Press, 1997.

Bricka, Carl Frederik. *Dansk biografik Lexikon.* Copenhagen: Gyldendalske Boghandels Forlag, 1887–1905. runeberg.org/dbl/12/0301.html.

Brighton, Ray. *The Checkered Career of Tobias Lear.* Portsmouth, NH: Portsmouth Marine Society, 1985.

Burg, B. R. *Boys at Sea: Sodomy, Indecency, and Courts Martial in Nelson's Navy.* Basingstoke, UK: Palgrave Macmillan, 2007.

Burn, Helen Jean. *Betsy Bonaparte.* Baltimore: Maryland Historical Society, 2010.

Chapelle, Howard I. *The History of the American Sailing Navy.* New York: W. W. Norton, 1949.

Chernow, Ron. *Washington: A Life.* New York: Penguin, 2010.

Cleaver, Mark M. *The Life, Character, and Public Services of Commodore Jacob Jones.* Wilmington: Historical Society of Delaware, 1906.

Davis, Robert C. *Christian Slaves, Muslim Masters: White Slavery in the Mediterranean, the Barbary Coast, and Italy, 1500–1800.* Basingstoke, UK: Palgrave Macmillan, 2004.

Dearborn, H. A. S. *The Life of William Bainbridge, Esq.* Edited by James Barnes. Princeton, NJ: Princeton University Press, 1931.

Dearden, Seaton. *A Nest of Corsairs: The Fighting Karamanlis of the Barbary Coast.* London: John Murray, 1976.

De Kay, James Tertius. *A Rage for Glory: The Life of Commodore Stephen Decatur, USN.* New York: Free Press, 2004.

Deutsch, Alexandra. *A Woman of Two Worlds: Elizabeth Patterson Bonaparte.* Baltimore: Maryland Historical Society, 2016.

Dye, Ira. *The Fatal Cruise of the* Argus: *Two Captains in the War of 1812.* Annapolis, MD: Naval Institute Press, 1994.

Dzurec, David J., III. *Our Suffering Brethren: Foreign Captivity and Nationalism in the Early United States.* Amherst: University of Massachusetts Press, 2019.

Estes, J. Worth. *Naval Surgeon: Life and Death at Sea in the Age of Sail.* Canton, MA: Science History Publications, 1998.

Folayan, Kola. *Tripoli during the Reign of Yūsuf Pāshā Qaramānlī.* Ife, Nigeria: University of Ife Press, 1979.

Footner, Geoffrey M. *Tidewater Triumph: The Development and Worldwide Success of the Chesapeake Bay Pilot Schooner.* Mystic, CT: Mystic Seaport Museum Press, 1998.

Fowler, William T. *Jack Tars & Commodores: The American Navy 1783–1815.* Boston: Houghton Mifflin, 1984.

Friedenberg, Zachary B. *Medicine Under Sail.* Annapolis, MD: Naval Institute Press, 2002.

Frykman, Niklas. *The Bloody Flag: Mutiny in the Age of Atlantic Revolution.* Oakland: University of California Press, 2020.

Gilje, Paul A. *Liberty on the Waterfront: American Maritime Culture in the Age of Revolution.* Philadelphia: University of Pennsylvania Press, 2004.

Gleaves, Albert. *James Lawrence: Captain, United States Navy.* New York: G.P. Putnam's Sons, 1904.

Glenn, Myra C. *Jack Tar's Story: The Autobiographies and Memoirs of Sailors in Antebellum America.* New York: Cambridge University Press, 2010.

Goodin, Brett. *From Captives to Consuls: Three Sailors in Barbary and Their Self-Making Across the Early American Republic, 1770–1840.* Baltimore: Johns Hopkins University Press, 2020.

Grant, Bruce. *Isaac Hull, Captain of Old Ironsides.* Chicago: Pellegrini and Cudahy, 1947.

Harris, Thomas. *Life and Services of Commodore William Bainbridge, United States Navy.* Philadelphia: Carey, Lea & Blanchard, 1837.

Hirschberg, J. W. *A History of the Jews in North Africa.* Vol. 2, *From the Ottoman Conquests to the Present Time.* Leiden, Netherlands: Brill Academic, 1981.

Irwin, Ray W. *The Diplomatic Relations of the United States with the Barbary Powers 1776–1816.* Chapel Hill: University of North Carolina Press, 1931.

James, Trevor. *Prisoners of War at Dartmoor: American and French Soldiers and Sailors in an English Prison during the Napoleonic Wars and the War of 1812.* Jefferson, NC: McFarland, 2013.

Jamison, Kay Redfield. *Robert Lowell, Setting the River on Fire: A Study of Genius, Mania, and Character.* New York: Vintage, 2018.

Jenkins, E. H. *A History of the French Navy, from its Beginnings to the Present Day.* London: Macdonald and Jane's, 1973.

Kitzen, Michael L. S. *Tripoli and the United States at War: A History of American Relations with the Barbary States, 1785–1805.* Jefferson, NC: McFarland, 1993.

Koedel, Barbara E. *Glory, at Last!: A Narrative of the Naval Career of Master Commandant Richard Somers: 1778–1804.* Somers Point, NJ: Atlantic County Historical Society, 1993.

Langley, Harold D. *A History of Medicine in the Early U.S. Navy.* Baltimore: Johns Hopkins University Press, 1995.

———. *Social Reform in the United States Navy 1798–1862.* Annapolis, MD: Naval Institute Press, 2015. (orig. pub. 1967).

Lavery, Brian. *Life in Nelson's Navy: The Ships, Men and Organisation 1793–1815.* Annapolis, MD: Naval Institute Press, 1997.

Leiner, Frederick C. *Millions for Defense: The Subscription Warships of 1798*. Annapolis, MD: Naval Institute Press, 2000.

Lewis, Charlene M. Boyer. *Elizabeth Patterson Bonaparte: An American Aristocrat in the Early Republic*. Philadelphia: University of Pennsylvania Press, 2012.

Lewis, Charles Lee. *The Romantic Decatur*. Philadelphia: University of Pennsylvania Press, 1937.

Linebaugh, Peter, and Marcus Rediker. *The Many-Headed Hydra: Sailors, Slaves, Commoners, and the Hidden History of the Revolutionary Atlantic*. London: Verso, rev. ed. 2012 (orig. pub. 2000).

Long, David F. *Gold Braid and Foreign Relations: Diplomatic Activities of U.S. Naval Officers, 1798–1883*. Annapolis, MD: Naval Institute Press, 1988.

———. *Nothing Too Daring: A Biography of Commodore David Porter, 1780–1843*. Annapolis, MD: Naval Institute Press, 1970.

———. *Ready to Hazard: A Biography of Commodore William Bainbridge, 1772–1833*. Lebanon, NH: University Press of New England, 1981.

———. *Sailor-Diplomat: A Biography of Commodore James Biddle, 1783–1848*. Boston: Northeastern University Press, 1983.

MacDougall, Philip. *Islamic Seapower during the Age of Fighting Sail*. Woodbridge, Suffolk, UK: Boydell Press, 2017.

Mackenzie, Alexander S. *Life of Stephen Decatur*. Boston: Charles C. Little and James Brown, 1846.

Malcolmson, Thomas. *Order and Disorder in the British Navy, 1793–1815: Control, Resistance, Flogging and Hanging*. Woodbridge, Suffolk, UK: Boydell Press, 2016.

Maloney, Linda M. *The Captain from Connecticut: The Life and Naval Times of Isaac Hull*. Boston: Northeastern University Press, 1986.

Martin, Tyron G. *A Most Fortunate Ship: A Narrative History of Old Ironsides*. Annapolis, MD: Naval Institute Press, 1997.

McCullough, David. *John Adams*. New York: Simon & Schuster, 2001.

McKee, Christopher. *Edward Preble: A Naval Biography, 1761–1807*. Annapolis, MD: Naval Institute Press, 1972.

———. *A Gentlemanly and Honorable Profession: The Creation of the U.S. Naval Officer Corps, 1794–1815*. Annapolis, MD: Naval Institute Press, 1991.

Melville, Herman. *White-Jacket*. Oxford: Oxford University Press, 1996. (orig. pub. 1850).

Miller, John Chester. *The Wolf by the Ears: Thomas Jefferson and Slavery*. Charlottesville: University of Virginia Press, 1991.

Miller, Melanie Randolph. *Envoy to the Terror: Gouverneur Morris and the French Revolution*. Washington, DC: Potomac Books, 2004.

Morris, Charles. *The Autobiography of Commodore Charles Morris, U.S. Navy*. Annapolis, MD: Naval Institute Press, 2002 (orig. pub. 1880).

Niles, John M. *The Life of Oliver Hazard Perry with an Appendix, Comprising a Biographical Memoir of the late Captain James Lawrence; With Brief Sketches of the Most Prominent Events in the Lives of Commodores Bainbridge, Decatur, Porter, and Macdonough*. Hartford, CT: Oliver D. Cooke, 1821.

The Oxford Companion to Ships and the Sea. Edited by Peter Kemp. Oxford: Oxford University Press, rev. ed. 1988.

Parker, Richard B. *Uncle Sam in Barbary: A Diplomatic History*. Gainesville: University Press of Florida, 2004.

Paullin, Charles Oscar. *Paullin's History of Naval Administration 1775–1911*. Annapolis, MD: Naval Institute Press, 1968.

Perla, Peter P. *The Art of Wargaming: A Guide for Professionals and Hobbyists*. Annapolis, MD: Naval Institute Press, 1990.

Peskin, Lawrence A. *Captives and Countrymen: Barbary Slavery and the American Public, 1785–1816*. Baltimore: Johns Hopkins University Press, 2009.

Pleadwell, F. L., and William M. Kerr. *Lewis Heermann, Surgeon in the United States Navy (1779–1833)*. New York: Paul B. Hoeber, 1923.

Pope, Dudley. *Life in Nelson's Navy*. London: Unwin Hyman, 1987.

Porter, David Dixon. *Memoir of Commodore David Porter, of the United States Navy*. Albany, NY: J. Munsell, 1875.

Reid, Chipp. *Intrepid Sailors: The Legacy of Preble's Boys and the Tripoli Campaign*. Annapolis, MD: Naval Institute Press, 2012.

———. *To the Walls of Derne: William Eaton, the Tripoli Coup, and the End of the First Barbary War*. Annapolis, MD: Naval Institute Press, 2017.

Rodger, N. A. M. *The Command of the Ocean: A Naval History of Britain, 1649–1815*. New York: W.W. Norton, 2005.

Said, Edward W. *Orientalism*. New York: Vintage, 1979.

Schroeder, John H. *Commodore John Rodgers: Paragon of the Early American Navy*. Gainesville: University Press of Florida, 2006.

Seiken, Jeff. "The Reluctant Warrior: Thomas Jefferson and the Tripolitan War, 1801–1805." In *Rough Waters: American Involvement with the Mediterranean in the Eighteenth and Nineteenth Centuries*, edited by Silvia Marzagalli, James R. Sofka, and John J. McCusker, 185-206. Vol. 44 of Research in Maritime History. St. John's, Newfoundland: International Maritime Economic History Association, 2010.

Sha´ban, Fuad. *Islam and Arabs in Early American Thought: The Roots of Orientalism in America*. Durham, NC: Acorn, 1990.

Shaw, Stanford J. *Between Old and New: The Ottoman Empire under Sultan Selim III, 1789–1807*. Cambridge, MA: Harvard University Press, 1971.

Spellberg, Denise A. *Thomas Jefferson's Qur'an: Islam and the Founders*. New York: Vintage, 2013.

Spencer, William. *Algiers in the Age of the Corsairs*. Norman: University of Oklahoma Press, 1976.

Symonds, Craig. "William S. Bainbridge: Bad Luck or Fatal Flaw?" In *Command Under Sail: Makers of the American Naval Tradition, 1775–1850*, edited by James C. Bradford, 97-125. Annapolis, MD: Naval Institute Press, 1985.

Taylor, Stephen. *Sons of the Waves: The Common Seamen in the Heroic Age of Sail*. New Haven, CT: Yale University Press, 2020.

Toll, Ian W. *Six Frigates: The Epic History of the Founding of the U.S. Navy*. New York: W.W. Norton, 2006.

Tucker, Glenn. *Dawn Like Thunder: The Barbary Wars and the Birth of the U.S. Navy*. Indianapolis: Bobbs-Merrill, 1963.

Tucker, Robert W., and David C. Hendrickson. *Empire of Liberty: The Statecraft of Thomas Jefferson*. New York: Oxford University Press, 1990.

Tucker, Spencer C. *Arming the Fleet: U.S. Navy Ordnance in the Muzzle-Loading Era*. Annapolis, MD: Naval Institute Press, 1989.

———. *Stephen Decatur: A Life Most Bold and Daring*. Annapolis, MD: Naval Institute Press, 2004.

Valle, James E. *Rocks and Shoals: Naval Discipline in the Age of Fighting Sail*. Annapolis, MD: Naval Institute Press, 1986.

Waldo, S. Putnam. *The Life and Character of Stephen Decatur*. Hartford, CT: P.B. Goodsell, 1821.

Wheelan, Joseph. *Jefferson's War: America's First War on Terror 1801–1805.* New York: Carroll & Graf, 2003.

Whipple, A. B. C. *To the Shores of Tripoli: The Birth of the U.S. Navy and Marines.* New York: William Morrow, 1991.

White, Jonathan W. *A House Built by Slaves: African American Visitors to the Lincoln White House.* Lanham, MD: Rowman & Littlefield, 2022.

———. *Midnight in America: Darkness, Sleep, and Dreams during the Civil War.* Chapel Hill: University of North Carolina Press, 2017.

Wiggins, Kennard R., Jr. *America's Anchor: A Naval History of the Delaware River and Bay, Cradle of the United States Navy.* Jefferson, NC: McFarland, 2019.

Wilson, Thomas. *The Biography of the Principal American Military and Naval Heroes.* 2 vols. New York: John Low, 1817, 1819.

Wright, Louis B., and Julia H. Macleod. *The First Americans in North Africa: William Eaton's Struggle for a Vigorous Policy against the Barbary Pirates, 1799–1805.* Princeton, NJ: Princeton University Press, 1945.

Zacks, Richard. *The Pirate Coast: Thomas Jefferson, the First Marines, and the Secret Mission of 1805.* New York: Hyperion, 2005.

Articles

Balinky, Alexander S. "Albert Gallatin, Naval Foe." *Pennsylvania Magazine of History and Biography* 82, no. 3 (July 1958): 293-304.

Barrett, Deidre, Zach Sogolow, Angela Oh, Jasmine Panton, Malcolm Grayson, and Melanie Justiniano. "Content of Dreams from WWII POWs." *Imagination, Cognition and Personality* 33 (2013): 193-204.

Berman, Jacob Rama. "The Barbarous Voice of Democracy: American Captivity in Barbary and the Multicultural Specter." *American Literature* 79 (March 2007): 1-27.

Bevan, Edith Rossiter. "Letters From Nicholas Harwood, M. D., U. S. N.: Prisoner of War in Tripoli, 1803–'05." *Maryland Historical Magazine* 40, no. 1 (Spring 1945): 66-70.

Blum, Hester. "Pirated Tars, Piratical Texts: Barbary Captivity and American Sea Narratives." *Early American Studies* 1 (Fall 2003): 133-58.

Brodine, Charles E., Jr. "'Children of the Storm': Life at Sea in the First Six Frigates." *Naval History* 23 (Aug. 2009): 14-23.

Bowden, Mark. "The Desert One Debacle." *Atlantic*, May 2006.

Brown, Eric. "A Sailor's Favorite Elixir: The Spirit Ration and the United States Navy, 1794–1862." Pts. 1, 2, and 3. *Journal of the War of 1812* 12 (Summer 2009): 17-24; (Fall 2009): 7-12; (Winter 2009): 15-18.

Budiansky, Stephen. "A Half-Pint of Rum, Hard Biscuit, and 20 Lashes." *New York Post*, Jan. 16, 2011.

Davies, George E. "Robert Smith and the Navy," *Maryland Historical Magazine* 14, no. 4 (Dec. 1919): 305-22.

Dye, Ira. "Early American Merchant Seafarers." *Proceedings of the American Philosophical Society* 120, no. 5 (Oct. 15, 1976): 331-360.

————. "The Philadelphia Seamen's Protection Certificate Applications." *Prologue-Quarterly of the National Archives* 18, no. 1 (1986): 46-55.

Estes, J. Worth. "Commodore Jacob Jones: A Doctor Goes to Sea." *Delaware History Journal* 24, no. 2 (Fall-Winter 1990): 109-22.

Frykman, Niklas. "Connections between Mutinies in European Navies." *International Review of Social History* 58 (2013): 87-107.

————. "Seamen on Late Eighteenth-Century European Warships." *International Review of Social History* 54 (2009): 67-93.

Hernberg, Sven. "Lead Poisoning in a Historical Perspective." *American Journal of Industrial Medicine* 38 (2000): 244-54.

Hunt, Livingston. "Commodore Ridgely's Account of the Last of Somers." U.S. Naval Institute *Proceedings* (June 1928).

Kitzen, Michael. "Money Bags or Cannon Balls: The Origins of the Tripolitan War, 1775–1801." *Journal of the Early Republic* 16 (Winter 1996): 601-24.

Langley, Harold D. "The Negro in the Navy and Merchant Service—1789–1860." *Journal of Negro History* 52 (Oct. 1967): 273-286.

Leiner, Frederick C. "Decatur and Naval Leadership." *Naval History* 15 (Oct. 2001): 30-34.

————. "Killing the Prisoners: What Did Decatur Order in Tripoli Harbor?" *Naval History* 32 (Dec. 2018): 26-31.

————. "Preble's Blockade of the Barbary Coast." *The Northern Mariner/le marin du nord* 25 (April 2015): 117-32.

LeJacq, Seth Stein. "Buggery's Travels: Royal Navy Sodomy on Ship and Shore in the Long Eighteenth Century." *Journal for Maritime Research* 17 (2015): 103-16.

McKee, Christopher. "Fantasies of Mutiny and Murder: A Suggested Psycho-History of the Seaman in the United States Navy, 1798–1815." *Armed Forces & Society* 4 (1978): 293-304.

————. "Foreign Seamen in the United States Navy: A Census of 1808." *William and Mary Quarterly*, 3d series, 42 (July 1985): 383-93.

Peskin, Lawrence A. "American Exception? William Eaton and Early National Anti-Semitism." *American Jewish History* 100 (2016): 299-317.

Ranlet, Philip. "Typhus and American Prisoners in the War of Independence." *Mariner's Mirror* 96 (Nov. 2010): 443-54.

Riche, Bouteldja, and Sabrina Zerar. "William Ray and Dr. Jonathan Cowdery Captivity Narratives: A Case of Political Partisanship in the Early American Republic." *International Journal of Arts and Sciences* 11 (2018): 357-74.

Schulman, Michael. "G.I. Jive." *New Yorker*, Jan. 9, 2017.

Taylor, Alan. "Hero or Villain, Both and Neither: Appraising Thomas Jefferson, 200 Years Later." *University of Virginia Magazine* 107 (Winter 2018): 48-51.

Tildesley, Jim. "The Influence of the Theories of John Clerk of Eldin on British Fleet Tactics, 1782–1805." *Mariner's Mirror* 106 (May 2020): 162-74.

Wilson, Gary E. "American Hostages in Moslem Nations, 1784–1796: The Public Response." *Journal of the Early Republic* 2 (Summer 1982): 123-41.

Unpublished Works

"The American captives emancipation/writen [*sic*] by A Tar; composed by Mr. R[aynor] Taylor." Musical score. Philadelphia: 1806. Rare Books and Manuscripts, Kislak Center for Special Collections, Keffer Collection of Sheet Music, University of Pennsylvania Library, Philadelphia.

Dunne, W. M. P. "Stephen Decatur, 1779–1820: A Critical Biography," 1995. Typescript manuscript in the possession of the author.

Frykman, Niklas Erik. "The Wooden World Turned Upside Down: Naval Mutinies in the Age of Atlantic Revolution." PhD diss., University of Pittsburgh, 2010.

Gale, Caitlin M. "The Role of the Barbary Regencies during Nelson's Command of the Mediterranean Fleet, 1803–1805." Paper submitted to Oxford University faculty of history, n.d.

Hicks, Dan. "True Born Columbians: The Promises and Perils of National Identity for American Seafarers of the Early Republican Period." PhD diss., Pennsylvania State University, 2007.

Mullen, Abigail G. "'Good Neighbourhood With All': Conflict and Cooperation in the First Barbary War, 1801–1805." PhD diss., Northeastern University, 2017.

Databases

Avalon Project: Documents in Law, History, and Diplomacy. Yale University, New Haven, CT. https://avalon. law.yale.edu.

Founders Online. National Archives, Washington, DC. https://founders. archives.gov.

Hammond-Harwood House Museum, Annapolis, MD. https://hammondharwoodhouse.org.

Medical Dictionary. The Free Dictionary. https://medical-dictionary.thefreedictionary.com.

Thomas Jefferson Memorial Foundation, Charlottesville, VA. https:// www.monticello.org.

Topkapi Palace, Istanbul, Turkey. https://www.millisaraylar.gov.tr/saraylar/topkapi-sarayi.

～ ACKNOWLEDGMENTS ～

THE SEED FOR THIS BOOK WAS PLANTED A LONG TIME AGO. What was then the US Naval Historical Center awarded me the Admiral Edwin P. Hooper Prize in 1993–94 to research the school for officers in Tripoli. Often over the years, I considered writing a book on the captive Americans but hesitated because I was unsure I could find enough original material. Christopher McKee, an excellent and generous scholar of the early navy, pointed me not only to the unpublished letters of Keith Spence at the Huntington Library in San Marino, California, and to Dr. Lewis Herrmann's illuminating and almost unknown account of Decatur's raid to burn the *Philadelphia* in the National Archives, but he also provided me with a reel of the microfilmed letters of French consul Beaussier from the French Archives Diplomatiques. Edward C. Papenfuse, the retired archivist of the State of Maryland, who is a treasure trove of information and ideas about many subjects, reminded me about the seamen's protection certificates at the National Archives, which the late Captain Ira Dye first discovered and so effectively analyzed, and Ed also forwarded many original materials to me. In addition, I gratefully acknowledge the advice from historians and other experts regarding various facts and themes, notably William S. Dudley, David M. Rappaport, Spencer Tucker, Seth LeJacq, and Myra Glenn.

My French language skills leave much to be desired, but my old friend and classmate, Seth Winnick, a former diplomat, worked wonders at translating Beaussier's letters to Talleyrand, some of which appear here for the first time.

In one of his letters, Nicholas Nissen referred to his native language as "almost a cypher," meaning he did not need to encrypt his letters because almost no one understands Danish. I certainly do not. Brian Kalhøj at the Rigsarkivert, Copenhagen, provided me with digital scans of some of Nissen's overlooked letters, as well as transcriptions of them (Nissen's handwriting being nearly illegible, another form of cypher). Troy Wellington Smith, a PhD candidate in Scandinavian at the University of California, Berkeley, translated them, making them accessible for the first time. Bjørn Okholm Skaarup provided me with Danish sources unknown to Anglophone historians, translated certain tracts, and found an image of Nicholas Nissen (previously unknown to the American historical literature).

Research can be frustrating. Fatih Tetik examined the Ottoman archives for documents about the *Philadelphia* or the captured Americans for me but found no letters or reports from Tripoli to the Sublime Porte in the Ottoman and Topkapi Palace archives. Another frustration was learning that in 2017, an auction house sold the diary of an unidentified *Philadelphia* officer in captivity in Tripoli; the owner did not respond to my requests to examine it. These points underscore the notion that history is never complete, and a future historian may have access to information that enhances the story.

The coronavirus pandemic made research difficult and caused delays. When a visit was impossible, Connie Griffith Houchins, then the executive director of the Andalusia Historic House and Gardens in Pennsylvania, provided me with digital scans of Midshipman James Biddle's letters. Rachel Lovett, the curator and assistant director of the Hammond-Harwood House Museum in Annapolis, Maryland, shared information about Nicholas Harwood and his family. Much of the research for this book dealt with online archival newspapers, an amazing resource and one impossible to imagine just a few years ago; searches in those newspapers recovered letters and other material that had long been forgotten. The staffs of the National Archives, the Maryland Center for History and Culture, the Huntington Library, the British National Archives at Kew, the Enoch Pratt Library in Baltimore, and the Kislak Center for Special Collections in the Rare Books and Manuscripts Department of the University of Pennsylvania Library all assisted in providing materials for this book.

My thanks go also to my new old friend Tim McGrath, a sailor and writer, who introduced me to Westholme Publishing and its publisher, Bruce H. Franklin, who decided almost instantly to publish this book and then patiently waited for the manuscript to materialize.

Edward C. Papenfuse, James Vescovi, Ben Leiner, and Joshua Leiner each read drafts of the manuscript, pointing out errors of substance and style and questioning interpretations. Their advice has helped immensely. It is conventional for an author to state that any errors of fact or interpretation that remain are entirely his, but it is entirely true.

Finally, without my wife, Jill Leiner, none of this would have been possible, and she has my gratitude and love.

INDEX